BETRAYAL: Left Behind

Prisoners of War and Military Veterans

....

Jerry Kiley

BETRAYAL: Left Behind
Prisoners of War and Military Veterans

POST-CAPTURE PHOTOGRAPHY OF
CAPTAIN DAVID L. HRDLICKA, USAF

Post-capture photograph of Capt. David L. Hrdlicka, USAF
He remains unreturned to this day.

Dedication

I'm dedicating this book to the grunts that fought in the jungles of Vietnam, and those unfortunate hundreds of grunts and pilots who were captured by the enemy and never returned.

One soldier I know blames himself for the death of his field combat sergeant. His sergeant, after a long period of trying, finally convinced him to take one week of R&R, something we all lived for. The sergeant made arrangements for his R&R and ordered him to go. The sergeant was killed in combat while he was gone and he never forgave himself.

When he told me his story, I immediately said, "You're not responsible for his dying."

He replied with determination, "Yes, I am." He looked at me with tears in his eyes and said, "He never would have died if I had been there."

For the ones who didn't come home…
…and the ones who did.

Introduction

When I started writing my memoirs over ten years ago, my only thought was to pass this along to my two sons so that they could pass it along to any future grandchildren. I've lately come to believe it might be more than that.

Betrayal has grown into something more. It's become a glimpse into the United States government's betrayal of the living American Prisoners of War left behind after World War I, World War II, the Korean War, and Vietnam. The first betrayal I experienced was returning home to find Americans' hatred of Vietnam veterans, but even worse was the outright rejection from our fellow veterans of previous wars. Since my awakening, I've seen the systematic betrayal of veterans through the government's lies about the effects of Agent Orange, the denial and cover-up of Post-Traumatic Stress Disorder, the characterization of Gulf War Syndrome as an individual mental problem, and numerous violations of the promise to provide quality healthcare to men and women following their honorable service to our country.

The fact that at least one veteran will commit suicide every hour is a testament to that systematic betrayal. In the time it takes to read 15 pages of this book, another veteran will have committed suicide. By the time you finish reading the book, 20 veterans will have taken their lives.

Was it really, as many claim, the billions of dollars the USG saved by characterizing those veterans from WWI, WWII, and Korea as having individual personal problems -- implying weakness of character -- instead of treating their mental conditions as they finally did after the Vietnam War? I have to wonder whether an equally strong motivator was the reluctance to admit how many more veterans were damaged during their service than the official numbers showed.

The POW betrayal did not occur in a vacuum. Every President, past and present members of Congress, governmental agencies, and the mainstream media have actively or passively participated in the charade for almost a century. After thirty years of involvement with veterans' issues, I look back on the good old days when I could believe the government wouldn't do these things and I realize ignorance was truly bliss.

The mainstream media has played an important role by under-reporting, misreporting, or completely ignoring the devastating facts of these issues, often likening them to conspiracy theories about UFOs and Sasquatch.

The way these stories have been covered forces those who know the essential facts to wonder whether the bias is intentional. My personal experience with misquotes, partial quotes, quotes out of context, and summaries of my comments written in a way that completely missed my central point—sometimes so badly worded it could leave readers with the impression that I was a drooling nutcase—leads me to the conclusion that the mainstream media rarely allows the facts to interfere with their preferred storyline. I have, admittedly, become very skeptical of anything our government and our mainstream media claim.

For those of you who are less skeptical than I, I urge you to at least read the first chapter of this book, if you read nothing else. "The Cover-Up of U.S. POWs Left Behind in Vietnam" was written by one of the few people in mainstream media to exhaustively investigate the issue, Pulitzer Prize-winning author, Sydney Schanberg.

Chapter One
The Cover-Up of U.S. POWs Left Behind in Vietnam

The reason I have a story to tell is that long after I came home from the war, I became aware of overwhelming evidence that our government had knowingly left many U.S. prisoners of the Vietnam War in enemy hands, and for political reasons, denied their existence. I couldn't walk away from that.

Before I wade into those depths, consider the investigative reporting of Pulitzer Prize-winner Sydney Schanberg, author of *The Death and Life of Dith Pran,* the book upon which the movie *The Killing Fields* was based. He is an internationally known columnist at *The New York Times* and *Newsday,* an award-winning media critic for *The Village Voice,* and a two-time winner of the George Polk Award for excellence in journalism.

The article below, written by Sydney Schanberg, appeared in his most recent book, *Beyond the Killing Fields,* and is reproduced here by permission of The Nation Institute.

The Cover-Up of US POWs Left Behind in Vietnam
HOW JOHN MCCAIN BURIED INFORMATION ON AMERICAN PRISONERS ABANDONED BY WASHINGTON

Author's Note: I have been writing about the missing US POWs since the 1990s, when John McCain bonded with John Kerry and Dick Cheney to bury the voluminous evidence that hundreds had been left behind in Indochina. Kerry was chairman then of a special Senate committee created, supposedly, to get at the truth. McCain was the most powerful member on the panel. Cheney was the Pentagon chief.

The lengthy investigative piece I have chosen to present here is representative of my larger body of POW work. The detailed evidence in this piece has never been refuted. With the election of Barack Obama, the scandal has endured across eight presidencies. And the national press is still too scared to tackle the issue.

September 18, 2008, The Nation Institute (nationinstitute.org)

John McCain, who has risen to political prominence on his image as a Vietnam POW war hero, has, inexplicably, worked very hard to hide from the public stunning information about American prisoners in Vietnam who, unlike him, didn't return home. Throughout his senate career, McCain has quietly sponsored and pushed into federal law a set of prohibitions that keep the most revealing information about these men buried as classified documents. Thus the war hero who people would logically imagine as a determined crusader for the interests of POWs and their families became instead the strange champion of hiding the evidence and closing the books.

Almost as striking is the manner in which the mainstream press has shied from reporting the POW story and McCain's role in it, even as the Republican Party has made McCain's military service the focus of his presidential campaign. Reporters who had covered the Vietnam War turned their heads and walked in the other direction. McCain doesn't talk about the missing men, and the press never asks him about them.

The sum of the secrets McCain has sought to hide is not small. There exists a telling mass of official documents, radio intercepts, witness depositions, satellite photos of rescue symbols that pilots were trained to use, electronic messages from the ground containing the individual code numbers given to airmen, a rescue mission by a special forces unit that was aborted twice by Washington—and even sworn testimony by two Defense secretaries that "men were left behind." This imposing body of evidence suggests that a large number—the documents indicate possibly hundreds—of the US prisoners held by Vietnam were not returned when the peace treaty was signed in January 1973 and Hanoi released 591 men, among them Navy combat pilot John S. McCain.

Mass of Evidence

The Pentagon had been withholding significant information from POW families for years. What's more, the Pentagon's POW/MIA operation had been publicly shamed by internal whistleblowers and POW families for holding back documents as part of a policy of "debunking" POW intelligence even when the information was obviously credible.

The pressure from the families and Vietnam veterans finally forced the creation, in late 1991, of a Senate Select Committee on POW/MIA Affairs. The chairman was John Kerry. McCain, as a former POW, was its most pivotal member. In the end, the committee became part of the debunking machine.

One of the sharpest critics of the Pentagon's performance was an insider, Air Force Lieut. Gen. Eugene Tighe, who headed the Defense Intelligence Agency (DIA) during the 1970s. He openly challenged the Pentagon's position that no live prisoners existed, saying that the evidence proved otherwise. McCain was a bitter opponent of Tighe, who was eventually pushed into retirement.

Included in the evidence that McCain and his government allies suppressed or sought to discredit is a transcript of a senior North Vietnamese general's briefing of the Hanoi politburo, discovered in Soviet archives by an American scholar in 1993. The briefing took place only four months before the 1973 peace accords. The general, Tran Van Quang, told the politburo members that Hanoi was holding 1,205 American prisoners but would keep many of them at war's end as leverage to ensure getting war reparations from Washington.

Throughout the Paris negotiations, the North Vietnamese tied the prisoner issue tightly to the issue of reparations. They were adamant in refusing to deal with them separately. Finally, in a February 2, 1973, formal letter to Hanoi's premier, Pham Van Dong, Nixon pledged $3.25 billion in "postwar reconstruction" aid "without any political conditions." But he also attached to the letter a codicil that said the aid would be implemented by each party "in accordance with its own constitutional provisions." That meant Congress would have to approve the appropriation, and Nixon and Kissinger knew well that Congress was in no mood to do so. The North Vietnamese, whether or not they immediately understood the double-talk in the letter, remained skeptical about the reparations promise being honored—and it never was. Hanoi thus appears to have held back prisoners—just as it had done when the French were defeated at Dien Bien Phu in 1954 and withdrew their forces from Vietnam. In that case, France paid ransoms for prisoners and brought them home.

In a private briefing in 1992, high-level CIA officials told me that as the years passed and the ransom never came, it became more and more difficult for either government to admit that it knew from the start about the unacknowledged prisoners. Those prisoners had not only become useless as bargaining chips but also posed a risk to Hanoi's desire to be accepted into the international community. The CIA officials said their intelligence indicated strongly that the remaining men—those who had not died from illness or hard labor or torture—were eventually executed.

My own research, detailed below has convinced me that it is not likely that more than a few—if any—are alive in captivity today. (That CIA briefing at the agency's Langley, Virginia, headquarters was conducted "off the record," but because the evidence from my own reporting since then has brought me to the same conclusion, I felt there was no longer any point in not writing about the meeting.)

For many reasons, including the absence of a political constituency for the missing men other than their families and some veterans' groups, very few Americans are aware of the POW story and of McCain's role in keeping it out of the public view and denying the existence of abandoned POWs. That is because McCain has hardly been alone in his campaign to hide the scandal.

The Arizona senator, now the Republican candidate for President, has actually been following the lead of every White House since Richard Nixon's and thus of every CIA director, Pentagon chief and national security advisor, not to mention Dick Cheney, who was George H. W. Bush's defense secretary. Their biggest accomplice has been an indolent press, particularly in Washington.

McCain's Role

An early and critical McCain secrecy move involved 1990 legislation that started in the House of Representatives. A brief and simple document, it was called "the Truth Bill" and would have compelled complete transparency about prisoners and missing men. Its core sentence reads, "[The] head of each department or agency which holds or receives any records and information, including live-sighting reports, which have been correlated to United States personnel listed as prisoner of war or missing in action from World War II, the Korean conflict and the Vietnam conflict, shall make available to the public all such records held or received by the department or agency."

Bitterly opposed by the Pentagon (and thus McCain), the bill went nowhere. Reintroduced the following year, it again disappeared. But a few months later, a new measure, known as "the McCain bill," suddenly appeared. By creating a bureaucratic maze from which only a fraction of the documents could emerge—only records that revealed no POW secrets—it turned the Truth Bill on its head. The McCain bill became law in 1991 and remains so today. So crushing to transparency are its provisions that it actually spells out for the Pentagon and other agencies several rationales, scenarios and justifications for not releasing any information at all—even about prisoners discovered alive in captivity. Later that year, the Senate Select Committee was created, where Kerry and McCain ultimately worked together to bury evidence.

McCain was also instrumental in amending the Missing Service Personnel Act, which had been strengthened in 1995 by POW advocates to include criminal penalties, saying, "Any government official who knowingly and willfully withholds from the file of a missing person shall be fined as provided in Title 18 or imprisoned not more than one year or both." A year later, in a closed House-Senate conference on an unrelated military bill, McCain, at the behest of the Pentagon, attached a crippling amendment to the act, stripping out its only enforcement teeth, the criminal penalties, and reducing the obligations of commanders in the field to speedily search for missing men and to report the incident to the Pentagon.

About the relaxation of POW/MIA obligations on commanders in the field, a public McCain memo said, "This transfers the bureaucracy involved out of the [battle] field to Washington." He wrote the original legislation, if left intact, "would accomplish nothing but create new jobs for lawyers and turn military commanders into clerks."

McCain argued that keeping the criminal penalties would have made it impossible for the Pentagon to find staffers willing to work on POW/MIA matters. That's an odd argument to make. Were staffers only "willing to work" if they were allowed to conceal POW records? By eviscerating the law, McCain gave his stamp of approval to the government policy of debunking the existence of live POWs.

McCain has insisted again and again that all evidence—documents, witnesses, satellite photos, two Pentagon chiefs' sworn testimony, aborted rescue missions, ransom offers apparently scorned—has been woven together by unscrupulous deceivers to create an insidious and unpatriotic myth. He calls it the "bizarre rantings of the MIA hobbyists." He has regularly vilified those who keep trying to pry out classified documents as "hoaxers," "charlatans," "conspiracy theorists" and "dime-store Rambos."

Some of McCain's fellow captives at Hoa Lo prison in Hanoi didn't share his views about prisoners left behind. Before he died of leukemia in 1999, retired Col. Ted Guy, a highly admired POW and one of the most dogged resisters in the camps, wrote an angry open letter to the senator in an MIA newsletter—a response to McCain's stream of insults hurled at MIA activists. Guy wrote, "John, does this [the insults] include Senator Bob Smith [a New Hampshire Republican and activist on POW issues] and other concerned elected officials? Does this include families of the missing where there is overwhelming evidence that their loved ones were 'last known alive'? Does this include some of your fellow POWs?"

It's not clear whether the taped confession McCain gave to his captors to avoid further torture has played a role in his postwar behavior in the Senate. That confession was played endlessly over the prison loudspeaker system at Hoa Lo—to try to break down other prisoners—and was broadcast over Hanoi's state radio. Reportedly, he confessed to being a war criminal who had bombed civilian targets. The Pentagon has a copy of the confession but will not release it. Also, no outsider I know of has ever seen a non-redacted copy of the debriefing of McCain when he returned from captivity, which is classified but could be made public by McCain.

All humans have breaking points. Many men undergoing torture give confessions, often telling huge lies so their fakery will be understood by their comrades and their country. Few will fault them. But it was McCain who apparently felt he had disgraced himself and his military family. His father, John S. McCain II, was a highly regarded rear admiral then serving as commander of all US forces in the Pacific. His grandfather was also a rear admiral.

In his bestselling 1999 autobiography, Faith of My Fathers, McCain says he felt bad throughout his captivity because he knew he was being treated more leniently than his fellow POWs, owing to his high-ranking father and thus his propaganda value. Other prisoners at Hoa Lo say his captors considered him a prize catch and called him the "Crown Prince," something McCain acknowledges in the book.

Also in this memoir, McCain expresses guilt at having broken under torture and given confession. "I felt faithless and couldn't control my despair," he writes, revealing that he made two "feeble" attempts at suicide. (In later years, he said he tried to hang himself with his shirt and guards intervened.) Tellingly, he says he lived in "dread" that his father would find out about the confession. "I still wince," he writes, "when I recall wondering if my father had heard of my disgrace."

He says that when he returned home, he told his father about the confession, but "never discussed it at length"—and the admiral, who died in 1981, didn't indicate he had heard anything about it before. But he had. In the 1999 memoir, the senator writes, "I only recently learned that the tape . . . had been broadcast outside the prison and had come to the attention of my father."

Is McCain haunted by these memories? Does he suppress POW information because its surfacing would rekindle his feelings of shame? On this subject, all I have are questions.

Many stories have been written about McCain's explosive temper, so volcanic that colleagues are loathe to speak openly about it. One veteran congressman who has observed him over the over the years asked for confidentiality and made this brief comment: "This is a man not at peace with himself."

He was certainly far from calm on the Senate POW committee. He browbeat expert witnesses who came with information about unreturned POWs. Family members who have personally faced McCain and pressed him to end the secrecy also have been treated to his legendary temper. He has screamed at them, insulted them, brought women to tears. Mostly his responses to them have been versions of: How dare you question my patriotism? In 1996, he roughly pushed aside a group of POW family members who had waited outside a hearing room to appeal to him, including a mother in a wheelchair.

But even without answers to what may be hidden in the recesses of McCain's mind, one thing about the POW story is clear: If American prisoners were dishonored by being written off and left to die, that's something the American public ought to know about.

10 Key Pieces of Evidence That Men Were Left Behind

1. In Paris where the Vietnam peace treaty was negotiated, the United States asked Hanoi for the list of American prisoners to be returned, fearing that Hanoi would hold some prisoners back. The North Vietnamese refused, saying they would produce the list only after the treaty was signed. Nixon agreed with Kissinger that they had no leverage left, and Kissinger signed the accord on January 27, 1973, without the prisoner list. When Hanoi produced its list of 591 prisoners the next day, US intelligence agencies expressed shock at the low number. Their number was hundreds higher. *The New York Times* published a long, page-one story on February 2, 1973, about the discrepancy, especially raising questions about the number of prisoners held in Laos, only nine of whom were being returned. The headline read, in part, "Laos POW list Shows 9 from US—Document Disappointing to Washington as 311 Were Believed Missing." And the story, by John Finney, said that other Washington officials "believe the

number of prisoners [in Laos] is probably substantially higher." The paper never followed up with any serious investigative reporting—nor did any other mainstream news organization.

2. Two defense secretaries who served during the Vietnam War testified to the Senate POW committee in September 1992 that prisoners were not returned. James Schlesinger and Melvin Laird, both speaking at a public session and under oath, said they based their conclusions on strong intelligence data—letters, eyewitness reports, even direct radio contacts. Under questioning, Schlesinger (also former CIA Director) chose his words carefully, understanding clearly the volatility of the issue: "I think that as of now that I can come to no other conclusion … some were left behind." This ran counter to what President Nixon told the public in a nationally televised speech on March 29, 1973, when the repatriation of 591 was in motion: "Tonight," Nixon said, "the day we have all worked and prayed for has finally come. For the first time in twelve years, no American military forces are in Vietnam. All our American POWs are on their way home." Documents unearthed since then show that aides had briefed Nixon about the contrary evidence.

Schlesinger was asked by the Senate committee for his explanation of why Nixon would have made such a statement when he knew Hanoi was still holding prisoners. He replied, "One must assume that we had concluded that the bargaining position of the United States … was quite weak. We were anxious to get our troops out and we were not going to roil the waters …" This testimony struck me as a bombshell. *The New York Times* appropriately reported it on page one but again there was no sustained follow-up by the Times or any other major paper or national news outlet.

3. Over the years, the DIA received more than 1,600 firsthand sightings of live American prisoners and nearly 14,000 secondhand reports. Many witnesses interrogated by CIA or Pentagon intelligence agents were deemed "credible" in the agents' reports. Some of the witnesses were given lie-detector tests and passed. Sources provided me with copies of these witness reports, which are impressive in their detail. A lot of the sightings described a secondary tier of prison camps many miles from Hanoi. Yet the DIA, after reviewing all these reports, concluded that they "do not constitute evidence" that men were alive.

4. In the late 1970s and early 1980s, listening stations picked up messages in which Laotian military personnel spoke about moving American prisoners from one labor camp to another. These listening posts were manned by Thai communications officers trained by the National Security Agency (NSA), which monitors signals worldwide. The NSA teams had moved out after the fall of Saigon in 1975 and passed the job to the Thai allies. But when the Thais turned these messages over to Washington, the intelligence community ruled that since the intercepts were made by a "third party"—namely Thailand—they could not be regarded as

authentic. That's some Catch-22: The US trained a third party to take over its role in monitoring signals about POWs, but because that third party did the monitoring, the messages weren't valid.

Here, from CIA files, is an example that clearly exposes the farce. On December 27, 1980, a Thai military signal team picked up a message saying that prisoners were being moved out of Attopeu (in southern Laos) by aircraft "at 1230 hours." Three days later a message was sent from CIA station in Bangkok to the CIA director's office in Langley. It read, in part, "The prisoners . . . are now in the valley in permanent location (a prison camp at Nhommarath in Central Laos). They were transferred from Attopeu to work in various places . . . POWs were formerly kept in caves and are very thin, dark and starving." Apparently the prisoners were real. But the transmission was declared "invalid" by Washington because the information came from a "third party" and thus could not be deemed credible.

5. A series of what appeared to be distress signals from Vietnam and Laos were captured by the government's satellite system in the late 1980s and early '90s. (Before the period, no search for such signals had been put in place.) Not a single one of these markings was ever deemed credible. To the layman's eye, the satellite photos, some of which I've seen, show markings on the ground that are identical to the signals that American pilots had been specifically trained to use in their survival courses—such as certain letters, like X or K, drawn in a special way. Other markings were the secret four-digit authenticator numbers given to individual pilots. But time and again, the Pentagon, backed by the CIA, insisted that humans had not made these markings. What were they, then? "Shadows and vegetation," the government said, insisting that the markings were merely normal topographical contours like saw-grass or rice-patty divider walls. It was the automatic response—shadows and vegetation. On one occasion, a Pentagon photo expert refused to go along. It was a missing man's name gouged into a field, he said, not trampled grass or paddy berms. His bosses responded by bringing in an outside contractor who found instead, yes, shadows and vegetation. This refrain led Bob Taylor, a highly regarded investigator on the Senate committee staff who had examined the photographic evidence, to comment to me, "If grass can spell out people's names and a secret digit codes [sic], then I have a newfound respect for grass."

6. On November 11, 1992, Delores Alfond, the sister of missing airman Capt. Victor Apodaca and chair of the National Alliance of Families, an organization of relatives of POW/MIAs, testified at one of the Senate committee's public hearings. She asked for information about data the government had gathered from electronic devices used in a classified program known as PAVE SPIKE.

The devices were motion sensors, dropped by air, designed to pick up enemy troop movements. Shaped on one end like a spike with an electronic pod and antenna on top, they were designed to stick in the ground as they fell. Air Force planes would drop them along the Ho Chi Minh trail and other supply routes. The devices, though primarily sensors, also had rescue capabilities. Someone on the ground—a downed airman or a prisoner on a labor gang—could manually enter data into the sensor. All data were regularly collected electronically by US planes flying overhead. Alfond stated, without any challenge or contradiction by the committee, that in 1974, a year after the supposedly complete return of prisoners, the gathered data showed that a person or people had manually entered into the sensors— as US pilots had been trained to do—"no less than 20 authenticator numbers that corresponded-exactly to the classified authenticator numbers of 20 US POWs who were lost in Laos." Alfond added, according to the transcript, "This PAVE SPIKE intelligence is seamless, but the committee has not discussed it or released what it knows about PAVE SPIKE."

McCain attended that committee hearing specifically to confront Alfond because of her criticism of the panel's work. He bellowed and berated her for quite a while. His face turning anger-pink, he accused her of "denigrating" his "patriotism." The bullying had its effect—she began to cry.

After a pause Alfond recovered and tried to respond to his scorching tirade, but McCain simply turned away and stormed out of the room. The PAVE SPIKE file has never been declassified. We still don't know anything about those twenty POWs.

7. As previously mentioned, in April 1993, in a Moscow archive, a researcher from Harvard, Stephen Morris, unearthed and made public the transcript of a briefing that General Tran Van Quang gave to the Hanoi politburo four months before the signing of the Paris peace accords in 1973.

In the transcript, General Quang told the Hanoi politburo that 1,205 US prisoners were being held. Quang said that many of the prisoners would be held back from Washington after the accords as bargaining chips for war reparations. General Quang's report added, "This is a big number. Officially, until now, we published a list of only 368 prisoners of war. The rest we have not revealed. The government of the USA knows this well, but it does not know the exact number . . . and can only make guesses based on its losses. That is why we are keeping the number of prisoners of war secret, in accordance with the politburo's instructions." The report then went on to explain in clear and specific language that a large number would be kept back to ensure reparations.

The reaction to the document was immediate. After two decades of denying it had kept any prisoners, Hanoi responded to the revelation by calling the transcript a fabrication.

Similarly, Washington—which had over the same two decades refused to recant Nixon's declaration that all the prisoners had been returned—also shifted into denial mode. The Pentagon issued a statement saying the document "is replete with errors, omissions and propaganda that seriously damage its credibility," and that the numbers were "inconsistent with our own accounting."

Neither American nor Vietnamese officials offered any rationale for who would plant a forged document in the Soviet archives and why they would do so. Certainly neither Washington nor Moscow—closely allied with Hanoi—would have any motive, since the contents were embarrassing to all parties, and since both the United States and Vietnam had consistently denied the existence of unreturned prisoners. The Russian archivists simply said the document was "authentic."

8. In his 2002 book, Inside Delta Force, retired Command Sgt. Major Eric Haney described how in 1981 his Special Forces unit, after rigorous training for a POW rescue mission, had the mission suddenly aborted, revived a year later and again abruptly aborted. Haney writes that this abandonment of captured soldiers ate at him for years and left him disillusioned about his government's vows to leave no men behind.

"Years later, I spoke at length with a former highly placed member of the North Vietnamese diplomatic corps, and this person asked me point-blank: 'Why did the Americans never attempt to recover their remaining POWs after the conclusion of the war?'" Haney writes. He continued, saying that he came to believe senior government officials had called off those missions in 1981 and 1982. (His account is on pages 314 to 321 of my paperback copy of the book.)

9. There is also evidence that in the first months of the Ronald Reagan's presidency in 1981, the White House received a ransom proposal for a number of POWs being held by Hanoi in Indochina. The offer, which was passed to Washington from an official of a third country, was apparently discussed at a meeting in the Roosevelt Room attended by Reagan, Vice President Bush, CIA Director William Casey, and National Security Advisor Richard Allen. Allen confirmed the offer in sworn testimony to the Senate POW committee on June 23, 1992.

Allen was allowed to testify behind closed doors and no information was released. But a San Diego Union-Tribune reporter, Robert Caldwell, obtained the portion relating to the ransom offer and reported on it. The ransom request was for $4 billion, Allen testified. He said he told Reagan that "it would be worth the president's going along and let's have the negotiation." When his testimony appeared in the Union-Tribune, Allen quickly wrote a letter to the panel, this time not under oath, recanting the ransom story and claiming his memory had played tricks on him. His new version was that some POW activists had asked him about such an offer in a meeting that took place in 1986, when he was no longer in government. "It appears," he said in the letter, "that there never was a 1981 meeting about the return of POW/MIAs for $4 billion."

But the episode didn't end there. A Treasury agent in the Secret Service on duty in the White House, John Syphrit, came forward to say he had overheard part of the ransom conversation in the Roosevelt Room in 1981, when the offer was discussed by Reagan, Bush, Casey, Allen and other cabinet officials.

Syphrit, a veteran of the Vietnam War, told the committee he was willing to testify but they would have to subpoena him. Treasury opposed his appearance, arguing that voluntary testimony would violate the trust between the Secret Service and those it protects. It was clear that coming in on his own could cost Syphrit his career. The committee voted 7 to 4 not to subpoena him.

In the committee's final report, dated January 13, 1993 (on page 284), the panel not only chastised Syphrit for his failure to testify without a subpoena ("The committee regrets that the Secret Service agent was unwilling…"), but noted that since Allen had recanted his testimony about the Roosevelt Room briefing, Syphrit's testimony would have been "at best, uncorroborated by the testimony of any other witness." The committee omitted any mention that it had made a decision not to ask the other two surviving witnesses, Bush and Reagan, to give testimony under oath. (Casey had died.)

10. In 1990 Colonel Millard Peck, a decorated infantry veteran of Vietnam then working at the DIA as chief of the Asian Division of Current Intelligence, asked for the job of chief of the DIA's Special Office for Prisoners of War and Missing in Action. His reason for seeking the transfer, which wasn't a promotion, was that he had heard from officials throughout the Pentagon that the POW/MIA office has been turned into a waste-disposal unit for getting rid of unwanted evidence about live prisoners—a "black hole," these officials called it.

Peck explained all of this in his telling resignation letter of February 12, 1991, eight months after he had taken the job. He said he viewed it as "sort of a holy crusade" to restore the integrity of the office but was defeated by the Pentagon machine. The four-page, single-spaced letter was scathing, describing the putative search for missing men as "a cover-up."

Peck charged that, at its top echelons, the Pentagon had embraced a "mind-set to debunk" all evidence of prisoners left behind. "That national leaders continue to address the prisoners of war and missing in action issue as the 'highest national priority' is a travesty," he wrote. "The entire charade does not appear to be an honest effort, and may never have been . . . . Practically all analysis is directed to finding fault with the source. Rarely has there been any effective active follow through on any of the sightings, nor is there a responsive 'action arm' to routinely and aggressively pursue leads."

"I became painfully aware," his letter continued, "that I wasn't really in charge of my own office, but was merely a figurehead or whipping boy for a larger and totally Machiavellian group of players outside of DIA. . . I feel strongly that this issue is being manipulated and controlled at a higher level, not with the goal of resolving it, but more to obfuscate the question of live prisoners and give the illusion of progress through hyperactivity." He named no names but said these players are "unscrupulous people in the government or associated with the government" who "have maintained their distance and remain hidden in the shadows, while using the [POW] Office as a 'toxic waste dump' to bury the whole 'mess' out of sight." Peck added that "military officers . . . who in some manner have 'rocked the boat' [have] quickly come to grief."

Peck concluded, "From what I have witnessed, it appears that any soldier left in Vietnam, even inadvertently, was, in fact, abandoned years ago, and that the farce that is being played is no more than political legerdemain done with 'smoke and mirrors' to stall the issue until it dies a natural death."

The disillusioned colonel not only resigned but asked to be retired immediately from active military service. The press never followed up.

My Pursuit of the Story

I covered the war in Cambodia and Vietnam, but came to the POW information only slowly afterward, when military officers I knew from that conflict began coming to me with maps and POW sightings and depositions by Vietnamese witnesses.

I was then city editor of *The New York Times*, no longer involved in foreign or national stories, so I took the data to the appropriate desks and suggested it was material worth pursuing. There were no takers. Some years later, in 1991, when I was an op-ed columnist at Newsday, the aforementioned special Senate committee was formed to probe the POW issue. I saw this as an opening and immersed myself in the reporting.

At Newsday, I wrote thirty-five columns over a two-year period, as well as a four-part series on a trip I took to North Vietnam to report on what happened to one missing pilot who was shot down over the Ho Chi Minh trail and captured when he parachuted down. After Newsday, I wrote thousands more words on the subject for other outlets. Some of the pieces were about McCain's key role.

Though I wrote on many subjects for *Life*, *Vanity Fair* and *Washington Monthly*, my POW articles appeared in *Penthouse*, the *Village Voice* and *APBnews.com*. Mainstream publications weren't interested. Their disinterest was part of what motivated me, and I became one of a very short list of journalists who considered the story important.

Serving in the army in Germany during the Cold War and witnessing combat firsthand as a reporter in India and Indochina led me to have great respect for those who fight for their country. To my mind, we dishonored US troops when our government failed to bring them home from Vietnam after the 591 others were released—and then claimed they didn't exist. And politicians dishonor themselves when they pay lip service to the bravery and sacrifice of soldiers only to leave untold numbers behind, rationalizing to themselves that it's merely one of the unfortunate costs of war.

John McCain—now campaigning for the White House as a war hero, maverick and straight shooter—owes the voters some explanations. The press were long ago wooed and won by McCain's seeming openness, Lone Ranger pose and self-deprecating humor, which may partially explain their ignoring his record on POWs. In the numerous, lengthy McCain profiles that have appeared of late in papers like *The New York Times*, the *Washington Post*, and *The Wall Street Journal*, I may have missed a clause or a sentence along the way, but I have not found a single mention of his role in burying information about POWs. Television and radio news programs have been similarly silent.

Reporters simply never ask him about it. They didn't when he ran unsuccessfully for the Republican nomination in 2000. They haven't now, despite the fact that we're in the midst of another war—a war he supports and one that has echoes of Vietnam.

The only explanation McCain has ever offered for his leadership on legislation that seals POW files is that he believes the release of such information would only stir up fresh grief for the families of those who were never accounted for in Vietnam. Of the scores of POW families I've met over the years, only a few have said they want the books closed without knowing what happened to their men. All the rest say that not knowing is exactly what grieves them.

Isn't it possible that what really worries those intent on keeping the POW documents burying is the public disgust that the contents of those files would generate?

How the Senate Committee Perpetuated the Debunking

In its early months, the Senate Select Committee on POW/MIA Affairs gave the appearance of being committed to finding out the truth about the MIAs. As time went on, however, it became clear that they were calling the shots, even setting the agendas for certain key hearings. Both agencies held back the most important POW files. Dick Cheney was the Pentagon chief then; Robert Gate, now the Pentagon chief, was the CIA director.

Further, the committee failed to question any living President, Reagan declined to answer questions; the committee didn't contest his refusal. Nixon was given a pass. George H.W. Bush, the sitting President, whose prints were all over this issue from his days as CIA chief in the 1970s, was never even approached.

Troubled by these signs, several committee staffers began asking why the agencies they should be probing had been turned into committee partners and decision makers. Memos to that effect were circulated. The staff made the following finding, using intelligence reports marked "credible" that covered POW sightings through 1989: "There can be no doubt that POWs were alive . . . as late as 1989." That finding was never released. Eventually, much of the staff was in rebellion.

This internecine struggle continued right up to the committee's last official act—the issuance of its final report. The "Executive Summary," which comprised the first forty-three pages—was essentially a whitewash, saying that only "a small number" of POWs could have been left behind in 1973 and that there was little likelihood that any prisoners could still be alive. The Washington press corps, judging from its coverage, seems to have read only this airbrushed summary, which has been closely controlled.

But the rest of the 1,221-page report on POW/MIAs was quite different. Sprinkled throughout are pieces of hard evidence that directly contradict the summary's conclusions. This documentation established that a significant number of prisoners were left behind—and that top government officials knew this from the start. These candid findings were inserted by committee staffers who had unearthed the evidence and were determined not to allow the truth to be sugarcoated.

If the Washington Press corps did actually read the body of the report and then failed to report its contents, that would be a scandal of its own. The press would then have knowingly ignored the steady stream of findings in the body of the report that refuted the summary and indicated that the number of abandoned men wasn't small but considerable. The report gave no figures but estimates from various branches of the intelligence community ranged up to 600. The lowest estimate was 150.

Highlights of the report that undermine the benign conclusion of the Executive Summary:

* Pages 207-209: These three pages contain revelations of what appears to be either massive intelligence failures or bad intentions—or both. The report says that until the committee brought up the subject in 1992, no branch of the intelligence community that dealt with analysis of satellite and lower altitude photos has ever been informed of the specific distress signals US personnel were trained to use in the Vietnam War, nor had they ever been asked to look for any such signals at all from possible prisoners on the ground.

The committee decided, however, not to seek a review of old photography, saying it "would cause the expenditure of large amounts of manpower and money with no expectation of success." It might also have turned up lots of distress signal numbers that nobody in the government was looking for from 1973 to 1991, when the committee opened shop. That would also have made it impossible for the committee to write the Executive Summary it seemed determined to write.

The failure gets worse. The committee also discovered that the DIA, which kept the lists of authenticator numbers for pilots and other personnel, could not "locate" the lists of these codes for Army, Navy or Marine pilots.

They had lost or destroyed the records. The Air Force list was the only one intact, as it had been preserved by a different intelligence branch.

The report concluded, "In theory, therefore, if a POW still living in captivity [today], were to attempt to communicate by ground signal, smuggling out a note or by whatever means possible, and he used his personal authenticator number to confirm his identity, the US government would be unable to prove such confirmation, if his number happened to be among those numbers DIA cannot locate."

It's worth remembering that throughout the period when this intelligence disaster occurred—from the moment the treaty was signed in 1973 until 1991—the White House told the public that it had given the search for POWs and POW information the "highest national priority."

* Page 13: Even in the Executive Summary, the report acknowledges the existence of clear intelligence, made known to government officials early on, that important numbers of captured US POWs were not on Hanoi's repatriation list. After Hanoi released its list (showing only ten names from Laos—nine military and one civilian), President Nixon sent a message February 2, 1973, to Hanoi's Prime Minister Pham Van Dong, saying, "US records show there are 317 American military men unaccounted for in Laos and it is inconceivable that only ten of these men would be held prisoner in Laos."

Nixon was right. It was inconceivable. Then why did the President, less than two months later, on March 29, 1973, announce on national television that "all of our American POWs are on their way home"?

On April 13, 1973, just after all 591 men on Hanoi's official list had returned to American soil, the Pentagon got into step with the President and announced that there was no evidence of any further live prisoners in Indochina (this is on page 248).

* Page 91: A lengthy footnote provides more confirmation of the White House's knowledge of abandoned POWs. The footnote reads:

"In a telephone conversation with Select Committee Vice-Chairman Bob Smith on December 29, 1992, Dr. Kissinger said that he had informed President Nixon during the 60-day period after the peace agreement was signed that US intelligence officials believed that the list of prisoners captured in Laos was incomplete. According to Dr. Kissinger, the President responded by directing that the exchange of prisoners on the lists go forward, but added that a failure to account for the additional prisoners after Operation Homecoming would lead to a resumption of bombing. Dr. Kissinger said that the President was later unwilling to carry through on this threat."

When Kissinger learned of the footnote while the final editing of the committee report was in progress, he and his lawyers lobbied fiercely through two Republican allies on the panel—one of them was John

McCain—to get the footnote expunged. The effort failed. The footnote stayed intact.

  * Pages 85-86: The committee report quotes Kissinger from his memoirs, writing solely in reference to prisoners in Laos: "We knew of at least 80 instances in which an American serviceman had been captured alive and subsequently disappeared. The evidence consisted either of voice communications from the ground in advance of capture or photographs and names published by the Communists. Yet none of these men was on the list of POWs handed over after the Agreement."

  Then why did he swear under oath to the committee in 1992 that he never had any information that specific, named soldiers were captured alive and hadn't been returned by Vietnam?

  * Page 89: In the middle of the prisoner repatriation and US troop-withdrawal process agreed to in the treaty, when it became clear that Hanoi wasn't releasing everyone it held, a furious chairman of the Joint Chiefs of Staff, Admiral Thomas Moorer, issued an order halting the troop withdrawal until Hanoi complied with the agreement. He cited in particular the known prisoners in Laos.

  The order was retracted by President Nixon the next day. In 1992, Moorer, by then retired, testified under oath to the committee that his order had received the approval of the President, the national security advisor and the secretary of defense. Nixon, however, in a letter to the committee, wrote, "I do not recall directing Admiral Moorer to send this cable."

  The report didn't include the following information: Behind closed doors, a senior intelligence officer had testified to the POW committee that when Moorer's order was rescinded, the angry admiral sent a "back-channel" message to other key military commanders telling them that Washington was abandoning known live prisoners. "Nixon and Kissinger are at it again," he wrote. "SecDef and Sec-State have been cut out of the loop." In 1973, the witness was working in the office that processed this message. His name and his testimony are still classified. A source present for the testimony provided me with this information and also reported that in that same time period, Moorer had stormed into Defense Secretary Schlesinger's office and, pounding on his desk, yelled, "The bastards have still got our men." Schlesinger, in his own testimony to the committee a few months later, was asked about—and corroborated—this account.

  * Pages 95-96: In early April 1973, Deputy Defense Secretary William Clements "summoned" Dr. Roger Shields, then head of the Pentagon's POW/MIA Task Force, to his office to work out "a new public formulation" of the POW issue; now that the White House had declared all prisoners to have been returned, a new spin was needed. Shields, under oath, described the meeting to the committee. He said Clements told him, "All the Americans are dead." Shields said he replied, "You can't say that." Clements shot back, "You didn't hear me. They are all dead." Shields

testified that at that moment he thought he was going to be fired, but he escaped from his boss's office still holding his job.

* Pages 97-98: A couple of days later, on April 11, 1973, a day before Shields was to hold a Pentagon press conference on POWs, he and Gen. Brent Scowcroft, then the deputy national security advisor, went to the Oval Office to discuss the "new public formulation" and its presentation with President Nixon.

The next day, reporters right off asked Shields about missing POWs. Shields fudged his answers. He said, "We have no information at this time that there are any Americans alive in Indochina." But he went on to say that there had not been "a complete accounting" of those lost in Laos and that the Pentagon would press on to account for the missing—a seeming acknowledgment that some Americans were still alive and unaccounted for.

The press; however, seized on Shields' denials. One headline read, "POW Unit Boss: No Living GIs Left in Indochina."

* Page 97: The POW committee, knowing that Nixon taped all his meetings in the Oval Office, sought the tape of that April 11, 1973, Nixon-Shields-Scowcroft meeting to find out what Nixon had been told and what he had said about the evidence of POWs still in Indochina. The committee also knew there had been other White House meetings that centered on intelligence about live POWs. A footnote on page 97 states that Nixon's lawyers said they would provide access to the April 11 tape "only if the Committee agreed not to seek any other White House recordings from this time period." The footnote says that the committee rejected these terms and got nothing. The committee never made public this request for Nixon tapes until the brief footnote in its 1993 report.

McCain's Catch-22

None of this compelling evidence in the committee's full report dislodged McCain from his contention that the whole POW issue was a concoction by deluded purveyors of a "conspiracy theory." But an honest review of the full report, combined with other documentary evidence, tells the story of a frustrated and angry President, and his national security advisor, furious at being thwarted at the peace table by a small, much less powerful country that refused to bow to Washington's terms. That President seems to have swallowed hard and accepted a treaty that left probably hundreds of American prisoners in Hanoi's hands, to be used as bargaining chips for reparations.

Maybe Nixon and Kissinger told themselves that they could get the prisoners home after some time had passed. But perhaps it proved too hard to undo a lie as big as this one. Washington said no prisoners were left behind, and Hanoi swore it had returned all of them. How could either side later admit it had lied? Time went by and as neither side budged, telling the truth became even more difficult and remote. The public would realize that

Washington knew of the abandoned men all along. The truth, after men had been languishing in foul prison cells, could get people impeached or thrown in jail.

Which brings us to today, when the Republican candidate for President is the contemporaneous politician most responsible for keeping the truth about this matter hidden. Yet he says he's the right man to be the Commander-in-Chief, and his credibility in making this claim is largely based on his image as a POW hero.

On page 468 of the 1,221-page report, McCain parsed his POW position oddly: "we found no compelling evidence to prove that Americans are alive in captivity today. There is some evidence—though no proof—to suggest only the possibility that a few Americans may have been kept behind after the end of America's military involvement in Vietnam."

"Evidence though no proof." Clearly no one could meet McCain's standard of proof as long as he is leading a government crusade to keep the truth buried.

To this reporter, this sounds like a significant story and a long overdue opportunity for the press to finally dig into the archives to set the historical record straight—and even pose some direct questions to the candidate.

***

Sydney Schanberg's devotion to this issue is impressive and nearly unique among the most respected U.S. journalists. It is a sad fact that speaking the truth on subjects that threaten to shatter the public impression of a well-meaning government is often a thankless pursuit.

Fortunately, some journalists outside the U.S. don't face the same threats to their careers. For example, a German producer has released a video that chillingly documents the United States government's abandonment of POWs in every 20th Century war: World War I, World War II, Korea, and Vietnam. Go to powhrdlicka.com to find this 50-minute video. You can also view the most famous photo of a healthy David Hrdlicka, who was shot down in Laos and is in enemy hands. Carol Hrdlicka is 100% sure this is her husband. A father of three children, David never came home. The Vietnamese know his fate.

Chapter Two
Vietnam

As I completed my final edit of the following account of my life as a POW/MIA activist over the last 30 years, I found it interesting that, for someone who is not politically motivated or connected, I met with many politically influential people.

Considering my primary role has been a hard-core activist, it is surprising that I had face-to-face meetings (not always friendly) with the following people in chronological order: New York City Mayor Ed Koch; nationally recognized anthropologist Dr. Michael Charney; Cardinal O'Connor and Duke University Trustee Anthony Drexel Duke; White House Communications Director Pat Buchanan; former Navy Captain, POW, and Heritage Foundation Vice-president Eugene Red McDaniel; Reagan's Education Secretary William Bennett; Reagan's Secretary of Interior William Hodel; Senate Minority Leader Bob Dole; President of the Stanton Group Paul Weyrich; former UN Ambassador Jeanne Kirkpatrick; Secretary of State James Baker's wife at their home; President Reagan's Chief of Staff Donald Regan and his wife at their home; American Legion Executive Director John Summers; Vice-president GHW Bush; Presidential Nominee Governor Michael Dukakis; Presidential candidate Jesse Jackson; H. Ross Perot; Vietnamese Special Ambassador Can; Prime Minister of Vietnam Phan Van Khai (on two occasions); President of Vietnam Nguyen Minh Triet; Swift Boat vet John O'Neil, Pulitzer Prize winning author of *The Killing Fields* Sydney Schanberg; John Syphrit, a member of the Secret Service detail, and Jacob Stein, one of the most respected lawyers in D.C., who successfully defended one of the Watergate lawyers.

After receiving national attention for a flag incident in 2003, and then getting directly involved in the presidential race in 2004 between Senator John Kerry and George Bush, Jr. after Kerry's surprising victory in the Iowa Democratic Primary, I decided to record my 20-plus years as an activist for future generations of my family. I began writing this story more than 20 years after beginning my life as a POW/MIA activist, and 38 years after I was drafted into the U.S. Army.

I wanted to leave a legacy to my grandchildren that demonstrates the ways one dedicated person can make a difference, no matter how many obstacles are thrown in his way. I started writing, not knowing what the outcome would be; however, I began to believe in 2004 that there was an end game somewhere down the road.

Discipline, tenacity, and high energy can carry a person beyond the apparent limits of natural ability. Considering I had an average intellect, below average writing skills, and very poor oral presentation skills in 1983, my activism became a very challenging work in progress. I first had to force myself to overcome my greatest fears: the fear of public speaking and the fear of failure. The fact that I was a stutterer and had an additional speech impediment early in life and that I didn't graduate from first grade on my first try obviously contributed greatly to my lack of self-confidence.

Entering Army basic training blind, intimidated and fearful, I had several experiences that handed me a big boost in confidence that I badly needed. I think I would not have been able to do many of the things I later did without those experiences.

The following account of my life begins at age 19, the average age for a draftee in the Vietnam War. Looking back now, I realize how many times I was the beneficiary of dumb luck…my next few years could have been so much worse or so much shorter!

I received my draft notice in the summer of 1966 and shortly after that my mother suffered a stroke, paralyzing her entire right side. This would prove to be the defining moment in my life. I did actively try to get into the National Guard and Reserves to avoid having to go to Vietnam because of the fear I had that going there would possibly kill my mother. I guess from a selfish point of view I had no desire to be hurt or killed or do the same to anyone else. I do believe that if I had died in Vietnam that would have been a crushing blow that my mother never would have recovered from.

I was inducted into the U.S. Army in August, 1966. I served the typical two months of basic training at Fort Gordon, Georgia, then four months of Advanced Individual Training at Fort Jackson, South Carolina. I received specialized training as a Radio Teletype Communication Center Operator (Encryption and Morse code).

Basic training at Fort Gordon was an eye opener, to say the least. As we departed from the train that left from New York City, middle-aged men in uniforms were screaming at us to do something. At that point, I just followed the crowd. We had about 250 in our company, almost all from New York City.

Upon arriving at Fort Gordon, my first trip to the bathroom was eventful. There was a huge inductee next to me at the urinal. He was grunting and groaning. I've learned over the years from living in the city, especially going to high school in the middle of Harlem, to avoid eye contact in strange situations, but without looking directly I could see that he was masturbating, apparently without a care in the world. I zipped up— almost too soon—and got the hell out of there. On the way out, I heard him say, "Tell them what I'm doing." I found out later that he was discharged as an undesirable, which was what he was apparently trying to accomplish.

My basic training was generally uneventful except for a situation that probably changed the course of my life. The motto in the service is never volunteer for anything, no matter how good it appears at the time. The first situation I witnessed supporting this was when the sergeant asked for volunteers for fireman training. It actually was cleaning out the coal-fired heating units. The soldier from our barracks who volunteered came back every night covered in black coal dust. They didn't use safety masks back in those days. I wonder how many of them survived later in life.

Since the company commander's assistant slept near me in my barracks, we developed a friendly relationship. Shortly after this fireman situation, the same sergeant again asked for volunteers for driver training, and I was the only person who raised my hand. My friend had told me in advance that this was a legitimate request. The sergeant had to threaten the entire company before several others volunteered.

I trained on driving three-quarter and two-and-a-half ton Army trucks. This duty, driving supplies, not only got me out of marching out and back every day in the hot sun, it also made me exempt from company duty such as kitchen patrol (cleaning dirty dishes). Remember, this was August in Georgia. Needless to say, when my friend and I went out drinking, I bought.

We had to qualify with our M14s on the firing range, and I was very surprised how proficient I was considering I had never fired a weapon in my life. One day, the guys were in a reckless frame of mind on the range. Luckily, I was driving that day. I usually had to wait for them to arrive before the kitchen opened. This day the company punishment was low crawling up and down Big Red—a very steep hill of hard red clay—several times with their M14s. When they finally arrived, all of them were bleeding from their elbows and knees.

As it turned out, I was one of only three in my company that had a perfect qualification, 60 out of 60 shots from four different positions. I wore my expert shooting medal proudly whenever we wore our dress uniforms.

Basic training was very intense because the drill sergeant's job was to emotionally strip us of our individuality and make us think of ourselves only as members of a team. Since this was the greatest build-up of the war, it was a foregone conclusion we were all going to Vietnam. Certainly, it was a catastrophic change from living at home where all my needs were attended to by my mother. At 19, I had a job, car, money, and a girlfriend. The major decision in my life at that time was whether to take out my girlfriend or go to the local Irish bar.

There were very few humorous moments in Basic Training; however, there was one situation that invoked laughter. There was a Hispanic soldier from Brooklyn, I believe he was Puerto Rican, who looked and sounded very tough. Even though he was shorter than my five-foot-nine-inch height, he was very intimidating because of his Hispanic Brooklyn accent and scarred face.

I'm not sure how we started the harmless, light-hearted banter regarding his boys in Brooklyn versus my boys in the Bronx, but over time, we wound up with an all-out, in-your-face yell-down about whose boys were tougher. Naturally, we used the Army vernacular, which included a generous dose of vulgarity. The purpose of this exercise was to see who would laugh first. In the beginning, he won, hands down. Eventually, I had to adapt and started speaking like a mobster from Brooklyn even though I normally had a Bronx accent.

Over time I won. The other guys in our company would gather around us, laughing and cheering us on to be even more aggressive verbally. One time, we were in line when we started and the sergeants all came running over, thinking it was a riot. We had to be careful when and where we did this and eventually stopped because some were taking it too seriously. After that we would joke about not getting each other started! This turned out to be my first friendship with a Hispanic person since there were no Hispanic or black people in my Irish/German Bronx neighborhood.

There were five events we trained for at the end of Basic: the run-dodge-jump, low crawl, monkey bars, grenade tossing, and one mile run. Each company in the battalion was in competition to be the best. Besides being an expert in qualifying with the M14 rifle, I was one of the best at run-dodge-jump.

There was only one other person in my company that competed with me. I beat him most of the time when we were timed with a stopwatch, and one sergeant, who had been a drill instructor for many years, said I had the best time he had ever seen.

Even though my overall score was excellent, certainly at the top of the battalion scores, I didn't get the maximum points for the grenade throw. There had to be more than 1,000 guys in our battalion and some received the maximum score on all five events.

Our future assignments and training were posted just before we completed Basic. The one assignment no one wanted was infantry. Everyone understood that infantry meant no further training, and that they would be shipped out to Vietnam immediately following our leave to go home. Since I had no skills that would prevent me from becoming infantry, I hoped my scores would qualify me for something else, anything else.

I remember the look of desolation and despair on the faces of the soldiers who saw "Infantry" next to their names. One in particular was a person who seemed lost in whatever situation he was subjected to, the last person we would expect to be in infantry. In retrospect, it looked like they thought he was expendable. The joy and happiness I felt when I qualified for Morse code /radio teletype communication center training was dampened by my sadness for this poor guy.

We all wondered what criteria they used to determine this life-defining moment. We had no doubt that even if he wasn't killed in combat, he would never survive mentally. I have no idea what happened to him. It would not surprise me if he were one of the thousands of Vietnam veterans who committed suicide, assuming he made it home. We all thought he was a dead man walking.

Having figuratively dodged a bullet, I thought back to when I was a senior at Rice High School and Brother Otto had encouraged all of us to take typing as an elective because computers were going to be a big thing in our future. I picked up that skill very quickly, typing 60 words a minute with few or no mistakes. To say Brother Otto was a life changer would be an understatement. Now that he has passed away, I regret not going back to tell him he saved my life.

At the completion of Basic Training we were given a two week leave. Coming off our leave, I reported directly to Fort Jackson. As soon as we arrived, we were all questioned about our basic training skills. When I told one of the sergeants my run-dodge-jump time he immediately brought me into the First Sergeant, the top ranking Non-Commissioned Officer in charge of that company. When I told him, he immediately called in the Company Commander to get clearance to use me. In amazement, they both questioned my time, saying it wasn't possible.

I was dumfounded with their insistence that I was wrong. The sergeant finally said to the commander, "I'll have one of my sergeants bring him over to try out." They walked me over to the course in front of the companies getting ready to compete.

This was an all-day battalion competition that First Sergeant took very seriously. Before I left his office he told me that his company had dominated this event in the past and he expected to win this one. He was a hard ass, as we referred to those career men, who didn't take no for an answer.

The sergeant in charge of this event had already selected their four in a relay run-dodge-jump. He reluctantly agreed to time since the Company Commander and First Sergeant wanted to see if I could perform as I had indicated. Before starting, he told me not to try too hard, just run a safe race as I would in the competition.

When I finished, I was disappointed because I knew this wasn't my best race. I was coming off a two-week leave and didn't have the focus and intensity I'd had in Basic. When I told him that wasn't my best time, he immediately turned around and asked the other coaches where they should place me. They asked if I would be comfortable in the third spot. I said it didn't matter, but I knew I could give them an early lead if I was in the lead off position.

After a lengthy discussion, the sergeant explained that they thought I could either make up any ground if the first two fell behind or pull away if we were in the lead. I said no problem. Before starting the race, I asked the sergeant what my time was; it was only one second slower than my Basic Training record.

The sergeant cautioned me to just run a safe race and we'd have it in the bag. Our first two legs were good and gave me a very small lead, which I built into a very big lead. The fourth leg could have jogged around and won, but he held the lead. Since they didn't time the splits of all the racers I don't know exactly what my time was, but I know it was one of my better performances, certainly better than my earlier time trial.

They congratulated all of us; later the sergeant told the First Sergeant about our win and about my performance. The First Sergeant was very pleased about our decisive win and my contribution, that we set the tone for this competition.

I observed the rest of the day's competition until the final event. The closest two teams were trying to push a huge ball about eight feet high over the opponents' goal line. The winner of this event would win the competition. All of the First Sergeants and the Company Commanders were on the sideline, cheering for their companies. The cheers coming from our First Sergeant sounded more like a direct order to succeed, or else.

I asked the sergeant in charge to include me in this event. Without being introduced, he said, "I know who you are. We're using our biggest and strongest men for this event, and you already did your job." To put things in perspective, I was 5'9" and 130 pounds soaking wet, certainly one of the smaller competitors.

As I found out later on, the person I replaced in the third leg of our opening event was their weakest runner, and the rumor spread that I was the difference maker.

As the event wore on, the sergeant came over to me and said, "This event has a tendency of being a marathon so if I put you in later on, I want energy and toughness; we have to win this event."

I looked him in his eyes and said, "I'm ready." He finally inserted me as a replacement and even though I didn't push the ball over the goal line, the ball never got past me when I got my hands on it. I helped stop several attacks by our opponents, and at the end I kept driving it forward with my teammates until we pushed it over the line for the win.

I spent my first night at Fort Jackson celebrating in a tent with my teammates from the run-dodge-jump. Unfortunately, I had too much to drink. They actually woke me up in a panic saying I had to get back to the tent I'd been assigned before roll call. When I arrived, I was told I had to report to the First Sergeant's office.

When I arrived, the First Sergeant asked me what happened and I explained. He said I was AWOL. I played the "I helped you win the event card," and that didn't work. I was literally in tears when he said rules were rules. He did show some compassion when he said the punishment is only an Article 13 (company punishment), which wouldn't follow me or hurt my military career.

I was awakened an hour early every morning for the next week or two to pick up cigarette butts on company grounds. The worst part of all was cleaning out the "the pit," a disgusting accumulation from all the grease and cooking oil. The stench was unbearable.

The First Sergeant never told me "good job," but he always looked me in the eyes and nodded whenever we passed each other, a sign of respect. I have no idea what his background was; I just always assumed he was a combat veteran. He was definitely old enough to be a veteran of the Korean War. He was probably the biggest hard ass I've ever met, and I say that with great respect.

I successfully completed my training with a good score in tuning both a receiver and transmitter in an enclosed mobile unit. One of them required over 100 checks to tune it properly. Even though this required about a month of training, it would prove to be easier than learning Morse code.

Since I wasn't sure how to describe Morse code, I used the Wikipedia Definition so you'd see its elegant simplicity:

Standardized sequences of short and long signals called "dots" and "dashes," or "dits" and "dahs." Each character (letter or numeral) is represented by a unique sequence of dots and dashes. The duration of a dash is three times the duration of a dot. Each dot or dash is followed by a short silence, equal to the dot duration. The letters of a word are separated by a space equal to three dots (one dash), and the words are separated by a space equal to seven dots. The dot duration is the basic unit of time measurement in code transmission. For efficiency, the length of each character in Morse is approximately inversely proportional to its frequency of occurrence in English. Thus, the most common letter in English, the letter "E," has the shortest code, a single dot.

Reading that even gives me a headache, and I already understand it.

Our instructor told us from the start that learning this code would be mentally exhausting. When putting on the headphones for the first time and listening to what was expected of us, we all wanted to quit, thinking there was no way we could ever decipher words or even letters at this extremely rapid pace. It sounded like a continuous flow of sounds with no breaks. Headaches and sleepless nights were the norm until we started to get the hang of it.

When we became demoralized, our instructor knew the right thing to say to motivate us: "Failure means being immediately shipped out to Vietnam as an infantryman." In the end, I mastered sending and receiving Morse code at the pace we'd heard in the original demonstration, and much faster than required.

After another leave to return home, I arrived at Ben Hoa Airbase, Vietnam, in March, 1967. We were told that it could take several days before shipping out to our final destinations. One day seemed like a week, not knowing what our fate would be. Upon landing, my friend and I, both truck drivers during basic training, were approached by a low-level NCO asking if we had civilian and military drivers' licenses.

He then asked if we were interested in joining a convoy, explaining this was a better assignment than our MOS (Military Occupational Specialties) which would include carrying a backpack through the jungle with an antenna sticking in the air advertising to the Viet Cong, "Shoot me first." Basic warfare strategy is to take out the communication first. The jungle is no exception.

My gut told me something was wrong so I followed the "never volunteer" motto. We had been advised by some of the other low-level specialists working at the center that it could be a convoy on the Ho Chi Minh Trail. Half of them were attacked by the enemy.

Unfortunately, my friend didn't heed their advice, and he volunteered only to find out it was a convoy on this trail. His face was drained of blood, and to say he was upset would be an understatement. He'd rolled the dice and lost. I tried to console him, but we both knew the outcome. He would definitely see action, the only question was whether he would survive.

The day after he shipped out, I was told to get in a jeep with two other soldiers heading to Long Bien, six miles away, where we would depart for our final destination, Cu Chi. The driver of the jeep was from Brooklyn. He asked if any of us had both civilian and military driving licenses. Since I was the only one that had both, he asked if I wanted to drive a Colonel. I said no, explaining how I had just dodged a bullet.

He assured me that this was a legitimate offer. He was the Colonel's driver and was leaving to go home. He told me that I was going to Cu Chi to replace the communication specialist who was recently killed. Cu Chi was a secure post and home base for search and destroy patrols. This post was partially overrun by the VC, according to my driver.

This was sounding strangely familiar; a convoy would be a better job. I was so gun shy at this point that I said, "Unless this is verified and promised by someone in authority, I will not consider the offer."

He laughed and said, "Someday you'll thank me."

An interview was set up with the company First Sergeant where I would live. He approved me for an interview with the Sergeant Major in charge of the 2nd Signal Group, the highest ranking NCO in the Army. After he approved me, Colonel Byrd, who was in charge of the group, gave the final interview. We hit if off right away. He explained that we would be driving from Long Bien to Saigon, 20 miles away, on a regular basis in an open jeep.

Since he appeared very intelligent and didn't exhibit a macho, gung ho mentality, my gut told me he would do everything possible not to place us in harm's way. Given the alternative, Cu Chi, I gladly accepted the position.

Shortly after I became the Colonel's driver, the General from Division Headquarters contacted him to switch vehicles. The General earned his star on the battlefield and didn't want to drive around in his air conditioned Ford Fairlane, preferring the more "macho" jeep. My Colonel was more than happy to make the switch and I couldn't have agreed more.

Our Signal Group lived in tents several miles from Group Headquarters. Even with the sides of the tents rolled up it was brutally hot. What made it worse were the rats that had a tunnel complex running through all of the tents, surrounded by sandbags.

When I first arrived, the tent next to ours caught a rat in a cage. They doused the rat with lighter fluid, lit the rat on fire, and opened the cage. The rat squealed as it ran down the dirt road until it expired. The rat was then placed outside the tent to keep the other rats away; this usually worked pretty well for a couple of days.

Welcome to Vietnam.

That's probably how the VC got the nickname "tunnel rats," for their complex of underground tunnels in the jungle.

Shortly after arriving, I encountered the company commander, Lt. Friend, who was a bit arrogant and very impressed with himself. He tried to portray himself as a hard-ass, and he was disliked by nearly everyone. Late one night after we'd had a few too many drinks, we entered the company headquarters tent looking for one of the guys on duty. I saw the picture of Lt. Friend hanging on the side of the tent when I got the brilliant idea to cut out his name tag and replace it with a handwritten piece of paper saying "Lt. Fiend." When the Lt. found out, he was furious and demanded that I be given company punishment.

The Sergeant Major I reported to at Group Headquarters said he would take care of it. The Lt. actually confronted him, saying he would decide what the punishment would be. The Sergeant Major was beyond upset and told the Lt. to leave our headquarters immediately. The Colonel and Sergeant Major agreed that they would handle my situation which meant no punishment. They disliked the Lt. so much that I actually ingratiated myself with both of them. The Sergeant Major was my mentor, and the relationship I developed with him was second only to the one I had with my Colonel.

Eventually, we moved from the rat-infested tent area to brand-new aluminum huts right next door to our headquarters building. We were very grateful the rats didn't follow us.

Many of the young Vietnamese boys in the area were responsible for feeding their families. I remember seeing one boy walking with a pole over his shoulder and fish tied to the line hanging behind him. At first, he looked like Tom Sawyer. As I approached, I was shocked to see rats hanging on his line, not fish. It took a very long time to get that thought out of my head.

I always thought back to that incident when I was telling my sons to be grateful for the food on our table and to finish everything they put on their plates.

After moving into our new barracks, our First Sergeant had us build bomb shelters. He called in engineers for the construction phase and then had us fill sandbags to fortify the shelters against a direct hit.

His next project was to build a volleyball court complete with sand, taped out of bounds markers, and a tower for the referee. We had a volleyball league within our company that was very competitive. It turned out to be the best way to release our tension and anxiety, not only from being in a war zone but also being away from our homes and families.

Looking back, the First Sergeant probably started volleyball to build teamwork and a sense of unity. Even when our team wasn't playing, we were there cheering and trash talking. The bonds we built as a group would never be broken.

The heat in Vietnam is oppressive, so air conditioned anything was heaven. Our headquarters was not air conditioned, and I remember sitting in my own sweat, wishing the Colonel would call for a trip to anywhere. I became an on-call volunteer to run errands for the Sergeant Major just so I'd have a chance to cool down, so he took full advantage of the situation. It was a win for both of us.

I planned on going to college, if I made it home, so I enrolled in a three-credit correspondence course to fill in my time at headquarters. It was difficult keeping the paper dry because of all the sweat on my arms and wrists. Back then, every module was sent and returned via the Post Office. I eventually completed and received the three course credits.

Colonel Byrd and I developed a good relationship over the next seven months during our half-hour drives to Saigon. The Colonel was relatively young, and he talked about his specialized training in Army Warfare at West Point. It was obvious that his opinion was valued at high-profile meetings in Saigon with four-star General Westmoreland and his eventual replacement, General Abrams. Even though I didn't personally meet these generals, I was in their company when they arrived or departed from meetings.

On several occasions, I drove one-star and two-star Generals who visited, and I drove the Colonel to private meetings at their homes in Saigon. Even though I ate with the cooks and servants in the kitchen, we ate the same food as the generals, and they ate like kings.

The generals didn't eat the local version of "beef," which was water buffalo; they ate good old-fashioned American steak. Whatever was on the menu, even in the officers' quarters in Saigon where the drivers slept in bunks, we ate top shelf food. As drivers, we learned from our predecessors to get on the good side of the cooks.

Whenever the Colonel attended a high-profile meeting in Saigon, I would always hang out with the other drivers. One day, we discussed the reason why we were in Vietnam and based on the conversations we heard in the back seat of the vehicles we drove, the consensus was oil. Even though we had great respect for the officers we drove, we thought they were crazy because there was no oil in the jungles of Vietnam.

After arriving home, I heard about the conflict between Vietnam and China over the Spratly Islands. There is a very large oil reserve in the ocean floor near these islands. Whoever owns these islands also owns the oil rights potentially worth billions. It's ironic that the USA is now looking to re-enter Vietnam in a big way, possibly to assist them in their ongoing conflict with China over these islands. One reason cited for not launching an all-out invasion of Communist North Vietnam during the war is that China had threatened to enter the war if we did.

China is claiming ownership of these islands now as payback for their support during the war. Without China's threat, we most likely would have invaded North Vietnam, which would have been a game-changer in the outcome of the war.

The soldiers in our barracks were primarily from the east and west coasts. This group of guys became my extended family and very much like the saying, "opposites attract," we bonded and developed a camaraderie that is unexplainable. The California and Southern boys were laid back and mellow while the New York boys were not.

Every night about ten of us would get together and form a circle with our chairs for at least a couple of hours, either talking or just listening to music. One night we played "Under My Thumb" by the Rolling Stones twenty-seven consecutive times, claiming that it set a new Guinness record. We had no idea if there was a record to break and didn't care. That was our claim and we stuck to it. We also agreed never to do that again.

The most popular album by far was the new release by the Beatles, *Sergeant Pepper's Lonely Hearts Club Band*. Many of our nights went well into the morning hours.

One morning after a very late night, one of the guys set his reel to reel on full blast so when the lights were turned on, controlling the electricity, the theme song to the album started. It came on with a crowing rooster, followed by "Good morning" repeated three times.

Usually we got up cranky, bumping into each other and communicating in a grunting style. That morning, we woke up laughing. Even though it was funny, we enjoyed it even more talking that night and months after that. I know the humor will never translate completely to those who were not there; however, this is one of my fondest memories.

I can remember several mornings when I walked into the headquarters building and the Sergeant Major looked at me and never said hello as he normally did. He just looked down at the Colonel's schedule to make sure it was clear and said, "Get the hell out of here; go back to the barracks. I'll send someone if I need you." It was good to know that the Sergeant Major always had my back.

There were mornings when I did have to drive the Colonel in less than ideal conditions. Thankfully, my experience hanging out in Irish Bars in the Bronx paid off. That may be part of the reason why they liked New York boys as drivers. The driver I replaced came from Brooklyn and the other driver for our Lt. Colonels also was from Brooklyn.

Some of the guys from California tried to convince me that it would be a good idea for us to use the Fairlane to travel to many of the Enlisted Men's clubs on post. These posts had live Vietnamese bands playing American rock and roll music, so we made it our mission to visit every one on post.

The Long Bien base was very long and narrow, and there was no direct route through it from one end to the other. The simplest way from our end was to leave the base, drive to the other end on HWY 1, then re-enter at a gate near our destination. Jeeps were not allowed to leave at night without a good reason—which usually meant an official pass—but automobiles could. They were probably trying to prevent a bunch of jerks from using them for drinking expeditions.

At first I said, "No way, it's too dangerous." Over many days, perhaps weeks, they wore me down until I issued my conditions: only one or two could ride in the rear seat—which would make them look like chauffeured officers—with the rest in the trunk. They said, "Hell no, if we're gonna play the part of generals, you're gonna have to treat us with respect." All of us were E2s and E3s, near the very bottom of the food chain.

I finally relented and agreed to use the Fairlane to visit one of the clubs on the northern part of the post. Even though I prepared them to return the salute of the MPs at the main gate when we left, I remember how tense it was not knowing if the gate guards would look inside the car.

As I approached the main gate, the MPs raised their arms to salute and I didn't hesitate hitting the gas pedal. I never gave them the option to stop us. My Fairlane had a metal grill in front that would hold a plate designating the general's rank if he was in the car. It also had a white top signifying a high ranking General. Even though I never used the plate the previous general had left—the possible punishment for that would be too severe to risk it—the empty grill at least put doubt in MPs' minds. They didn't want to get chewed out by a general for stopping him when they shouldn't have.

Once we turned onto HWY 1, we all started yelling, thinking about the bullet we'd just dodged. We never thought about the possibility of real bullets heading in our direction from the VC while driving on the highway. We were too young and stupid to worry. I quickly had to get them under control because several minutes later we had to re-enter the post up north.

By now, we were seasoned officers. No one could stop us. In the half dozen or so trips we made with the Fairlane, we never were stopped by the MPs.

When using the Fairlane, I always made sure we were on our best behavior for obvious reasons; however, when we used the jeeps to visit the clubs near us in the southern part of the post, things sometimes got out of hand. The EM clubs had a strict no dancing rule. We danced individually standing at our table; however, after one warning they would kick us out.

We would form a line and dance on the way out the door with the other soldiers cheering us on. Our favorite song, along with those cheering us on, was always "We Gotta Get Out Of This Place" by the Animals. We always left with a lot more soldiers than when we arrived.

I came to realize later in life that my enjoyment of music not only helped me get through Vietnam, it helped in difficult times throughout my life.

My Colonel was a cool guy. When we slept over in Saigon he'd say, "Kiley, there's no bed check in the Officer's Quarters; just make sure you're back on time and ready to drive me at 8 AM sharp." The nights I spent in Saigon were very interesting, to say the least.

My luck in driving through the streets of Saigon, narrowly missing the thousands of bicycles, was amazing. I never hit one. That's something a New York cab driver would be proud to claim.

We generally drove with our windows part way down because the Colonel liked to hear the hustle and bustle and smell the aromas of Saigon; however, there was a rash of car/jeep bombings. The VC would throw bombs into our jeeps so as a precaution we opened the windows on the Fairlane only a couple of inches.

The Colonel was always aware of the time because he wanted to get back to Long Bien before dusk. HWY 1 was fairly safe during the day but very dangerous at night. I remember one situation when we left a meeting much later than usual. Realizing that it was already dusk and we would arrive in the dark, he said, "Kiley, put your gas pedal to the floor and don't let up until we get home. Make sure your rifle is loaded with the safety off." He took his .45 out of his holster to do the same and laid it on his seat.

I don't remember exactly how fast we were going. I know it was the fastest that Ford Fairlane could travel. After leaving Saigon, we never saw another vehicle on the Highway the entire trip. Most of the ride back was pitch-black because it was overcast that night. If a sniper disabled our vehicle, I knew I would have to help us get out of a jam. That's why when I was able to practice firing a .45, I took it seriously. I realized I might get only one shot.

When we arrived back at our base he said with a big sigh of relief, "It's good to be home." He then said almost apologetically, "Kiley! That will never happen again."

I realized that my responsibility in a combat zone wasn't only to drive the Colonel but also to protect him. No matter what happened, we were joined at the hip and he had confidence in me that I would do anything to protect him. He was smart; he treated me with respect and knew I was loyal to him personally.

We carried a loaded .45 with the safety on when walking guard duty at night within our own company. Even though Long Bien was guarded by the Military Police (MP) at the entrances, we decided to guard our company after a very disturbing incident. A Vietnamese barber who cut our hair directly across the road from our company was shot down along with his VC friends one night by the MPs. They'd been attempting to fight their way through our main gate.

That was the uneasy feeling we had when dealing with the South Vietnamese people. You could never distinguish between the VC versus the overwhelming majority of Vietnamese who either supported our occupation or didn't want to take a side. Some of the men in my company recounted that this same person shaved their necks with a straight razor. Needless to say, that barber shop was shut down.

That incident caused the military to reevaluate allowing Vietnamese businesses to operate on our posts.

I guess this is the time I should talk about the other situations that scared the living hell out of me. Let me qualify the following by saying that what I experienced was nothing compared to what the grunts were subjected to in the jungle. When I finally made it home I said, "Thank you, God, for sparing me the horror of war." I know if I were a grunt I probably would not be writing this story. The horror of that war would have destroyed me mentally, if not physically. The Army and Marine grunts are the true heroes of the war.

Even though it may seem odd, once a week we watched an outdoor movie within the company. One night while watching a movie, I clearly heard incoming mortar rounds. I jumped up and yelled, "Incoming." As I began to run toward our bunkers, everyone started laughing and telling me to sit down. I looked at the sergeant and company commander, who'd remained seated. They were telling me to sit down and be quiet. I was very embarrassed, until we were hit with a barrage of mortar shells quickly running up on us.

Everybody ran for the bunkers and, needless to say, I was the first one there. If there had been one or two more rounds in the "walking" sequence, we would have had several casualties at the very least. Our bunkers' design would supposedly withstand a direct hit. I was glad we never found out if that was true.

It turned out to be friendly fire from our artillery unit in Bearcat. They overshot the valley the VC would use if they tried to enter the post.

The company commander and the First Sergeant who'd built the bunker said, "Whenever you think there is incoming, please don't hesitate to tell us. We'll believe you next time."

There was one lighter moment in this event. It was normal for us to pick up our chairs when the movie ended and return them to our barracks. When the First Sergeant flicked on his lighter in the bunker, we were all holding our beach chairs. Either we'd grabbed them without thinking or we thought saving our chairs was as important as saving our lives.

Also, with all the preparations we'd made, it was funny that our First Sergeant had to stand there in the middle of the bunker with his lighter on. We had forgotten to wire it for light.

I'm not sure how this translates to civilian life; however, in times of extreme stress, situations like this are transformed from merely humorous to hilarious. It's a normal release of tension when you realize how close you came to dying.

The reason I knew the mortars were incoming was that when I sat on the sand bags surrounding our aluminum hut each night, either writing a letter home or listening to a tape from my family, I could frequently hear the VC trying to shell our ammo depot over a mile away. We, in turn, would try to kill them with our own mortars. I was able to distinguish between incoming and outgoing, and obviously my hearing was very acute.

We had to take turns standing guard duty to protect the perimeter of the post. The beer and soda storage area was located next to the valley where the VC would try to infiltrate the post, so we were supposed to pay particular attention to that area. One night when I was on duty, one of our helicopters apparently was called in for an air strike against infiltrators. All of a sudden, the mini-machine gun containing red tracer bullets opened fire, leaving what appeared to be a solid red beam of light. It looked like a red laser beam.

The first problem was that we could not see anything with all the dust created by the mini-gun; a bigger problem was that the chopper was driving the VC towards us rather than driving them away. Had there been a substantial number of them they could have overwhelmed us because there were very few of us.

I guess I should include a third problem; like everyone else who ever guarded that area, we were able to get our hands on the gigantic stacks of beer, so we were not even close to sober. All the cans that should have been on the exposed outside corners of those cases within reaching height were missing in action.

Needless to say, we didn't get any sleep that night. We barely slept in that bunker because the rats would run over your body, scratching your poncho when you were trying to sleep.

I enjoyed working for seven months with this Colonel until he was reassigned. I heard he was promoted to General when he arrived stateside.

His replacement was a Lt. Colonel who was obnoxious. I asked my Sergeant Major if he could get me reassigned to the teletype communication center next door, which was my primary MOS. He was able to make that happen because nobody messes with a Command Sergeant Major, including my new Colonel, who would defer to him.

I worked my last seven months in the 2nd Signal Group teletype communication center, having received a security clearance before shipping out to Vietnam. We received teletype messages from Division Headquarters and forwarded them to the five companies in our group. Conversely, we sent company messages to Division Headquarters. This was a 24/7 operation. As the newbie, I would work either the evening or graveyard shift.

While working in the communication center another situation occurred when the persistent VC finally had a direct mortar hit on our ammo depot over a mile away. A huge explosion shook the ground so hard it almost knocked me off my feet. The aluminum building that held our communication center shook so much so that the light fixture that hung by chains from the ceiling fell to the ground. The lights went out, and we couldn't see anything through all the dust.

I immediately grabbed my loaded M14 and took the safety off. Eventually, we were told it was all clear. When the lights were restored, we resumed as though nothing had happened.

The VC had directly hit our stockpile of mortar shells that was stored above ground. Eventually, we built an underground facility, and we never experienced another direct hit.

The scariest situation of all involved the Tet Offensive. The Vietnamese celebrate their New Year in January. This particular year, 1968, the VC decided that they would celebrate by invading South Vietnam with an all-out assault through the Demilitarized Zone separating the North from the South. We had captured many documents leading up to Tet indicating what their plans were.

Our entire military was on alert in preparation for this final conflict. The timing could not have worse for me because I was scheduled to leave Vietnam two months later. I was a short timer, counting down the days to wake-up (back home). I eventually extended my tour by two months, leaving in May 1968, because that would mean an early discharge upon arriving back in country.

Nearly everyone was pulled from their normal duties and reassigned, including my Sergeant Major. Since he was on the verge of retirement, I knew this was serious when they pulled him out. They also removed all the aircraft from Tan Son Nhut Air Base in Saigon.

When I said everyone was pulled out of Long Bien, the exceptions were communications and the prisoners at LBJ, the Long Bien Jail that we could see from our company. Our post had 55,000 troops assigned to it although they were never all there at the same time. I'm going to guess that there were only a couple of hundred left, spread out over a 33 square mile post (three miles wide by eleven long). The only thing stopping the VC from entering our post were some MPs at the main gate.

You can imagine what I was thinking when I received a very rare hotline message from Division Headquarters. They said battalions of VC were moving past Long Bien heading south toward Saigon. We realized if they wanted to enter the post, they would only need to knock out communications. We would all be dead meat. Later, I wondered if they had entered our post, whether the American prisoners in LBJ would have been released to help us defend the post.

Sergeant Major told me the only reason the VC didn't enter Saigon after they knocked out the police stations was a breakdown in communication. We recovered in time to scatter the VC surrounding Saigon, thus preventing a breach of the city. Had they taken Saigon, we would have eventually routed the VC, but it would have been after a very bloody battle. The mainstream media in America, who inaccurately reported the Tet Offensive as a major victory for the VC, would have had a field day if they had occupied Saigon.

Weeks after the Tet offensive was squashed, my Sergeant Major told me a story about how the VC made it appear that they were all gathering north of the Demilitarized Zone and getting ready for one final invasion of South Vietnam. He related this to the strategy used by the Indians to draw in Custer and his men by setting up empty teepees and fires. Sergeant Major said that this wasn't common knowledge and perhaps I would never see this reported in the media; however, it was a major embarrassment to the U.S. Military.

Before I left for home, the First Sergeant tried to get me to re-enlist for another two years with the understanding that I would be promoted and be vetted for a top secret security clearance to train on the upgraded encryption equipment that was replacing the obsolete teletype machines. I thanked him, but declined.

When I first arrived in the 2nd Signal Group, I was surprised by the emotion shown by the veterans leaving for stateside and their friends. They would hug each other with tears in their eyes, saying, "I'll see you on the other side." Growing up in the streets of the Bronx, I never saw that type of emotion toward friends, even though we were fiercely loyal to our neighborhood and to each other.

I didn't completely understand until some of my friends began leaving to go home. Because I extended my tour two months for an early out, I saw most of my friends go before me. When I finally left Vietnam, I had mixed emotions. I was very happy to go home but also very sad to leave my other family. It was then that I fully realized what our special camaraderie and friendship meant.

I felt very fortunate that I had dodged so many bullets. I was very thankful that I didn't experience some of the horrors that the combat grunts did. In fact, I do feel a little guilty that, looking back, I actually had a good time while serving in Vietnam. What I could not see coming was the terrible experience of returning home.

Chapter Three
Brutal Homecoming

When we landed in San Francisco in May, 1968, there were school buses waiting to bring us to the discharge center. I asked the bus driver why the school bus had metal bars on the windows. He sat all of us down and said we might experience war protesters at the discharge center entrance and not to leave our seats even though they may throw rocks, bottles, and eggs, or spit and curse at us when we enter. It was evening time, and, fortunately, they left before we arrived; we were discharged at dawn so we were spared the degradation of being spit and cursed at.

The NCO who gave all of us our final debriefing said that we should not wear our uniforms in public when we left the center because of the negative reaction it might generate. After we stopped laughing, thinking it was a joke, he became very upset and said in an angry tone that he was serious.

Realizing that most of us came from urban areas, he continued in the same angry tone and said, "If you are riding in a cab, don't even tell the cab driver you served in Vietnam!"

For additional emphasis, he said, "Nobody cares that you served, forget you ever served, and put this behind you or else you will be hurt." I left the discharge center mentally numb from what we were just told. I later learned that it was true, that some Vietnam Veterans who wore their uniforms were spit on and physically attacked in commercial airports.

What was most disturbing was realizing later on that the grunts, the true heroes of the war, experienced this after literally placing their lives on the line for our country. That will haunt me until my dying days.

I called and met a recently-discharged friend of mine from Brooklyn who I served with in Vietnam. He was the driver for the Lt. Colonels at Group Headquarters. We asked each other what was going on because we were confused and realized that our protective families had created an unrealistic assessment of our support. The only explanation we could come up with was that we were being blamed for the war.

Shortly after my reunion with my friend, I visited the Veterans of Foreign Wars post off Fordham Road in the Bronx to get some answers. I approached the bartender and a member sitting at the bar to request how I could join their organization. The bartender asked me what war I had served in.

When I said Vietnam, they both laughed and said that Vietnam was never a declared war by Congress; it was "just" a military holding action.

When I said it sure looked like a war where I was, they said "No way!" because Congress never declared it a war; therefore, I could not join their organization.

As I was walking out the door, the bartender said, loud enough for me to hear, "Imagine that, they disgrace us and now they have the nerve to try to join our post." At that point, I was so hurt I eventually buried my thoughts and feelings to protect myself from the pain and anger I was feeling.

I spent that summer trying to make up for lost time. I went back to my company, started working, and then realized that I wanted to take advantage of the GI Bill that would pay me over $300 a month to subsidize my college attendance.

The first semester I attended was at the height of the peace demonstrations protesting the Vietnam War at my school. I had arranged all my classes at night except for one course that was only available during the day. Demonstrations increased with students laying down in the main lobby trying to shut down the school. I literally had to step around and over these demonstrators to get to my class every week.

It became so difficult to get to class that the college completely shut down the school just before our final exam. We all received a Pass or Fail grade for all of our courses that semester.

Even though it did not affect me in receiving an Associate's Degree, it did hurt me later on when I considered going for a Bachelor's. Colleges would not accept a Pass grade when transferring credits so I would lose an entire semester. Had I received those credits along with Life Experience credits I would only need two full-time semesters to get my BA. The thought of retaking those courses discouraged me from continuing.

Reagan Presidency 1981 – 89

In early 1981, Ronald was just elected President when the U.S. Embassy hostages held in Iran for over a year were released. As fate would have it, they landed at Stewart Airport and were transported by bus to West Point just 20 minutes north of where I lived.

My sister and I and my two sons (7 and 5 years old) wanted to welcome them home, so we parked on an overpass overlooking thousands of people lining their route waving American flags, shouting, and cheering.

The excitement and patriotism we felt was indescribable. This was a great day that I would never forget, for several reasons.

As we drove home following this historic moment, I initially felt elated, then, unexpectedly, deflated. My sister later recalled my being very upset on the drive home. Later that evening watching the 11:00 news, I saw a Vietnam Veteran saying that this was great for the hostages, but there was a painful contrast to the way we were treated like dirt when we returned from Vietnam.

Realizing what we had missed out on, being treated like scapegoats rather than being appreciated, the anger and feelings I had repressed for over 12 years resurfaced. This day was the beginning of the healing process that would get me ready for the next phase of my life.

There were three unusual events that took place before I would find the direction my life would take.

In the winter of 1981, I volunteered to mentor Junior Achievement high school students with two other management employees from my company. Our project was to create multiple businesses that would sell their products at a special JA Fair. The high school that made the largest net profit would win the contest.

One of the male students mentioned that he learned to read Tarot Cards from his grandmother who did this her entire life. He lacked confidence and was quickly withdrawing his offer when I asked him to give me a reading on my future to see if it was worth the risk. The upside was no overhead, just a pure profit.

He was doing a good job explaining what each card meant in relation to the others when he stopped and said someday you will be in a national leadership position not related to work. When I asked for more information, he could not provide any specifics; however, he said the time frame would be within the next 5 years.

When I pressed him, he stood firm and stated that his reading was accurate even though I told him I was not involved in any organizations except the company I worked for.

At that point, he became very philosophical and said everybody has the opportunity during a lifetime to do something special with their lives; however, most people are afraid to walk through the doors that are open to them.

He went on to say that those people who had the courage to walk through those doors found options that they would not have had otherwise. He said the more doors you open, the more opportunities you will have. Also, he said that those who did not have the courage of their own convictions usually lived to regret not having made those choices.

Even though I didn't put any stock in predicting the future, this young man left a lasting impression on me. I believe the confidence and determination I had in many situations later in life was at least in part a result of remembering this young philosopher's words.

I convinced him that he should set up a table at the fair and, as a result, he was the team member that made the most money, charging $5 a reading, and we won the competition.

Shortly after that, one of my former bosses requested that I work for him in a job that would result in a promotion. When I expressed interest, he said, "You are the most qualified; however, you have no chance because the job would go to a minority female supervisor we both know and respect." This was in a time when our division was under the company quota for promoting women and minorities.

My boss stated that the State laws against discrimination would dictate the next promotion. A Vietnam Veteran friend of mine, who worked in the Law Department and was a member of our Vietnam Veterans Association, told me that our State had recently included Vietnam Veterans as a group who could not be discriminated against in this same law.

I immediately told my boss about this change in the law and he said he would pass the information along to our General Manager who normally decided who would be promoted. Soon thereafter, the GM uncharacteristically passed the promotion decision on to the group of branch managers under him. As I would find out later, 4 of the branch managers voted in my favor and I was moved into the new position within several weeks of my State Law declaration. Ironically, my new job was with the one Branch Manager who did not vote for me.

The company immediately sent around an email to every employee in the company informing them of the change in the law to include Vietnam Veterans.

During this time-frame, our newly formed Vietnam Veterans Association was battling the powerful industrial American Legion Post and the company about flying the POW/MIA flag. The American Legion Post, comprised of WWII veterans, told our company executives it was illegal to fly the POW/MIA flag on the same single staff along with the American Flag. We had to get a copy of the congressional record stating that only the POW/MIA flag could fly directly underneath the American Flag on a single staff.

We finally won that fight after we threatened to join the American Legion Post in large numbers and take over their organization. I was the first Vietnam Veteran allowed to join their post. After I convinced them that we did not want to threaten their power base, they gave their approval and the company began to fly the POW flag. Subsequently, I was asked to speak about the plight of U.S. prisoners of war at the yearly Veterans Day ceremony in the lobby of our headquarters building.

Through all of this only one person in upper management supported us, the Vice-President of my division. Perhaps the greatest lesson the Vietnam Veterans Association learned was that we no longer had to allow people to push us around.

We stood tall and we stood proud. This time it felt like we won the battle and the war. The company began flying the POW/MIA flag from its workout locations system-wide and continues to this day.

In the summer of 1983, my company had received tremendous criticism for not having an evacuation plan in case there was an emergency at a major facility. This was a big public relations problem the company faced, and it had reached its climax during a time when our union was on strike.

I volunteered to assist in the first evacuation plan as a bus driver. The volunteer drivers received 3 days training to answer media questions about our facility and the evacuation plan and additional time in bus driver training.

Since I was in the first training class, we received tremendous attention from the media and politicians. This was a hot button issue that consumed the Chairman and Board of Directors.

During the first day of training, in a very large parking lot, we received a visit from the Lt. Governor and a reporter from the CBS local TV station. The trainer on our bus had already selected the most qualified person to drive the bus anticipating a CBS crew arrival. That person had driven buses and trailer trucks and was driving our bus for over an hour waiting for the TV crew who were very late.

He asked to be relieved until the crew arrived, so I took the wheel when the CBS crew drove up in a mad rush and almost cut me off. The interviewer and cameraman immediately jumped on our bus, so the trainer told me to stay seated and start driving.

The cameraman filmed me as I managed to drive through the orange cones, without error, and then sat me down in the bus for an interview. I had just received 3 days of training so I had all the answers to their questions. Afterwards, our public relations person who listened to the interview said I did a great job. I appeared on the 6 PM and 11 PM CBS local news show.

The company Public Relations representative informed me that the President, Chairman, and members of the Board saw me on TV and were impressed with my performance. Up to this point, the media had been brutal in their criticism of our efforts.

This was not only recognized as the first time we had received positive news coverage on our evacuation plan but was also considered to be the turning point in our public relations effort.

I was notified by a public relations person that I would receive a letter for my file from a company executive, perhaps the President, commending me for my performance.

I had surprised myself by performing well under pressure. I have often thought that this positive experience for me played a big role in my willingness to accept more and more responsibility for difficult assignments in the future.

Chapter Four
How I Became an Activist

On Veterans Day 1983, my wife asked me if I was aware that the U.S. had left behind live American prisoners of war (POWs) from the Vietnam War. I said that all of our POWs had been released before the war was over. She showed me the article she had just read in the newspaper. Congressman Bill Hendon from South Carolina was quoted in an Associated Press article, stating that we left men behind after the war ended in 1975.

The following morning, I looked up his home phone number, and surprisingly, he picked up his home phone and spoke to me for over an hour. Bill Hendon convinced me that President Nixon, whom I had voted for twice, had lied in 1973 when he said all of our POWs were coming home; living U.S. POWs had actually been abandoned.

The anger I felt at that moment was so intense that I tried to convince myself that it could not be true.

Through the winter and spring of 1984, I began my search for the truth. I visited many American Legion and VFW posts asking for any information on groups that were involved in the POW issue. A representative from the Yonkers VFW Post I visited asked why I had not joined the VFW. I told him about my being denied membership, and he defiantly said that was not the VFW policy. After I told him it was the Fordam Road (Bronx) Post, he sheepishly said, "We've had trouble with them."

This same person advised me that Tom Burch, Chairman of the National Vietnam Veterans Coalition (NVVC), newly formed out of Washington, D.C., had recently spoken to them about the POW issue. I called Tom the next day. He asked me about my background and then immediately referred me to Margaret and John Nevin, the founders of "Homecoming II."

"Operation Homecoming" was the title given to the release operation of the 591 POWs who had returned in 1973. Homecoming II was an all-volunteer project to establish the truth and gain the release of U.S. prisoners still held against their will in Southeast Asia. I was overwhelmed with very credible-sounding articles detailing evidence of their existence and explaining how, for a number of domestic political reasons, the decision had been made to consider them casualties of war and write them off. I was forced to conclude that there was a great deal of truth in what I had been reading. I decided I had to get more involved.

Tom also asked me to contact Ted Sampley, who was considered to be the most aggressive Vietnam veteran POW/MIA activist in the country. My relationship with Ted would grow over the years to the point that we covered each other's backs when involved in our attention-seeking acts of civil disobedience. (Ted had received numerous decorations for the heroics of his Special Forces unit; however, he could never get an individual award since his best work was "unofficial," behind-the-lines with anti-Communist insurgents in Cambodia and Laos.)

I eventually met Tom Burch in D.C. and he asked me if I had any experience with the media. I told him about my positive experience the summer before giving a CBS interview on my company's evacuation plan.

As I went through this process, and thought back to the young high school student's words to me several years earlier, I couldn't help but wonder whether I would have had the courage to step through this first doorway without his putting that thought in my mind.

In the early part of the summer (1984), I met with Congressman John LeBoutillier to discuss the POW issue. John was a Congressman from Long Island who was passionate about this issue. He suggested the best way for me to have the greatest impact was to become an activist and look for opportunities that most people would not consider.

We discussed options and events that I could be involved in and we came up with the Alfred E. Smith dinner, which was a Roman Catholic fundraiser at the Waldorf Astoria, promoted by Cardinal John O'Conner. The reason LeBoutillier had focused on this dinner was because it was an election year and the two nominees, President Reagan and Governor Walter Mondale, would be the invited guests and therefore draw national media. This would be the first of many demonstrations that I planned.

Tom Burch immediately endorsed this demonstration as a NVVC sponsored event. He also asked me to be his Communication Director. I would represent the coalition at Mayor Koch's Planning Committee meeting that summer for the first Vietnam Veterans Homecoming Parade the following year.

Mayor Koch held his first meeting in the spring/summer 1984 to address all the veteran representatives and express his support. He showed a desire to recognize our contributions as veterans, something that he said was long overdue.

As he was leaving, I positioned myself so he would have to pass by me. I asked him to say a few words at our POW demonstration outside the Waldorf Astoria during the Alfred E. Smith dinner in October. He agreed, and his aide made the arrangements. I suspected the Mayor's helping hand when we were assigned the prime corner closest to the hotel during the permit process, even though there were at least five other groups demonstrating.

During the summer of 1984, I visited any American Legion Post or VFW Post I became aware of, trying to rally support for the demonstration. I was told someone named Joel Cook was very knowledgeable about the issue and had some connection to the White House. I made an appointment to meet Joel at his house to find out what he knew. I also wanted to see if he could pass the word along to President Reagan in hopes that he would also say a few words at our demonstration.

About five minutes into our conversation, Joel received a phone call. He spoke in a very low voice in the kitchen, but I heard him say, "He just arrived. I'll call you later and let you know." When he returned, he said that was George Brooks, former director of the National League of Families, who was considered to be a very important person in the POW movement.

Joel continued our conversation and made it clear that he was in constant contact with Dick Childress, who worked in the White House. I asked him to pass along my request to have President Reagan join Mayor Koch in saying a few words to our group, and he said he would. My gut instinct said there was something wrong if there was so much concern about one new person to this movement, but I was excited that the President might stop by to say a few words.

Later I found out that Dick Childress, who worked for the National Security Council in the basement of the White House next to Colonel Oliver North, declined my invitation. As it turned out, Childress was instrumental in trying to keep a lid on the POW issue and would later publicly denigrate all POW activists in an attempt to control the issue.

I was naïve to have believed that President Reagan knew about and cared about the POW issue and would do right by those abandoned men. My excitement would soon turn into bewilderment. I had already voted for Reagan when he first ran in 1980, and felt certain that if he only knew, he would do something.

We had over a hundred people show up for the Alfred E. Smith demonstration in October 1984. As promised, Mayor Koch joined us in demonstrating our concern for our POWs left behind after the Vietnam War. We thanked the Mayor and gave him a POW/MIA t-shirt, along with other items. At least four TV camera crews filmed his appearance. We both gave several interviews, and our demonstration appeared on several local news channels at 11:00 PM.

What I liked most about Mayor Koch was his apparent sincerity and candor. The Mayor was the first major political figure in New York and one of the first in the country to outwardly show his support for Vietnam veterans, something he would show again the following summer with the New York City Homecoming Parade.

At a time when we were still being treated like pariahs, the Mayor proved to be a great friend and supporter. We will never forget that he came to our rescue when we were still being kicked around. Back then, there was no political correctness; many blamed the warrior for the war. Mayor Koch helped pick us up off the ground and dusted us off so we could begin the process of building our confidence and senses of self-worth.

As we grew into leadership roles throughout the veteran community and country, we developed a quiet resolve: "Never again!" Future generations of veterans would never again experience what we went through.

In May, 1985, I marched with the NVVC across the Brooklyn Bridge into Manhattan and down the Broadway "Canyon of Heroes" for a ticker tape Welcome Home Parade for all Vietnam veterans. Over a million people were cheering and yelling in support of our service to our country. It was our finest hour, if not our proudest moment, since returning home. It was long overdue.

That weekend, I organized a NVVC breakfast meeting at the New York Penta Hotel where we had many guest speakers, including Congressman John LeBoutillier. The breakfast was as big a success as the Alfred E. Smith Dinner demonstration. That same weekend, I organized a rally at Dag Hammarskjold Plaza across from the United Nations building; then we marched to the U.S. Embassy where they allowed me to enter the embassy and leave our handout for the Ambassador to read.

During this same period, Tom Burch asked me to put together a press conference for Dr. Michael Charney, a world-renowned forensic anthropologist who had discovered that the remains returned from Vietnam as an alleged U.S. serviceman were actually animal bones, not human remains.

I arranged the press conference at the New York Penta Hotel and contacted all the New York media. Our panel consisted of Dr. Charney; the family members of the missing serviceman (Fuller); Ann Hart, whose husband was known to be alive in enemy hands; Jeff Donahue, whose brother was missing; Tom Burch, and me.

Dr. Charney had the relatives hold about seven small bone chips in a white cloth and said these bones fragments were not Fuller's remains, they were not even human remains; they were animal bones. He proceeded to say how someone from the United States government (USG) must have picked up these animal bones off the ground, placed them in a plastic bag, and given them to the Fuller family to pretend the recovery of one more missing man. Dr. Charney then said that it was a disgrace for having done such a shoddy job in their analysis of these bones and it was, in fact, so obviously wrong that it was hard to believe it could have been inadvertent.

This was one of our most successful media events in terms of media attendance. We had about a dozen TV cameras with a total of about twenty media personnel present. We received good local TV and newspaper coverage with some national coverage of the event that night and the next day. More importantly, there was a shake-up in the processing of remains in Hawaii as a result of our efforts.

The NVVC marched in the 1986 Los Angeles Vietnam Veterans parade and then Joan Rivers honored us that afternoon on her talk show by having us stand up in the audience to a loud ovation. Every event across the country helped to bolster our confidence and solidify what became the Vietnam veteran movement.

Chapter Five
High Profile Encounters

During the remainder of the Reagan administration, from about 1986 to 1988, I was involved in a number of high-profile meetings and personal visits to the homes of his closest advisors.

In the spring of 1986, Tom Burch arranged a day of high-profile meetings in D.C. in support of the Vietnamese community. Tom was a member in the Stanton Group, a coalition of conservative groups, headed by Paul Weyrich, who played an important role in making this arrangement. Paul Weyrich wanted to meet me so he could evaluate whether I would pass muster, so Tom arranged the meeting. Paul, as he preferred to be called, personally asked me to participate in the day's events.

We began the day at a breakfast in the capitol building with Senator Dole. After the meeting was over, I approached the Senator and asked him to accept a POW/MIA bracelet inscribed with the name of a POW, a man whose two daughters I knew and who were very active in pressing the government for information: COL. ROBERT L. STANDERWICK, USAF 2-3-71 LAOS.

Dole's response was that he didn't need one because he had several in his drawer at home. I looked at him in disbelief and said in an annoyed tone, "Senator, the purpose of the bracelet is to wear it in public to promote more public awareness of the problem." His aide, realizing he was in trouble, immediately whisked him away. My immediate thought was that this was the Republican Senate Whip and former WW II disabled veteran; no wonder we can't make any progress on this issue.

In 1991, Senator Dole would prove to be the biggest impediment to resolving the POW issue when he agreed with Clinton to appoint Senator Kerry as Chairman of the Senate Select Committee on POW/MIAs, along with John McCain as a member of the committee.

I told Tom what had happened with Bob Dole and wanted to apologize to Paul Weyrich if this offended him. Paul walked directly to me in a very assertive manner and made it very clear the reason why he invited me was to shake things up. To emphasize his meaning, he said the main reason I was invited was to do the same, if not worse, at the Pat Buchanan meeting at the end of the day. I breathed a tremendous sigh of relief.

I came to realize why Paul was the head of the Stanton Group; he was a pit bull and I loved it. He's one of the few people I have met in Washington, D.C. who had a backbone and the courage to fight for his conviction. Unfortunately, he passed away in 2008.

The second meeting was with Secretary of Education Bill Bennett, who was gracious with the Vietnamese representatives. They had asked for an appointment of one of their people to a newly formed Education Committee. He asked them to submit the name of the person they wanted and, as I learned, he later followed through with his promise. It was a very pleasant experience in contrast to the encounter with Bob Dole.

The next meeting was a luncheon with Secretary of the Interior William Hodel and Former Navy Commander and Vietnam War POW Red McDaniel, who was then with the Heritage Foundation in D.C. Red was considered to be one of those quiet heroes, well respected by his peers. We discussed how the Secretary was going to fix the problem that caused hairline cracks in the Vietnam Veterans Memorial, and repair it.

The last meeting took place at the White House with Communications Director Pat Buchanan. There were about ten of us in attendance. Just before the meeting Paul called me over to say that he brought me along for this moment. He wanted me to be blunt and to make sure Pat Buchanan understood how we felt about the POW issue.

As White House protocol would have it, Pat Buchanan sat at the head of a very long table where President Reagan sat every morning when he received his National Security briefing.

The person sitting to his immediate right in the first chair was the most important person in that delegation, Paul Weyrich, then order-of-importance would shift to the first chair on the left side, the Vietnamese representative, then back to the right second chair, Tom Burch, and to the second chair on the left, me. This was considered to be a position of authority at this meeting. I waited until the Vietnamese had discussed all of their issues, and then it was my turn.

Either Paul or Tom introduced me as the vice chairman of the NVVC and said, "Jerry wants to ask you some questions concerning the prisoner of war issue."

Even though I was surprised at the sudden introduction, I was satisfied with my two-minute presentation, laying out our position and describing the frustration from the lack of support from politicians, government officials, and especially the resistance from the intelligence community.

Pat listened carefully and then responded that he could only state the obvious, which was to get the information from the CIA files. I said that we had good evidence that they were at the heart of the problem and that they were withholding a vast amount of relevant classified information that would prove definitively that live American POWs were knowingly abandoned after the end of the war.

Buchanan said, "If what you're saying is true, and I'm not saying it isn't, I don't know how anyone from the White House can help, including the President himself." He then said, with great conviction, "If I ever saw one shred of credible information that any were still alive, I would go through a wall to get them home." I told him that we had pictures of live POWs captured and never returned, and that there were thousands of reports from refugees about sightings of individuals they believed to be detained Americans. He said to send him whatever we had and he would take a look at it.

After the meeting, Paul Weyrich said I did a great job and that I wasn't intimated by the surroundings as he had feared. He said that I did exactly what he wanted and now we would see what happened.

I appreciated Pat Buchanan's candor in how he responded and have no doubt he would go through a wall to get them out, but the dirty little secret in D.C. is that there are too many people who don't want them to return after all these years because of the way it would so conclusively prove more than a decade of official lies. Many political careers rest on the public belief that our government would never do such a thing.

There are numerous credible-sounding reports of another dirty secret regarding POWs held in Laos: the CIA and others used opium poppy and processed opium—acquired largely in Burma—as a means of payment to anti-Communist fighters in the mountains and jungles of Laos. The CIA is said to have documented where the POW camps were located in order to avoid them, not wanting to have their activities witnessed by Americans who might one day go home. Unfortunately, these "left-behinds" were ultimately written off as casualties of war, just as was done to many after WWII and Korea. But that is another story every bit as complex as this one.

In November, 1986, John LeBoutillier introduced me to Anthony Drexel Duke, a trustee of Duke University. Because of his legitimate and deep feeling to do the right thing and bring these men home, Mr. Duke set up a meeting with Cardinal O'Connor, LeBoutillier, and me to discuss the POW issue. I was very impressed by how humble and sincere Mr. Duke was before, during, and after the meeting.

The purpose was to ask the Cardinal to contact President Reagan and suggest that he take an active and aggressive role in determining what happened to live American POWs we left behind after the war ended. The emphasis was to take action now; with only two years left in President Reagan's second term, time was running out.

John LeBoutillier opened with a compassionate and factual statement regarding the importance of taking action now, and Mr. Duke told the Cardinal that he would consider it a personal favor if he could pursue this issue as it was very important to him.

The Cardinal surprised me when he said he was also a veteran who had served in Vietnam as a chaplain. Unfortunately, he was slipping and sliding on the issue of calling the President. It was my job to insist that he use every means necessary to help rescue the men we left behind. When he talked about helping veterans that had come home from the war, we thanked him. I reminded him that POWs couldn't defend themselves and that we had to speak for them.

The Cardinal tried to appease us by volunteering to dedicate the next Sunday Mass to the POWs. I pushed as hard as I could without insulting him, but I don't believe additional coercion would have made him more aggressive. He was initially reluctant to contact the President by phone even though he acknowledged speaking to Reagan once a week. I was very assertive in stating that as a Vietnam veteran he had a special obligation to do everything possible to save these men.

The Cardinal eventually committed to sending what turned out to be a very effective letter rather than a phone call to the President. He also contacted the media and held a press conference on the steps of Saint Patrick's church after service that Sunday.

After that meeting, Mr. Duke continued to ruffle many feathers while pushing for action on this issue. Finally, someone ordered a truckload of boulders dumped on his driveway. I thought, "If they did that to a man who was close to Vice President Bush and had raised over a million dollars in a Long Island fundraiser, what would they do to me?"

I was shaken up and scared by this incident and had to reevaluate my commitment. I knew that there were two choices: either completely stop all my activities, or make a commitment to go forward no matter what the consequences might be.

I thought long and hard, again taking into account my family, especially my two children. I cut back on my normal participation for several months and finally decided that I could not live with myself knowing that I didn't do everything possible to get our men home. As fate would have it, the Cardinal and I would meet again two years later in a very unpleasant confrontation.

John LeBoutillier arranged for the two of us to meet with former United Nations Ambassador Jeanne Kirkpatrick. At the time we met, she had a nationally syndicated column and quickly agreed to write a story about the issue. She seemed very concerned about the POWs left behind and expressed her commitment to our cause. She said it would take a little while to get all the facts together, which we were more than happy to supply.

Shortly after the meeting, Ms. Kirkpatrick was accepted as a member of the Tri-lateral Commission, which consisted of very powerful and wealthy people around the world. Their mission, as they describe it, is to study, consider, and share information regarding international relations and the domestic policies which could affect them. According to LeBoutillier, she had been very frustrated in her past attempts to join this organization. She was seen as something of an "inside outsider" and loose cannon, not a characteristic the organization seems to favor. The timing of her acceptance seemed somewhat suspicious to us. Bottom line: we never heard from her again.

I received a tip from someone close to me who gave me the home address of former White House Chief of Staff and current Secretary of State James Baker. His house was difficult to find since the house number couldn't be seen from the street. I literally knocked on doors in this very exclusive neighborhood until someone finally identified his home.

I drove into the semi-circular driveway with my sister and two sons in my car and knocked on the door. To my surprise, Mrs. Baker opened the door in a sweater. I asked if her husband was home since it was the weekend and she said, "No, he just left on a trip, I can't remember where." I gave her information on the POW issue for her husband to look at and left my name and phone number in case he had any questions. She then asked me for my license plate number and I laughed and said, "You have my name and number."

Uninvited visits to the homes of those in power were important because it sent a strong message that we know where you live, we take this personally, and you are as vulnerable as we are.

This same friend gave me the address of Don Regan, who replaced James Baker as White House Chief of Staff. We searched for hours trying to find his street until we pulled into what we thought was a driveway. It was actually his street hidden by low hanging tree branches. We didn't have GPS in those days.

Don Regan assumed greater authority during the last two years of the Reagan Presidency because of Reagan's failing health. Some felt he made many of the "Presidential" decisions. Our first encounter involved the arrest of Margaret Nevin and the Standerwick sisters, whose father was missing. They had locked themselves in a bamboo cage in Mr. Regan's driveway while he attended Sunday mass. Charges of trespassing were dropped at a later date when he decided not to pursue these charges.

The next time we visited Don Regan was during Christmas week because Patty O'Grady Aloot, whose father was missing, sent a letter stating that we were coming to sing Christmas songs. She never received a response so we slowly walked up their brightly lit driveway, expecting the worst. I had the family members walk behind us in case someone overreacted to our trespassing on their property.

There were about eight of us who gathered directly in front of his front door waiting for someone to appear. After about a minute wait, it became apparent that no one was coming out, and we started to believe that they were not home, like the last time. The group volunteered me as the person to ring the doorbell, which I did with great apprehension. We waited for about a minute before I rang again and waited by the door. When the door opened, I was startled.

Don Regan was dressed in pajamas and a robe, with a newspaper folded under his arm and a pipe in his hand. He walked outside and said hello. It was very disarming. Patty explained who we were and why we were there and Mr. Regan smiled and said let me get my wife. He went back inside and shut the door.

I immediately warned everyone to get ready to run. I envisioned Regan returning with a shotgun but instead he reappeared with his wife, who was also dressed in a robe and carrying their small dog. He introduced his wife, who graciously thanked us for coming and encouraged us to sing.

We had substituted the Christmas choruses with POW/MIA wording and sang for about ten minutes. When we stopped, they both appeared very pleased and Mrs. Regan thanked us for coming. Don Regan said he was a World War II veteran and that he sympathized with our cause. Patty was very compelling in stating specific case history as well as the overwhelming evidence proving Americans were left behind.

Don Regan said if we had definitive proof, the President would take action. Again I raised the issue of credibility of our intelligence agencies. Mr. Regan said because we didn't have diplomatic relations with Vietnam, he had no leverage to discuss the issue with them, but if he received timely information on POWs the President would take immediate action.

He even mentioned that a strike force was ready around the world if we received credible and timely information. At that time, we thanked them. I wanted to hate him, but he and his wife were so gracious and sincere that I could not help but like both of them.

I know he had a reputation for being a hard ass, but we saw the softer side of a man who at that moment was the second most powerful person in the world. Some would say he was the acting President and the most powerful person because President Reagan's mental state was very questionable toward the end of his second term in office. I recently heard a news report that said Don Regan had died, and I felt a deep sense of sadness.

Over the three years from 1985 to 1988, I worked through the normal political process and came away extremely frustrated with the belief that the overwhelming majority of the politicians in Washington, D.C., were corrupt. Again and again we were promised some political step that the Congressman or Senator was fully able to take, but it rarely happened. We got the distinct impression that many of them were sincere when they made the promise, but when or before they started that step, they were "talked to," either by other party members who knew this was a "don't touch" issue or by Pentagon or intelligence community representatives.

Almost all of them suffered from Potomac Fever, allowing power, money, and the desire to win another term to corrupt their morals and values, if they ever had any to begin with. I began to wonder about what a friend of mine said: politicians are people who seek the authority and power to make decisions for other people, and this is the last kind of person to whom we should give that authority.

They allowed the lies concerning the POW and Agent Orange issues to continue through the years. Realizing that there was no way they would do the right thing, I decided that a more aggressive strategy was needed to get their attention, or at least the attention of the public.

John Nevin and Lynn Standerwick, the daughter of an F-4 pilot missing in Laos, had a private meeting with Ross Perot in his Dallas office. Perot told them a remarkable story about the first aggressive non-public attempts to shut down his efforts on behalf of living POWs in Vietnam. It involved Perot's attempts to get Richard Armitage, an Assistant Secretary of Defense, removed from office. John felt Perot's reason would be Armitage's obstructionism on the POW issue, but it was something else.

Armitage is a character with a shady background in covert operations and was deeply involved in Iran Contra. He became the point man for managing the POW issue for the Reagan Administration and successfully set up many roadblocks to families and veterans trying to dig for the truth. We were confident that Reagan never grasped the extent of Armitage's role, or even knew much about Armitage's POW activities. If Reagan did know, he was complicit; he knew quite well that the Vietnamese were holding living Americans because there was an offer in 1981 to return them for the billion dollars Nixon had promised for postwar reconstruction.

Armitage had close ties to several notorious CIA covert operations people: Richard Secord, Ted Shackley, Tom Clines, Dewey Clarridge, and Edwin Wilson, as well as some slick operators, Elliot Abrams, William Clements, and Heinie Aderholt. He was also joined at the hip to Colin Powell, starting at least as early as 1969 when Powell was appointed to lead the initial investigation into the My Lai massacre. (Powell's investigation reported that the allegations were false. It wasn't until a later investigation occurred that the facts were eventually uncovered.)

Perot was going after Armitage because of a 1984 investigation. In this incident, Nguyen O'Rourke, a Vietnamese woman who was charged with running a gambling and prostitution ring, had a close relationship with Armitage going back to his days in Southeast Asia during and after the war. When O'Rourke was charged, Armitage wrote a letter to the judge in the case on Department of Defense stationery, praising her character and recommending leniency. This was highly unethical, but probably not sufficient grounds to fire an Assistant Secretary of Defense. Perot believed it revealed something about Armitage's character that should make the President reluctant to keep him in such an important position.

Perot spoke with Vice President George Bush, whom he felt was his friend. After detailing to Bush a number of reasons Armitage was "bad news" and should be removed, Bush said he really couldn't do anything, but if Perot had evidence of Armitage's misfeasance or malfeasance in office he should give it to the FBI.

Perot met with the FBI person that Bush suggested and awaited developments. Within a few weeks, Perot received a call from National Security Advisor Frank Carlucci. Carlucci asked Perot to come to Washington to discuss some issues surrounding satellite computer software that Perot's company, EDS, was providing to the Department of Defense. Perot arrived in Washington and checked into the Hay Adams Hotel.

At the appointed time, he called the White House for Carlucci, who came on the line and said, "Where are you, Ross?" Perot told him, and Carlucci said he'd be right over.

Perot said that in all the years and all the occasions of having an appointment with White House personnel at any level, he had always met in the White House or its annex, the Old Executive Office Building. He thought it quite strange that Carlucci was going to come to his hotel room.

Before I continue this story, I need to point out that before telling John and Lynn this tale, Perot said, "I don't want to read this in the newspaper, but you need to know what I'm up against." Due to the passage of time and change in circumstances, John Nevin felt it was okay to repeat it here.

When Carlucci arrived, before even the most minimal greeting, he said, "Ross, you need to understand that Rich Armitage is extremely important to many of the things we're trying to do here, and you need to stop this crusade against him. You need to realize that he's right in the middle of the group of people you'd have to come to for help if, God forbid, you were ever in a position to need our help. With your money and notoriety, you and your family are some of the most high-profile targets in this country for any group who wanted to use violence to get something they wanted. A word to the wise, you need to drop this vendetta you have against Rich."

Perot was dumbfounded. He was a "true believer" in the essential goodness of the people who led his country. Without Perot specifically saying so, John and Lynn both had the strong impression that this experience had caused a corner to be turned in Perot's thinking.

When Perot later ran for President and then dropped out, John was convinced that a threat much stronger than disruption to his daughter's wedding had been made, and the wedding was simply the public excuse.

In fact, John and I both know the individual who delivered the alleged "wedding threat" to Perot. We think he sincerely believed he was doing

Perot a favor by passing the info along, but we think he was bamboozled specifically to give Perot a convenient excuse.

During this time, I became heavily involved with the family members of those POWs and hard-core activists such as Ted Sampley, unquestionably the leader of the POW/MIA activist movement, Margaret and John Nevin from Homecoming II, and many others who participated in peaceful civil disobedience on many occasions. My dilemma was the guilt I felt at being considered one of the leaders and yet never pushing any of my civil disobedience activities far enough to get me arrested, as so many others had done. Admittedly, pushing to the point of getting arrested seems foolish on one level, but when people are frustrated by repeated attempts to work "within the system," they sometimes feel compelled to go to extraordinary lengths to grab public attention for their cause. The media fascination with civil disobedience arrests is almost certain to get a number of TV cameras to the scene (if they are strategically informed in advance).

I've always believed in leading with my actions rather than my words; however, I feared that if arrested I could be fired from my position in management with no safety net or union to fight for me. Being married with two children and a mortgage, I struggled with my desire to join Margaret, Ted, and others in their many arrests.

In June 1988, Beth Stewart, a daughter of a POW, asked me to join her and other family members on Father's Day when they planned to chain themselves to the White House fence. This turned out to be the most difficult decision I've ever made in my life. Before making that decision, I called my father to tell him that I was considering supporting these family members.

My father's reaction was predictable; he said I would disgrace the family and that he would have nothing to do with me, would disown me, if I did get arrested. This was no idle threat. He and my sister had several arguments where they wouldn't talk to each other for six months at a time. But in all the years that they had their disagreements, he'd never vowed to disown her.

Within several days, I decided to join the family members. I knew it could cost me my job, my life as I knew it, and my relationship with my father, which had been good up to that point. Besides Beth, some other members were Patricia O'Grady Aloot (daughter), Michael Clark (son), Doctor Bruce Adams (brother), and Vietnam era veteran Bill Sullivan. We practiced the night before and the plan was simple.

That Sunday morning at nine, we stood at the fence facing the back of the White House as spectators waited for the Presidential helicopter to land on that back lawn. We found out that President Reagan was going to Canada for a historic meeting with the Prime Minister to discuss acid rain and other issues.

Reagan had only seven months left in office, so we saw this as a last hoorah to draw attention to the POW issue. Secret Service policy is to move all spectators across the street and away from the fence before allowing the chopper to take off. When it landed, we gathered together and hand cuffed ourselves to a thick chain that was wound around the fence and padlocked.

A rookie cop came over several times to tell us to move; then he finally realized we were chained to the fence. He told us if we didn't unhook ourselves and move, we would be arrested. I asked him to give us a couple of minutes to discuss this, then the Captain of the Park Police came over and told him to arrest us in a very stern voice. I'd been hoping to stall as long as possible, but we only bought ourselves another minute.

It turned out that they couldn't find the bolt cutters while we (and the President) waited. When they finally found the cutters, we were escorted into the police van. We delayed the President at least fifteen minutes and later found out that the captain, who was sympathetic to our cause, had "misplaced" those cutters.

Most of the police and secret service agents at that time were Vietnam veterans. We had a very strong network in Washington, D.C., which resulted in a great deal of support, respect, and sometimes inside information from within the White House and Executive Branch Departments (including, most importantly, the Pentagon.)

The main reason why I joined the family members was to make sure they were not hurt and to show support for their struggle. While in jail, the Secret Service agents interviewed the family members, as protocol would dictate, and let them know that the President asked why he was being delayed and they told him that the daughters and sons of the POWs had chained themselves to the fence. Unfortunately, Reagan did nothing, just like all seven Presidents have done since the end of the Vietnam War.

I never called my father, knowing how stubborn he was. To my surprise, he wound up calling me several months later, asking why I had not called him. I was stunned to find that my father had a new level of respect for me that made our relationship even better.

This event didn't receive national coverage, so there was never any retribution at work. Subsequently, I became more vocal as an activist and soon my comrades were calling me an activist leader.

That same summer, I organized a demonstration with local Vietnam veterans at Vice President George Bush's Kennebunkport summer home. Even though they claimed that Bush wasn't there, I spoke to the Secret Service agents protecting his home to pass along a message that we held him accountable for the POWs that we believed were still being held alive in Vietnam. The one agent seemed confused and asked why, so I gave him a history lesson of Bush's past, including his role as CIA Director when the war ended in 1975. There's no possibility that he didn't know about the abandonment of at least some of the POWs.

An interesting thing happened a couple of months later. I wasn't directly involved in it, but it underlines the kind of support we had from "inside."

We had obtained a demonstration permit from the D.C. Park Police for some activities we were planning for Veterans Day weekend. There was apparently some concern in the White House that we might be up to something more radical than we had ever done before. A number of Secret Service agents were dispatched around the country to interview some of the individuals seen as leaders.

John and Margaret Nevin of Homecoming II were at home in Kansas City, and by good fortune it happened that Tom Ashworth, a former Marine Corps pilot and an expert on the history of U.S. handling of POW issues, was present. The doorbell rang and John found a Secret Service agent at his door. He was invited in, and after he explained why he was there, the four of them sat down to talk at the dining room table. Tom Ashworth had done hundreds of media appearances, lectures, and addresses regarding the POW issue and he knew what the typical intelligent person found hardest to believe about the subject. He had the facts and the documentation to overcome the doubts of anyone honestly seeking the truth.

The discussion of our "radical" activities was quickly dispatched. By coincidence, the agent had sat down in the chair immediately in front of a photograph under the table's glass cover. It was picture of John and Margaret with Ronald Reagan, and they each had an arm over Reagan's shoulder. Reagan was wearing a POW T-shirt. "Reagan" was actually an enlarged photographic cut-out that some enterprising photographer had made and used to offer to tourists for photos "with the President," but the agent didn't realize that. Soon after the discussion began, he pointed at the photo and said, "You guys are obviously no threat to the President, and if he likes you, I like you."

This moved the discussion to the agent's interest in why we were demonstrating, and Tom Ashworth took the floor. Within thirty minutes, our movement had a new convert. As he left he said, "All I can say is, go get 'em guys."

I had come to Kennebunkport alone, even though I had heard that some of the members of the local Vietnam vet group were planning to get physical with me. They thought Bush was a good guy and didn't like an outsider from New York interfering in their affairs. My feeling was the same as it had been from the beginning, which was bring it on. Once I explained who I was and why I was protesting, they left without an incident.

I also organized a separate demonstration at the Bush Presidential Campaign Headquarters in New Hampshire. The people inside locked the front door and refused to talk to us, so later in the day I walked around to the back of the house and walked through the back door with the media following close behind.

They were embarrassed and insisted the media leave. I later told the media what we discussed and that Vietnam veterans were used to being treated like second-class citizens, so entering through the back door was expected.

Tom Burch recently reminded me of this incident and the fact that it was the first of many situations that earned me the reputation as The Stealth Activist, a title coined by former U.S. Congressman John LeBoutillier in 1993.

In October, 1988, I arranged another demonstration outside the Waldorf Astoria during the Alfred E. Smith Roman Catholic fundraiser. At that time, the presidential nominees were Vice President George Bush and Michael Dukakis. I checked out how I could get into the main ball room and attempt to deliver the Vice President a letter explaining how I had met with the Cardinal several years before. I figured if they stopped me before I reached the Vice President, presenting the letter would indicate that I meant no harm to anyone. I left my sister outside with over a hundred supporters and told her that if I didn't come back in about a half hour to ask the police if someone had been arrested inside and to bail me out of jail.

I was walking down a spiral staircase in the back of the hotel, checking out plan A, when all of a sudden I stopped in my tracks. Secretary of State Alexander Haig was walking up the staircase with a horde of media behind him. He walked past me and responded to my greeting with a friendly, "Hello." I could not get past the media, so I joined the group and followed along.

As I followed Haig up the staircase, I asked one of the media people where everyone was going and he said he didn't know; Haig had said there was going to be a photo opportunity with the Cardinal and the two presidential candidates. This seemed to be a good plan B, so I followed them to a long narrow walkway lined with tables and Secret Service agents on one side and the media on the other.

The security for this event was much tighter than I had ever seen. Agents conducted searches and even demanded we empty our pockets and bags. Photographers were forced to take the telescopic lenses off their cameras for inspection and there was close inspection of TV cameras.

As usual, I was dressed in a very nice suit and tie. I proceeded to calmly walk through all the media people saying, "Excuse me, please," until I walked into a very large room with about a hundred chairs set up in front of a small stage area. The area that was lit up was a platform about six inches high with velvet ropes in front of it.

I was one of the first to arrive so I immediately joined the few reporters in the second row to avoid drawing attention to myself. I realized that in the frenzy of the moment I had forgotten to put on what appeared to be media credentials that Ted Sampley had sent me. I slowly reached in my pocket and took out a chain with an attached laminated card labeled "Veterans Affairs Newspaper" and hung it around my neck.

At this point I'm laughing inside because I not only slipped past a hallway full of Secret Service agents, I did so without my fake credentials. What really surprised me is that there was no metal detector to walk through, so I could have brought in a weapon. Since the agents were located on the side of the platform, and not directly in front, anyone in the front two rows could have reached the three of them with no resistance.

We waited for about an hour until finally Cardinal O'Connor entered. There were about fifteen to twenty TV cameras and about a hundred total media personnel including radio and newspapers. I thought it was sad that there were as many media people at a photo-op as there were people outside demonstrating for the return of our POWs.

The Cardinal said in a very firm tone that there would be no questions allowed because this was for pictures only. He then introduced Governor Dukakis and as they were smiling for the cameras, I asked in a very loud voice so everyone could hear, "Governor Dukakis, we left live American Prisoners of War behind from the Vietnam War; if you're elected, will you appoint Ross Perot as a special envoy to Vietnam?"

The Cardinal immediately said, "Governor, don't answer that question," and then quickly moved in front of Dukakis and said in an annoyed tone, "Please, I asked that no questions be asked; this is only a photo-op." He then placed his hand up to shade his eyes from all the bright lights to see who it was. He could not see me even though I was in the second row only ten feet away.

He then introduced Vice President Bush, and I asked him the same question. Now the Cardinal was very pissed off and said in an angry tone, "Didn't I tell you not to ask any more questions?" It had become very personal. Realizing that the Cardinal had just lost it, the Vice President jumped in and said, "If elected President, I'll ask the Cardinal for his advice." The funny thing was when I asked the first question, many of the media were shushing me, and when I asked the second question they were all shushing me. But as Yogi says, "It ain't over 'til it's over."

As the three of them were walking off the platform I said in a very loud and authoritative voice, "Cardinal O'Connor, I'm Jerry Kiley, the Vietnam veteran who met with you and John LeBoutillier two years ago; you said you were going to help resolve the POW issue." The Cardinal turned around abruptly with a red face and just stared at me with anger I haven't seen since my Bronx schoolyard childhood.

As he began to walk away I said in an angry tone, "Two years later and nothing has happened; what are you going to advise the Vice President?" The Cardinal turned abruptly toward the sound of my voice and his body language indicated that he wanted to come back and challenge me, but the Vice President started talking to him and ushered him out of the room.

I immediately turned, thinking the Secret Service agents were going to knock me to the ground and arrest me; however, they all left with Bush. The media people were sarcastically telling me good job and a few bumped into me as I left to let me know how unhappy they were with what I had done. I told Ted what had happened, and he said there was nothing on any of the wire services, implying that he doubted my story.

He then called an Associated Press reporter who he knew was there, who confirmed what I did. The reporter said the security was so tight this time, primarily due to our demonstration outside, that if they printed what I did, the security would get even worse next time. I was very disappointed that the media would not report this story, but I shouldn't have been shocked: they had shown very little interest up to that point in reporting on the POWs we left behind, and I would soon realize that there was a widespread view among them that the story was one of the "untouchables."

My focus was to create some pressure to appoint Perot as special envoy to Vietnam because he was one of the few people we believed in, one of the few who had the character to do the right thing and convince Vietnam to return our men. It turned out that VP Bush was elected President and appointed insider General Vessey instead of Perot; that ultimately began the downfall of the POW issue.

As Vice Chairperson of the National Vietnam Veterans Coalition, I was called upon to perform other duties unrelated to veteran's issues. Two such events involved our support of the Baltic States Revolution against the Soviet Union. We were asked to join Lithuania's cabinet members, sent to America by their President, for a rally at the Russian Embassy in New York City. I was scheduled to speak immediately after Senator Alfonse D'Amato before a crowd of about 2,000 people.

Realizing that Pepsi Cola had a bottling and distribution plant in Russia, I drew a big red circle with a line through it on a Pepsi 2 liter bottle. I thought the Senator would be a hard act to follow; however, he spoke in a monotone throughout his speech. I began by committing the support of our organization and then went right into chanting, "Pepsi Nyet," while holding up the bottle of Pepsi. The crowd's reaction was so explosive and intense that it initially scared me.

We ended when I spoke to them about one final chant that would be heard around the world. I yelled "Freedom!" and they responded by yelling "Now!" I had taken a group who were very quiet and reserved until I spoke and left them cheering and yelling. When I left the stage area, which was a microphone set up on a flatbed truck, all those involved treated me like a hero and posed for pictures with me holding the Pepsi bottle.

That picture appeared on the front page of Ted's Veterans Affairs newspaper. At least six months to a year later this newspaper was lying at the base of the Vietnam Veterans Memorial with other memorabilia when it was gathered up and appeared in a display at the Smithsonian Institute. I never saw it myself, but several people said they saw my picture in that display.

Shortly after that rally in NYC, they had an even bigger rally of 5,000 on the steps of the U.S. Capitol. I spoke immediately following a talk by the son of the President of Lithuania. The results were the same and I was honored to join them in their fight for freedom. The revolution eventually succeeded with the Soviet Union's breakup and all three Baltic States were freed.

George H.W. Bush Presidency 1989 – 1993

Vice President Bush was elected President in November 1988 and, predictably, he never appointed Ross Perot to any position involved in the POW issue for fear he might actually succeed.

For the 1990 Rolling Thunder, Ted Sampley came up with an idea to erect a stage next to the Vietnam Veterans Memorial where all the bikers parked their bikes after the Rolling Thunder ride past the White House on Memorial Day. There were 25,000 bikers who participated in this ride, which started from the Pentagon parking lot in Virginia, proceeded past the Lincoln Memorial down Constitution Avenue to Pennsylvania Avenue, and then back to the two huge fields next to the Vietnam Veterans and Lincoln Memorials.

The theme each year was to draw attention to the POW issue to make sure the politicians and White House would not forget we left live American servicemen behind from the Vietnam War.

We had a professional stage erected and a sound system for a six-hour event. Three different bands each played for forty-five minutes each hour, with special guest speakers for the remaining fifteen minutes of each hour. Ted asked me to be the emcee of the event, and stepping out on stage with my two young sons was a thrill for me as well as for them.

I was very nervous before the event, but once we started I was surprised at how relaxed I felt and how confidently I handled everything. As emcee, I added additional comments that were appropriate after each speaker, and when the crowd got restless I would get them chanting "Freedom! Now!"

After the event, we invited the bikers to join us at the Lao Embassy to demand the release of the Americans. We had over a dozen demonstrations at this embassy; Vietnam controlled Laos, but with no diplomatic relations between the U.S. and Vietnam, Vietnam had no embassy here.

When I arrived at the Lao Embassy with my two sons, we heard a loud bang inside and the front door knob immediately flew out between us. We think a gun must have been fired; if a bullet made it through the door, it fortunately did no harm to anyone outside.

Even though we moved everyone away from the door, the gunshot incited us to be more vocal and aggressive. There was a constant roar of motorcycles up and down the narrow one-way street. There were times when it was deafening.

Late 1980s through early 1990s

Over the years I organized about a dozen demonstrations, half of them at the Vietnamese Mission at 20 Waterside Plaza in Manhattan where the Vietnamese Ambassador and his United Nations delegation lived. As many as 500 people marched and chanted right outside their building.

One of the Vietnam veterans from my company researched getting permits and discovered that the park in the middle of this very large apartment complex on the East River was subsidized by New York City. That thereby allowed us to demonstrate in this large area right in front of their building. Prior to that, demonstrators had stayed out on the street and so far away from the Vietnamese building that the Vietnamese could not see or hear them.

September thru October 1991

I attended the annual Rolling Thunder rally from New Jersey which traveled up FDR Drive past the Vietnamese Mission. I sneaked into the Vietnamese Mission building through the parking garage and left a pewter eagle clutching a POW/MIA banner in the middle of what looked like a pool of blood in front of the Vietnamese apartment. Since this had been a gift I had given to my son, I apologized to him, saying I would try to replace it. He understood. Unfortunately, I was never able to find another pewter spread eagle clutching the POW/MIA banner.

In this same time, I met three times with Vietnamese Ambassador Can, who had been sent by the government of Vietnam as a special Ambassador to deal exclusively with the POW/MIA issue. I joined the Rolling Thunder delegation on one occasion and on a second occasion joined with the Vietnam Veterans of America Chapter from Bayonne, N.J.

I arranged a third trip representing the NVVC, which was a one-on-one meeting with Ambassador Can. He spoke to me for over an hour to try to convince me that they were not holding any American POWs. Can was very calm but very firm in stating that there was no reason for Vietnam to hold our prisoners. His position was, of course, unchanged when I told him we had always assumed they had held them as leverage to guarantee the payment of nearly $5 billion in postwar reconstruction aid they had been promised by President Nixon but never received.

We spoke almost exclusively about the POW issue, with some talk of the human rights violations in his country and also how Agent Orange had devastated his country and his people. He had no interest in discussing the human rights issue, but I did express empathy for those hurt by Agent Orange, stating we did have a common issue since our veterans were also suffering.

I moved on to say we knew men were left behind, and we placed much of the blame on Nixon and Kissinger, who had promised the postwar aid. Nixon, Kissinger, and their apologists blamed Congress, but Nixon had never submitted a request for the aid to Congress. In fact, the promise itself was kept secret until exposed during the Carter Presidency.

We discussed and argued our points with my main message being that we were not seeking retribution and would consider their release of the men a courageous, humanitarian act; however, the American Vietnam veterans would never rest until the POW issue was resolved and we were prepared to fight them for the rest of our lives, until our dying breaths, if necessary. Vietnam veterans wanted justice, not revenge. I said our mantra is "Never forget," but we would not hold a grudge if they did the right and courageous thing by releasing our men.

Since I had already made my points in a very assertive manner, I wanted to end the meeting on a reconciliatory note. I told Can we were even prepared to accept without argument their predictable claim that the POWs were found in isolated areas in Laos. Soon after that meeting, they appeared more open to veteran delegations visiting Vietnam; however, their interest died several months later. Can eventually returned to Vietnam after unsuccessfully trying to do everything possible to convince us to give up our fight.

I observed that the Saturday before each one of my Sunday demonstrations my phone had a very distinct clicking sound. It would be gone by the time I got back home after the demonstration was over. At the time I thought it might be an act of intimidation by some government characters that had an interest in my activism, but it couldn't have been more than that. After all, if one of the intelligence agencies really wanted to monitor my calls, I was sure their technology would make it possible to do so without the clicks.

These incidents, along with several other odd occurrences, got me thinking paranoid thoughts. Even though I knew that if they were paying attention to me at all, they would know by now that non-violent civil disobedience was the worst I would do, but it did appear that I was on their radar screen.

During this period, I travelled to D.C. several times a month. Preparing for one of these Friday night trips, I said goodbye to my wife and two boys and headed toward my car carrying my luggage. Just then a very low flying helicopter passed over my house. As fate would have it, my sons chose that moment to playfully shine a spotlight beam at me which hit full-power on the side of my face. Thinking the beam was from the chopper, I dropped my luggage and ran back into the house in a panic.

My boys didn't understand my panicked reaction until I explained. Then they both broke out in hysterical laughter and have been laughing at my expense ever since. I'm forced to hear this story every few years. No helicopter before this incident or after has ever flown over my house that low.

I attended two meetings at the State Department. One was arranged by John LeBoutillier with the person rumored to be in charge of issues related to U.S. POWs and a couple of his staff people. I was there to stir things up if we were being led down the old, "We are trying our best," path. We did receive the typical bull story: If they knew about POWs, they would take immediate action.

They said there was a strike force on alert 24 hours a day, seven days a week. When we told them to visit the CIA because they have the classified information you want, they said certain information is not available to them and what they were able to see wasn't specific enough to take action.

Ted Sampley jumped all over them, and when things started to calm down, I threw fuel on the fire. Naturally, we accomplished nothing except to let them know we were not buying their lies.

The second meeting—set up by John Brown, whose relative was Deputy Secretary of State—was also supposed to be with top-level State Department employees. There were only five of us at this meeting, two of them and three of us. The person in charge gave us the same old story and John Brown and a friend he had brought along seemed to agree with this person, until I started to challenge his statements.

The other person he had at this meeting emphatically said, "If I knew where the POWs were, I would go over there right now to rescue them."

I said even more emphatically, "If you tried, they would stick you in the corner counting pencils for the rest of your career."

With that he leaped to his feet as if to come after me. I leaped to my feet and started at him. The person in charge yelled for him to sit down and repeated that several times before he complied. After that, I said we were wasting our time here because they were giving us the same old bullshit story.

What annoyed me most was the fact that John Brown, who talked a big game, was apologetic to this idiot who escorted us out the door. I yelled to John to go; as we were leaving, he said he believed that we were set up and that those two were CIA agents. If that was the case I could understand his anger. I'd knocked the CIA during the entire twenty-five minutes meeting. I hope they were CIA so they understood why we held them responsible for the POW cover-up.

Summer 1991

The National Alliance of Families with Delores Alfond and Ted Sampley invited Ross Perot to be their guest speaker. Perot was a self-made billionaire whose claim to fame was state-of-the-art computer software, as well as some bells-and-whistles hardware that was in great demand within the U.S. government. He was also famous for having rescued several of his employees from an Iranian jail and his undying support for the live Americans we left behind from the Vietnam War.

The National Alliance of Families is an organization comprised of family members of missing servicemen and women from all the wars, going back to World War II. Mike Bates and I were designated to be Perot's security for the day.

We met Mr. Perot at his car and brought him to a private meeting with Delores, Ted, and several people prior to his speech. The discussion centered on the obstacles surrounding resolution of the issue.

After Perot finished his speech to the hundred members in attendance, he grabbed his briefcase and began to walk to the front entrance where his car was waiting. All of a sudden, he was surrounded by everyone, wanting to talk to him about their cases and asking for his autograph.

Even though Mike and I were slowly moving the large crowd, I could see the family members getting increasingly agitated because of Perot's inattention. As a result, Perot was becoming frustrated because the family members were becoming more vocal and aggressive, preventing us from moving forward. He had been raising his briefcase as an excuse for not being able to make contact with them when I said in a very assertive tone, "Mr. Perot, I'll hold your briefcase for you."

He looked at his case and continued walking as if he didn't hear me. Several seconds later he turned, looked me straight in the eye as if to say, "Can I trust you?" When I reached out my hand to take it, I was surprised he gave it to me.

The tension immediately dissipated and the entire group began moving again. It took about ten minutes to get to the front entrance. Perot entered his car but immediately jumped out, panicked and saying, "Where is my briefcase?" I was in the process of stepping toward the car to hand him the case when I jumped back, startled by his reaction. He was relieved, embarrassed, and thankful when he shook my hand and disappeared in his car.

My impression was that he is a humble and modest man who felt embarrassed when people wanted to touch him and wanted his autograph. Perot doesn't believe he deserves such praise. The undying loyalty the family members felt for Perot is due to their trust in him. They'd been sold out by so many politicians and government agencies over the years that they simply worship him because his motives seem to be pure. In many ways, it's a sad commentary on the character and integrity of our political system and government.

Chapter Six
Stopping the Runaway Train 1991

President George H.W. Bush's strategy, or that of his surrogates, was to solicit the support of the major veterans' organizations like Vietnam Veterans of America, Disabled American Veterans, American Legion, and Veterans of Foreign Wars.

The one organization that they could not influence was Disabled American Veterans, who held true to their values and were the most vocal in their support of the men we left behind. The other three were a work in progress that Ted and I worked on in order to stop them from endorsing the normalization of relations with Vietnam.

Tom Burch held a very important national position of Adjutant in the VFW; however, he could not stop them from appeasing those who were in the strongest positions of political influence over the POW issue, in this case Clinton, Kerry, and McCain. The VFW was going along with Clinton's effort to pursue normalization when Tom asked Ted and me to take some action at the VFW national convention meeting in D.C. The Standerwick sisters, Ted, and I sneaked into their policy meeting of about hundred people.

Ted had filled a plastic baggie with ketchup that he planned on pouring out to symbolize the blood of those POWs left behind. He started to worry about the bag leaking so he reinforced it with another baggie that he hid inside his raincoat. The Standerwick sisters and I stood in the back, took posters out from under our shirts, and started yelling as a diversion to draw security away from the podium area.

As everyone was focused on us, Ted calmly walked to the podium, took out the bag, and made his statement to a shocked audience. As security started running back to the podium, Ted panicked and could not open the baggie. He laid it down on the podium so he could break it open with his fist. He hit it once and then in a panic, as security was closing in on him, he came down on the double baggie as hard as he could. All I can remember is an explosion of ketchup covering him and all the American Legion members sitting in the first ten rows.

I really felt sorry for those who were wearing white caps and white shirts. There was a collective moan and then dead silence. We all stood in shock, including Ted. Security escorted us all out of the room. He cleaned up his ketchup-drenched raincoat in the bathroom. VFW national leadership was extremely mad at Tom Burch when they found out later that Ted and I were the two vice chairmen of the NVVC, reporting directly to him.

The VFW national leadership never supported the POW issue; however, they didn't support normalization as they had intended before our visit. They backed off supporting McCain, knowing that we would be back if they didn't "shut up and sit down." We put them in their place and I enjoyed every second remembering how the VFW members had humiliated me when I tried to join their organization back in 1968. The same theme seemed to repeat itself: what goes around comes around.

July thru August 1991

Next was the American Legion. I was the spokesperson at a press conference held at the Press Club in Washington, D.C., introducing guest speakers John LeBoutillier, Red McDaniel, and others concerning the POW issue. After the press conference ended, Dave Christensen, American Legion Communication Director in D.C., approached me and expressed concern about this issue. After a ten minute discussion, he sounded very interested in learning more.

Dave indicated that the American Legion was having trouble recruiting Vietnam veterans, and he feared that they would eventually become extinct as the WWII veteran population dwindled. I told him the problem is that the major veteran organizations stayed away from controversial issues like Agent Orange and the POW issue, so we weren't going to join organizations that didn't support our cause.

I'd recently read an American Legion article in which they were challenging the government over Agent Orange and even used the word "cover-up." I said, "If you believe the government can cover up a medical issue right in front of their eyes, why do you find it difficult believing there is a coverup of men being held halfway around the world?"

"If you guys truly got behind both of these issues, not just lip service, you would save the American Legion from extinction." He told me that if I put that in a letter he'd make sure the American Legion Executive Director, John Summers, read it. As usual, John Nevin helped me write the letter that resulted in an invitation for us to meet with John and Dave at their headquarters in D.C.

Ted and I met with John and Dave and gave them our best information on the POW issue. We explained that if they supported normalization it would be their deathblow; however, if they opposed it, we would actively encourage Vietnam veterans to join the American Legion. They were aware of our activities, and I was surprised with the amount of respect they had for us.

At the end of the meeting, John Summers made a joke about us backing down. I said, "We may decide not to leave," and then I asked Ted, "Did you bring the handcuffs?"

"I told you to bring them."

"Damn, we messed up; now they'll have to drag us out the door."

John and Dave laughed. Dave later told me that they really respected what Ted and I were doing for our fellow veterans. We had mutual respect and admiration for both of them for having the courage of their convictions, something very rare in D.C.

This was a big morale boost for us considering the trashing we were receiving from politicians, government officials, the media, and almost everyone else who wasn't either a Vietnam veteran or a family member of a missing man or woman. John and Dave used our meeting to pressure the National Commander, Rivers, on the membership side of the organization.

The best feeling was when the American Legion took a strong position opposing normalization. John Nevin and I wrote a thank you letter to the American Legion leadership, pledging to help them recruit Vietnam veterans. Their actions spoke much louder than their words, and membership grew in subsequent years.

August 21 thru 25, 1991

There was one more veterans organization to turn around, Vietnam Veterans of American (VVA), the toughest of the three. VVA was born from the leadership of Vietnam Veterans Against the War (VVAW) and had John Kerry as their spokesperson.

This was the one organization he could count on to support normalization since VVA had opposed the POW issue on the grounds that it took away from the other more important veterans' issues. They also feared that the POW supporters might eventually try to overthrow their entrenched people once the door was open.

VVA was the most credible politically because it was exclusively Vietnam veterans. The organization was very outspoken and politically effective in their support for Clinton and Kerry.

Since I knew someone had to take on the national organization, I looked for a VVA chapter that was behind the POW issue and would cover my back. Finding little or no support from the chapters where I lived and worked, I decided to join the Bayonne, N.J., VVA Chapter with Sal Mione as their chapter president. Sal and his brother Jim were very outspoken on the POW issue.

As a side issue, I was actually referred to the Bayonne Chapter in New Jersey by the Black Veterans for Social Justice, whom I had visited in Brooklyn when recruiting organizations. They were interested in the POW issue, but with limited resources they were focused primarily on social issues and the effects of Agent Orange (AO).

When I told them I was on a post in Vietnam and wasn't exposed to Agent Orange, they became very annoyed and asked if my post had any vegetation. I was stunned and replied no. Their leader said my post had been

77

cleared with AO and the dust I'd breathed in for those fourteen months was toxic. Also, the clothing we wore was washed by the Vietnamese on the side of the river bank that had been sprayed with AO. The 55-gallon drums that had been cut in half to collect our waste in the latrines were AO drums. We would use gasoline to burn that waste for hours at a time and then replace it under each stall for reuse. After they told me the effects of Agent Orange might not surface until years later, I left the meeting feeling numb, stupid, and embarrassed for my lack of knowledge. The saddest thing of all is that these black veterans came home to the same prejudice and hatred they had experienced before they placed their lives on the line for our country.

I felt very comfortable visiting the Bayonne Chapter to give updates on what the activists were doing in D.C. and around the country. I attended most of their monthly meetings and was elected as one of the convention delegates, as I had hoped.

I announced my intention to be a candidate for VVA National president. The current president of the national organization, Mary Stout, and her current vice president were both running for the presidency. There was friction between them because Mary wasn't stepping down as she had previously promised.

I attended the three-day convention where amendments to their by-laws would be voted on as well as an election held. There were 300-plus delegates to the convention representing chapters from around the country.

I was aware of many proposed amendments from National that would destroy any possibility of supporting the POW issue, so the Bayonne chapter submitted their own amendments in support of the issue. Even though the convention met to discuss each amendment, the VVA's leadership controlled the meeting with Robert's Rules of Order in concert with their own people to subvert the voice of the membership, especially those who disagreed with them.

I quickly realized that the same people kept rushing to the microphones to prevent those in disagreement from speaking before voting on an amendment. Fortunately, they tipped their hand on insignificant amendments so when it came time, I got to the microphone before the debate began.

As it turns out, I set the stage for a slam-dunk against the VVA leadership when I addressed the convention on the very first POW amendment. I made the point that the membership was stagnant because it had not taken a stand on the POW issue and that National was an impediment to the issue.

I told the members that those of us who had devoted our lives to the POW issue had no intention of taking away from the other issues. I asked them to give us the ability to increase the VVA membership across the country by passing these amendments in support of our POWs.

The most important amendments proposed by VVA national were negative because they supported normalization and were critical of our Last Fire Base vigil across from the Lincoln Memorial. Ted Sampley was personally attacked as someone committing fraud while taking advantage of the family members.

The most important POW amendment we supported came at the end of many. They'd made sure I wouldn't be able to get to the microphone while they trashed Ted, so I walked around to the far side, up to a microphone that was hardly used.

They rotated the order of the microphone locations and were shocked when I interrupted their second call for a vote. Since they had skipped past my microphone, they were forced to stop the vote and recognize me after consulting with their expert on Robert's Rules of Order.

I began by criticizing those who would trash a fellow Vietnam veteran and said our government had trashed us enough, that it was a disgrace that we would do it to someone who was a war hero with four Bronze Stars, earned while serving two tours of duty in Vietnam in the Special Forces.

I tried to cut the tension by saying that it was true when government officials called Ted Sampley stubborn, arrogant, and belligerent, and those were his best attributes. I then said he was also the best friend the POWs ever had. I believe this was the speech that turned the convention around.

The membership overwhelmingly passed our POW amendments and defeated the VVA national leadership POW amendments that would have supported Kerry's position. I saw Senator Kerry standing by one of the side doors observing the convention while his/Nationals' amendments went down in flames.

The convention ended when the three candidates, the president, vice president, and I, answered questions on stage prior to the election. The final question concerned the loyalty of the vice president to the president, which was one of the biggest conflicts at the convention.

Mary answered first and naturally knocked her VP for being disloyal. I was next and respectfully said I'm passing on this one, which caused some loud laughter. At the same time I moved my chair, which was situated between both of them, back three or four feet and then made a gesture with my hands for both of them to get it on.

The entire convention broke out in a second wave of laughter. That threw off the VP, who'd been trying to answer during the noise. It was so funny that the VP stopped talking during a round of laughter.

I've always had a knack for saying or doing something to break the tension. I guess the final joke was on me because I came in a distant third; even though I lost that battle, I felt like I definitely won the war.

The outcome of this VVA convention would have been different had I not attended, and I view my role in turning things around as one of my toughest and greatest accomplishments. Without the support of the Bayonne VVA chapter, none of it would have been possible. They walked the walk and displayed tremendous character in the face of adversity.

Ted and I stripped our adversaries of the cover they were looking for from these three veterans' organizations. Unfortunately, our adversaries included President George Bush, Senator John Kerry, Senator John McCain, Dick Cheney, Paul Wolfowitz, Richard Armitage, Richard Childress, their CIA, DIA, and ONI friends, and the entire intelligence community.

We delivered a crushing defeat to Kerry's hoped-for "veteran strategy." I suspect that he already knew that the Senate Select Committee on POW/MIA Affairs was going to be formed four months later to "review" all POW-related information.

This was the one organization Kerry could count on to help him destroy the POW issue once and for all. Ted and I and our many veteran and family member supporters managed to get all four major veterans' organizations to support the POW issue, taking away Kerry's leverage to discredit those of us who refused to back down in the fight for our abandoned comrades-in-arms.

I have to say that choosing the right VVA Chapter, developing an effective strategy to counter the national organization amendments with our own, and successfully implementing that strategy at the convention was one of my most difficult achievements.

Unfortunately, I did go back on my promise to the Bayonne Chapter that I would remain and fight within the VVA. The success we had at the convention made me a lightning rod for POW controversy within the organization. I was forced to conclude that my continued presence would only impede any further progress.

The people we went up against in VVA National were tough, hardened veterans who'd had years of experience going back to when they opposed the Vietnam War in the '60s and '70s.

December 1991

The Senate Select Committee was allegedly formed to investigate the POW/MIA issue. Even though President Bush touted the CIA/DIA line that the activists in the country were the lunatic fringe and that we had no substance to our charges of government cover up, our constant attack was instrumental in the creation of the committee.

Bush continued his agenda of burying the POW issue when he supported the Democrats' appointment of our sworn enemy on this issue, Senator John Kerry, as Chairman, and Senator Dole's choice of Senator John McCain. Both of these Senators had a history of supporting and even praising the brutal Communist regime in Vietnam. They were the worst possible choices because they vehemently denied that we left POWs behind, and Bush supported that same belief.

The committee conducted a sham of an investigation, attacking the family members and activists who said there was a cover up and then scripting the government testimony to bury the issue. McCain yelled and scolded family members while praising and hugging the former Vietnamese officer he claimed beat him while he was held in captivity.

It was clear that the investigation wasn't going well for us when Kerry and McCain attacked the activists who had pressured the government to form this committee. They called us radicals and accused us of profiting from the grief of the family members.

Summer 1992

We were thoroughly frustrated until President Bush made one politically fatal mistake; he decided to attend the National League of POW/MIA Families meeting before the election against Clinton because of the criticism from POW groups and family members.

Since this was the yearly meeting for the families of those missing from the Vietnam War, the game plan was simple: embarrass Bush for his role in helping to cover up the POW issue. The feeling was that four more years of Bush meant no chance to succeed, whereas with Clinton as President there was at least a slight chance.

As in American politics, it was the lesser of two evils. As John Nevin has said, the problem with that dilemma is that we are always voting for evil. As usual, I had already checked out how I could get through security, but the families asked us to back off. They guaranteed us they were going to lodge a protest inside the meeting when Bush appeared.

Normally, I would have been skeptical. We'd been let down before by promises of tough action by League of Families members that never materialized. John LeBoutillier and Jeff Donahue worked with the family members and in this case, they hit a grand slam.

As Bush began his speech, about a dozen or more family members stood up in protest; as he talked about how he supports the POW issue, they began to chant. Eventually, he became so frustrated that he said in an angry tone, "Shut up and sit down."

It appeared on the news that evening and played for several days around the country. The family members said they did it because they were frustrated in his stonewalling on the POW issue, and what goes around comes around. I believe that incident and the negative publicity it generated for him played a role in Bush's defeat in the November election.

Outside, we were having fun chanting against Bush. The police were playing games with us trying to keep us away from the front of the hotel.

When we refused to leave, Ted basically cut a deal to get himself arrested instead of the whole group. As Ted entered the police van, about a hundred of us shook the van while chanting, "Free Ted!"

As the van drove off I turned to the detective who cut the deal and said, "You made a big mistake."

He got in my face with about a dozen detectives behind him and said, "What are you going to do about it?"

"Leave him in jail." They all froze and looked at me in disbelief until I said, "He's your problem now; we never wanted him."

They broke out laughing for a minute or two, so I milked it for all it was worth. I told them we'd been trying to get rid of him for years and said things like, "Boy, did you guys screw up."

The detective eventually laughed along with us, and in the end he told me where we could bail him out.

"Hell no! I'm going in the opposite direction!"

He slapped me on the shoulder as we parted company, still laughing. We did bail Ted out of jail and then gathered for dinner, as we usually did after one of our activities, to revel in our dirty deeds.

There was a demonstration on Pennsylvania Avenue in front of the White House that turned out to be a great event because of President Bush's overreaction. Ted asked everyone to bring their combat boots and throw them over the White House Fence to symbolize each POW still missing in action.

The White House lawn was filled with agents and there were at least twenty sharp-shooters on the White House roof, in addition to all the normal D.C. and Park police. I would guess there were at least two hundred officers in all. Disabled veterans in wheelchairs led our demonstration. The local media made the White House look ridiculous with their armed overreaction.

Bush set the table for normalization of relations with Vietnam. Ironically, three allegedly conservative Republicans played the most important role in normalization, Bush, Dole, and McCain.

The Morton Downey Show on WPIX at one point wasn't only conservative but also very popular. Unfortunately, I got caught in a competitive cross-fire between former Congressman Bill Hendon of South Carolina and Ted Sampley of North Carolina on who would set up a presence on the Thailand/Lao border in case anyone took advantage of the $7 million reward guaranteed by seven Congressman for the return of a legitimate American POW from the Vietnam War.

I was representing Ted when I was thrown off the show with extreme prejudice in typical Mort Downey fashion. Bill Hendon, who orchestrated my removal, later apologized, but our relationship was never the same.

I found out that Jessie Jackson was supposed to have a rally in support of a possible Presidential bid right outside the office I managed. He was using this event to enhance his political influence in an election year. I waited in the very large crowd so that I could attempt to give him a POW/MIA bracelet and ask him to support the issue. I could not pass up this opportunity.

About five minutes later, he showed up and waded through the very large crowd. I placed myself between him and the stage area as he slowly moved towards me. Since I was one of the few white people in this crowd, he was aware of me even though he was a distance away.

I finally shook his hand and gave him the bracelet while he enthusiastically said he had always supported the freeing of POWs left behind in Vietnam. With that he put his arm around me and brought me up on stage with him. The next day, I was on the front page of the local newspaper with Jesse Jackson as one of his supporters. I have no doubt that he would have jumped at the chance to negotiate for the release of these men.

Tom Burch and the NVVC were instrumental in helping a former Vietnam veteran win the governorship of Kentucky. The governor later bestowed the state militia honorary title of "Kentucky Colonel" on Tom and me. I was told that it is considered to be one of the most prestigious honorary appointments due to the fact that it is among the oldest and most recognizable titles in the country.

Technically, if the governor declared a state of emergency or had to call out the state militia, I would be immediately promoted to colonel. God forbid! The actual benefit to this title is attending the Kentucky Derby and the formal political events with the governor, including the formal ball. I never did attend any of those events.

Clinton Presidency 1993 – 1995

Some dates in this timeframe are only as reliable as my memory, but precise dates rarely have importance to the narrative. January 1993 was significant because Clinton was inaugurated the same month that Senator John Kerry, chairman of the Select Committee to investigate the POW issue, and Senator John McCain, member of that committee, released their final report which said: "While the Committee has some evidence suggesting the possibility a POW may have survived to the present, and while some information remains yet to be investigated, there is, at this time, no compelling evidence that proves that any American remains alive in captivity in Southeast Asia."

What escaped the media's attention was the fact that neither Kerry nor McCain—nor anyone else in the U.S. government—had questioned or pressed Vietnam for direct, specific answers about what happened to many of the live POWs we knew by name who were being held but had never been returned.

Former Secretaries of Defense Melvin Laird and James Schlesinger—who was also a former CIA Director—testified before the committee that they believed back in 1973 and still believed to that day that we left men behind. That story ran nationally for a day or two, but was never substantially followed-up on by any major media outlet. Neither the fact that President Nixon had lied to the American people in 1973 when he said all our POWs were coming home, nor the fact that some living Americans were very possibly still being held captive in Southeast Asia seemed important enough to pursue.

John McCain berated Delores Alfond, whose brother was missing, to such a degree that she broke down and cried. The angry McCain that many of us have witnessed over the years surfaced while he attacked her. Delores was the leader of the National Alliance of Families, a group that has been involved in locating missing POWs going back to the Korean War.

This despicable act, the many instances of his explosive temper towards family members and veterans, and his underhanded, aggressive attempts to bury the issue—not to mention some critical evidence of his behavior as a POW in Vietnam—combine to explain why he is held in such low regard by those who have studied this issue carefully.

Kerry and McCain's manipulation of witness lists, treatment of witnesses, ignoring of staff investigators' recommendations regarding some of the best evidence, and even destruction of evidence have all played a significant role in the final abandonment of our POWs. There is little satisfaction in the fact that their behavior later undermined their further political ambitions. This issue played a role in bringing down a sitting President (GHW Bush) and helped prevent Kerry and McCain in their bids to become President of the United States.

Unfortunately, when Clinton became President, the table had been set by former President Bush, Senator Dole, Senator Kerry, and Senator McCain to slam-dunk the POW issue. At one time, it was the only obstacle to normalizing relations with the Communist government of Vietnam.

October 17, 1993

The "Captains of American Industry" gathered at New York City's Crown Plaza Hotel to honor Deputy Prime Minister Phan Van Khai with a cocktail party and dinner. I had already checked out the hotel earlier that evening to see if there were any obvious entry paths that would allow me access to the event.

Unfortunately, my effort turned out to be a waste of time because I didn't know exactly where the event was going to be held.

My first roadblock was getting into the reception area for people who had attended the business meetings to promote trade in Vietnam. I always dressed in a very nice black power suit at these events, one that had been custom fit by the head tailor at West Point (he lives a couple of blocks away from me), paired with a pink shirt and a black and wine colored tie.

I walked past the reception table unnoticed. Two security guards stood at the foot of a spiral staircase leading to the second floor where I was sure the banquet for Khai would be held. I recognized them as Secret Service agents from my 1988 encounter at the Alfred E. Smith dinner in New York. They all wear the same pins at an event. I could feel my heart pounding.

Since I was one of the first people to enter the ground floor cocktail area, I immediately began serving myself jumbo shrimp to avoid suspicion. One of the attendees started up a conversation with me, stating that the presentations were excellent. I responded by saying that I thought they were too long and quickly ended that conversation after he awkwardly agreed with me.

My game plan to get past the agents was neither A nor B. I had no game plan except to wait and observe for a possible opening to make a move.

To my surprise, I saw a friend of mine who was also a veteran activist (Mike Van Atta) on the other side of the shrimp. Without making eye contact, Mike quietly said he would create a disturbance to distract the Secret Service agents.

As promised, Mike became very loud and drew the agents to him. I quickly walked up the staircase, through the unmanned metal detectors, and into a large room where several people were engaged in a heated discussion. I continued to walk away from them and into another large ballroom that was already set up for dinner. Upon entering this ballroom, I saw a full table; I was about to sit at a table away from them when they all stood up, their Secret Service pins on their lapels.

Instinctively, I turned toward the stage area as they started walking toward me. I climbed several stairs and walked over to the podium and began playing with the microphone to make sure everything was working correctly. They glanced in my direction as they left the room, thinking that I was with the hotel event staff.

After they left, I took a deep breath and sat down at one of the tables in the back corner to wait patiently for my meal. I was scared, but I couldn't help but laugh as I sat in the main banquet hall all alone. About twenty minutes later, an agent saw me and said, "Sir, you will have to go down stairs and re-enter (through the metal detector)." He escorted me to the top of the spiral staircase and then left as I descended down the stairs.

As good fortune would have it, the agents at the bottom of the staircase allowed some people waiting patiently to ascend the same staircase I was coming down. I allowed the first couple to pass me then followed behind them. At the top of the staircase where the metal detectors were placed, I stood next to them as if we were together, waiting for the agents to allow us through. When the agent waved for us to walk through, I gestured for them to go first, but they insisted that I go.

I've learned that decisiveness is an asset in these types of situations, especially considering I was supposed to be a captain of some kind of industry. It's not easy acting like a captain when you feel like a scared cook. Upon entering the reception area for a second time, I walked quickly to the hors d'oeuvres and took a long time checking out all the food. I ended up with the same jumbo shrimp I was eating on the first floor where I'd met Mike.

Avoiding eye contact at all costs, I occasionally said hello to several people who were friendly, giving the appearance that they knew me. My stomach was churning as it had been at the Alfred E. Smith dinner, and I started to shake slightly because I was so nervous. After about fifteen minutes, a gentleman who was running the show announced that the reception line should start forming to his left where I was already standing.

One couple walked in front of me, so I was second in line (I had positioned myself there because I couldn't stand waiting around any longer.) There were four or five Vietnamese standing around, so at first I wasn't sure which one was Khai since I had never seen him before. This was his first visit to the U.S., the historic first unofficial visit by a Vietnamese dignitary since the war ended in 1975.

While being introduced as an AT&T representative, I took out my American Legion cap and put it on. I took out a small POW/MIA flag on a stick and handed it to Khai as I clutched his other hand in a death grip handshake. His smile quickly vanished as I told him that I represented hundreds of thousands of Vietnam veterans and millions of Americans who believed Vietnam was lying about live POWs held in their country. I told him we would never rest until every one of them come home.

I also told him America knew about his government's brutal history and that Americans would never believe that Vietnam had changed until they gave their own people human rights freedoms, and until they set all the POWs free. I cannot accurately say how long it was because in the heat of the moment time is suspended. My guess is that it was about thirty seconds but seemed like minutes.

At that point, Khai's entourage began to yell for the Secret Service agents. They approached me and politely asked me to leave. As I made my way across this very large banquet room of over two hundred people, I realized the agents were protecting Khai and that no one was escorting me out. I stopped in the middle of the room and said in a very loud voice, "Excuse me, ladies and gentlemen, could I have your attention please?"

I said that twice until the room became quiet and then said, "I'm a Vietnam veteran and I want you to know that all of you here today representing American business have betrayed living American POWs left behind in Vietnam after the war. You have betrayed their families, you have betrayed Vietnam veterans, you are betraying the American people. You are betraying the Vietnamese people and their hope for democracy and human rights by supporting a government with one of the worst human rights records in the world. I hope you are proud of yourselves, because you have disgraced yourselves and your country."

The Secret Service eventually approached me a second time and escorted me down the spiral staircase and out to the main lobby. Even though there were thirty media people who witnessed this, someone told me only one print media mentioned an aging veteran wearing a veteran's cap.

There were a handful of TV cameras. I would give anything to get the video of Khai holding the POW/MIA flag as I berated him during my speech. As fate would have it, I would have another "interesting" meeting with Khai twelve years later at another banquet in Washington, D.C,, on 6/21/05.

July 16, 1994 - I attended the National Alliance of Families meeting in Washington, D.C., and decided that we needed to do something dramatic because Senator Kerry and Senator McCain were positioning themselves to give President Clinton the cover he needed to lift the embargo and normalize relations with Vietnam without a full accounting of the live POWs we abandoned.

I had met Jane Gaylor, whose son was missing from the Vietnam War, the previous year when she expressed her frustration at the government officials who had lied to her. I approached her at the meeting and said I was thinking of chaining myself to the White House fence. Jane wanted to make one last statement to President Clinton, so she agreed to chain her wheelchair to the White House fence. I made the announcement of Jane's intention and requested support for her courageous act at the meeting.

We usually had a difficult time getting people to join us, but this time we limited the number to a dozen because we could not afford the bail money for the twenty-five who volunteered. Even at twelve, this was the largest arrest I had ever seen, and so I affectionately named them the Dirty Dozen.

We'd spent a lot of money in the past buying large heavy link chains and handcuffs, but the police always had bolt cutters that cut through the large links like a hot knife through butter. We knew we could not delay the inevitable, so I went to a local hardware store with my sons, Mike and Dave. My youngest, Dave, suggested we buy the cheapest bicycle wire and a tiny lock to secure Jane's wheelchair to the White House fence.

As luck would have it, the big bolt cutters crushed and twisted the wire but could not cut through it and the lock was so tiny that it kept slipping out of the cutter. After at least fifteen minutes, they gave up and asked us for the key because it was a hot day and Jane was starting to feel faint.

Ted Sampley, who was handling the media that day, was yelling at me to give the police the key. But I had given the key to Dave, who was across Pennsylvania Avenue in the park with the supporters who were cheering us on. When Dave finally gave a police officer the key, Jane was immediately placed in an air-conditioned police car and was released without being jailed.

It may sound hard, but I would have preferred Jane be arrested. I'm unsure if her release was an act of kindness or political CYA. The last thing Clinton and his people wanted was the embarrassment of a wheelchair-bound POW mother being sent to jail. When I organized this event, my goal was to cause that embarrassment to force a response.

As we were being arrested one at a time, the large group supporting us started singing "Happy Trails," Roy Rogers' and Dale Rogers' theme song. Since I was the organizer, I was the last to be arrested. Just before my arrest, I held up the POW/MIA flag upside down, the sign of distress, and immediately heard the chant, "Jerry! Jerry!" This was a popular chant on TV for Jerry Springer. Even though moments like this were very serious, we often enjoyed the much-needed humor to break the tension.

President Clinton normalized relations with Vietnam 7/11/95, thus killing any chance for resolving the POW issue. Even though it is understandable why a liberal Senator from Massachusetts who opposed the Vietnam War would be in favor of normalization, it is totally unbelievable that a self-proclaimed Conservative Senator from Arizona—and a pretend "war hero"—would be the most instrumental person in giving Clinton the political cover he needed from the Republican side of the aisle.

McCain is loved by the mainstream media and portrayed as a war hero even though he committed treasonous acts while held as a POW. He gave the enemy military information for the promise of better medical treatment, signed a confession admitting to acts against civilians that was a lie, and repeated that lie on radio Hanoi broadcasts.

We do not condemn him for these acts because we know the kind of pressure that can be put on a person in his situation. We do think, however, that these acts should preclude his being seen as a hero. We condemn him for his actions that undermined possibilities for honest investigation and actions to free his former comrades-in-arms. He's caused immeasurable pain to families of the missing, knowledgeable Vietnam veterans and concerned citizens who know the truth but have been powerless to do anything about it.

The North Vietnamese used McCain in their propaganda to try and convince the American people and the world at large that they treated the POWs very well. McCain was the only POW to rehabilitate in a hospital where he received and carried on lengthy conversations with Communist reporters and military generals. His captors knew McCain as "The Crown Prince," whose father was an Admiral and commander of the entire military force in the Pacific theater.

Even though McCain claimed to be tortured, no one ever witnessed any physical abuse against him. In fact, his Senior Ranking Officer (SRO) at the POW camp, Ted Guy, told John LeBoutillier and me that McCain was never tortured at his camp. Ted Guy said that McCain was taken from the camp on a regular basis, sometimes for weeks and months at a time, and McCain never talked about where he had gone or what he did when he returned.

The wounds McCain suffered were from his landing in a lake after being shot down, not torture.

Considering how obsessed McCain is with his undying support of a brutal Communist regime in Vietnam whom he claimed tortured him, one can speculate that the Vietnamese government might be holding something over his head. McCain has supported almost every piece of legislation favorable to Vietnam and his support is seen by many as being essential to the early normalization of relations.

We'd given it our best shot, but our efforts didn't prevent the collaborative effort of Senator Kerry, Senator McCain, President Clinton, and a biased media from normalizing relations with Vietnam on 7/11/95, almost one year to the day after our arrest. That was the moment I believed there was no hope for saving our men, and so I retired as an activist. After Clinton normalized relations in 1995, I became inactive in the POW movement for the next 8 years until an unrelated event in 2003 brought me back from seclusion.

Chapter Seven
Coming Out of Activist Retirement

G. W. Bush Presidency 2001 – 2005
February 23, 2003 (Sunday)

Eight years later, I walked onto the Manhattanville College basketball court to confront a female player, Toni Smith, who repeatedly turned her back to the American flag during the playing of the national anthem. Her photo and story of this protest appeared on the front page of my local newspaper two days earlier. She was protesting the fact that the President might go to war in Iraq.

Saturday morning, I called Manhattanville College and asked to speak with her in order to explain the disappointment and even anger felt by veterans like me. I already planned on suggesting an option to stay in the locker room during the playing of the anthem.

The college's public affairs representative called me back on Saturday afternoon. She was belligerent when she told me there was no way I could speak with the player. She said the president of the college was on a business trip and unavailable. When I warned the rep that if they didn't stop her, I would protest her actions, she threatened to have me arrested if I stepped foot on campus. That afternoon I did a recon of the main entrance to Manhattanville College and realized that the back entrance was my best option.

I was surprised when a captain in the Harrison Police Department called me the night before the game and told me they had tripled security and that he would have to do his job even though he supported my position. I thanked him and said I understood that he had a job to do and that whatever I did it would be peaceful. I did explain that I had been a veterans' rights activist and had a track record of peaceful demonstrations.

On Sunday, the day of the game, I first tried to enter in the rear entrance to the college, but it was closed. I walked to the top of the driveway where a security guard appeared and asked me who I was. I responded that I was a reporter and he told me to go to the front entrance. Apparently, they saw me coming; there were cameras set up at the entrances and throughout the campus. I drove up to the security shack at the front entrance and they refused to let me enter because the basketball game was invitation only.

Finally, I drove around the back past the rear entrance to an area I had checked out on Saturday. Unfortunately, there had been a heavy snow storm, so I decided not to attempt climbing over high metal fencing, but I saw a path where the snow was shoveled from the dormitories to the main campus.

As I began to walk down a very long path I saw a campus security vehicle on the other side. I waited patiently in the dormitory foyer and, to my surprise, the security vehicle drove away.

I approached the building where the game was being played, but I still didn't have a ticket. I started up a conversation with a man and his young daughter with the hope of slipping through as they handed in their tickets. I saw a side door and opened it, then walked directly onto the court, immediately behind the opposing team's seats.

You would think by now I would handle these situations calmly. Wrong! As usual my heart was pounding, working its way to my throat.

Both teams' benches were against the wall where I was standing and everyone else, fans and security, were on the other side of the court. The students were in the second floor balcony seats overlooking the court. Since security had stopped me from entering, I was late and the game was in progress. About one minute after I arrived, there was a foul called in front of where I was standing. Toni Smith, the female player who'd turned her back on the flag, was standing on the base line waiting for her teammate to take a foul shot when I approached her.

I opened up a flag from my pocket and held it up in front of her, saying, "This flag symbolizes the sacrifice of brave women and men who give you the right of free speech; don't abuse that right by using the flag as a political tool." I was removed from the court and held for about five minutes near the front entrance. There were about a dozen people trying to get at me. I couldn't tell what they were saying until they were allowed to approach, then they told me they were relatives of the players and that they, along with almost all of the team, had been against Smith's protest. They praised me for my effort and asked for my phone number.

I later received a call from one of the players on the basketball team. She told me that almost the entire team supported what I did. The coach had tried to get Smith to remain in the locker room during the anthem, but she rejected that idea. When it looked like Smith was going to be forced to comply, the coach and majority of the players were overridden by the president of the college.

Eventually, the Harrison Police appeared at the main entrance and the captain who had phoned me introduced himself, shaking my hand. He explained that the campus police would drive me to the front entrance of the college and release me unharmed. On the drive to the entrance, I complimented the two security guards by telling them I'd slipped past Secret Service on two occasions and was never stopped.

"You guys stopped me twice, at both entrances," I told them.

One guard said, "I'd appreciate your telling us how you got on campus." When I told him, he said, "See? They didn't listen to us when we told them to place a camera on that dormitory path."

As promised, the captain was waiting for me and we talked as he drove me to my car. Since the drive to the back of that campus was dark and deserted, I was still apprehensive that something bad could happen. My fear was unfounded. During the short drive, I gave him a quick recap of my history as a POW/MIA activist.

He made it clear that the entire Harrison Police Department supported me, including the Chief of Police. He shook my hand again and told me it was an honor to meet me.

"If they win tonight, I'll see you again at the playoff game," I said. He was laughing as he drove away.

One local cable station, Channel 12, filmed the event. It appeared across the country—even on ESPN—for the next two weeks. Since this was on the front page of my local newspaper, I felt compelled to send a clear message to our children that even though you have the right to disrespect our flag, it does not make it right and when you do something wrong there are consequences. If no veterans spoke up or took any action, it would have given the appearance to our younger generation of Americans that we condone such actions.

I spoke to a couple dozen radio stations from around the country over the next two days. Even though I took two vacation days to devote myself to getting out my message, I could not accept many of the requests. Several stations made me hero of the week, even though I insisted I was no hero. Two New York TV stations stopped by my house to film me with the flag I'd held up to Smith's face. Those interviews appeared many times over the next few days.

Fox Cable Network called the following Monday afternoon and asked if I would come into their New York location to give an interview. I declined since I had already scheduled interviews for the following day. They were persistent, calling me several times and even offering to pick me up in a limousine. What finally convinced me was the debate they set up between me and the President of Manhattanville College. I couldn't resist because his basketball team was going to play Tuesday night in the first round of the playoffs.

Since I'd never owned a cell phone, I borrowed my son's and gave interviews in the back seat of the limo on the way to NYC. The director and producer came up to me and seemed genuinely grateful that I was appearing on their show. I'd learned to be skeptical of mainstream media during my years as an activist, but they sat me next to Shepard Smith, one of the few people I admired because of his thoughtful and objective commentary.

Shepard—knowing I was a Vietnam Veteran—immediately struck up a conversation because his brother had had some problems since returning from Vietnam. I said many Vietnam veterans suffer from Post-Traumatic Stress Disorder (PTSD) due to combat; however, many who escaped that horror had even more problems from being treated like dirt when returning from the war. When they gave him a one minute heads-up to go live, he said, "You have my appreciation and maybe someday we will talk again."

I debated the Manhattanville College president on the cable station for about ten minutes, calling him a disgrace and then talking about my demonstration that night in front of his college. About fifty people, mostly veterans, showed up with dozens of flags. A contractor who'd worked a large crane at Ground Zero for six months during the 9/11 clean-up effort displayed American flags on five plastic tubes, all 20 feet high. It was a great visual, and the hoard of media that showed up an hour early to interview me turned the event into a feeding frenzy.

I met with the demonstrators who showed up and said the mainstream media had already distorted my message in the past. To ensure they would not be misled by leading questions, I gave them the following talking points with the understanding they would add their own appropriate comments:

* Our flag represents the blood and sacrifice of those brave men and women who gave the player the right to speak her mind; she inherited this right.

* Don't use the flag as a political tool.

* Even though she has the right to turn her back on the flag, it doesn't make it right.

* We have the right as Americans to protest what she is doing.

* Our protest has nothing to do with supporting a possible war in Iraq.

I gave about twenty interviews in a 75-minute time frame. Local and national TV and radio stations and the print media made this an extraordinary event. ESPN replayed my court appearance over the next two weeks. AP sent out a national wire story picked up by the print media around the country for both the Sunday and Tuesday events. Every TV station in New York ran the story for three days.

When challenged as to why I was doing this, I said that as an American and Vietnam veteran I had the right to protest her protest. Also, I made the point that she had inherited the right of free speech because of the sacrifice of millions of brave men and women.

I became very emotional when I saw a young boy of about five years old make a statement on camera about supporting our flag. His mother had obviously done a great job explaining to her young son why we were there.

After the horde of media left us to film Smith's disrespect of our flag, the police Captain called me aside and asked if I wanted to go inside. At first I laughed and then said I didn't have a ticket; realizing he was serious, I also told him I didn't have a flag on me. He told me we didn't have time to get a flag, just to get into the police car and he'd drive me in. We pulled up in front and one of the Harrison police officers escorted me into the building. I promptly walked to the edge of the court where Smith and her teammates were warming up by taking lay-ups.

I decided not to walk onto the floor because I feared one of her teammates might get hurt in all the confusion. It didn't feel right; my gut reaction was to back away. Later, I realized it could have been perceived as a Vietnam veteran stalker, which could have been twisted against me and my message. Much of the mainstream media had already implied that I was for a war in Iraq, when actually I was very skeptical about the drumbeat for war orchestrated by Dick Cheney, one of the people who seemed to have done his best to undermine the POW issue.

I'd made my way up to the balcony to observe the playing of the anthem when a camera suddenly appeared in my face. It turned out to be HBO, so I was giving my normal interview until the student body realized it was me. They supported Toni Smith and began yelling at me. I got in their faces and yelled back. The police officer who'd been following me the entire time said it was time to leave. We left the building while I was engaged in a heated argument. I didn't back down from the mob who seemed to hate me.

I gave the HBO cameraman my phone number and received a call requesting an interview for *Real Sports* with Bryant Gumbel. Even though I agreed, I never heard from them again and as far as I know they never did a story about Toni Smith.

On that Wednesday I turned down an appearance with O'Reilly on Fox Network's *O'Reilly Factor* and Bill Maher on HBO's *Politically Incorrect* shows because I didn't want to make the issue about me. I'd made my point and moved on.

After a whirlwind of activities over a three-day period, there was one that stood out over all the rest. As the veteran demonstrators and I were parting to leave the college after the Tuesday demonstration, the contractor, Mark Volpe, who had worked cleaning up Ground Zero called me aside.

He reached in the back of his truck and retrieved a stained, sun-damaged American flag, folded in the traditional triangle. He said, "I promised myself that I would never give this flag that hung on my crane for six months at Ground Zero to anyone." He handed me the flag and said, "I want you to have it."

With a lump in my throat, I looked at him and said, "Are you sure you want to part with it?"

"Yes," he said with conviction, "You've earned it, you deserve it." I was deeply touched and honored to accept it.

Author's Note

The first part of this book is the story I want to leave behind for my kids and my grandkids, a way for them to know the truth about our abandoned POWs and to know that we must never give up on doing what is right. We have to fight against corruption, lies, and self-serving greed in every instance, and we must never be content with excuses.

What follows are the journal entries I kept to chronicle the work that we did once I realized a day by day record was needed.

January 2004

In January, when John Kerry won the first Democratic primary state of Iowa, and then looked like he was going to win New Hampshire, I contacted John Nevin and told him I needed to do something to stop this guy politically. John said to call Ted Sampley because he was starting a website called VietnamVeteransAgainstJohnKerry.com.

Ted and Mike Benge were just starting a new Vietnam Veterans Against John Kerry organization and asked if I would like to join them. Naturally, I said yes. When I told John I wanted to send a letter to the New Hampshire *Manchester Union Leader* newspaper, we discussed the content and he wrote the letter that I faxed on January 24, 2004. I emailed it to Governor Dean's campaign, the Democratic candidate running against Kerry (see below).

One week later, Terry McAuliffe, the Democratic Party National Chairman, came out of nowhere to attack and criticize President Bush for his National Guard service. I suspect that this letter, email, and the website created a knee-jerk reaction from Kerry and the Democrats. I'm sure they thought we were George Bush's surrogates, and they launched their counter strategy prematurely on February 1, 2004, nine months before the election.

From:

Jerry Kiley <gwkiley@hotmail.com>

Sent:

Sunday, January 25, 2004 4:43 PM

To:

kgard@deanforamerica.com

Subject:

Vietnam Veterans Against Kerry

As a follow-up to my telephone call today, I would appreciate your sending the following statement to Governor Dean or his closest advisors, preferably Mr. McMahon. I sent this to the Union Leader yesterday; however, they were not interested, stating that I was an outsider. Copies will be sent to UPI, AP and media outlets in South Carolina.

As indicated below we have a website that will continue to update articles regarding Senator Kerry. You may also want to visit another website,WWW.NEWSMAX.COM, and read an interesting article titled, What You Don't Know About John Kerry, written by Chuck Noe dated 1/20/04.

I've been a POW/MIA activist for many years and have never voted for a Democratic Presidential Candidate. In fact I have not voted for either party's candidate over the last four elections choosing a third party or write-in candidate.

I'm offering you my services because I believe Governor Dean is the only candidate that has a chance to change the direction of a misguided government.

Last year, a misguided female Manhattanville College (NY) basketball player turned her back on the American flag during the playing of the national anthem in protest of government policies. A Vietnam veteran confronted her on the basketball court by holding an American flag in front of her face while explaining that the flag symbolized the sacrifice of brave men and women who gave their lives allowing her to protest and that the flag should not be used as a political tool. I was that veteran.

If you think I can be of assistance in the Governor's campaign please let me know.

Letter faxed to the New Hampshire Manchester Union Leader newspaper on January 24, 2004.

Vietnam Veterans Against Kerry

There's a widespread but glaring misperception about the depth of support John Kerry enjoys from U.S. veterans.

John Kerry is a fraud and a large segment of the U.S. veteran community knows it.

On returning from Vietnam, John Kerry led a pro-Communist demonstration calling the war genocide against the Vietnamese people and calling fellow American military men war criminals.

Kerry was a supporter of the "People's Peace Treaty," a supposed "people's" declaration to end the war, reportedly drawn up in Communist East Germany. It included nine points, all of which were taken from Viet Cong peace proposals at the Paris peace talks as conditions for ending the war. One of the provisions stated: "The Vietnamese pledge that as soon as the U.S. government publicly sets a date for total withdrawal [from Vietnam], they will enter discussion to secure the release of all American prisoners, including pilots captured while bombing North Vietnam."

Had the nine points -- particularly the one regarding U.S. withdrawal prior to any prisoner negotiations -- of the "People's Peace Treaty" favored by Kerry been accepted by American negotiators, the United States would have totally lost all leverage to get the Communists to release POWs captured during the war years, including the 591 that were released in 1973.

Kerry became something of a radical celebrity during a highly publicized stunt when he threw Vietnam service medals, which the press reported were his, over a barricade and onto the steps of the Capitol. Kerry never mentioned that the medals he so gloriously tossed were not his own. When a *Washington Post* reporter asked Kerry about the incident, he said: 'They're my medals. I'll do what I want with them." In later years, Kerry's own medals were seen hanging on the wall of his Senate office.

In Kerry's run for election to the U.S. House in 1972, he found it necessary to suppress reproduction of the cover picture appearing on his own book, *The New Soldier*. His political opponent pointed out that it depicted several unkempt youths crudely handling an American flag to mock the famous photo of the US Marines at Iwo Jima.

Sydney H. Schanberg, associate editor and columnist for *New York Newsday* and Pulitzer Prize-winning journalist veteran of the Indochina War whose book, *The Death and Life of Dith Pran*, became the subject of the Academy Award-winning film *The Killing Fields*, chronicled some of Kerry's more blatant pro-Hanoi biases in several of his columns.

In a Nov. 21, 1993 column, Schanberg wrote:

"Highly credible information has been surfacing in recent days which indicate that the headlines you have been reading about a 'breakthrough' in Hanoi's cooperation on the POW/MIA issue are part of a carefully scripted performance." The apparent purpose is to move toward normalization of relations with Hanoi.

"Sen. John F. Kerry, chairman of the Senate Select Committee on POW/MIA Affairs, is one of the key figures pushing for normalization. Kerry is currently on a visit to Vietnam where he has been doing two things: (1) praising the Vietnamese effusively for granting access to their war archives and (2) telling the press that there's no believable evidence to back up the stories of live POWs still being held.

Ironically, that very kind of live-POW evidence has been brought to Kerry's own committee on a regular basis over the past year, and he has repeatedly sought to impeach its value. Moreover, Kerry and his allies on the committee - such as Sens. John McCain, Nancy Kassebaum and Tom Daschle - have worked to block much of this evidence from being made public."

In December of 1992, not long after Kerry was quoted in the world press stating "President Bush should reward Vietnam within a month for its increased cooperation in accounting for American MIAs," Vietnam announced it had granted Colliers International, based in Boston, Massachusetts, a contract worth billions designating Colliers International as the exclusive real estate agent representing Vietnam.

That deal alone put Colliers in a position to make tens of millions of dollars on the rush to upgrade Vietnam's ports, railroads, highways, government buildings, etc. C. Stewart Forbes, Chief Executive Officer of Colliers International, is John Kerry's cousin.

In its 1993 final report, Kerry's Select Committee determined that live U.S. prisoners of war were left behind in the hands of the Vietnamese after the end of the war, but concluded its business without demanding answers to two obvious questions: (1) What happened to those U.S. prisoners of war who the Select Committee said were alive in 1975, and; (2) if they were not still alive, who was responsible for their deaths?

For the families of the missing and U.S. veterans who watched Kerry's role in closing the investigation, those two questions still resound. Instead of demanding answers from the government of Vietnam, Kerry became the most vocal public figure in praise of their "spirit of cooperation" in "resolving" the fate of the missing.

John Kerry is a fraud, even to the extent of allowing people to think for 30 years that he was of Irish ancestry. His long record of deceptive behavior should alert any thinking American -- especially his fellow veterans whom he called "war criminals" -- that this is a man who cannot be trusted.

For more information regarding John Kerry's pattern of deception, visit the Vietnam Veterans Against Kerry

----

Jerry Kiley

The website was up and running and recorded over 10 million hits in the first three months, from the end of January until the end of April. I immediately organized two demonstrations in New York in February and two in Boston in July during the Democratic National Convention.

The first New York event, Saturday 2/24/04, was a demonstration of about one thousand people at John Kerry's headquarters on Park Avenue in Manhattan. This was a success not only because of the media attention we received but mostly because we were united with the Vietnamese-American community. I had already nurtured a new relationship with the Vietnamese community by attending some of their events and meetings. Half of the groups were veterans and concerned citizens, and the other half were Vietnamese-Americans primarily from New York and Boston.

Shortly after arriving at his headquarters, we realized that the American flag in his window was backwards. The flag should be facing the correct way for those on the outside. The media didn't seem interested in reporting that oversight.

The following day (2/25/04), there was a Presidential debate at the CBS TV station, hosted by Dan Rather. There were about eight areas surrounded by metal railings that were designated "Free Speech" areas for the groups that were demonstrating. (Apparently the powers that be think our right to free speech means we can say whatever we want as long as we say it where and when they dictate.) Naturally, Kerry's group had the prime spot.

The New York permit I obtained placed us all the way at the end, completely away from the front entrance. When the media came out to interview the groups, I told all of our people to charge into the street. We marched in front of the Kerry's people and put on a show for the media. When a police officer told us to go back down to the bottom of the hill, I said, "Where is your commanding officer?"

The captain threatened to arrest us. I made it clear that I was an activist who had been arrested many times. I said, "We are going to that vacant area next to Kerry's group or we are going to jail." Disgusted, he said, "Take the spot you want."

We immediately moved as close as we could to this group, literally yelling in their faces, "Kerry is a traitor." When the Kerry people realized who we were and what we were chanting, they were stunned. I think we actually broke their spirit, because soon after we arrived their numbers started to dwindle and their chants became weaker.

March 2004

This was the time when I began writing my life story. It was a very slow process trying to recall events that went back to 1968.

About five months later, I arrived in Boston for the Democratic National Convention at the Fleet Center and stayed at the home of a Vietnamese-American friend of mine. As usual, I did an advance recon of the holding area where they place all of the protest groups. It was some distance from the Fleet Center. Upon first glance, I was very disappointed and knew we would need to separate ourselves if we were going to have any impact at all.

I had a permit to demonstrate for two days, both beginning at Kerry's Boston Senate office, marching to the Fleet Center, and back to Kerry's office. The first demonstration, either that Tuesday or Wednesday, was a dismal failure because we were in that holding area with many other groups. Even if the people at the Fleet Center could hear us, they would not be able to discern what was being said with all the groups yelling at one time. It seemed to be a tactic to discourage groups from returning.

The second demonstration was on Thursday, July 29th, the final night of the convention when Kerry would accept the nomination. We had a much larger and more vocal group of demonstrators chanting, "Kerry lied while good men died." When I chanted, "Is John Kerry a traitor?" the group yelled an emphatic, "Yes," while we marched toward that holding area. We also carried a huge banner; it was about twelve feet long by eight feet high, with pictures of John Kerry and Jane Fonda wearing the traditional hats of the common Vietnamese worker. Under their pictures it read "Hanoi John" and "Hanoi Jane."

I had already planned on taking a location near the entrance of the holding area so we could exit quickly, hopefully before the police would react. If we were stopped, my plan B was to disband our demonstrators and tell them to filter down the dead end street until they were in front of the path leading to the center where all the delegates would pass. I was prepared to get arrested if there was coverage, and I felt it was necessary to make a statement.

To my surprise, we entered the holding area, and it was completely empty. I immediately stopped the demonstration and led them to the front of the dead end street, then told the commanding officer that we planned to march to the convention center. He said, "Go ahead, march down the street," pointing to the center. As I paused to make sure we were all together in a tight group, there were dozens of people between us and the center and hundreds lining the sidewalk on both sides of the street.

We quickly found out these people were not there to support us. They were there to yell at us. We had a good practice march about a mile or so from Kerry's office to the center, so we began chanting as we marched while drowning out any opposition.

We were there for about thirty minutes, chanting and yelling at the delegates who were about fifty feet away; they heard everything we were saying. I pulled our people out when I sensed that a physical confrontation was becoming more likely. I got into a heated argument with a group next to us, then one of the Vietnamese who was sent to protect me said it was time to go. I looked around and my demonstrators were at the other end of the street, turning the corner and heading back to Kerry's office.

The Vietnamese individual who literally covered my back was also there at other events I attended in New York and Washington, D.C. I'm embarrassed to say that I don't remember his name. Unfortunately, forgetting names is one of my flaws that I've never been able to overcome. I do know that this gentleman, based on his stature and demeanor, was one rough SOB. I put him in the Ted Sampley level of toughness which by my standard is a great compliment.

As my bodyguard and I were running down the street to catch up with my runaway demonstration, we passed the police officer in charge. He tipped his hat to us and said, "Great job."

The situation was very tense. I later overheard one veteran tell his wife on his cell phone, "We were just in the belly of the beast." I laughed and thought, "Damn right." Our adrenaline was still pumping when we approached Kerry's office where we were supposed to disassemble. I asked them through the bullhorn if they were ready to pay a visit to John Kerry at his residence, about ten minutes away. Naturally, they were ready.

We passed the disassembly point, then the officer in charge came up to me and asked where we were going. When I told him, he gave a very short command, like, "Go." Immediately, vehicles came from every direction imaginable, including black trucks unloading what looked like SWAT teams and approximately a hundred police dressed all in black with bullet proof vests and helmets.

To say it was intimidating would be an understatement. We had to walk up a very long hill that was lined on both sides by policeman. I ran up the hill in front of them to make sure we would be able to make the right turn onto his street when all of a sudden the police came to attention and saluted.

When one of the police sergeants realized what had happened, he began screaming that the captain didn't want them saluting. I was stunned that they were saluting and then very surprised at the sergeant's response. Without thinking, I started shaking their hands, thanking them for their service. I still get chills up my spine just thinking about the entire police contingent saluting us.

I found out later that year from one of the demonstrators that when the group behind me started passing the police, they all came to attention. I was about a hundred feet in front of the group so I didn't know it had happened. Conversely, the protestor didn't know about the saluting because they had stopped after the sergeant's command.

I was ready to make that right turn when he told me to continue up the hill. I asked, "Are you bringing me to Kerry's residence?" and he said yes. We made a right turn at the top of the hill, passing City Hall. We arrived at a fenced-in area and Kerry's residence was a good distance from our location; we were even more motivated to chant so he could hear us. The Secret Service was in force on the other side of the fence.

We stayed there for about thirty minutes and then returned to his office building to discuss the day's events. A young policeman approached me, smiling. I tried to shake his hand, but he quickly stepped back and said he could not. They had been given orders not to shake our hands or salute. He said, "I can tell you how proud we are of your service, and that you did yourselves proud today." I thanked him for taking the time to visit us and for his service as a policeman. He waved and walked away.

I knew from the many demonstrations I've participated in that the police supported what we were doing, but I'd never realized just how strong that support was until that event.

The local ABC station covered our demonstrations. While Kerry was standing in a live shot after accepting his party's nomination, ABC cut to a reporter saying not all veterans supported Kerry. The station inserted our demonstration and our chant, "Kerry lied while good men died." Mission accomplished.

September 2004

Larry Bailey, former commanding officer in charge of Navy SEAL training, organized a great demonstration of about 5,000 veterans in a park where the Capitol building was the backdrop to the stage area. The theme was "Kerry Lied While Good Men Died," a reference to his distorted testimony before the Fulbright Senate Committee during the Vietnam War.

John O'Neill, representing the Swift Boat Veterans, was the guest speaker, and it was the first time I met him. The Swift Boat Veterans were a group of Navy Officers who detested John Kerry for his lies and false statements characterizing himself as a hero. They were devastating in their attacks on Kerry's character and integrity and were instrumental in his defeat as the Democratic nominee for President. Ted, Mike, and I spoke at the very end of the event about our research into Kerry's background and our demonstrations in New York and Boston. I asked the crowd the same question I asked at the demonstrations, "Is John Kerry a traitor?" and naturally, they answered yes.

A week after this demonstration, Kerry's people demonstrated in front of John O'Neill's home. John O'Neill's daughter was being married that day and Kerry's people deliberately showed up to disrupt the family on one of the most important days of their lives. Fortunately, John and his family were not home, having decided to spend the night in a hotel as part of the wedding plans and celebration.

The following week, the end of September, Ted, Mike, Larry Bailey, and I, along with a number of other veterans, demonstrated in front of John Kerry's home in Georgetown. Most of the people on that block didn't appreciate our presence and one woman said we didn't have the right to demonstrate on their street. I said, "I'm a Vietnam veteran who *earned* the right to speak my mind; you *inherited* those rights, so don't tell me how and when I can enjoy them."

We stood directly in front of his house for about two hours, and had even posed for pictures on his steps, when a USPS worker delivered a box, accepted by Kerry's maid. She seemed shocked when she saw us standing and chanting a couple feet away from the front entrance.

I was amazed that there was no security to stop us if we'd had evil intentions. About twenty minutes later, two local D.C. police came and told us that if we didn't stop the demonstration, they would have to arrest us. Ted asked me what I thought about that and I said, "We aren't going anywhere; I'd rather go to jail than move." The police officer didn't know how to react to that, but he didn't have to decide because very shortly after this confrontation two Secret Service Agents showed up.

Ted talked with them for a long time; he asked me when the last time the Secret Service interviewed us was. I hesitated and then answered, "In jail." Everybody, including the agents, laughed out loud.

When Ted stopped laughing, he said, "Seriously, when did they last interview us?"

"Is this a trick question?" That prompted another round of laughter.

Annoyed, Ted said, "Seriously."

I thought for a moment and said, "I'll stick with jail. And that's my final answer!" I walked away as the Secret Service agents continued to laugh.

As was common for police and Secret Service, it was clear they supported what we were doing, but they did their best to appear objective. In this case, they probably went over the line because they were very friendly and gave us Secret Service pins, one of which was really nice in the shape of the United States.

When Mike Benge realized that we might go to jail, he apologized and said he couldn't. I laughed and said there was no way we would ever consider him going into a jail cell after what he went through as a POW. I explained that his job would be to bail out Ted and me. Mike looked at me with that deadpan stare and said, only as he could, "I'll have to think about that."

When I asked what he meant by that, he said, "I have to think about the crime of releasing both of you back into society."

We eventually moved down the block and then I took out a portable sound system in a plastic case. One of the newer agents had me place the case on the ground while he brought over a bomb-sniffing dog to clear me. We didn't know whether Kerry was in the house, but I broadcasted a number of choice things I knew he wouldn't enjoy if he heard them. Near the end I started saying, "Come on, John, won't you come out and plaaaaay with us?"

The Secret Service agents and even more from the D.C. police started to laugh. They all waved at us when we left.

October 2004

That year's Alfred E. Smith fundraiser at the Waldorf Astoria came and went without incident. Cardinal Egan didn't invite President Bush and Senator Kerry, even though the event usually included the presidential candidates. I was disappointed, considering I'd done some of my best work in two events at this hotel, but it did make me wonder (even hope) if the Cardinal didn't invite them because he was afraid I'd show up.

November 2004

Following Kerry's defeat in the election, Larry Bailey, the SEAL training officer, organized a victory dinner in Rhode Island. John O'Neill, spokesperson for the Swift Boat Veterans, was the guest speaker. I sat with John, his wife Anne, and Larry Bailey. John is very humble and dedicated, and his wife is very gracious.

John and I were the only speakers. John introduced me to his wife as one of the veterans who demonstrated in front of Kerry's Georgetown home in September 2004. That was after Kerry's people had fired a warning shot at O'Neill by demonstrating at his home the night before his daughter's wedding. After shaking my hand, they expressed their gratitude for returning the favor to Kerry the following weekend. John signed his *Unfit for Command* book for me. The inscription read, "To Jerry Kiley. He never came back to picket my house after you showed up in Georgetown."

After John addressed the group, I spoke about Ted, Mike, and my involvement in creating the website. I ended by stating that John Kerry might run again so that we were maintaining the site for 2008. One of the vets who attended the dinner was the person who'd told me about the State Police coming to attention as we marched towards Kerry's home in Boston.

Something else interesting happened. Larry Bailey asked me to drive a friend of his to a house close to where we were dining. His name was Jack Wheeler. He told me that the group he had been in charge of during the Reagan administration developed what came to be known as the "Reagan Doctrine." He said Washington's political culture and media gave him the credit, even though it was a group venture. When he asked me what I knew about the doctrine, I said the premise was to get the USSR to increase military spending that would ultimately ruin them economically.

He said that is what most people think; however, the basic premise was to build up the USSR's global military image to the extent of making them invincible in the eyes of the Communist bloc. Once that image was cracked by one of four non-Communist nations under their control, Communist countries in their orbit would start falling away like dominos. He said that the plan worked to perfection after the USSR withdrew from Afghanistan. He said that the amusing part of this scenario was that Afghanistan wasn't one of the four nations they thought would successfully escape the USSR. That was an unexpected surprise.

I thought it was pretty amazing that I had been able to spend that time with one of the people instrumental in orchestrating the fall of the Soviet Union, first symbolized by the fall of the Berlin Wall.

A strange thing happened to me in January 2007, over two years after this November 2004 victory dinner. I brought in the book *Unfit For Command* to work to show one of my friends John O'Neill's inscription. The next page had an inscription by his wife Anne. I never knew she'd written in the book.

I was very touched by her remarks, placed directly above John's dedication line: "To Anne O'Neill, the most courageous person I ever met— JO." Anne wrote, "Jerry—Congratulations! Fondly, Anne O'Neill."

John's comment about Anne's courage stems from her struggle while enduring a kidney transplant, a kidney that John himself provided. I could tell she was far from healthy, but she never complained. Anne sat there for the entire night in support of her husband. Anyone who had any doubt about John's sincerity or character would have been convinced that he and his wife were the real deal. Two people who were so humble, and so down to earth, and they left a lasting lifetime impression wherever they went.

March/April 2005

I wanted to send President George W. Bush an article I'd written for my local newspaper (see below). I know someone whose best friend is a former White House employee who worked for George W. during his first term. He delivered my article and letter to his contacts close to the President. I have no idea if the President actually read the letter, but that wasn't the purpose.

The letter wasn't delivered until the end of April and several weeks later we heard about Bush's June 21st White House invitation to Prime Minister Pham Van Khai. Initially, I didn't believe it. I questioned the former White House employee who delivered the letter why the president would invite Khai and give the Communist government credibility. He said the president invites dignitaries to the White House for two reasons, to recognize and prop them up, or to twist their arms. Khai's visit was supposedly the latter.

"Vietnam Veteran Leader Opposed to Vietnam Visit" – *Rockland Journal News* (NY), March 30, 2005

Vietnam continues to be one of the most repressive Marxist regimes in the world today, second only to North Korea. As recently as this past Easter Sunday, hundreds of Christian Montagnards were slaughtered by Vietnamese Communist security forces in the Central Highlands of Vietnam for conducting peaceful prayer vigils.

Six months before this slaughter Amnesty International called on the international community to end the harsh repression of the Montagnards, urged access for outside observers, and called for the immediate and unconditional release of prisoners arrested for the non-violent expression of their religious beliefs.

Montagnards fought with American forces against the Communist North Vietnamese during the Vietnam War and now there is a genocide being committed against them because religious observance is not tolerated in Vietnam.

The Montagnard population when the war ended in 1975 was approximately 1,500,000; thirty years later it has been reduced to less than 750,000. The US State Department has declared Vietnam a "Country of Particular Concern," which means they are placed on a watch list because of brutal human rights violations.

The second critical issue is Vietnam's continued failure to tell us what happened to the American Prisoners of War who are known to have been held by them, but never came home. It is well documented that the North Vietnamese kept exhaustive records on our missing. There are even pictures of some of these men in captivity, interviews of them in the French, Soviet, and Cuban press, and thousands of first hand live sightings of Americans in captivity that never came home.

I'm opposed to any American visiting Vietnam, especially an American Vietnam Veteran, because it lends to the Vietnamese government an air of legitimacy it doesn't deserve at a time when their economy is faltering and the repressive regime is under pressure from many quarters on human rights issues.

Wouldn't it be ironic to see Vietnam fall as part of a reverse domino effect as numerous totalitarian regimes around the world are being pushed in the direction of more freedom and human rights for their own people.

I have a dream that someday soon the Vietnamese people will have the freedom to speak their minds and practice their own religions without fear; that we will once and for all be able to find out what happened to the live Americans we left behind; and that we Vietnam veterans can finally declare Victory, not for us, but for the 58,000 brave women and men who paid the ultimate price so that the Vietnamese people could live in peace and freedom.

--Jerry Kiley served in the US Army in Vietnam 1967-68. A long time Vietnam veteran leader and activist, he is the former Vice-Chairperson and Communication Director of the National Vietnam Veterans Coalition, member of the Board of Directors of Veterans of the Vietnam War, and the nominee for the presidency of Vietnam Veterans of America.

April 13, 2005

Dear Mr. President:

Even though we have never met, I believe our paths have crossed on several occasions. I'm the Vietnam veteran who walked on the basketball court and held the American flag in front of the female college player who turned her back to the flag during the playing of the national anthem on February 23, 2003. That act engendered a wave of patriotism across America in newspapers, radio talk shows, and television reporting over the next several weeks. Shortly after that, you sent a letter to the House and Senate on March 18th, stating your intentions to go after terrorists and you have never wavered from that position, something I admire, having lived through an era when people didn't have the courage of their own convictions.

Almost a year later, on January 25, 2004, as co-founder of the newly formed Vietnam Veterans Against John Kerry organization, I sent damaging information about John Kerry's past to the Manchester Union Leader and to Governor Dean's campaign headquarters. John Kerry had already gained tremendous momentum by surrounding himself with a handful of veterans while pretending to be a hero. John Kerry was exposed as a phony and a fraud over the next three months when 10 million people visited our website (www.VietnamVeteransAgainstJohnKerry.com), creating a floodgate of criticism. Our site is still on line in preparation of his 2008 Presidential run. We have also reserved the rights to www.AgainstHillary.com that will be available in 2006.

I spoke to Sydney Schanberg, Pulitzer Prize winning author of *The Killing Fields*, who said that the last five Presidents prior to your administration have turned their backs on the human rights violations committed by one of the most brutal Communist regimes in the world—Vietnam. We discussed their religious intolerance underscored by the 30-year genocide that has reduced Vietnam's Christian Montagnard population from 1.5 million to less than 750,000 today. The repression culminated in the slaughter of Christian Montagnards on Easter Sunday last year in the central highlands of Vietnam.

The government of Vietnam is in clear violation of the freedom of emigration criteria of our own Jackson-Vanik amendment. Emigration requests are routinely denied even in family reunification cases, particularly those involving Christian Montagnards who have escaped and wish their loved ones to join them. Your administration has waived Jackson-Vanik provisions with regard to Vietnam.

I respectfully request the following:

1) Make a strong public statement condemning the brutal treatment the government of Vietnam regularly inflicts on its own citizens for their peaceful worship—especially the Montagnards.

2) Suspend the Jackson-Vanik waiver until Vietnam meets specific benchmarks on freedom of emigration and improvements in religious freedom and human rights.

3) Call for the government of Vietnam to allow international observers—perhaps UN NGOs—to monitor and report on any abuses of religious freedom and human rights, and to ensure that there is no retribution against Montagnard refugees that are returned to Vietnam.

You have shown a passion and determination for those issues you believe in, and now it's time to stop the bloodshed in Vietnam. We can talk about Christian values; however, it's time to walk the walk, Mr. President, as you have in Iraq. I ask that you show the same passion and compassion for the Vietnamese people who have been brutalized for the last thirty years as you have toward the Iraqi people. If not for them, then do it for the 58,000 brave women and men who gave their lives so the Vietnamese people could speak their minds and worship their own religion in peace and freedom.

Sincerely,
Gerard W. Kiley

June 2005

Quyen Le, a Vietnamese-American leader in the Maryland/Virginia/D.C. area, called me as soon as he knew about Khai's invitation to the White House. This visit was very significant, even historical, because this was the first U.S.-sanctioned visit to the White House by a Vietnamese government official.

Quyen Le requested my participation in the D.C. events because he knew of my reputation supporting the Vietnamese community in its fight to expose the brutal Communist regime in Vietnam. He wanted my help in creating chaos during Khai's visit. I also received a similar request from a Vietnam veteran friend of mine who should remain nameless.

I was an invited guest on three Vietnamese radio programs prior to a demonstration I helped organize on Saturday, June 18th, to take place across from the White House.

One was on shortwave radio that was listened to by the Vietnamese community in the United States and around the world in Canada, Europe, Australia, and Vietnam. The second interview was played primarily in California, Boston, and Georgia. The third was a radio station that was received exclusively in Vietnam, so I knew my comments were heard by the Communist government officials as well as the Vietnamese people.

My general response to why I was involved was that I was a Vietnam veteran speaking for those who could not speak for themselves, the 58,000 brave American men and women who gave their lives so that the Vietnamese people could live in freedom, the hundreds of thousands of Vietnamese who gave their lives to be free, the millions of Vietnamese people oppressed in Vietnam, and the living American POWs who were abandoned in Southeast Asia after the war ended.

I spoke directly to the Vietnamese people when I said it had been thirty years since we abandoned Vietnam; however, we have not forgotten them and their struggle for freedom and that we would not allow those who sacrificed and died to have done so in vain. I also discussed the following points:

1. The brutal and godless Communist treatment in beating, torturing, jailing, and killing their religious leaders in Vietnam as witnessed in the 2004 Easter morning slaughter of hundreds of peaceful Montagnard Christian worshipers in the central highlands. Genocide was being committed against the Montagnards who fought along with American troops and other Vietnamese anti-Communist forces. There were 1.5 million Montagnards in 1975 when we abandoned Vietnam and currently, thirty years later, there are less than 750,000 even though Vietnam has seen a dramatic increase in their general population during that same time frame.

2. The State Department declared Vietnam a Country of Particular Concern (CPC) because of their horrible human rights record, religious

abuses, and the fact that they will not allow any independent monitoring by the United Nations or human rights organizations.

3. We should call on George Bush to repeal his suspension of the Jackson-Vanik bill that specifically allows the United States to levy sanctions on any nation that does not allow emigration.

4. My message to the Vietnamese-American community was that I saw problems in the way they look at their role in America, that they are foreigners in a foreign country. They were American citizens now and represented the morals and values that make America great, and in that vein they also have a responsibility and an obligation to speak for those who cannot speak for themselves. They need to assert themselves with the politicians and government officials who are supposed to represent them; this is their country as much as anyone who was born here.

5. My message to the Communist leaders in Vietnam was that we will never allow the war to end. We will continue to fight until our dying breath to free the Vietnamese people and the live American POWs we know were never returned. As I discussed with Vietnam's Ambassador Can back in the early 1990s, American Vietnam veterans are not looking for revenge, we are looking for justice; if the other side does the right thing, we have the ability to forgive.

6. My additional message to the people in Vietnam was that America didn't have the character to finish what we started, we cut and ran and abandoned them thirty years ago, and that I hold the politicians and government officials in Washington, D.C., accountable for their disgraceful actions. I committed my support to them no matter how long it takes. Even though I will never set foot in Vietnam while its people remain oppressed under a brutal, godless regime, my dream was to visit a free Vietnam before I died.

Friday, June 17, 2005

I spoke before the National Alliance of Families to solicit their participation in my demonstration the following day. It had been over ten years since my last involvement with Jane Gaylor when she chained her wheelchair to the White House fence, supported by "The Dirty Dozen."

When I tried to say that Jane had passed away since that arrest, dying without ever knowing if her son were alive or dead, I lost my composure and struggled to continue. I finally said that I was back and that I would once again be active until we finally obtained an honest accounting of the men we abandoned after the war and until the Vietnamese people in Vietnam were free.

Chapter Eight
Second Confrontation with Khai

Saturday, June 18, 2005 - We demonstrated across the street from the White House to protest Prime Minister Khai's visit to the U.S. We had about 300 people at this event, three days before his visit to the White House. I met Quyen Le for the first time and, at his request, stayed at his house until I left D.C. the following Thursday. This proved to be a powerful alliance that would result in my most effective personal protest on the world stage.

I celebrated Father's Day at Quyen Le's house with his family. Earlier that day, I drove into Washington, D.C., to check out the Mayflower Hotel and to visit the Korean, WWII, and Vietnam Veteran Memorials. I always stop at the Vietnam Veteran Memorial to ask them to give me the courage needed when confronting a difficult and potentially dangerous situation. Thinking about their courage and their sacrifice always reminds me that what I'm doing is easy compared to what they faced.

I realized it was going to be next to impossible to get into the Grand Ballroom where Prime Minister Khai was to be honored. I did figure out a possible way to get to the large open lobby outside the ballroom where I was hoping he would have a reception before the dinner.

That night, Quyen Le and I were relaxing and drinking some wine when he said over ten years before he'd been in New York demonstrating with about fifty other Vietnamese when a Vietnam veteran confronted then-Deputy Prime Minister Khai. I asked whether that was at the New York Plaza Hotel in October 1993, where the American Captains of Industry honored Khai. I told him I was that veteran, and proceeded to tell him how I had sneaked past Secret Service and confronted Khai on the reception line.

I called John Nevin and told him that, even though I believed everyone makes his or her own destiny, in this case, if I were able to get into the ballroom, I'd have to consider it my destiny. Normally, John would rebuke any comment regarding destiny; however, this time, he laughed and said, "Maybe, but have you ever considered the possibility that you're getting behind-the-scenes help you don't even know about?"

John and I were aware that people within the Pentagon, intelligence agencies, and law enforcement quietly supported our efforts whenever they were in a position to help. I doubt that this explains my ability to get to places I didn't belong—especially those guarded by Secret Service—but it's a possibility that can't be completely discounted.

No matter what the reason is for my success, Quyen Le was ecstatic when learning that I was the veteran known as the Stealth Activist. I have to admit that I'm very proud of this nickname.

Tuesday, June 21, 2005

I attended a Vietnamese protest of about 1,000 people, possibly the most exciting protest I've ever attended. Similar to the June 18th demonstration the Saturday before, Ted Sampley, Mike Benge, and I kept order and handled the police at the request of the Vietnamese people.

I discussed what we planned to do with the officer in charge before the event, as we usually did before a demonstration. There had been a misunderstanding between him and some of the Vietnamese leaders before I interceded on their behalf.

The D.C. Park Police have nearly always been supportive of everything we did over the years, and these two demonstrations were no exception.

At some point, the Secret Service tried to prevent us from crossing the street to the White House side of the street, so Ted and I straightened that out so we could cross.

Ted and I began to incite the demonstrators who were waiting for Khai. As he arrived through the front gate, we charged the White House gate and the crowd exploded into chants and yelling. I used a bullhorn placed against the White House fence, yelling at maximum volume. Normally, they don't allow a loud speaker pointed at the White House. They stopped me once, but then let me yell at a deafening level throughout Khai's visit. This implied to me that the White House wanted to use this as leverage to gain a political advantage.

I later spoke to a Vietnamese reporter about his experience at this meeting and he said we were making so much noise in front that they had to move the President and Khai from the Rose Garden in the back to inside the White House. Even then he said we disrupted their event because they had to speak louder so the media could hear them. The final insult was Khai having to leave through the side exit rather than the front.

I was surprised how demonstrative the Vietnamese were at this event. I've been involved with the Vietnamese-American community many times and have never seen them even come close to this level of anger and hostility.

We broke up this demonstration about noon so we could have lunch before going over to the Mayflower Hotel where the Communist delegation was conducting business meetings during the afternoon, and where American business people were sponsoring a banquet honoring Khai that night. Quyen Le organized the afternoon and evening demonstrations, which were attended by a couple hundred Vietnamese-Americans.

At about 6:10 PM, I changed into a suit and tie in the back seat of my car, then Quyen Le moved my car a block away while I entered the hotel.

My plan was to disrupt Khai's event, stay over at Le's house one last night, and then leave for home Wednesday morning.

I entered the hotel through the bar entrance. I went immediately to the basement where I took an elevator to the third floor conference rooms. I then walked to another elevator that would bring me back to the first floor but at the back of the hotel where the banquet would be held. This was the route I had discovered two days earlier, but I wasn't optimistic.

The first problem was that the elevator that would bring me back to the first floor was shut down by the Secret Service. Looking around for an exit sign leading to a stairwell, I discovered a staff stairwell and walked to main level. I walked through two swinging doors right into the huge lobby directly outside the Grand Ballroom.

I immediately started walking around with a handful of other people that I quickly realized were all Secret Service Agents. There were no other people in that area because I saw everyone being held up by other agents at the beginning of the lobby, which meant that I had already bypassed security.

I went downstairs to a bathroom that I had checked out during my previous reconnaissance. Bathrooms are a great place to go to take the pressure off when you're in trouble. I sat in one of the stalls for about thirty minutes and went up to the lobby to see if there was a reception line forming for Khai. While sitting in the stall, I thought of plan B if they stopped me from getting into the ballroom. I would wait in the lobby and try to create a disturbance in case Khai crossed the lobby to enter the ballroom. I would have considered that action to be a success.

There was no reception, so I went back to the stall for about another thirty minutes. When I heard three or four people enter the bathroom, I came out of the stall to find three agents, one of whom was washing his hands next to me. I avoided eye contact and proceeded to wash my hands then go back upstairs to the lobby.

I was able to avoid the dozen or more Secret Service agents protecting Khai and attended the banquet.

When I reached the lobby at about 7:20 PM, there were about ten other people walking around so I wasn't that obvious. I looked over the big posters praising Kerry and McCain until the first group passed through security and into the Grand Ballroom. I walked behind them and sat at their table since there were several empty chairs, in order to blend in. This was the third row of tables from the dais.

Eventually the round table for ten filled up. They asked me if I was at the right table because one of their people was standing, trying to figure out what happened. I said they must have made a mistake in my seating arrangements, so I moved to the next table, two rows from the head table.

The dais ran parallel to the three-foot-high stage area that held a very large podium.

The second table filled up and everyone at this table was double checking their names to make sure they were correctly seated because again, an extra person again was standing. I had already slipped the name of a woman who was supposed to be sitting in my chair into my pocket, anticipating this problem. At this point, my first table became aware of the same problem, so I couldn't leave again. Thankfully, the woman who was supposed to be sitting in my seat graciously said she would join her friends at another table.

The event started sometime after 7:45 PM and the young Vietnamese woman to my left started asking me questions. My cover story was that I owned a travel agency in Crystal City, Virginia, involved with travel to Vietnam. She asked how I got visas for my clients, and I said they get them as everyone else does. She said they needed special permission from the Vietnamese government, and I recovered by saying that I was there to solicit information for future travel.

Realizing that she wanted to continue our conversation, I ate the salad and main meal very slowly so it would be obvious that I was in no position to converse with her. Every table had their own toast by standing up and taking a sip of wine, which I did by simply putting the glass to my lips without drinking.

I originally was looking for red tomato juice; however, they didn't have any so I ordered red wine as a substitute. I found out later that the P&G sign in the middle of our table stood for Proctor and Gamble Corporation, who'd paid $10,000 for a ten-seat table. I ate the $1,000 chicken dinner to avoid drawing attention to myself and then waited patiently for Khai to be introduced.

At about 9 PM, Senator John McCain introduced the Prime Minister. As the crowd stood and cheered, I grabbed my glass of red wine and slowly moved past the first row of tables to the head table. I wanted to use red wine to symbolize the blood on Khai's hands and of his brutal Communist regime's killing of their own people, religious leaders, and American POWs.

My intention was to first get Khai's attention while a very loud crowd was cheering him. I waited for the cheering to start dying down and threw the symbolic red wine at his empty seat. I walked up to the head table and threw the wine at the seat, then placed the glass on the table. I then picked up what I thought was an empty cup and waved it over my head to get everyone's attention. The cup apparently contained a clear tea that wasn't noticeable when I picked it up. The wine or tea never came close to Khai.

This all happened in a matter of seconds; time was running out so I shouted, "Khai, you and your government are killing your religious leaders." I then turned to John McCain and said, "McCain, you're a traitor to the live

American POWs we left behind after the war." As I was escorted out of the room I yelled, "Free Vietnam."

Immediately outside the Grand Ballroom, a female Secret Service agent who appeared to be in charge released me within thirty seconds and stated, "Let him go; he didn't do anything wrong."

The hotel security people who escorted me out were very pissed off, even saying I was lucky the Secret Service was closely following to ensure my safety. They said they would be in trouble because of my actions, and I said that wasn't my intent. When I told them why I did it, they didn't care. Just before they released me, I asked them to do me a big favor: please tell the chef he overcooked the chicken and it was too dry to enjoy. With that, they shoved me out the side entrance.

As I walked down the side street, Quyen Le spotted me and crossed the street to meet me. As I approached the corner, two Secret Service agents (Phillips and Hughes) ran after me, yelling to come back. Phillips, who wasn't in the ballroom when I threw the wine, asked me what happened. After I told him what I did, he said, "You threw wine on Khai." I corrected him and said the wine never came close to hitting him. He repeated that it hit Khai, so I asked if he was in the room. He said someone told him this story. I told him the story was incorrect.

When I asked why I was being detained, he said that tossing the wine was considered simple assault. They asked permission to search my car, and since I had nothing to hide, I agreed. I explained how I entered the Grand Ballroom, thinking that it would help secure my release. We waited for over an hour for the Assistant District Attorney on call to make a decision whether to arrest me, which they did around 10:30 PM.

When I arrived at the federal booking facility across town and walked out of the paddy wagon chained to four black men who were dressed like boys in the hood, the Secret Service agent started laughing. One of his men had asked, "Who's the Vietnam veteran?"

His reply was, "Isn't it obvious?" which prompted a loud laugh from all the agents and detainees, including me. Strangely, this gave me "street cred" with the other four detainees. When I told them what I had done, they all said it was cool.

It turns out that I was the only one wearing dress shoes and pants. What wasn't funny was the night in jail with at least twenty drug dealers and pimps. As prostitutes passed through to be booked and finger printed, the guys made obscene cat calls, telling the girls what they wanted. I really lucked out having to spend the night in a cell with a young black kid who was clearly not a hardened criminal. He sobbed quietly during the night. Maybe someone took pity on me and it wasn't luck at all.

The next morning, everyone who'd been arrested that night was moved to two large holding areas. I looked around and spotted someone who looked Vietnamese. It suddenly dawned on me that this was probably the person who'd knocked out one of the people in Khai's entourage. He introduced himself as Tuan Le.

We spoke for hours about what we did to get arrested. He talked about how he'd been mentally and physically tortured by the Vietnamese government agents who despised Amerasians—their fathers were American servicemen and their mothers were Vietnamese—and treated them like dirt.

Many of these mothers disowned their children, who then had to live out on the street to survive. Eventually these young kids came to be called "Children of the Dust."

Tuan Le had tears in his eyes recalling the bayonets thrust into his body around a campfire at night to make him dance. I was horrified. When he saw my disillusioned look he started to show me all the scars all over his body, thinking I didn't believe him.

When he smiled as he told me about hitting one of Khai's people in the throat, knocking him out instantly, I immediately told him never to smile when telling that story going forward. I said he needed to show remorse. He initially disagreed with me. After I explained that he could be deported back to Vietnam, he realized the seriousness of his action. I explained this to his court-appointed attorney who told Tuan to say nothing at his initial hearing before the judge.

After a night and day in jail, I was finally presented for arraignment to a federal judge in Washington U.S. District Court around 5 PM, represented by the same court-appointed attorney assigned to Tuan.

The charge of simple assault, as explained to me by the agent before my arrest, was changed to "willfully intimidated, coerced, threatened and harassed a foreign official, an official guest of the United States government, to wit, Phan Van Khai, Prime Minister of the Socialist Republic of Vietnam and obstructed the Prime Minister in the performance of Prime Minister Khai's official duties."

Eventually that changed again when the Secret Service and District Attorney charged me under Title 18, United States Code, Section 112(B). The two counts finally submitted to the federal judge hearing my case were changed to "involve the Act of or Intent of willfully threatening, intimidating, coercing, harassing, obstructing, and interfering in the official duties of a foreign official on American soil."

The Assistant D.A. argued that I was a flight risk, but the judge released me on my own recognizance citing my family ties and long-term employment with a large corporation. He set my arraignment for July 8, 2005, for a status update to determine if I hired a lawyer. I was released after signing an agreement not to go anywhere around the White House, Khai, or his delegation while they were still in the United States.

I was released later on that evening, sometimes after dark; I had no money to even make a phone call. The officer who released me said my personal belongings were taken by the local police department completely across town. When I asked to make a phone call, he said that wasn't their policy. I begged him to let me use the phone, otherwise, I would literally have to beg for money on the street to make a phone call. When he realized how desperate my situation was, he let me make a call.

I called Quyen Le, who traveled by train to pick me up. He verified that the attorney who represented me was only a few blocks away so I arrived and waited in his office. This was a fitting ending to the scariest arrest and detention I was ever involved in.

We were sure Senator McCain was behind my being arrested. He was quoted saying that he and Khai were splashed. There is no way Khai was splashed because it never came close to him, and this is proven by a look at the CSPAN tape. Khai had no idea what was going on until he saw the agents converge on me. The tape clearly shows that McCain did have wine on his shirt, as well as a few others at the head table.

McCain not only sat next to Khai at the dais, he introduced Khai as his long-time friend. As Prime Minister of Vietnam, the most powerful position in their government, Khai not only sanctioned the killing of his own people, he also had to be at least indirectly involved in the deaths of some American POWs over the years.

This again raises questions about McCain's stability and motives. The following is a handout John Nevin and I put together for the media; however, the underlying problem is that the American mainstream media has made McCain a hero despite his treasonous behavior during the war. They never allow the facts to get in the way of a good story line, and of course McCain plays the phony "hero" image to the hilt.

Hero, Fraud, or Worse?

A former military officer—whose own father was one of the highest-ranking officers in the same branch of service—wrecked three aircraft during his pilot training. Despite earning the nickname "Crash" from his fellow trainees, he was granted his Wings.

In Vietnam, he flew 23 missions totaling only 20 hours in the air, but received more decorations than Audie Murphy. [1]

He received the second-highest decoration his service could offer—the Silver Star—despite the absence of the required two witnesses; information

119

on which the award was based could only have come from him. [1]

On his 23rd mission, he crashed again, this time apparently as a result of a North Vietnamese surface-to-air missile or anti-aircraft fire. Surviving but badly injured, he was captured by the enemy.

Four days later, he called a North Vietnamese officer into the room in which he was being held, and said, "Okay, I'll give you military information if you take me to the hospital." [2]

Thirteen days after his capture, Hanoi press quoted him giving specific military information, describing the number of pilots in his wing and aircraft in his flight, information about rescue ships, and the order of which his attack was supposed to take place. [3, 4, 5]

He participated in several interviews by French, Cuban, and Vietnamese Communist journalists and two North Vietnamese generals, enjoying coffee, tea, cookies, cakes, and oranges during several of these visits (extravagant items other POWs never received). [4, 6]

He signed and taped a "confession" in which he called himself a "black pirate" and "admitted" to bombing civilian targets. The tape was played over the POW camp loudspeakers, undermining the morale of his fellow prisoners. [5, 7]

He personally made a Radio Hanoi propaganda broadcast in which he "admitted" to attacking non-military targets and saying he had received excellent medical care while in North Vietnamese hands. [7, 8]

He later claimed that he had been tortured to extract his confession and radio broadcast, but his two Senior Ranking Officers (SRO) at the time—Col. Swede Larsen and Col. Ted Guy—have publicly stated that they don't believe it. [9]

Since his return from Vietnam, as a member of the U.S. Congress, he has voted for the brutal Socialist Republic of Vietnam's favored position on every issue of relevance to them.

About this man, Pulitzer Prize winner Sydney Schanberg wrote, "There is one part of his record, however, that the press almost never asks him about. They never ask why this decorated Navy pilot and Vietnam P.O.W. has spent so much of his time and energy as a Senator pushing through legislation to block the release of information about American P.O.W.s and M.I.A.s who are still not accounted for.

"Working hand in hand with the Pentagon and the intelligence community, [he] has kept hidden critical documents about a body of prisoners who were alive but secretly held back by Hanoi when the war ended as bargaining fuel for war reparations. They were never returned...

"Incidentally, [he] was a pivotal member of that [Senate Select] P.O.W. committee, which was co-chaired by his friend, Senator John Kerry. The committee's final report, in early 1993, whitewashed the evidence that men were left behind." [11]

Giving military information to the enemy in time of war puts the mission in jeopardy as well as endangers the lives of one's comrades.

Participating in interviews while a POW with journalists known to be friendly to the enemy and engaging in discussions with general officers of the enemy military are both clear and serious violations of the U.S. military Code of Conduct.

Making propaganda broadcasts on enemy radio, admitting crimes he didn't commit, and praising the treatment he had received as a POW undermined the mission and morale of his compatriots. [8, 10]

All three of the above acts qualify as giving "aid and comfort" to the enemy in time of war, the specific definition of treason named in the U.S. Constitution.

Who is this man? None other than Senator John "Crash" McCain.

Is it any wonder that some who know McCain's real record and his "reliability" as an advocate for the Socialist Republic of Vietnam call him the "Senator from Hanoi?"

1. Colonel David Hackworth - www.hackworth.com
2. Article Written by John McCain in *US News and World Report* dated May 14, 1973

3. *Faith of My Fathers,* written by former POW John McCain, Pages 193 – 194

4. Declassified Department of Defense document dated November 9, 1967

5. *The Nightingale's Song* by Robert Timberg

6. Havana Granma January 24, 1970

7. Saigon – UPI wire story dated June 4, 1969

8. New York Daily News dated June 5 1969

9. The Phoenix New Times dated March 25, 1999

10. The Washington Post dated June 5, 1969

11. Sydney H. Schanberg, Pulitzer Prize winning author of *The Killing Fields,* wrote *Senator Goes Missing* dated June 7, 2005

Rumors have been rampant for years among POW family members, veterans, and his fellow former POWs about what may have motivated McCain to be such a reliable advocate for the interests of the Socialist Republic of Vietnam.

During the 2008 Presidential election, CNN was very persistent in arranging an interview with me, even to the point of tracking me down in a place near my home where they conducted a half hour interview. Several days later, Wolf Blitzer criticized me for even considering the ridiculous possibility of McCain being turned while he was isolated from the other POWs at the time when he was first captured.

They ignored my explanation that McCain was treated differently because his father was the Commander of the entire Pacific Operation, including the Vietnam War. They didn't allow any of the facts I spoke about during the half an hour interview to get in the way of their goal, which was to discredit me and Ross Perot in the same story. They killed two birds with one stone. It's the same strategy almost all the mainstream media obsessively pursued.

Immediately following my June 21st arrest, I called John LeBoutillier concerning legal representation that I could afford. He referred me to a very high-priced lawyer in D.C., but his fee was too high for me, which started at $1,000 an hour. He said a friend of his, Ken Robinson, who had been an Assistant Prosecuting Attorney in the '60s, now defended the people he used to put in jail. He also told me that his friend's fee was more reasonable.

End of June 2005

My Vietnam veteran friend picked me up at my attorney's office and took me to a restaurant to talk. He thanked me for my courage at the Mayflower Hotel and explained how important it was to the POW issue. He had made contact with a Vietnamese citizen who had contacts in the

Vietnamese Communist government but held no government position. His Vietnamese contact had made arrangements to meet him in D.C. to discuss the POW issue on November 9, 2005, specifically because of what I did.

He also said that other friends of ours didn't want me convicted of a misdemeanor nor to do any additional jail time, so they recommended taking a plea deal in return for community service.

I told him that fundraisers were being organized in the Vietnamese-American community to pay for my legal representation. He said, "They will never be able to raise the money needed to pay for a D.C. lawyer. Times are tough for them financially, and good legal representation in D.C. is quite expensive."

July 8, 2005

Quyen Le and I visited Ken Robinson's office the morning before my first court appearance. We hammered out an agreement where my defense fund would pay Ken a flat fee of $15,000 if he got me off with no trial, or $20,000 should there be a trial. Considering his normal fee is $500 an hour, which he estimated would cost over $30,000 for a two or three day trial, it appeared to be a bargain.

As I found out later, Ken visits the National Vietnam Veterans Memorial Wall once in a while to remember and pay respects to his best friend. Ken became very emotional when discussing his friend. He believes he could have made a difference had he gone with his friend to Vietnam. It never occurred to me that a civilian back home could also suffer from survivor's guilt.

The Assistant District Attorney met with Ken and me privately to make sure I understood that the plea bargain deal he offered would result in no jail time with only community service. I said that was my understanding and that I would not accept a deal. He came back again to convince me without success and appeared surprised that I would not jump at his offer. I had become very optimistic through my conversations with Ken, so I said, "I'm not guilty and I plan on winning this case."

We appeared at 9AM in front of Magistrate Judge Debra Robinson to set my trial date. Ken said of the pool of six judges, she was the best judge we could have gotten because she was a strong believer in civil liberties. The other five were white male judges who might have limited the testimony and were more likely to find me guilty. Ken Robinson represented me even though we didn't pay him because the Le and Kiley Defense Fund Foundation had just been formed. The first fundraiser event was scheduled for July 22nd in Atlanta, Georgia.

July 9, 2005

Quyen Le arranged a picnic, as he does each year, at a state park near his home in Maryland. It was attended that year by over a hundred Vietnamese-Americans. It was my first exposure to the Vietnamese community since the Mayflower Hotel incident and I was surprised and humbled by their attention and praise. The biggest problem with this event—as with others later—is that I don't speak or understand Vietnamese and the only time English was spoken was when someone was speaking to me. Even though many have excellent command of English, their different cadence, and sometimes accent, often made it difficult for me to be sure what was being said.

On July 22, 2005, the Atlanta (Georgia) Vietnamese-American community flew me in for a fundraiser, with Tuan Le as the other guest. There were three hundred people there and we received over $7,000 in donations that night. Everyone wanted to take a picture with me during the three-hour event. It was overwhelming.

I told the Vietnamese and their families how humble I felt before thanking them for their support, but all the attention and praise was somewhat disorienting. I wasn't used to anything like that and my speech didn't have the normal fire and passion. Even though I experienced some of this at the picnic on July 9th, I was blown away by this event. Fortunately, I did recover enough to end with my standard chant of, "Freedom," to which they responded, "Now."

The following day I met a former vice chairman of the U.S. Vietnamese community who asked me how I was being treated and I said like royalty. He responded by saying, "Yes, you are Ki-ley."

"What?" I asked.

He answered emphatically, "You are Khai-Le," indicating that I was now considered royalty by the Vietnamese people. The name Le is one of the original family names in Vietnam.

I laughed when I understood his meaning, and then he became very serious and said the Vietnamese people around the world will be forever grateful for what I did and that they owed me a debt of gratitude that could never be repaid. I was speechless, except to thank him for his gracious remarks. I struggled to regain my breath.

Before leaving Georgia, I was invited to Tuan Le's house to celebrate our successful fundraiser. The event was far more successful than we originally realized because it generated substantial donations of money over the next month from those who could not attend.

Tuan Le invited his tight-knit group from the Amerasian community in the Atlanta area and, naturally, the architect of the fundraiser, Quyen Le. Traditional gatherings for the Vietnamese include sitting around a huge burner-heated pot of seafood broth in the middle of a room. Quyen Le made the broth the day before from fish heads. Surrounding the pot were bowls of shrimp and assorted fish that would periodically be placed in the pot to cook for everyone to eat at their leisure. Alcohol was consumed, and along with energetic conversations, the celebration started in the afternoon and lasted well into the evening hours.

At least forty people came and left during this get-together. I've never experienced anything like this before. The passion and camaraderie of the Amerasian community—many of whom had been brutalized physically and mentally since they were born—was inspiring, to say the least. I'll never forget the spirit they still had when most would have been broken.

The August 26, 2005, fundraiser in D.C. was the most exciting event because about four hundred people paid $50 per person to attend. Besides my attorney Ken Robinson and my son David, co-activist Ted Sampley, former POW Mike Benge, NVVC Chairman Tom Burch, Tuan Le and his attorneys were all there.

Tom, Ted, Mike, and I all spoke to the crowd. They were very vocal. I stole the show by using the big bullhorn used at the White House when I turned up the volume to maximum and repeatedly yelled, "Khai, go home." We netted $9,000 for the defense fund, including funds from an auction at the end of the dinner. I went around to every table to thank everyone.

This was the first event where I felt I was back on my game and didn't feel overwhelmed. At the end of the night, Tom Burch said he was blown away by their response and that I was right to place my faith in their ability to raise this money. Tuan Le's attorneys, who were dealing with the Immigration and Naturalization Service, sat at our table and said they had never seen anything like this in the twenty-plus years they'd been involved with different cultures. They praised the loyalty of the Vietnamese community in their support of our cases.

The fund was closed shortly after this event because we had reached our goal of raising $55,000 in only seven weeks. Quyen Le, who was responsible for this incredible demonstration of support by the Vietnamese community, had committed $20,000 of this fund to my defense and $35,000 to Tuan Le's defense.

Tuan Le was represented in his assault trial by Ken Robinson, who did a good job of getting Le into an anger management program rather than a prison term after his felony conviction for assault. A separate husband and wife team, specializing in deportation, was hired to keep Le in this country. They successfully argued that returning Le to the brutal government of Vietnam would result in torture at the very least. Tuan Le was released after nine months of rehabilitation on the assault charge and was allowed to remain in the USA provided he didn't break any laws in the future.

Tuesday, October 18, 2005
First Day of Trial

The prosecutor, Assistant United States Attorney Bruce Hedgy, opened with brief remarks stating that he would prove that I had been obsessed with the POW/MIA and human rights issues in Vietnam for the last twenty years. This would prove to be fatal because this was also my attorney's strategy. My attorney had told the prosecutor what he was going to do, but Halley had probably thought he was bluffing.

In his opening statement, Ken Robinson also said he was going to discuss my activism over the last twenty years to show that I was a dedicated, loyal, and peaceful person who is respected and admired by other Vietnam veterans and the Vietnamese-American community.

The first witness for the prosecution was Virginia Foote, head of the Asian/American Trade Council, who sponsored the June 21, 2005, banquet for Khai. She described the atmosphere at the banquet as fearful and terrifying following my tossing of the wine and calling Khai a killer and McCain a traitor. Her testimony actually helped me; she saw the liquid land on the head table, which verified that it could not have landed on or even near Khai who was feet away and standing behind a large podium. She also tried to describe Khai as fearful even though he was laughing and puzzled, unaware of what was happening in the prosecutor's CSPAN video.

My attorney was outstanding in his cross-examination. After skillfully asking her many questions while both of them watched the C-Span tape of the event at the dinner, he put her in a position that she had to admit Khai was enjoying himself or she had to dodge the answer. Foote chose to dodge the answer, and the judge repeatedly told her to answer yes or no, eventually threatening to hold her in contempt if she didn't answer my attorney's questions. Foote verified that Khai didn't speak English so my attorney asked how he could feel threatened if he didn't understand what I said.

Ken also asked her about other occasions when Ms. Foote had confrontations with the National Vietnam Veterans Coalition at other sponsored events supporting her Communist friends. He induced her to contradict herself. In her struggle to avoid saying that Khai was laughing on the tape, she described Khai's face as a "dead face," a claim that the judge could see was ridiculous. She did verify that (1) Proctor and Gamble paid $10,000 for the table I sat at where I patiently ate my salad, chicken dinner, and dessert; (2) the fact that Congressman Miller from California and two Fortune 500 executives were the individuals who actually escorted me out of the Grand Ballroom, rather than Secret Service agents as I had assumed, and (3) the official number in attendance was six hundred.

By the time Ken Robinson was through with her, Virginia Foote had destroyed her own credibility.

Next up was the Vietnamese lady at my table who tried to talk to me while I ate my chicken dinner. She said I claimed to be an owner of a travel agency and verified that I moved toward the head table even though she didn't see what happened with regard to my tossing the wine. My attorney immediately made a major case about her needing an interpreter during the trial when she not only spoke to me in English; she also spoke to the Secret Service Agent in English, and then signed the statement written by the agent in English.

At one point Ken asked her a question and before it could be interpreted she answered and the prosecutor objected which the judge overruled. When Ken asked her to read the English statement written by the agent she read it with no problem. He made it seem clear that the interpreter was being used as a device only to give her more time to consider her answers. I felt that he had eliminated any value she might have to the prosecution but her credibility declined even more when it was revealed that she worked for the Vietnamese Embassy.

The third and final witness for the prosecution was Special Agent Phillips, who was said to be in charge of investigating security violations. He proved to be a great character witness for me by testifying that I answered all his questions honestly and truthfully even pointing out that I helped the Secret Service by explaining how I slipped past their security. He explained how composed I was and later verified that I said I would not have thrown the wine had I known that I would be arrested. Even his claim that I threw wine on Khai did not hurt me because he wasn't even in the banquet hall when I tossed it. It didn't matter anyway because the C-Span tape clearly showed that the wine never got close to Khai.

I could not believe that the prosecutor rested his case without impugning my integrity. My attorney immediately requested a dismissal of all charges based on a lack of evidence that I committed or had the intent to throw wine at or on Khai. There was a tremendous battle between the prosecutor and the judge, with my attorney throwing fuel on the fire. The prosecutor argued that I willfully entered a hotel he claimed I had no right to be in, willfully sneaked past security, willfully attended a banquet without purchasing a ticket, and willfully threw wine in the direction of Khai and therefore, a willful act as applied to this statute constitutes guilt.

Judge Robinson said that willful does not constitute guilt and ruled that the first count of the indictment indicating that I had threatened, intimidated, harassed, obstructed, and interfered with Khai in the execution of his official duties was never proven. The prosecutor was outraged and continued to argue with a vengeance that surprised me. It was so confrontational and dramatic that it reminded me of an unbelievable, overdramatic Hollywood version of a court trial. The prosecutor's vehemence made me suspect that he was under a lot of pressure from someone up the federal food chain to get a conviction.

As the trial transcript will show, the judge overruled most of the prosecutor's objections and the tension between them was felt to an extreme degree throughout the trial. The judge did let stand the second charge, exactly as the first except that it involved my intent to threaten, intimidate, harass, obstruct, and interfere with Khai. If I intended to throw the wine on Khai and failed, I would be found guilty. The judge called on my attorney to present the defense witnesses.

Our first witness was Anh Thu, who holds a government contract job. Anh testified to participating with me in five demonstrations, one in New York and two in Boston against John Kerry, and the two in D.C. in June 2005 against Khai. She confirmed my peaceful demeanor and honesty; however, the most important part of her testimony was talking about our permit to demonstrate directly in front of the Mayflower Hotel and our being moved across the street with the promise from the police that we would be able to come back when Khai arrived. His instructions were that we could yell anything we wanted to at Khai as long as we didn't touch him. If we touched him, we would be arrested.

The prosecutor immediately objected saying that it cannot be admitted as a true statement without verification from the source. The judge said this testimony wasn't considered a true statement but would be considered probative information germane to the case. The prosecutor continued to argue this point beyond what I considered to be reasonable. He clearly was on a scorch and burn mission, probably to put on a good show for the dozen Communist embassy officials attending the trial every day. Instead, he completely burned his bridge with the judge.

The prosecutor may also have been looking to impress his boss, the District Attorney, who had opposed Judge Robinson's reinstatement for another eight-year term as one of the three magistrates appointed by a federal panel. The DA wanted her replaced supposedly due to his conviction rate being hurt by Judge Robinson's rulings against his office.

The prosecutor tried to get Anh to say that the NAM360 website was my site. She said very firmly that it was Duc Tran, a Vietnamese scientist from Philadelphia, who had created the website and placed Khai's picture with the red X across his image.

He asked if that meant we wanted him dead and she again said, very assertively and with some disdain, "No." When asked what it meant, Anh said we didn't want him in America. When the prosecutor tried to get Anh to say something negative about me, she said the Vietnamese-American community thought I was their hero and that four hundred of them had met in Virginia to raise funds for my defense.

He then tried to trap her into saying that I was wrong and broke the law and illegally entered the hotel and banquet. She said she was in the hotel for the same reason and that it is our right under the First Amendment to freely speak our minds. Anh was great, and set the tone for the next day when our defense was confident, assertive, and credible.

Wednesday, October 19, 2005

Second Day of Trial

Tuan Tran, a pharmacist in Boston and a lieutenant in the South Vietnamese Army during the war, was our second witness. Tuan talked about his brother being killed in a reeducation camp where he and the former South Vietnamese military personnel were held for years after the war ended. Many were tortured and killed.

Tuan was a good character witness who confirmed that I was peaceful in the five demonstrations he participated in with me. He called me a hero and said he had great admiration and respect for the commitment and loyalty I have for the American POWs and Vietnamese people. The prosecutor established that we had only known each other since the year before.

Mike Benge is a former POW who was held for over five years. He was a civilian with the Peace Corps prior to his capture, and later was involved in rebuilding parts of Vietnam. He made the point that he'd known me ever since we participated in a demonstration in the mid-80s, as well as the Vietnam Veterans Against John Kerry demonstration in New York in February 2004 and the two June 2005 demonstrations in D.C. Mike vouched for my character and truthfulness.

The prosecutor had Mike verify my signature on the June 18, 2005, D.C. permit, and then asked him if he agreed with the section that stated all U.S. laws and regulations should be adhered to. Mike answered that also included the First Amendment, which gave us the right of free speech.

The prosecutor was surprised by his answer and asked Mike, "Are you a lawyer?" He responded with a deadpan expression, stating indignantly, "I certainly hope not."

I burst out laughing, and his remark ignited the entire courtroom, including the judge who turned her face and held up her hand to disguise her laughter.

The prosecutor ended his cross-examination several questions later. Mike never smiled until I spoke to him during the next break.

Tom Burch is the former National Vietnam Veterans Coalition Chairman and an attorney-at-law. There was a huge battle between the prosecutor and the judge regarding an "advice and consent" defense on the first day of the trial before we called our witnesses. The judge said that wasn't our defense and that the information is probative.

The prosecutor then complained that he didn't know Tom was an attorney until the day before the trial. Tom was moving to a new office and didn't get the fax to which he was supposed to respond with his credentials.

The judge sarcastically asked the prosecutor whether he wanted to delay the trial because Tom didn't get a fax. The judge ruled against the prosecutor and said we could mention that Tom was an attorney.

Tom and I had known each other for over twenty years. Since I'd worked for him as the coalition Communication Director and Assistant Chairman, he knew me as well as anyone. His testimony to my integrity was perhaps the most important.

Tom made the point that a positive image of the Vietnam veteran was one of the goals of the NVVC and that we'd always made arrangements with the police prior to planned peaceful civil disobedience events at the White House. The prosecutor showed Tom a law that would make my actions illegal back in 1993 when Tom had authorized me to approach Khai. Tom pointed out that the law wasn't enacted until 1996, thus embarrassing the prosecutor who reluctantly gave him the document to read. It almost appeared that the prosecutor was either caught in a deception or had no idea of this date. In either case, he looked very bad. The prosecutor ended his cross-examination soon after that response.

I was the last person to testify for my defense. Ken asked me about my involvement in dozens of demonstrations over the last twenty years. I stated that I personally organized twelve demonstrations, including six in front of the Communist Mission to the United Nations in NY. I also said that I'd had three meetings with Special Ambassador Can, who'd been sent from Vietnam specifically to manage the POW/MIA controversy and public relations problem Vietnam had here. The discussion had centered primarily on the live POW issue, along with human rights violations in Vietnam. I made the point that if the Communist regime did the right thing on the POW issue and made substantial progress on human rights, we would support them; otherwise we would continue to fight them.

Ken Robinson then asked me to discuss my three other arrests related to the POW issue. I explained that on two occasions I chained myself to the White House fence. One was at the request of a sixty-year-old mother, Jane Gaylor, whose son was missing from the Vietnam War.

The other arrest was at the request of the sons and daughters of missing serviceman who had already decided to chain themselves to the White House fence on Father's Day in June 1988, during the Reagan Administration. I explained that the third arrest was a mistake because of holding a sign in the air on park property, which is illegal in D.C. The sign called Vice President Gore a traitor to the POWs because he was technically their comrade-in-arms, having served a month in-country as a writer.

Ken Robinson then questioned me about four situations when I had walked past security during private events. Three of the four involved the Secret Service. I first spoke about the October 17, 1993, Captains of Industry dinner/reception when I had handed a small POW/MIA flag to Deputy Prime Minister Khai while I berated him.

Ken asked me if Khai spoke English and I explained that he didn't understand until one of his interpreters stepped in. I said that his smile turned into a dead face, in reference to Virginia Foote's testimony. The Secret Service politely asked me to leave and I left with no discussion of an arrest.

Ken asked me if I considered the 1993 and 2005 banquets official government business. I said in both cases it was American big business lobbying the Communist government, and not a government-sponsored event.

I then discussed the fundraising dinner sponsored by Cardinal O'Connor, involving then VP George HW Bush and Governor Dukakis. Even though the cardinal was furious with me, the Secret Service left without approaching me.

Another was the incident involving a female basketball player who turned her back on the flag. I told how I'd approached her on the basketball court and held up the flag. The Harrison Police captain had let me go.

We then went over the details of the June 21, 2005, arrest. The main point had been the wine, which symbolized the blood of innocent people, and had been thrown at Khai's chair and not at Khai himself.

Ken made an excellent point, that I could have thrown the wine directly on Khai who'd been sitting directly in front of me for over an hour.

Another point was that the female Secret Service agent told the other agents to let me go since I hadn't done anything. Also, we had been instructed by the police outside the hotel that it would be all right for us to yell whatever we wanted to at Khai as long as we didn't touch him. Ken Robinson said that I followed the policeman's instructions at the banquet as well as Tom Burch's advice as chairman and lawyer of the NVVC.

The prosecutor tried to involve me as the originator of the NAM360 website. I told him the Coalition for Human Rights and Religious Freedom in Vietnam was a loose organization involving many people and that I had no idea how to start or update a website. I said Duc Tran was the originator of the site.

As a last resort, the prosecutor made a desperate attempt to get me to admit I had the intent to intimidate, coerce, and harass. I denied every accusation and made it clear I was exercising my First Amendment right of free speech. He even tried to get me to admit to annoying the Prime Minister, at which time the judge stopped him even though the prosecutor said the word annoy appears in the dictionary under harass.

The clincher was when I said Secret Service Agent Phillips, whom I'd testified the day before was an honorable man with integrity and that I have tremendous respect for the Secret Service agents, wasn't in the banquet hall. He'd been told incorrectly that I had thrown wine on Khai. He maintained that later on when he wrote his report, even though I had told him otherwise. I reminded the court that the agent confirmed during his testimony that I said I would not have thrown the wine had I known it would get me arrested.

The agent didn't take notes during the ninety minutes we were together. He eventually wrote two reports in two completely different time frames.

The prosecutor had one final question. "Is it true that you're called the Stealth Activist because you have an uncanny ability to get past security?"

I said "Correct."

Thursday, October 20, 2005
Third Day of Trial

The closing arguments from both the prosecutor and my attorney took about ninety minutes. The judge repeatedly interrupted the prosecutor for making unsubstantiated remarks not supported by trial testimony. The prosecutor disrespected the judge in his frustration to try to finish his remarks without interruption by asking the judge to hold all her questions until the end of his remarks. She asserted herself by overruling his objection, indicating that statements unsubstantiated by the testimony would not be allowed.

Her questions to the prosecutor would usually began with, "Did I miss something in the testimony?" and "Is it your contention that you presented this information?" The prosecutor would always acknowledge that he didn't submit his statement into testimony and the judge repeatedly overruled him. He additionally insulted her by emphasizing that anyone with "any common sense" would view the tape of the incident the same way he did. Debra Robinson disagreed and overruled him.

Comically, the prosecutor described my four previous activities in slipping past security as surreptitious and clandestine. He said Khai's visit was historic because it was the first time a Vietnamese (Communist) leader had been invited and officially recognized by an American President in thirty years.

The prosecutor also made the point that Senator McCain was so embarrassed that he felt compelled to apologize to Khai for my actions. He tried to disparage me by repeating the fact that I was known throughout the activist community as the Stealth Activist, even though I had been given that nickname by a former U.S. Congressman.

My attorney called me an American patriot who was dedicated, honest, peaceful, and trusted by Vietnam veterans and the Vietnamese community. He emphasized my twenty years of peaceful and non-threatening activities.

Ken also made the point that Khai could not have felt threatened, harassed, or intimidated as witnessed by the tape because he does not speak

English and didn't understand what I said. He finished by making an impassioned plea for my release and said even the prosecutor didn't attempt to impugn my reputation during the trial, a fact that further confirms my honesty and truthfulness. He also pointed out that I had honestly stated how much respect I had for Secret Service Agent Phillips even though Phillips was testifying against me.

The judge said she would take under advisement the prosecution's motion to quash the testimony about the police officer's instruction not to touch Khai and the overall testimony before ruling on this case.

As a side issue, the testimony from the prosecutor's witnesses strengthened and confirmed our case that the wine never came close to Khai. It was in direct conflict with McCain's statement the day after the banquet that he and Khai both had wine splashed on them. He was half right, because it did hit him. The point is that he deliberately lied because he knew my arrest was predicated on wine hitting a foreign official. Ironically, in his desire to have me prosecuted and convicted, he had enhanced my reputation in the Asian anti-Khai community.

My attorney was brilliant. I was very fortunate to have found him and I felt I had gotten the best representation money could buy. In this case, it was the $20,000 the Vietnamese community had raised for my defense. He earned my eternal friendship and loyalty, the same loyalty I have for the POWs we abandoned over thirty years ago.

Funny story: on one of the breaks during the trial, I found a very attractive Secret Service agent engaged in conversation with my son Michael. When I asked what they were talking about, Mike said they were talking about some of my visits to D.C. This agent had been assigned as a consultant to the prosecutor and attended every minute of the trial.

I reminded him that the woman was an agent for the people behind my prosecution, and very politely ended the encounter by saying, "Good try."

She silently gestured with a shrug of her shoulders, as if to say, "I had to try."

I actually acknowledged her job and said, "I understand."

She told me I had a very nice son and naturally I thanked her.

Wednesday, November 9, 2005
The Verdict

The verdict of not guilty was based on the discredited testimony of Virginia Foote and the failure of the prosecutor to prove that I had any intent to threaten, intimidate, harass, obstruct, or interfere with Khai in his official duties. The prosecutor told my attorney that the Communist embassy of

Vietnam protested my verdict, that they were outraged and demanded I be recharged.

He also told my attorney that the D.C. District Attorney was definitely going to file additional charges of unlawful entry in the local Appellate Court, which carries a six-month sentence. He admitted that this was a politically charged issue; our government, in particular the District Attorney's office, is working for a Communist government.

I can't even imagine the rage McCain felt when he heard the verdict. There is no doubt that he once again was acting as Vietnam's surrogate.

I received a call at 3:30 PM from my attorney's clerk stating the verdict. The transcript I received later indicated that "Having completed due deliberations the Court finds Mr. Kiley not guilty of Count two. The Court finds that the government has failed to carry its burden to prove each element of the remaining offense beyond a reasonable doubt." She had already dropped the first count near the end of the trial.

The following is the most compelling part of Judge Deborah Robinson's verdict: "The Court also at the government's invitation looked very carefully at the expression of the Prime Minister and the reaction of the guests and finds that the version of events offered by the government during the government's closing argument wasn't at all supported by the Court's view of the video tape. By the same token the Court finds that the testimony of the government's eyewitnesses, most particularly Ms. Foote, wasn't supported by the videotape, the other evidence in the case.

"To the extent that this means that credibility is an issue as it is in every instance in which a defendant and other witnesses testify the Court credits the testimony of Mr. Kiley regarding his actions and his purpose and his intent and his state of mind at the time of the relevant events. The Court does so for several reasons.

"First, his testimony was corroborated by the government's evidence, that is, the videotape. More specifically, the Court finds that what Mr. Kiley said regarding where he stood, what he did and the reactions of those around him were the very observations that the Court had upon viewing the videotape. Witnesses testified on behalf of Mr. Kiley regarding Mr. Kiley's reputation for truth and veracity and peace and good order. Neither Mr. Kiley nor any of those witnesses were impeached.

"On the other hand, the testimony of a witness on whom the government placed particular reliance, that is Ms. Virginia Foote, was impeached. The Court determined during the government's case-in-chief and set forth the determinations in great detail on the record that Ms. Foote demonstrated that she wasn't amendable to answering the questions of Mr. Kiley's counsel on cross-examination, that her own testimony with respect to her interest in the event and her planning of the event warrant the inference that her capacity to testify objectively with respect to any disturbance of the event was compromised. Ms. Foote was impeached on several occasions during her cross-examination.

"And finally, the Court notes that Ms. Foote's testimony wasn't corroborated by the videotape. That is there was no evidence of any change in expression of the Prime Minister, no evidence of any fear on the part of any of the individuals, and of the guests who attended the event. Indeed, no evidence that a crowd was required to usher Mr. Kiley from the ballroom. Indeed, the videotape shows that only one person approached Mr. Kiley. Mr. Kiley offered no resistance, didn't continue to make any comments and left without saying anything or taking any action, further corroborating his testimony regarding his intent, his purpose, his state of mind and the description of the events that he undertook."

I called everyone to tell them the good news. Coincidentally, my Vietnam veteran friend who'd asked me to create a problem with Khai was at a meeting with his Vietnamese friend in D.C. when I called. I had delivered on his requests.

Immediately after my arrest in June, this friend of mine called to say that his Vietnamese contact was delighted with the results of our actions and had asked for this meeting on November 9th because of our success.

The meeting was just ending when I called. The Vietnamese contact spoke to me for a minute, profusely thanking me and saying my actions had international significance. He said that he could never repay me for what I had done, and I said we would never be able to repay him if we finally received a full and honest accounting of our POWs. I ended by offering my services again if that were necessary to get the job done.

In conversations on November 9th and later when we met face-to-face on November 22nd, my friend told me that his Vietnamese contact had surprised him by bringing an active Major General of the Vietnamese Army. This man claimed to be in charge of two POW camps that they referred to as Group 42.

I confirmed with one of our people in attendance that he knew of this code name and confirmed the General's authenticity, even though he didn't believe the man was directly in charge of our POWs.

The General, titled Deputy Commandant, claimed that the camp in Vietnam had 43 American POWs, while the camp in Laos had eleven, for a total of 54; however, he also indicated that there could be more in other camps not under his control. Their ages ranged from 65- to 78 years old. The General wanted to know how we would respond if they were to release three POWs, claiming that they had found them in a remote area of Laos. He went on to ask about our willingness to accept a promise that the remainder would be released at a later date. The expected time frame for this possible release would be the latter part of 2006, after Khai's scheduled replacement in June. My friend said we would support their effort to release these POWs with the following stipulations:

1. The three POWs are healthy, have all their mental faculties, and want to come home;

2. Are legitimate POWs and not in any other category (i.e., deserter, "stay-behind," etc.);

3. The release would be unconditional, not contingent on any financial exchange or any promise, explicit or implied, from us.

The preliminary details worked out were that this situation would not be considered unless my friend and his contact signed off on it. If they both agreed then a letter would be sent to my friend from the Vietnamese Communist government asking him to visit Vietnam for the purpose of this release. He would bring this letter to the Vietnamese Embassy in D.C. to verify its authenticity.

When verified, he would then take a delegation to Vietnam only to bring those men home, not for negotiation purposes. He made it clear that there would be no ceremonial visit similar to the one that embarrassed Bobby Muller when he was used as a propaganda tool by laying a wreath at gravesites of our enemy.

Since the General came from Vietnam and was staying that night at their embassy in D.C., it seemed clear that the Politburo approved this trip. The General said he was satisfied that we had standing to speak for a significant portion of the Vietnam veteran community and that we would look favorably on the release of a small number of POWs, even if it were explained in a less-than-honest manner. Then he raised a related issue that appeared to be a potential problem.

The General presented himself as representing a more progressive, open-minded element in the "new" Vietnam government. He stated that this more open thinking had become the majority view in the upper echelons of the government, but a significant roadblock to more rapid reform was fears held by some of the old hard-liners that easing government controls might lead to various forms of retribution against them. Both groups, the reformers and the hard-liners, saw the danger of keeping the remaining U.S. prisoners, and knew it was a threat to future relations with the West if it were not resolved favorably.

One major sticking point that they recognized, and the reason they were talking to us rather than to the U.S. government, was that these remaining prisoners, whose existence had been denied by both governments for over thirty years, were as big an embarrassment to the U.S. government as to Vietnam. Vietnam, at least, could claim (honestly, according to the General) to have turned over a new leaf, but the U.S. wouldn't have that out. The U.S. would have to admit to massive lies over several decades, or at least massive intelligence failures over the same period.

We were informed that the Politburo's ruling body contained sixty members who were elected by the 150-member Assembly consisting of six committees. The General was a member of the Assembly's Military Committee.

My friend assured the General that we had no inclination to pursue retribution and simply wanted to end this nightmare, but then he made it clear that we would obviously not be able to speak for everyone, and couldn't even promise what we would do. We could only make clear our thoughts, feelings, and what we considered the best strategy. "Unconditional" meant no promises from us.

He said we would not think it wise for us to challenge any statements concerning where they were held or found, continuing to reassure the General that we would appreciate their courageous action to do the right thing.

The General was going back to the embassy that night and would tell them that they should request no further charges be filed against me for the wine-throwing incident. More importantly, he said he would report that we were not inclined toward revenge in any form.

I was glad the General was going to recommend that Embassy officials act to end my legal troubles, but it was doubtful the District Attorney would pursue an unlawful entry charge anyway. Local D.C. law requires a person be warned first, preferably in writing, that he/she is not allowed at that premises in the future. The other part of that law says that if a person initially resists when asked to leave, he/she can be arrested at that time.

The lobby of a hotel is generally considered to be a public place and the fact that one of the Vietnamese protesters had given me a key to his room as an invited guest strengthened my case. I was advised that any attempt to file charges should be thrown out immediately by the judge. The General also said the feeling against Tuan Le was much harder and, therefore, he would not make any commitment to help him.

The following article was written by Ted Sampley, posted to our website www.usvetdsp.com and was then sent through the Internet worldwide. Even though some Vietnamese in Vietnam would read this, more importantly, Vietnamese government agents would definitely monitor it.

The Vet Now Faces New Charges After Communist Vietnamese Complain About The Verdict.

Ted Sampley
US Veteran Dispatch
November, 2005

A Vietnam veteran, and dedicated protester against human rights abuses still occurring in Vietnam, has been absolved of charges of assault against a Vietnamese official, but faces new charges of illegally entering a $1,000-a-plate dinner for Phan Van Khai.

Khai, Vietnam's Prime Minister, was in the US in June to meet with President George W. Bush, Sen. John McCain, Sen. John Kerry and other American officials and business leaders to discuss trade with the Communist country.

Vietnam veteran Jerry Kiley, a longtime POW/MIA activist, threw a glass of red wine on Khai's vacated seat in front of Khai shortly after the prime minister rose to speak to diners in a ballroom at the Mayflower Hotel. The wine, which Kiley said symbolized innocent blood that continues to be spilled by the brutal and godless Communist regime, splashed onto McCain, a former Vietnam POW, but did not strike Khai.

A US court, after hearing over two days of testimony against Kiley, ruled that the veteran did not assault Khai, as prosecutors alleged.

Pressure from the Communist Vietnam embassy, McCain's office, and the US State Department, however, may now result in new charges that Kiley illegally entered the ballroom where the reception for Khai was being held.

Neither McCain's office nor the Vietnamese embassy would comment on their involvement in the fresh charges.

The incident stemmed from a protest that began outside the White House and the Mayflower Hotel on June 21. Kiley, former vice president of the National Vietnam Veterans Coalition, and Ted Sampley, publisher of the online US Veterans Dispatch, were among the leaders of the demonstrators. Over a thousand Vietnamese and concerned Americans joined together in protesting against trade with Vietnam while at the same time urging Bush not to embrace the Communist leader.

Demonstrators reminded Bush that last year he promised Rolling Thunder President Artie Mueller that he never would abandon American prisoners left in Vietnam. Rolling Thunder is one of the largest veteran activist organizations in the country.

The US initiated trade restrictions in 1975 after Vietnam violated the Paris Peace Agreement by rolling tanks and massive infantry from North Vietnam into South Vietnam. Communist troops captured all of South Vietnam.

Upon occupying the country, the North Vietnamese uprooted millions of non-Communists from their homes, killed hundreds of thousands and threw others into concentration/reeducation camps. A lucky few escaped into the ocean and became known as the "boat people."

President Reagan sustained the embargo when North Vietnam refused to answer questions about the fate of American servicemen known to be alive in POW camps or reveal the location of others known to have died and whose bodies had not been recovered.

The Clinton administration, goaded by McCain, a former Vietnam POW and Sen. John Kerry (who after serving in Vietnam, vigorously protested the war and supported the Communist terms for US withdrawal), opened the door to trade and diplomatic relations.

McCain and Kerry worked closely with Virginia Foote, head of the US-Vietnam Trade Council, and successfully lobbied Clinton and Congress to lift the embargos on trade and diplomatic relations, although both men knew about the existence of Americans still held captive by Vietnamese Communists.

Human Rights Watch recently named Vietnam as one of the world's most egregious violators of human rights. Vietnamese, Montagnard, Cambodians, and Laotian refugees continue to present evidence to the United Nations that Vietnam Communists are systematically exterminating anti-Communist and pro-religious groups in that country.

After the demonstration earlier that day, Kiley, a guest at the Mayflower Hotel, changed into a business suit and tie at the garage where his car was located to avoid suspicion of those hosting the Khai dinner. The gala affair was sponsored by the US-Vietnam Trade Council, the US ASCAM Business Council and the Communist Vietnamese Chamber of Commerce and Industry.

Court testimony during Kiley's trial revealed that a Communist Vietnam representative was seated at every table. A Vietnamese woman from the Vietnamese embassy named Hung Young-Ahn Pham sat next to Kiley.

According to testimony, Kiley entered the Mayflower's Grand Ballroom after slipping past numerous Secret Service agents. He quickly found an empty chair and seated himself. The table at which he sat, he soon discovered was sponsored and paid for by Fortune 500 company Proctor & Gamble for $10,000.00. No one questioned his presence or asked him to leave.

McCain introduced Khai to the audience with a warm welcome. As the senator finished and sat down in a chair near the front of the stage, Khai walked to the podium.

Kiley left his seat and walked to the head table nearest the stage where McCain was sitting. He flung a glass of red wine across the table toward Khai's now-empty chair, inadvertently splattering McCain's shirt and tie. Kiley yelled that Khai and his government were killers and then pointed to McCain and said "Senator you are a traitor to the American POWs and Vietnamese people we abandoned after the war."

Dinner guests, momentarily surprised, laughed nervously, as did Khai.

C-span cameras focused close-up on a visibly furious McCain who was obviously struggling to gain self-control by attempting to force a smile. This action resulted in McCain's face appearing contorted as he twisted his mouth while rolling his eyes toward the ceiling.

California Congressman George Miller and two Fortune 500 Executives quickly grabbed Kiley, shoving him from the room.

Kiley's demonstration halted the momentum of the evening for less than a minute.

After Kiley was released outside the hotel by security, Secret Service agents intervened and questioned him. He cooperated and gave them permission to search him, his car and his hotel room.

Agents found nothing illegal or incriminating, but arrested him for assault. Kiley spent that night in jail and was released the following afternoon.

There was some evidence indicating that a thoroughly embarrassed McCain had demanded that the Secret Service arrest and charge Kiley.

Young-Ahn Pham, the Communist representative seated at Kiley's table, later became a prosecution witness during the two-day trial. She claimed not to speak English, but Kiley's attorney, Kenneth M. Robinson, arguing that she was just trying to avoid being tripped up during cross examination, forced her to acknowledge that she had given a statement to the Secret Service in English, without an interpreter, and that her statement was put in writing by the Secret Service.

Foote was one of the main witnesses against Kiley. She testified that right after Khai took his position behind the podium; she heard a commotion and saw a "sprinkling of a liquid falling on the head table." She claimed she heard a "loud thud" as a coffee cup rolled down the table. She pointed to Kiley when asked who was responsible for throwing a coffee cup.

Foote said that the incident caused a serious disruption of the meeting and that Khai's face "went flat" out of concern for his security.

The defense countered by playing a C-Span recording of the incident, which clearly showed Khai, and members of the audience laughing as Kiley was being pushed out. The defense then asked Foote to agree with the tape that Khai and the audience were laughing about Kiley's demonstration. Foote grew combative, refusing to answer with a direct yes or no.

On nearly every defense question afterward, she attempted to avoid answering direct questions by rephrasing the questions. She attempted to twist her testimony against Kiley so seriously that Judge Deborah Robinson (no relation to defense attorney Ken Robinson) warned her numerous times to properly answer the defense's questions.

The judge, apparently finally exasperated by Foote's continuous failure to follow the court's instructions, finally called a recess, and warned the prosecutor that continued obstruction by Foote would result in contempt of court charges.

A more subdued and cooperative Foote returned to the courtroom.

Prosecutors attempted to prove that Kiley had violated a new federal law forbidding the interference or harassment of foreign dignitaries while they are conducting official business.

The defense instead proved that Khai was not on official business at the dinner, which was a private meeting. The defense also proved that the wine Kiley threw was at Khai's empty chair and did not strike Khai, thus negating the assault charge.

Anh Thu Lu, a Vietnamese-American Defense Contractor, who became an American citizen in 1982, testified on Kiley's behalf. She said she had known Kiley for many years because of his unselfish participation in many "Freedom for Vietnam" and human rights demonstrations they both had attended. She said that Kiley is "a great man, friend and advocate for the Vietnamese people still suffering under a brutal Communist government in Vietnam."

Also, testifying for Kiley was; Mike Benge, a former Vietnam POW who is currently Senior Advisor for the Montagnard Human Rights Organization, Tom Burch, a Vietnam vet who founded the National Vietnam Veterans Coalition and is now a legal counsel for the Veterans Administration, Tuan Tran, a Vietnamese-American pharmacist/business owner who is a long time "Freedom for Vietnam" activist, and "Freedom for Vietnam" activist Quyen Le, who organized and led the Tuan Le and Kiley Defense Fund Foundation. Supporting Kiley in the courtroom and outside the courthouse were dozens of members of various Vietnamese-American communities.

McCain received a subpoena to appear in court and testify to the events. Kiley's attorney argued that McCain was not only present, but that the wine allegedly thrown by Kiley struck him, making him so angry that he insisted that Secret Service bring Kiley back into the hotel and charge him with a crime. The defense also argued that McCain had unique information that the other 600 guests did not have, such as what the dinner was about, who was there, why; he introduced Khai, and why he was a target of some of the remarks Kiley purportedly made.

McCain avoided the subpoena. His legal counsel successfully opposed all efforts to have the powerful senator testify and submitted a statement that McCain was so embarrassed that he personally apologized to Khai for the incident. His counsel also argued that the subpoena was unreasonable and oppressive, and that it is unduly burdensome to require the Senator to absent himself from legislative proceedings to testify.

Communist Vietnamese representatives carefully monitored both days of the trial. When the judge found Kiley Not Guilty of the charges, the Communists complained to the State Department.

The federal prosecutor launched an effort to file new charges against Kiley of illegal entry to the ballroom where the dinner was being held.

A trial date has not been set on the new charges.

The Mayflower protest is the second time Kiley successfully slipped through Secret Service security to confront Khai. In October 1993, at the New York City Plaza Hotel, when the "Captains of American Industry" hosted a reception/dinner for then Deputy Prime Minister Khai, Kiley slipped into a reception line reserved for the captains who were being introduced to Khai.

When it came time for Kiley to be introduced, he put on his American Legion cap, handed Khai a small POW/MIA flag, grasped the Communist leader's other hand in a "firm New York style" hand grip and began berating him about Vietnam holding live American POWS after the war and continued human rights violations in Vietnam.

It was that event in 1993 that prompted former congressman John LeBoutillier from Long Island, New York, to give Kiley the nickname "Stealth Activist" because of his uncanny ability to slip past security.

The Le and Kiley Defense Fund Foundation raised more than $55,000 in less than one month with fundraisers in Atlanta, Georgia, Falls Church, Virginia, and donations from Vietnamese communities around the world.

Kiley's defense cost for the three-day trial was $20,000. The remainder in the fund is set aside for Tuan Phuoc Le's defense by the same attorney.

Tuan Phuoc Le, 33, was arrested by federal authorities and accused of assaulting Nguyen Quoc Huy, vice chairman of the Vietnamese prime minister's office, outside the Willard InterContinental Washington hotel June 21, 2005. Huy was part of the delegation led by Khai.

Tuan Le's arrest and possible deportation have sparked outrage in the Vietnamese community in the United States. He has become a celebrated cause, with supporters collecting thousands of dollars for his defense and collecting more than 900 signatures in an online petition.

"It's very sad, very miserable for him," said Duc Tran of Philadelphia, a spokesman for the Coalition for Human Rights and Religious Freedom in Vietnam, one of the organizations that led protests against Khai's visit. "His father was American. They should not send him back."

Le has lived in the United States since 1993 and has permanent residency. After the incident, he was held without bond for weeks by immigration authorities in Virginia but has since been released and is back in Georgia working in construction.

--Ted Sampley

Chapter Nine
Continuing the Fight

November 22, 2005 - Quyen Le requested my participation at the Ronald Reagan building in D.C. to do my reconnaissance of the theater where the Vietnamese Embassy was planning a fundraiser that night for Hurricane Katrina victims.

Later that night, I demonstrated across the street from the Ronald Reagan Building/Theater with about one hundred Vietnamese, where the Communists had forced two of their professional singing groups to perform. The cause was good; however, we were protesting to expose the Vietnamese Communists as cold-blooded killers who are hypocrites that only do good deeds for propaganda purposes. In this case, it appeared to be orchestrated to help them gain acceptance into the World Trade Organization.

Even though I had figured out a way to slip into the event through the loading dock entrance, Quyen Le asked me not to go inside, so I honored his request. We had all the expatriate Vietnamese media there, TV, radio, and even Internet coverage, with the last two going out live around the world. We received live calls from freedom fighters in Hanoi and a radio station in Australia.

Several days later, Quyen Le told me there were over six hundred people at the fundraiser and they only raised $12,000 because most of the people were forced to go with very few American donors. I told Quyen Le that this demonstration was important for me. This was the first event I attended after my trial, and I wanted to send a message to the Vietnamese government that I would not be intimidated and would continue the fight.

On December 5 that year, John Nevin said it was important for my Vietnam veteran friend to insist on pilots who were shot down to be the first POWs to be released; that would eliminate any possibility that they might be deserters. That inference of desertion would be more credible and raise more doubt if the POWs had been infantry soldiers. John also said that our friend should ask his contact to remind the Vietnamese government that we have contended all along that the U.S. government has rebuked their numerous overtures to resolve the POW issue, with emphasis on their 1981 attempt with the new Reagan Administration. John said they also needed to be reminded that we had made many efforts to inform the public that the U.S. government refused to pay $4.25 - $4.75 billion in postwar reconstruction aid promised to them by President Nixon. We have not and will not imply that this justifies the continued holding of the prisoners of war, but it does explain Vietnam's actions as an attempt to use the little leverage they had to enforce the fulfillment of a promise of great economic importance to them.

We believe that the Politburo gave up trying to negotiate the release of POWs after finally realizing that the lack of interest grew out of fear of exposure; the U.S. government had knowingly left personnel in enemy hands, yet denied their existence. We have been told by multiple people in the Defense Department that many of those in leadership positions have taken the viewpoint that these POWs are simply additional casualties of war, and not worth the political cost of recovery.

I should mention that John Nevin has been my closest friend for over twenty years and has requested that he remain anonymous in my sensitive discussions. I've honored that request in the past, but he's let me know it's okay to reveal it here.

On January 24, 2006, Quyen Le called me to say that the BBC web site had an interview in Vietnamese with one of the Communist leaders in Vietnam. He was talking about a letter Hanoi had sent to the U.S. State Department complaining about my not guilty verdict, and our judicial system being slanted and prejudiced in my favor.

The Communist spokesman also said he wanted additional charges filed against me in D.C. court for unlawful entry. Fortunately for me, this was a dead issue.

These efforts are quite ironic; the Communist government of Vietnam has, at best, a kangaroo court system that tries and convicts anyone who disagrees with them. Many are taken from their homes for practicing their religion and never seen again. Others are thrown in jail for years without a trial or legitimate representation for simply questioning the authority and motives behind the government's action.

In March, Peter Nguyen, lawyer and current president of the New York Vietnamese-American Community, called to inform me that there was a seminar to be held by representatives from Vietnam's UN delegation. Even though Peter could not participate, he asked for my support. It was to promote investment in southern Vietnam, especially Saigon, by American business. The Communists refer to Saigon as Ho Chi Minh City, a name I refuse to recognize.

I called the Hyatt Hotel just before I left to verify the address and the operator confirmed that the seminar was on the third floor. When I arrived in front of the hotel, I told a former president of the group that I wanted him to bail me out of jail if I didn't come back in fifteen minutes. He laughed, thinking I was making a joke, but I looked in his eyes and said I wasn't kidding.

"I'm going inside to create a commotion. If I don't come out soon, find out what happened." He stopped smiling and said he would come get me.

As I entered the hotel, I had my game face on and immediately went to the men's room just in case things didn't go my way and I was arrested.

Based upon my previous experience, the time from arrest to booking can be very lengthy so I prepare myself for the worst-case scenario. I immediately went to the third floor where I saw the main entrance to the conference room in the middle of a long narrow corridor. I proceeded to a room at the very end of this hallway. It was a small servant's area where food could be brought into the conference room. The problem was that the door was locked with a key card entry and also had a large table blocking easy access to it.

I circled around by taking the narrow corridor past the main entrance and wound up on the other side of this very long room. I was inconspicuously making my way to the side entrance when several Vietnamese-Americans, who I recognized earlier demonstrating outside, yelled my name, saying, "Mr. Kiley, how are you?" I quickly walked up to them and asked them to please keep it quiet because I was trying to gain access. They immediately realized what I was doing and followed my instructions.

I checked out the staff room on that other side and saw the door was open a crack. When I opened it, I was at the very back of the long narrow conference room. I walked around several TV cameras on tripods, all the way to the front where someone was speaking at the podium. One of the Vietnamese saw me coming and pulled out a chair, offering me the seat located directly in front of the podium.

I waited patiently, sipping a cup of tea, until the Vietnamese speaker finished his comments about how he hoped this conference would be a huge success. He introduced the next speaker and without hesitation I walked up to the microphone and faced the room.

The person who'd been introduced had started toward the podium but stopped when he saw me arrive before him. He was Vietnamese and I thought they would come get me when they realized I wasn't the right person; however, he graciously sat down, making it appear that I was the next speaker.

Naturally, I was wearing a shirt and tie along with a very nice dress overcoat, so when I began talking to all of them I guess they saw me as a guest speaker. I introduced myself as Jerry Kiley, a Vietnam veteran, and said that I wanted freedom and democracy for the repressed Vietnamese people and freedom for the living American POWs that were still being held by the Communist government. Most of the Vietnamese were still smiling because they didn't immediately understand my intention.

I continued by berating the Americans who were there by calling them all a bunch of traitors. It was like looking at deer caught in the headlights; they were stunned, so I continued and repeated myself in case they didn't get it the first time.

I then told them I was the Vietnam veteran who was arrested the previous June for tossing wine in Khai's direction. By then, people were calling for my removal, so after I finished I left down the center aisle, pointing at all the Americans and calling them traitors to the repressed people of Vietnam and live POWs.

I was totally unprepared for a lengthy speech and was later disappointed that I had not mentioned the slaughter of the Montagnard people. My past experience involved situations where I made short statements and this situation caught me by surprise.

After slowly walking the length of the conference room, calling every American a traitor, I asked where the exit door was at the same time security entered and removed me from the room.

There was a very tall, well-dressed man (Walter Blocker, Chairman of AmCham Vietnam * HCMCity, contact@amchamvietnam.com, www.amchamvietnam.com) who was yelling at me outside the room. In response, I kept calling him a traitor.

It became so intense his security stepped in, asking him, as much as me, to back off.

As I started walking away, he yelled that I would be put on his list. When I corrected him by saying I was already on the Communist list and that I was proud to be on that list, I spelled out my name so he would get it right. I started walking back and said, "Since you have such a big mouth, give me your name so we know who you are, traitor." He gave me his business card and said his bio is on the Internet. As we disengaged, I made sure he didn't get the last word, otherwise I'd still be there.

I rejoined the Vietnamese-American demonstration outside the hotel and they gathered around to hear what I'd done. When I picked up my car in the parking garage and the garage ticket said that I had left it less than an hour earlier. It hit me how quickly I had gotten inside this conference and done my damage.

Reflecting later that night about what had happened, I realized that I wasn't surprised about finding an open key card door that should have been locked for security reasons. I've come to expect a door to be open, a staircase unguarded, or blind luck in evading the Secret Service.

On a personal level, I have to say that the apparent effect of my successful intrusions and my involvement in numerous other events and situations surpassed my expectations. Unfortunately, the bottom line is that they didn't lead to accomplishing the most important goal: freedom for long-suffering POWs and the people of Vietnam.

When I first became involved back in 1983, I actually thought it was simply a matter of putting together all the strongest evidence and showing it to important people in the government and media. It was hard for me to accept that they wouldn't do anything "if they only knew."

Even harder to accept was what turned out to be a mountain of evidence that there were actually people in important positions making a concerted effort to prevent the truth from being known, which in the end meant intentionally continuing the POWs' abandonment.

Looking back, I have to feel a sense of shame for the country I love so much. I'd have to believe that our forefathers would be embarrassed and ashamed of the lack of character and moral integrity shown by a country that once set the example for the world to follow. Conversely, I believe our forefathers would be proud of those POW activists who have shown a persistent, relentless, and unselfish devotion even in the face of ridicule from U.S. Presidents, Congress, governmental agencies, and a biased mainstream media.

Even though one person can sometimes make a difference, in this case it wasn't enough. I don't consider failure to be an option, but the reality is that I may be left with this one regret until my dying day. My mantra has been, since my Tarot card reading many years ago, to have no regrets on my deathbed. The only consolation may be the fact that I gave it my best effort with a selfless dedication to a worthy cause.

As my friend said, the struggle can be nobler than the outcome; however, I'll always feel that the struggle was in vain if we do not achieve freedom for the people of Vietnam and for our American POWs. Ultimate victory in Vietnam, even after all these years, would vindicate the sacrifice of the 58,000 brave American soldiers, hundreds of thousands of brave Vietnamese, and hundreds of thousands of disabled veterans still living with the physical and mental scars of war. The only way to put this war behind me would be total victory, something our politicians and mainstream media denied us nearly forty years ago.

In November 2006, Tom Burch contacted me to say that I should be sure to attend the National Vietnam Veterans Coalition (NVVC) breakfast the next week when John Syphrit would receive the NVVC's annual Veteran of the Year Award.

As reported by Sydney Schanberg, John was the Secret Service agent on White House detail who was present during President Reagan's secret staff meeting in January 1981 to discuss an offer from Hanoi to return a substantial number of American POWs for an amount of cash.

Further details of the meeting were uncovered by two Republican Congressmen who had relationships with a number of the attendees. The offer was made from Hanoi through the Canadian Ministry to Richard Allen, and was for 84 U.S. personnel to be returned for the $4.5 billion in Vietnamese "reparations"—which President Nixon and Henry Kissinger had called "Postwar Reconstruction and other Humanitarian Aid"—when they originally promised the payment preliminary to the signing of the peace agreement.

Other attendees in the meeting were Alexander Haig, George Shultz, and Jim Baker. After considerable discussion, the majority view was that Reagan was getting high marks from the public for resolving the Iranian Hostage crisis; acknowledging that Hanoi was holding live American POWs would create another hostage situation, since paying "ransom for hostages" wasn't an option.

To Reagan's credit, he wanted an analysis of options that might be available, including prospects for a rescue operation. Both Richard Allen and Director William Casey told Reagan they would look into it. Casey eventually told the President that a rescue wasn't possible. Many of his agents thought success was very unlikely. The CIA had previously been tasked with maintaining that no such prisoners existed, so acting now would give the CIA something of a black eye; a failed rescue attempt would make matters worse.

Casey said some agents didn't want angry POWs coming home talking about their knowledge of some of the CIA's clandestine operations during the war. Return of POWs at this late date would open a Pandora's Box that would be hard to close. These men should simply be considered casualties of war.

Reagan ultimately decided to take no action, but indicated that he wanted to remain open to rescue opportunities and possibilities.

Secret Service agent John Syphrit was aware of most of this but held it in confidence for several years. As mentioned earlier in the excerpt from Sydney Schanberg's *Beyond the Killing Fields*, Syphrit wanted to testify under oath about this meeting to the select committee allegedly investigating the POW saga. He couldn't do so without violating a secrecy oath unless he were subpoenaed, and the committee refused to subpoena him.

I attended the NVVC breakfast in D.C. and upon arriving Tom Burch introduced me to John Syphrit outside the ballroom where we were meeting. It was an honor to finally meet him.

As we sat for breakfast, I noticed that Tom had placed me between John and Tom's son. He said to his son, "That's Jerry Kiley."

John answered, "The great Jerry Kiley." I was surprised, but I figured Tom had told him about the Khai wine-tossing incident.

After breakfast, I wanted to see how responsive and open Syphrit would be in answering questions about President Reagan's meeting and his subsequent involvement in revealing the Vietnamese government's offer. If he was determined not to share any information with me, which would be understandable, my trip would have been pretty unproductive since that was the main reason I came. To my surprise, he was just the opposite. I struggled during the four-hour breakfast to restrain myself and to appear cool and calm while asking as many questions as possible. I realized that I was revisiting a very significant moment in history.

John said that his secrecy agreement with the government meant that he could not testify about the contents of the meeting, or even its existence, unless he were subpoenaed, placed under oath, and required to do so. He received intimidating calls from people he believed were other agents, saying that if he testified it would compromise the trust in Secret Service agents' confidentiality and thereby weaken the agency.

Knowing that his career was on the line, John showed tremendous courage and character when he finally made the difficult decision to reveal the meeting and its contents. Even though he was never given the opportunity—or the curse, as it may be—to testify under oath about the meeting, his willingness to do so painted him as a rogue agent and led to his resignation two years later.

I asked John whether the authorities thought he had leaked the information, and he said he didn't think so. According to investigators, leaks had come from one or more of the meeting's participants.

While the subpoena controversy was playing out, John was reassigned to the Chicago office. About two years later, he was called into a meeting with a large number of people who began to interrogate him about his expenses from fifteen years earlier. Naturally, he didn't know what they were talking about, but he was very familiar with this form of interrogation. He soon submitted his resignation after 28 years of service. Fortunately, John overcame the negative fallout from the "meeting" saga and is doing very well.

When I asked him about a pension, he said he hoped to get it when he turned sixty-two. His answer showed an uncertainty that was uncharacteristic. Perhaps it was being held over his head.

Tom's son asked where John had traveled and what he considered his toughest assignment. John talked about being in South America and Africa and said by far Somalia was the most dangerous place he served.

Tom's son was a very nice young man, about thirty years old. He'd recently quit his job as a manager to join the military police. He'd only asked that one question, but he listened as attentively to John's comments as I did.

There were several moments during the conference where both John and I tried to hold back our emotions. John lost it a little bit when he accepted his award and could not speak except to say how honored he was to finally be with us. When he came back to our table I gave him a big Vietnam veteran hug and a slap on the back.

Towards the end of the conference, I told John he should record his experiences for future generations to let them know that at least at the end of the 20th century there were still some men of character.

My overall impression was that John was very humble, yet he had a commanding presence. I was thrilled to have met him and I will never forget this encounter. I've met with many people who were supposed to be important, but none of them measure up to John Syphrit.

I was always curious whether they knew about the Alfred E. Smith dinner because that was my first activity of that kind. He said he was, so I asked him if he was there. John said, "I can't tell you that, but I heard everything."

He enjoyed the story of how I got caught up in the media frenzy in the back of the hotel with Alexander Haig and wound up walking past all the agents without any credentials showing. They had never figured out how I had done it.

John said his team, tasked with covering the event, was focused on Ted Sampley, who was never at this event, and missed me.

I went to Quyen Le's house in Maryland after the breakfast and spent the night before leaving for home in the morning. When I arrived, Quyen Le, a friend of his from Poland, and an American who did business with Vietnam greeted me. The American was said to be a friend of John McCain and Virginia Foote, so it was clear that we weren't going to see eye-to-eye on much of anything.

At one point, I reminded him of the Vietnamese practice of keeping meticulous records, which meant that they knew exactly what happened to most of the 2000+ Americans missing from the war, but they refused to tell us what they knew. He had no response.

I raised the argument that giving China World Trade Organization entry didn't improve human rights there, and since it didn't work in China, arguing to improve human rights as a reason to grant Vietnam better trade and diplomatic status was dishonest.

When Quyen Le saw our exchange getting heated, he tried to change the subject by asking how I liked the food and how my wife was feeling.

Quyen Le's Vietnamese friend, Le Dien Duc, who is the Co-Executive Editor of a Vietnamese newspaper in Warsaw, was his Polish guest. Duc had attended my defense fundraiser in Atlanta the previous year. He began praising me as a hero to the expatriate Vietnamese community and told me that someone was going to call me and ask for my help with the Amerasian children, most of whom were fathered during the war by U.S. servicemen and Vietnamese women. I said that I would be happy to help.

I called John Nevin later that night to tell him about the day's events and after hearing what happened with John Syphrit, he said, "It's good to know that the good guys know who you are as well as the bad guys." John thought that if any of the Secret Service guys had helped me in any way, John Syphrit would have at least hinted at that possibility. He suggested that the next time I talk to Syphrit I should ask if there were specific POW names mentioned in the Hanoi offer, and if so, would any of that information be available to a Freedom of Information request.

The following weekend, my two sons were critical of Syphrit for not coming out sooner than he did. I explained about the secrecy agreement he'd been required to sign many years ago. A violation could have resulted in his being arrested and jailed for divulging secret information. Hearing this, they seemed to understand.

Later that month, I called John Syphrit as a follow-up to my meeting with him on November 10th and asked him whether specific names were mentioned in Hanoi's offer. He said, "Not that I heard." He asked me if I knew Sydney Schanberg, and when I said I did, he said that Schanberg's account of the meeting was the most accurate version he'd seen of what actually happened.

According to Syphrit, after President Reagan received his normal morning national security briefing—I believe in the Lafayette Room—they then moved to the Roosevelt Room to discuss this offer. I asked John if there would be any records or files that we might be able to get by FOIA, and he said "Maybe." He then said that a producer for CBS's *20/20* had figured it out. John ended our conversation by saying that the next time he was in the New York area we could get together. He told me to write down all my questions, and he would answer as many as he could.

On November 22, 2006, Quyen Le and Mike Benge told me Congress was supposed to vote the week before to pass the Permanent Normal Trade Relations legislation that would give Vietnam World Trade Organization status. It should be no surprise that Senators McCain and Kerry introduced this bill in June, 2006.

President Bush visited Hanoi for the economic summit and tried to lay the foundation. If they were successful, big money would win out again as it usually does. However, if the PNTR vote had been delayed until the new Congress convened after January 20, 2007, we could have at least delayed what looked to be inevitable. If the Democratic Party gained control of both houses, we could have applied enough pressure to stop the vote, since a Vietnam WTO deal seems not to be of great interest one way or the other to a number of Democrats.

12/8/06 – I saw one of my best friends at a company Christmas party and mentioned a company Code of Conduct circular that raised the scenario of what to do if you were arrested. I said "I may be paranoid, but I can't help wondering whether it was directed at me."

My friend said, "They definitely know about your arrests because a memorandum was sent by our Division Manager to the Branch Managers in the 1988 or '89 time frame mentioning your arrest and saying they should do everything they could to protect you."

I was shocked when he told me, and he was surprised because he said we had discussed this many years ago. I think he must have made reference but without specifics because he assumed that I knew. I didn't know whether to be happy that there was intent to protect me or concerned that they knew a lot more about my activities than I had realized.

At this same party, I saw one of my Vietnam vet friends. He witnessed the deaths of almost his entire company, and suffered from survivor's guilt, the worst form of Post Traumatic Stress Disorder (PTSD). He said he'd attended group therapy every week for the last 15 to 20 years and he still couldn't sleep for more than two hours at a time. Sometimes, he stayed up all night or woke up abruptly in a cold sweat. Unfortunately, war leaves scars that last a lifetime.

12/17/06 – Final rally/Press Conference in Virginia for the Le/Kiley Defense Fund – Quyen Le made these arrangements to recognize Tuan Le and myself along with Le's immigration attorney, Parastoo G. Zahedi.

We held this press conference in a high school near the Eden Center with about 40 Vietnamese in attendance to support us and several representatives of International Vietnamese media.

I spoke briefly about my case and how ridiculous it was that Khai and his government kill innocent people, and I get arrested for tossing wine in his direction. I told them that the red wine symbolized the killing of the Vietnamese people and American POWs, and that I called Khai a killer and McCain a traitor to our POWs. Also, I mentioned my earlier encounter with Khai in 1993, and described how he kept smiling, not understanding what I was saying, while I maintained a death grip on our handshake and berated him.

They seemed to enjoy that story the most and were actually smiling and laughing which is uncharacteristic considering the serious nature of the press conference.

Just before we broke up the conference, I said we beat McCain in 2000, beat Kerry in 2004, and will beat McCain again in 2008. This engendered the strongest reaction from the gathering. I ended by saying that we will never give up the fight, and then solicited their response by chanting Freedom for Vietnam.

When I talked to Parastoo later, she was quite surprised that the immigration service dropped its case against Tuan after he had served only 3 months of his 9-month sentence. But, she said, if he did anything like that again he would be sent back to Vietnam.

Parastoo mentioned that her family name was famous because her father's cousin was a revolutionary who was found guilty by the Shah of Iran. He represented himself and when asked to make a statement to the court he said it would be a waste of time because he was going to be found guilty not matter what he said. He was executed for treason. She said that anyone who is Iranian always asks her if she is a relative of this famous Persian revolutionary.

12/30/06 – My Vietnam veteran friend who has a friend close to the government in Vietnam said his friend had been hoping to get a Vietnamese government position responsible for resolving the problem of U.S. POWs. Unfortunately, he had recently met with a group of government officials about the matter, and it didn't go well.

My friend said in disgust that this was the second time this had happened; there had been a similar meeting years ago where he came away with nothing because he may have asked or demanded too much. He said that we will now have to wait a couple of months until the next round of government changes to know for sure whether he can secure a substantial position or be passed over.

Chapter Ten
Getting Ready for McCain's Presidential Race

Ban Nguyen of Vietnam Vote asked me what I was planning in 2007. I told him we were raising money to produce radio and TV political ads against John McCain's run for the presidency in 2008. This was what we wanted to do against Kerry in 2004, but we didn't take the steps necessary to raise the money we would have needed.

Ban said he could help me raise that money, but wanted to add Kerry along with McCain because he was also running for the presidency again. I added that we planned on joining them together as two of the biggest phonies and frauds in government. Ban then suggested that he could raise more money and more interest if he could schedule me as a guest speaker. He then said that I might be surprised how much they can raise because his community was mostly lawyers, doctors, and other professionals who could be very generous. Ban indicated that they usually raise $30,000 to $40,000 per event.

He asked me how much I wanted to raise and I told him about $100,000. He asked how much the Swift Boat Vets had spent and I said they'd raised over $2 million; however, I didn't know how much was actually spent. He sounded surprised by how high that amount was so I quickly said we didn't need that much to be effective. We set November 2007 as the initial date to raise the $100,000 and I committed to at least two to three events in California.

Ban made it clear that they would not be directly involved with the filing of any forms or PACs and that I would be leaving these events with the checks in hand. Since I told him we would target Iowa, New Hampshire, and South Carolina in our ads, he suggested that I contact the Vietnamese community in each state and perhaps distribute fliers locally.

When I asked him for help in printing and distributing those fliers, he said that would be handled through the local communities. He said that they weren't computer professionals but learned quickly as a matter of survival. They learned how to bypass the firewall into Vietnam by not using key words flagged by the Communists, making the internet the most effective way of communicating around the world.

John Nevin and I decided that we should try to raise $250,000 to ensure adequate funding for producing these ads. He suggested that I contact John LeBoutillier and Bill Hendon to see if they were interested in helping with the media blitz.

Even though the Vietnamese-American community wanted me to represent them, I would have felt more comfortable knowing that people who had years of experience as Congressmen and exposure to the national media were involved in our media campaign.

In accepting Ban's offer to spearhead this fund raiser and in effect beginning a Political Action Committee (PAC), I'd opened another unexpected door. It had the potential to have more of an impact than anything I'd ever been involved in. I was very nervous, having seen the political blood bath between the Swift Boat Vets during Kerry's 2004 run, and McCain coming to his friend's aid. There was no way we would have that type of impact, but I'd put myself directly in the cross hairs of the political establishment. It had the potential to get very ugly if we were successful.

1/2/07 – Called Bill Hendon (former two-term Congressman from North Carolina) and he is about to release his book that is supposed to lay out the facts of McCain's involvement with Communist Vietnam and his opposition to those who demand the return of our POWs. Unfortunately, Bill will not be able to get involved with us because of restrictions imposed by lawyers of his book's publisher.

I called John LeBoutillier about joining us and as always he said, "Absolutely." Coincidentally, John just completed a TV commercial that will air in Iowa in a couple of weeks, one year before the primary. The ad will have five democrats saying that they will not vote for Hillary Clinton under any circumstances. John said that the ad costs $10,000 and about $500 for each of the four or five spots on a local channel. He also said that we didn't need as much as $100,000 to make an impact as long as we do it soon, before the campaign heats up.

I called Ted Sampley and asked if he was going to set up a site against McCain and he was already putting that together, Vietnam Veterans Against John McCain. I called Mike Benge and he was ready to assist us on a limited basis. I believe Mike, as with all the returned POWS, had difficulty criticizing another POW publicly.

Also called Ban Nguyen and told him we already had our team in place. He said to let him know when the checking account and mailing address was set up. Ban revealed that he was in a potentially difficult situation.

Ban was on Governor Arnold Schwarzenegger's campaign staff working for Steve Schmidt, who had just been hired by John McCain. Ban said Schmidt was very good and had a strike team on call 24/7 with the ability to attack immediately. Ban said that he made a commitment to follow through with us on this, no matter what. I told him that he was a man of character and that I was proud to know him.

We discussed that the April fundraiser would be best as a launching pad because April 30th is the 32nd anniversary of the fall of Saigon and the

Vietnamese-American community will be very emotional and upset. Ban may add more fundraisers to the two already scheduled.

Ban did emphasize the need for confidentiality because the Communists in this country are very devious and dangerous. He said he was concerned not only about his own security, but, more importantly, his family.

Last but not least, Ban said Rudolph Giuliani was coming to California in February for a Republican convention and that he was scheduled to meet face-to-face with him. He would try to get his people to support our fund raiser; however, I would think it is very unlikely since politicians want to keep their hands clean and stay as far as possible from activists like me.

1/6/07 – My two sons and I went to a friend's house to see a pay-per-view event. The friend is older than my boys—probably mid-40s—and has a very direct and dry sense of humor. He asked me at what college the flag incident had occurred, and I told him it was Manhattanville. He immediately started telling his son what I had done, and then he called me a patriot. I was touched by his comment since this is the way I'd like to be remembered.

I can't help thinking that our forefathers would approve of citizens who fight for what they believe in without personal, financial, or political gain, versus how disgusted they would be seeing the moral corruption of so many of our government functionaries as a result of corporate lobbyists and special interests groups. The final straw might be their witnessing government officials and mainstream media calling devoted activists "radicals" and "the lunatic fringe."

1/7/07 – Col. Swede Larson returned my call to discuss issues concerning John McCain. Swede was one of the two Senior Ranking Officers (SRO) in McCain's POW camp in Vietnam for several years.

I asked Swede if he knew anything about McCain being tortured or about his "confessions." He said he didn't because he was in and out of isolated confinement over a four-year period. He said that confessions were often read over the loudspeaker, but he didn't recall the name of a "confessor" ever being mentioned.

Swede did say that he was upset with Kerry and McCain's trips to Vietnam and their involvement to normalize relations with that government. He also said he was eighty years old, tired, and not willing to get involved with the media.

The other SRO in McCain's camp was Col. Ted Guy, whom I had met for dinner in the '80s along with John LeBoutillier. Ted had told me rather forcefully—more than once—that he wasn't aware of any U.S. POW being tortured in that camp while McCain was there, and he didn't believe McCain had been. The damage to McCain's arm and shoulder, that McCain liked for people to assume was a result of torture, was from injuries he received when he bailed out of his aircraft. Ted Guy also said that it was strange McCain was taken out of the camp for long periods on several occasions and would never explain why.

1/13/07 – I visited the FEC website and then made several phone calls to talk to their Information Division agents. Based on those calls, I put together a Word document explaining the Guidelines for Individual Donations, and two Excel reports for Itemizing Receipts and Independent Expenditures. This week I will need to speak with the IRS to determine any legal obligations regarding the disbursement of funds. In the end, I don't want to rely on anyone else controlling the most important parts of this endeavor: the finances, accuracy, and timeliness of the FEC reporting process.

1/24/07 – John Kerry announced on the floor of the Senate today that he will not run for President in 2008. One down and one to go; McCain's next.

1/30/07 – I called John Nevin to talk about how the mainstream media looks like they are starting to abandon McCain. Senator Hagel from Nebraska appears to be the new media darling replacing McCain.

As we spoke, I heard a familiar sound, continuous rhythmic tapping throughout our conversation that John also heard. The last time I heard that sound was on the Saturdays preceding my Sunday protests in front of the Vietnamese mission in the 1980s. John and I discussed it, and our opinion was that if it was something being done intentionally, the only purpose could be intimidation because the state-of-the-art technology available to anyone interested in us wouldn't be audibly detectable.

1/31/07 - I called my wife at home from my office phone and heard the same sound. She even commented about someone listening to our conversation. I then called John from work and there was no tapping sound that would indicate it was on my home phone. That night, cable TV mentioned President Bush had visited Wall Street in New York earlier in the day. I called John again from home and the sound was gone. My local newspaper the next day said the President's visit to Wall Street at 11 AM was "under publicized." I've always wondered whether someone was checking on me because of GW's visit.

If it was the Secret Service, they wanted me to know they were monitoring me. There is no doubt that I am on their watch list after my entire history was revealed at my trial. The Secret Service agent who filed the two misdemeanor charges of simple assault against me was there for the entire trial. She heard about my history, and how I got the nickname "Stealth Activist."

I found out during the Presidential race in 2004 that the FBI had my name at the top of their list as a person of concern even though I was considered to be a peaceful demonstrator. I met Ron, a captain in the New

York Fire Department, through friends of mine. Ron was in charge of the Fire and Evacuation Plan for Madison Square Garden during the Republican Party Presidential nominations. He was on a committee with the FBI and Homeland Security. His FBI contact confirmed my name was on their watch list because of my involvement with Vietnam Veterans Against John Kerry and the many demonstrations I had organized and attended.

February 2007 – I completed my research of the rules and regulations pertaining to the Political Action Committee we were forming to oppose John McCain's candidacy. I filed with the IRS and the Federal Election Commission, and established a bank account and a PO Box. On 2/28/07, the *Washington Post* printed a humorous article for the "In The Loop" section on page A17. It said that some PACs give themselves innocuous or misleading names, but it's refreshing to see one called Vietnam Veterans Against John McCain. It went on to say there was nothing innocuous about that.

3/4/07 – A veteran friend and I discussed how to use an article concerning Republican Party members' rebellion against McCain in his home state of Arizona, especially in his home district. This breakaway was named "The McCain Mutiny" in a *Nation* article by Max Blumenthal.

This mutiny was being led by a retired IBM manager, Rob Haney, who was the Arizona Republican Party state committeeman in McCain's home district.

Haney said, "The guy has no core, his only principle is winning the presidency. He likes to call his campaign the 'straight talk express.' Well, down here we call it the 'forked tongue express.'"

Max Blumenthal wrote that McCain's botched revenge had solidified his reputation in Arizona's Republican circles as a divisive, untrustworthy, and even dangerous figure. Haney hoped the general public would see this side of McCain before his penchant for angry reprisals is invested with the powers of the presidency. "This just shows that McCain is mentally unstable and out of control and vindictive," Haney said. "If he is determined to go through that much trouble to attack a district committee chairman, what does that say about his ability to handle real political problems?"

Another article, written by Amy Silverman from the *Phoenix New Times*, was titled "John McCain's Fame is Based on His POW Status, but He Has Abandoned Fellow Veterans," depicts the low opinion of him from veterans from his home state. During one of the debates, Obama vowed to get more help for veterans with Post Traumatic Stress Disorder:

McCain seemed incensed that President Obama would dare intrude on McCain's turf as, perhaps, America's most famous injured war vet.
"I know the veterans and I know them well," he said, his voice shaky with emotion. "And I know that they know that I'll take care of them. And

I've been proud of their support and of their recognition of my service to the veterans. And I love them, and I'll take care of them. And they know that I'll take care of them."

But he hasn't. McCain's had 25 years in Congress to help veterans, yet nearly all he's done is talk about his own experiences as a prisoner of war — and push the country to go to war again...

Veterans groups are finally speaking out about their frustration with McCain, who rides on his reputation as a war veteran while sitting on a long record of opposing legislation that would benefit vets.

McCain's campaign didn't return a call for comment about the work he claims to have done on behalf of veterans, both regarding his voting record and his constituent-services operations. To be fair, it's not that McCain has never cast a pro-veteran vote or helped a vet in need. But the overwhelming pattern of his actions is hypocritical: On the campaign trail, he pledges support. Listening to him, you'd think he's been the veterans' greatest champion. An examination of his record both in Washington, D.C., and Arizona just doesn't bear that out...

The senator didn't support a measure that would have closed tax loopholes to fund improvements at Walter Reed Army Medical Center in Bethesda, MD, though he surely must have wished he had when he saw the stories last year that documented deplorable conditions at the hospital. He has voted against help for victims of post-traumatic stress disorder. He has voted against programs to provide housing to low-income and special-needs veterans. He didn't support the latest GI Bill.

Brandon Friedman is a former Army officer who served in Iraq and Afghanistan and is now vice chairman of a national veterans support group called Vote Vets, which is devoted to electing veterans — with one notable exception — to public office.

Friedman calls McCain's statements in support of vets "a slap in the face." He says, "Coming from a guy who's kept us stuck in Iraq at the expense of the fight against al-Qaeda in Afghanistan — and who opposed the new GI Bill — [such comments don't] carry much weight. Those are empty words. John McCain is all talk when it comes to supporting veterans and his voting record shows it..."

His grandfather was a Navy admiral. His father was the commander of U.S. Naval forces in Europe and, later, the Pacific during the Vietnam War. John III landed softly in the arms of a well-to-do family and, later, his even wealthier second wife. John McCain never needed to line up at the VA to see a doctor; he's had the finest medical care money can buy. He never needed the government's help to pay the rent or find a job...

The Disabled American Veterans scored him at 20 percent [favorable voting regarding veterans' healthcare issues]...in 2006; 25 percent in 2005; and 50 percent in 2004.

And the Retired Enlisted Association gave him a 0 in 2006 and a rating of 18 percent in 2004.

Another organization, Veterans for Common Sense, posted this comment on its Web site earlier this year: "John McCain is yet another Republican . . . military veteran who likes to talk a big game when it comes to having the support of the military. Yet, time and time again, he has gone out of his way to vote against the needs of those who are serving in our military. If he can't even see his way to actually do what the troops want, or what the veterans need, and he doesn't have the support of veterans, then how can he be a credible commander in chief?"

John Adams retired last year as an Army brigadier general... [And became] the head of Arizona Veterans for Obama. "It's really disingenuous for him to say that he has taken care of veterans in any way," Adams says. "His voting record shows that he hasn't... "

If nothing else, John McCain's voting record on veteran's issues is a stunning example of hypocrisy, coming from a guy who owes his fame to his celebrity status as a former POW.

The saying goes, "Hate the war, love the warrior." In McCain's case, it almost seems reversed.

At a veterans' meeting at the Phoenix Veterans Center in 1984, McCain opposed [a veteran class action suit] suing the government and chemical companies over the use of Agent Orange. "His opinion was that it was unpatriotic to sue the government."

... "There was a lot of booing and hissing, and I think it was at that point that the suggestion was made that Congressman McCain leave."

Since 1987, McCain has voted against dozens of measures designed to assist veterans. Most recently, he skipped the vote on the Webb-Hagel 21st Century GI Bill, which funds higher education for post-9/11 veterans with a sliding payment scale depending on length of duty and disabilities sustained. [He opposed the bill but apparently didn't want to be on the record voting against it.]

Alfredo Gutierrez was a longtime McCain fan...But Gutierrez is furious with McCain over his voting record, particularly on the GI Bill. "So this guy who has built a whole political career on his status as a veteran and a POW," he continues, "he'll vote to send the guys to war . . . but he won't vote for the GI Bill. That's pretty amazing. It's stunning stuff to me. It's the height of hypocrisy.

"And," Gutierrez adds, it goes beyond the GI Bill. "His voting record is abysmal... "

Like Constantine O'Neill [who] spent 22 months in a German prison camp during World War II...

"McCain is, as far as I'm concerned, a jackass. He's not for the veterans. He never has been for the veterans [in] legislation that he's gone for . . . I would not recommend him for anything to anybody."

Disabled American Veterans, one of the largest veteran's organizations, scored McCain's voting record on health-care related veteran's issues in 2008. He was rated at 20% favorable, which was the lowest among Congress' 535 members. Let me also add that McCain is quick on the trigger when it comes to committing our brave men and women into combat but Missing In Action when it comes to taking care of those war veterans.

"Col. David Hackworth, Hero of Vietnam War, Dies at 74 "
Douglas Martin
The New York Times
May 6, 2005

Colonel Hackworth lied to enlist in the Army at 15 and won a battlefield commission at 20 to become the Korean War's youngest captain. He was America's youngest full colonel in Vietnam, and won a total of 91 medals, including two Distinguished Service Crosses, 10 Silver Stars, 8 Bronze Stars and 8 Purple Hearts.
In a 1971 interview with Nick Proffit of Newsweek, Gen. Creighton Abrams, a top commander in Vietnam, called Colonel Hackworth "the best battalion commander I ever saw in the United States Army."

The following is a blog post by Col. David H. Hackworth that outlines exactly what's wrong with many of the public sentiments towards Senator John McCain. (Spacing is the original author's design.)

"Defending America: Are McCain's Handlers Playing The Wrong Card?"
David H. Hackworth
Hackworth.com
January 25, 2000

John McCain is being hailed by the press as a "genuine war hero."
But is he a war hero in the conventional sense like Audie Murphy and John Glenn?

Or is his "war hero" status the creation of a very slick publicity campaign that plays on flag, duty, honor and country?

For sure, McCain has the fruit-salad -- a Silver Star, a Legion of Merit for Valor, a Distinguished Flying Cross, three Bronze Stars, two Commendation medals plus two Purple Hearts and a dozen service gongs.

On a purely medal count basis, he out-weighs Murphy and Glenn, who both for years repeatedly performed extraordinary deeds on the ground or in the air against an armed enemy.

McCain's valor awards are based on what happened in 1967, when during his 23d mission over Vietnam, he was shot down, seriously injured, captured and then spent 5 1/2 brutal years as a POW.

In an attempt to find out exactly what the man did to earn these many hero awards, I asked his Senate office three times to provide copies of the narratives for each medal. I'm still waiting.

I next went to the Pentagon. Within a week, I received a recap of his medals and many of the narratives that give the details of what he did.

None of the awards, less the DFC, were for heroism over the battlefield -- where he spent no more than 20 hours. Two Naval officers described the awards as "boilerplate" and "part of an SOP medal package given to repatriated (Vietnam-era) POWs."

McCain's Silver Star narrative for the period 27 October 1967 -- the day after he was shot down -- to 8 December 1968 reads: "His captors... subjected him to extreme mental and physical cruelties in an attempt to obtain military information and false confessions for propaganda purposes. Through his resistance to those brutalities, he contributed significantly towards the eventual abandonment..." of such harsh treatment by the North Vietnamese.

Yet in McCain's own words just four days after being captured, he admits he violated the U.S. Code of Conduct by telling his captors

"O.K, I'll give you military information if you will take me to the hospital."

A Vietnam vet detractor says, "He received the nation's third highest award, the Silver Star, for treason. He provided aid and comfort to the enemy!"

The rest of his valor awards -- issued automatically every year while he was a POW -- read much like the Silver Star. More boilerplate often repeating the exact same words. An example: "By his heroic endeavors, exceptional skill, and devotion to duty, he reflected great credit upon himself and upheld the highest traditions of the Naval Service and the United States Armed Forces."

Yet McCain's conduct while a POW negates these glowing comments. The facts are that he signed a confession and declared himself a "black criminal who performed deeds of an air pirate." This statement and other interviews he gave to the Communist press were used as propaganda to fan the flames of the anti-war movement.

Accounts by McCain and other writers tell of the horror he endured: relentlessly beatings, torture, broken limbs. All inflicted during savage interrogations. Yet no other POW was a witness to these accounts.

A former POW says "No man witnessed another man during interrogations... We relied on each other to tell the truth when a man was returned to his cell."

The U.S. Navy says two eye-witnesses are required for any award of heroism. But for the valor awards McCain received, there are no eye-witnesses, less himself and his captors.

And they're not talking.

Our POWs in Vietnam were treated appallingly. The Viets would either break a POW or kill him. POWs provided info beyond name, rank and serial number or they didn't come back.

Based on these stalwart men's horrific experiences, the Code of Conduct has been changed. A POW says, "Now the training is to give them something... don't risk permanent damage to health, mind or body."

McCain refused an early release. An act of valor? Three former POWs told me he was ordered to turn it down by his U.S. POW commander and he "just followed orders."

McCain certainly doesn't appear to be a war hero by conventional standards, but rather a tough survivor whose handlers are overplaying the war hero card.

In support of our effort to point out McCain's mental instability, Tom Burch mentioned an interview by Ron Reagan, Jr. with John McCain last year that went so badly Reagan ended by saying, "Senator, you just lost my vote."

Tom said he was warned from a friend of his working closely with McCain that they had already prepared an all-out assault on Tom if he attacked McCain. Tom said he admired what I was doing but to be careful.

Also, Tom dropped a bombshell that he had a tape of McCain's verbal attack of Dolores Alfond during the Senate Select Committee on POW/MIA Affairs in 1992. It was so bad that Sidney Schanberg wrote about it in an article saying that a red-faced McCain was shaking his fist and pointing his finger at Dolores even after she broke down crying. Our first commercial will be this confrontation showing how vicious McCain can be. The cost to edit the tape will be very little compared to our second ad that will require traveling around the country to film interviews with selected people.

3/6/07 – A reporter from my local paper (*The Rockland Journal News*) came by for an interview about our PAC. The photographer wanted something with a veteran look and I said no because I wanted to convey the image of a businessman which I am instead of the military look. He took a picture of the FEC website on my laptop and then a picture of me in front of the fireplace. The article appeared on the front page of the paper two days later. However, they didn't include my hard hitting remarks about McCain being emotionally unstable or The McCain Mutiny in his home state of Arizona that mirrored our charges.

Garnerville Veteran Organizes Anti-McCain Group
By SARAH NETTER

Jerry Kiley of Garnerville does research on the web to register his organization with the Federal Election Commission. Kiley, a Vietnam veteran, has organized a group of veterans against John McCain.

How to donate

- Vietnam Veterans Against John McCain

- A Web site is expected to be available within the week. For more information, visit www.vietnamveteransagainstjohnmccain.com (Original publication: March 8, 2007)

Jerry Kiley isn't impressed by John McCain. Actually, he downright dislikes the guy.

Kiley is so intent on not seeing the Arizona senator's name on the 2008 presidential ballot that he's formed Vietnam Veterans Against John McCain, a nonprofit, nonpartisan political action committee that will collect money for negative advertising in the months leading up to the primaries.

"If he had the power of the presidency, I'd really fear for this country," Kiley said.

The longtime Garnerville resident said Americans need to see that McCain, a Republican, has abandoned the causes of Vietnam veterans and prisoners of war, despite being a former POW himself.

Kiley, 60, was drafted into the Army at 19 and spent March 1967 through May 1968 in Vietnam, working in a communications center.

"I consider myself very lucky and fortunate not to have suffered any physical or mental wounds," he said.

Kiley remembers being loaded onto a bus upon his return to the United States and being told that the bars on the windows were to protect soldiers from being hit with objects thrown by demonstrators.

Kiley became involved with Vietnam veterans' causes in the early 1980s, at one point serving as chairman of the National Vietnam Veterans Coalition.

"I want what's best for America," he said. And according to Kiley and his supporters - whom he said include veterans, their families and some in the Vietnamese-American community - McCain isn't it.

"The issue is character, or lack of character," he said.

Kiley said he and others are frustrated by McCain's apparent unwillingness to open government POW records, even for families of the missing.

The veteran cited an article by Pulitzer Prize-winning reporter Sydney Schanberg, whose work inspired the acclaimed 1984 movie "The Killing Fields." Schanberg's 2000 APBNews.com article about McCain said the senator berated National Alliance for Families Chairwoman Delores Alfond, sister of a Vietnam POW, when she spoke before a POW/MIA committee hearing in 1992.

Schanberg reported that McCain reduced the woman, who asked that the committee not be shut down in two months as scheduled, to tears before he stormed out of the room. That type of temper shows that McCain would be unable to handle the pressures of the presidency, Kiley said.

Messages left at McCain's campaign and Washington Senate offices were not returned yesterday.

In 2004, Kiley formed Vietnam Veterans Against John Kerry. Kiley said Kerry, a Democratic senator from Massachusetts, went out of favor with many veterans after joining Vietnam Veterans Against the War after returning home.

Vietnam veteran Dennis Kelemen of Thiells said he had not heard of Vietnam Veterans Against John McCain. But he hasn't agreed with the senator on POW issues for years, he said.

It is a responsibility of the government to ensure that Americans aren't left behind in any war or conflict, Kelemen said, but it doesn't appear to be a priority for McCain.

"It seems like he wants to move on and it's not part of his thought process," he said.

Kelemen, who was in Vietnam for a year in 1966 and 1967, said he still regarded McCain as a hero for his experience as a POW and, after meeting him in Milwaukee, is reading his book.

"Some of his actions just do not wash with my beliefs," he said. Kelemen urged voters to research any presidential candidate and not decide based on surface appearances.

Jerry Donnellan, director of the Rockland County Veterans Service Agency and a Vietnam veteran, said that with so many bureaucratic layers in Washington, McCain or anyone else wouldn't be much of a threat on their own.

"I really don't think he's dangerous," he said.

Donnellan said he had heard about Kiley's PAC recently.

"Obviously, he has the right to do this," he said. "It's good he's out in the marketplace expressing his feelings because far too many people don't."

Reach Sarah Netter at 845-578-2433 or at snetter@lohud.com.

3/8/07 – The local cable station called after reading the *Journal News* article and I agreed to do an interview that night which ran all day on 3/9/07. They also avoided my reference to McCain's instability. This was the station that filmed my flag incident with the female basketball player, and they replayed that again during the two minute report.

3/23/07 – I viewed the one hour DVD by Bill Dumas titled "Missing, Presumed Dead." Bill is the nephew of Bob Dumas, whose POW brother Roger was known to have been alive in captivity during the Korean War but never returned. In that DVD, Tracy Usry—a senior staff member on the Senate POW committee—said that McCain made 32 propaganda tapes while he was in captivity.

The DVD mentioned that Bob Dumas had arranged a trip to North Korea to discuss the POWs left behind after the Korean War in 1953. I was scheduled to be a part of the delegation as Vice Chairperson of the National Vietnam Veterans Coalition, but the U.S. State Department would not issue visas to the delegation, so the trip was cancelled.

3/26/07 – I'm not sure what took me so long to realize that we didn't have to wait for the fundraiser at the end of April; we could compile a video presentation right away and put it on YouTube. We could use Usry's comment on the 32 tapes, Dornan on McCain threatening the Vietnamese if they release his POW records, McCain's passage of a bill that seals his POW records, Dolores Alfond's and Bui Tin's testimony at the 1992 Senate Select hearings, McCain's voting record since 1982, and end with a final question about what else the Communist government of Vietnam wasn't disclosing about McCain.

3/28/07 - I spoke to Navy Captain and former POW Eugene "Red" McDaniel tonight about McCain's propaganda "confessions." Red is a true hero and gentleman. He had no idea that McCain may have made as many tapes as Usry said. He mentioned that McCain was dropping quickly in the polls and I said he might make a comeback so we were going to stick a finger in his eye either way. Red said, "I'm glad you're on our side."

4/10/07 – Tom Burch called to tell me that Texas Tech only sent him one of the three tapes they have archived for him and it didn't contain Dolores's testimony in 1992. Tom said he'd call them the next day to get the other two tapes.

Dolores called to say she was in the process of copying three or four tapes and would send them later that week. She doesn't know exactly what testimony is on those tapes.

4/26/07 – Tom Burch called and suggested that we demonstrate against the visit of Vietnam's president to Washington, D.C., on 6/22/07. The Vietnamese Prime Minister was trying to upstage him with a visit at the beginning of June. These two are in competition for leadership of Vietnam, and the PM was said to be more likely to be amenable to "amnesty" for U.S. POWs still being held for "crimes."

As we understood it, a person with whom we had had previous and apparently fruitful discussions would accompany the PM. This could mean important opportunities for us.

I told Tom that Quyen Le had already asked me to join him on 6/21/07 to demonstrate against the President of Vietnam. I said the timing was perfect because I was going to San Diego the following day to discuss this with the Vietnamese-American leaders. I spoke to Ban Nguyen that night and confirmed that we were on the same page.

4/27/07 – Arrived in San Diego Friday morning and left Sunday night. I was invited to the very solemn commemoration of the 32nd anniversary of the fall of Saigon.

4/30/07 - The Vietnamese-American community treated me like a hero for what I had done against Khai. I spoke to about 250 on Sunday afternoon and was given a hero's welcome. I felt honored and humbled by their response. Here's how I was introduced:

"Ladies and gentlemen, we are happy and proud to have a good friend who has come from New York to be with us today. For over 20 years he has fought for the freedom of American Prisoners of War held by the Communist government of Vietnam after the war ended. He has fought to inform the American people of the terrible human rights record of the SRV; on numerous occasions he has confronted Vietnamese officials, often disrupting their public relations events here in the United States.

"He was a founding member of Vietnam Veterans Against John Kerry, and is here today as a founder of a new organization dedicated to exposing the truth about a famous American who is an enemy of the freedom loving people of Vietnam, the United States, and throughout the world. Ladies and gentlemen, the founder of Vietnam Veterans Against John McCain, our good friend, Mr. Jerry Kiley."

At their request, I spoke about my two encounters with Khai and then I proceeded to hammer McCain, calling him a collaborator both during the war and for the last 25 years since he was elected to Congress in 1982.

One of the Vietnamese I had dinner with personally knew our contact in Vietnam and said he would help us until he got whatever he was hoping to get out of it. Certainly not the ringing endorsement I was looking for.

5/1/07 – Ban said the Vietnamese President was a hard liner leaning toward China, and the Prime Minister was advocating a closer, friendlier relationship with the U.S.

When the PM's home was bombed we took it as confirmation that the Communist hard-liners opposed him.

5/2/07 – Former California Congressman Bob Dornan returned my call. He mentioned Hillary Clinton's spokesperson's comment about McCain's past history as a POW several months ago. The comment implied that McCain had a problem with his fellow POWs. Dornan said many of the former POWs have information that they will make public if McCain gets the Republican nomination for president.

Bob said that Admiral James Stockdale (ret), a former POW, hated McCain and that he would tell Bob something important about McCain before he died.

Unfortunately, Stockdale had Alzheimer's and never told him the story. Bob said Jeremiah Denton, another POW, also has a strong dislike for McCain and that he would contact him and let me know if there was anything I could use.

5/27/07 – Memorial Day, Washington, D.C. – I spent the weekend at the Rolling Thunder Rally featuring a motorcycle ride of many thousands of bikes riding from the Pentagon past the White House. Artie Muller, event organizer, met with President Bush and gave him a copy of Bill Hendon's book *An Enormous Crime*.

Bill and Beth Stewart, co-authors of the book, gave me a copy with an inscription from each of them. Bill's inscription touched me deeply: "To Jerry Kiley, whose efforts on behalf of the Indochina POWs put us all to shame. Thank you for your friendship and for all you have done for these brave men. I am proud to have known you; worked with you, and been your friend. Best always, Bill Hendon, Memorial Day, 2007."

Bill said that one of the most amazing facts he uncovered was that over 1,000 grunts were captured from about 1969 to 1973. Some were taken off the battlefield on a stretcher by the Viet Cong and literally carried into North Vietnam because at that time American POWs were a prize possession. Previously, we thought there were many fewer grunts captured, and the intelligence spin about them was that they were probably deserters.

Bill also talked about the satellite photo on the cover of his book taken in 1988. The letters U S A were over 30 feet long accompanied by the "walking k" that U.S. personnel had been taught to use as a distress signal. The letters had been dug out in a rice paddy when it was under about 18 inches of water; when the water level dropped during the dry season in January, the letters slowly appeared. McCain had twice claimed that these letters were made by a six-year-old Vietnamese child who saw USA on an envelope. Bill's eyes lit up when he told that story.

I met a contact in front of the Lincoln Memorial and he gave me the name of the Vietnamese two-star general who had told him that they were still holding 54 POWs. The general had implied that there were more POWs not under their control, presumably in Laos. The POWs were in seven locations in Vietnam and four in Laos that he knew about. The contact said that for undisclosed reasons he could not publicly associate his name with the information.

I talked to Lynn O'Shea of the National Alliance of Families and asked her if they would attend a press conference where the family members would express their displeasure with McCain. She said the organization could not officially endorse our press briefing but she would encourage family members to participate.

6/4/07 – I received a call from Ted Sampley asking me to call the son of a man who had been an Intelligence Officer in 1968-69. Ted said the father was dead and the sons were renovating the house when they found two plastic bags containing POW-related documents. Ted told the son to give me the documents.

The son was expecting my call and immediately explained what Ted had already told me. When I asked what the documents contained, he said one was a memo from President Ronald Reagan to the Department of Defense (DOD) saying that he wanted serious efforts to get POWs out. Another memo was from Vice President George Bush to DOD saying that getting the POWs out at that time would not be in the best interest of the country. He said I could listen to a tape his father made of Stephen Solarz when he was drunk, talking about the POWs.

The son also said his father was the one who broke the story about returning POWs placed under the witness protection program while receiving monthly Social Security checks. His father visited one of the houses in Connecticut where he believed a POW was living and found that the house was under protection, confirming what he already believed. Of course, we had all heard stories of POWs secretly returned, but it was unconfirmed and, since it might be exactly the kind of story put out to mollify or distract us by the very people we thought responsible for failure to bring them home, we were skeptical.

His father supposedly died of stomach cancer that appeared suspicious so they arranged for a special autopsy to be performed; the conclusion was said to be that the condition was very unusual and the cause unknown.

I told him that I would come to pick up the documents the following day, but he said he and his brother would deliver them to me later in the week.

6/6/07 – He called to say he was making copies of forty of the documents and that he would call me in a couple of days to deliver them to me. I called to see if John LeBoutillier was available, and without knowing what I wanted he said if I thought it was important, he would make the time.

That evening there was a Republican presidential debate. Giuliani actually made a point of saying how we were once at war with Vietnam and now we are friends. Add to that the other candidates, Duncan Hunter, Mitt Romney, and Fred Thompson, who say they are good friends with McCain, and the prospects for exposing McCain were looking bleak.

6/7/07 – I spoke to our contact about getting the documents and he said their plans had changed because they found that one of the documents, dated March 2005, was sent from President George W. Bush to the

Department of Defense with the names of seven American POWs believed to be alive in Vietnam. Another story that was entering the too-good-to-be-true category; along with repeated delays, I was becoming more skeptical.

Through contacts I was warned that if the documents were as described, some of them were almost certainly classified, and I could get into big trouble if I took them into my possession. I was still willing to help to get the documents into the right hands lawfully, but my suspicions that there was something going on here beyond simple truth made it even harder to know whom to approach. I was beginning to worry that either the source was mentally unbalanced, or perpetrating a scam, or being used in a clever ruse he didn't comprehend.

Bottom line, after several attempts to arrange contact between the source and someone lawfully authorized and trustworthy enough to receive them, all efforts failed and we were never able to see the documents or sort out what had been going on.

This was only one of several false leads, strange stories, and claims that we had to follow over the years. We had no choice, just-in-case.

Chapter Eleven
Warm Welcome for Vietnamese President

6/18/07 – Mike Benge was very upset that Quyen Le had not secured the permit for Lafayette Park in time for our demonstration on the 22nd and someone else took the spot. I told Mike we were going to make this work no matter what the obstacles were, and he was annoyed with me. The next day Quyen Le said we could join the person who had the permit for Lafayette Park on Friday. All would be well.

6/20/07 – As planned, Duc Tran had bought two tickets for the 1 PM luncheon honoring the President of Vietnam at the Asian Society in New York. Duc placed his name on the list of attendees; however, he simply said the other person was a friend of his. Unknown to them, the "friend" was the same person who had tossed red wine in Khai's direction two years earlier.

I was waiting for Duc Tran to arrive from the Philadelphia area, standing on a corner about a block away from where the Vietnamese-American community was demonstrating to avoid drawing unnecessary attention to myself. I suddenly saw four black SUVs come around the corner. I assumed they were part of Triet's Secret Service motorcade. An individual, probably an agent, opened his tinted window and stuck his head way out to look me right in the eye. He held his gaze for several seconds as the vehicle proceeded down the street. With this intense stare, there was no doubt in my mind that he not only made me but was letting me know I had been spotted.

I immediately called Duc on his cell phone and he said he was already inside, which was clearly not the original plan to meet outside and go in together. He told me to wait and I said no, I was just spotted and needed to make a quick move to have any chance of getting in even though I had a very bad feeling that I was being set up by someone.

I put my fear aside and immediately entered through the main entrance. Duc had to come back through the security checkpoint to register me as his friend. I gave them my driver's license and they entered my name into the computer; however, to my surprise, they let me in. The security person had me remove everything from my pockets, which included a small POW/MIA flag. Still, I wasn't stopped.

At this point I figured I must have been wrong about being spotted by the agent in the SUV because I thought they would never have let me into the event. I also felt more secure because even registering under my own name had not rung any bells, so they must not be looking for me.

As I stepped out of the elevator the obvious Secret Service presence gave me a queasy feeling in the pit of my stomach. Considering the agents later showed me my dossier complete with my picture, it became clear that they were expecting me and that I probably was recognized by the agent in the SUV as I originally suspected. I later saw this same agent in a *New York Times* photograph as part of McCain's security force. I have no idea what this all means, if anything beyond an odd coincidence.

Duc and I entered a very large banquet hall comprised of three areas and were seated farthest away from the already-full main. We immediately sensed a possible problem with security so we decided to sit at different tables, giving us two chances to succeed in making our point.

After the meal concluded, Triet was introduced and about a minute later I made the first move by getting up to go to the bathroom in order to get closer to the podium. A Secret Service agent stepped directly in front of me and said, "I'd like to talk to you." I said OK and then made a move to get past him by stepping to the right, waiting for him to take a step with me, then bolting quickly to the left. The years of playing football on the streets of the Bronx and later in life with my company's industrial football league paid off in a big way. As the saying goes, I left him standing in his shoes.

I ran into the main ballroom and stopped in front of Triet. About a dozen security people and Secret Service agents quickly converged as I yelled out, "Free Father Ly, free the Vietnamese people, and free the live American POWs you are holding." In an even louder voice, I looked directly at Triet and said, "Free Father Ly."

I was removed from the luncheon. As we waited for the elevator to arrive, I told the Secret Service agent that I did this to tell Communist Vietnam that we would not stop until Father Ly and all the political prisoners are released, the Vietnamese people are free from this brutal repressive Communist regime, and all the living U.S. POWs are returned home.

Before the elevator arrived, one of the event security guards who was massive in size, perhaps 6'5" and built like a stone wall, aggressively confronted me, asking how I got into the event. I didn't respond and the agents stood in front of me and told him to back away.

There was an older lady standing in the elevator as the door opened. In haste, the Secret Service agent sternly said to her, "You will have to leave; we need this elevator." He scared the life out of her; as she tried to exit the elevator we had her blocked and she didn't know which way to go. She said, "Please let me through," with a very confused and scared look on her face. I motioned with my arms inviting her past me.

As we rode down the elevator with three agents and three event security people, I was asked by one of the agents how I got into the event, and I said I'm not prepared to answer that question. The Asian guard yelled at me saying, "You have to tell us." I replied with a very arrogant New York attitude saying, "Hey pal, this is the United States; I'm a U.S. citizen, and

I'm NOT going to tell you anything." The hulk made a move toward me and the agents again assertively told him to stand down.

As we arrived on the main floor, the hulk was chomping at the bit, trying to question me. A female Secret Service agent, whose name I found out later was Sara, eventually asked him if he wanted to question me, and he said in a disgusted tone, "No, just get him out of here." With that, I said OK and started walking toward the door. Sara said, "Hold on, I want to talk to you," so I agreed and we went into the corner. As she asked her first question, the hulk interrupted and started to ask the same question in an angry tone. She directed him and everyone else to go to the other side of the lobby.

She asked me how I got into the building and I said I wasn't going to answer that question. She then asked me if I had done anything like this before, and I said, "Same answer." At that point, she opened a manila folder that had my picture in the top left corner with a full type-written page and other pages behind it. She said, "I have your record from two years ago concerning the Khai wine incident."

I said, "Oh yes, I seem to recall something about that," with a grin on my face. It was more of a nervous reaction, certainly no disrespect was meant.

I asked immediately whether she was going to arrest me and she said, "No, I'm not planning on arresting you." She then asked if I knew the reason why I was arrested last time and I said, "Tossing the wine." She said, "Correct," and I responded by saying that at least I learned from my mistake.

She smiled at my response and then she asked if I planned to harm Triet and whether I owned a gun. My answer was no to both questions. The follow-up to that was why I did this and what I planned to accomplish. I told her about the 58,000 brave Americans and millions of Vietnamese who died to preserve the freedom of the Vietnamese people and my message, personally delivered, was to let Triet know that we will never forget the Vietnamese people and the living American POWs still under their control who have lived under 32 years of Communist repression.

Several times during our conversation she almost apologetically said she had to ask these questions. I said in my 24 years as an activist I've never harmed anyone and have always been peaceful in my civil disobedience. She asked where I was going to go, and I said I'd go outside with the protestors and then home for the rest of the day.

"What are your plans?" she asked.

I said, "I'm not prepared to answer that question." At that point, she said she'd be right back and stepped away to make a phone call, leaving a young male agent to keep an eye on me.

This looked like a replay of two years ago in the Khai incident when they didn't arrest me at first, but after waiting over an hour for someone higher up to make a decision, they did. I said, "Am I under arrest?"

When the young agent said no, I got up and said, "I'll see you," and quickly walked to the exit. As I passed Sara, she had her back to me when I said goodbye.

All I heard behind me was, "Oh, shit, he's leaving, what should I do?"

I walked out the front door and never looked back.

That evening, two agents came to my house. When my wife asked who was at the door I said, "Secret Service agents, dear." She wasn't surprised. They questioned me for about thirty minutes, covering the same ground. They probed for names of people I was associated with and my response that we have a network of thousands around the country.

The agent said he wasn't judging me, that they had no intention of arresting me, and that I had the right to express my opinion. There were questions about whether I suffered any psychological problems from the Vietnam War or whether I received any medical help for any emotional problems, and I said that Vietnam had been no problem at all for me.

I did say that I worked for the same major corporation for over 40 years, had been married for over 36 years, had two fine boys who were very successful, and owned my house that was paid off. I said that I was very lucky because I've lived the American dream; however, that dream had turned into nightmare after experiencing the treated-like-dirt welcome home and seeing my government's lies about Agent Orange. That nightmare continues regarding the POWs we left behind, which is why I've continued this struggle.

They both shook my hand and thanked me for my patience.

Even though I never gave them Duc Tran's name, they realized he brought me into this event and questioned him briefly before releasing him.

6/21/07 – I traveled to Washington, D.C., on Thursday and attended a demonstration at the Ronald Reagan Building where Vietnam's President Triet was attending an event. We then marched to the Capitol building where we held a candlelight vigil. I spoke to the crowd and said the people in this building, and the people in the White House, betrayed the people of Vietnam, that George W. Bush did everything John Kerry would have done by giving Vietnam World Trade Organization status; however, he had one more chance left by making this right and holding Vietnam accountable on human rights. I received a big hand just before we chanted, "Free Father Ly!"

6/22/07 – The day began with a demonstration in front of the White House from 8 AM until the early afternoon to protest the meeting of Triet with President George W. Bush that was scheduled for 10 AM. I arrived a little after 8 AM and immediately began giving interviews with dozens of

Vietnamese media outlets, repeating much of what I had said at the luncheon on Wednesday.

The Vietnamese-Americans in attendance approached me all morning with requests to have my picture taken with them and expressing their appreciation and support for my efforts. They called me their hero and I could only respond by saying, "Thank you, thank you." Normally, I would say that I'm no hero, but it was coming at me in such a barrage I accepted as humbly as I could.

One person asked me if I knew who Le Tong is and I responded that I did. Tong is a world-renowned activist who flew many missions over Cuba and Southeast Asia, dropping freedom leaflets. He was arrested on three occasions and served a total of 21 years in prison, more than half of his life.

This person said that I was a hero like Tong and I stopped him immediately and said, "Le Tong is a true hero; you should not compare what I did to what he did." Uncharacteristically, he was persistent and almost defiant, insisting that I was the American version of Le Tong with a smile on his face, so I smiled and reluctantly said, once again, "Thank you, thank you." The sad thing is that all I really did was give a damn. They had no one else like me to respect.

A little after 9 AM, I realized that there were barriers on our side of Pennsylvania Avenue, preventing us from crossing to the other side; however, there was only a small police presence in front of the White House and the media inside were all waiting for Triet. I grabbed a bull horn and immediately ran to the end of the barriers where there was an opening for pedestrians to walk through and started yelling for the Vietnamese to follow me. We all wound up at the White House fence chanting for the next thirty minutes. The media inside came out as I anticipated and covered our protest. As usual, the mainstream media, whose biased coverage against the war undermined the chance to win it, didn't air our very vocal demonstration of 2,000 plus.

The *Washington Post* reported only "several hundred" protesters. I read *The New York Times*, supposedly the gold standard of the print media, and it didn't even mention that the meeting occurred. I suspect that a number of people associated with these press outlets are refusing to acknowledge the terrible human rights record of Vietnam because of their own guilt.

As we approached the 10 AM meeting time, the police slowly forced us back to the other side. I kept telling everyone to hold their ground, but the police were relentless. They brought in the horses to force us back to the park. When we all arrived in the park, the police lined the middle of Pennsylvania Avenue with twenty to thirty police vehicles, bumper to bumper so someone would have to jump over them to get to the other side, something I had never seen before. On the other side, in front of the White

House fence, were a large number of Secret Service agents, D.C. police, and visible snipers on the roof, all meant to intimidate us.

Just before 10 AM, a policeman came over to me and said he wanted to talk to me in the street. As the police opened the barrier so I could go into the street, I backed off and said, "I'm not going out there."

He responded that the Secret Service Agents across the street wanted to talk to me. We walked to the White House side of the street where an agent came over and said, "Mr. Kiley, it would be in your best interest and their best interest if no one attempts to get to this side of the street." I thanked him for the information and shook his hand.

As we approached 11 AM, Triet had not arrived through the front entrance when my greatest concern materialized; they had brought him in another entrance and were already meeting. It deprived me of an opportunity to rally the demonstrators into a frenzy that could only be achieved by his appearance. Also, we had planned on jumping the barriers when he arrived.

I ran the length of the park, telling everyone that Triet was already inside. Everyone rushed to the barrier to start chanting when I grabbed the megaphone and said to jump the barriers. Naturally, they waited for me to lead them and by the time I got to the barrier, about a dozen policemen rushed to the other side, preventing me from moving them or jumping over it. As I ran along the park to lose them, they followed closely so I could not make a move.

There were five policemen who came inside the demonstration area to talk with me. The leader said he was in charge of the SWAT team across the street. He said, "Mr. Kiley, you have had a very successful and very good demonstration so far; you have had a very good day and have made your point. If anyone attempts to cross the street, they will not reach the fence on the other side. I want this to end well for all of us."

I told him that I had a tremendous amount of respect for him and his people. We shook hands and they left.

I was now faced with a dilemma of having instigated most of the people, many of whom were ready to follow me no matter where I went. I instinctively knew that I had to take some dramatic action that would channel the crowd's energy into something positive. I again ran down the park, telling everyone to form together as one solid mass so we could all chant together as we did in front of the White House.

We began chanting: "VC Go Home, Freedom for Political Prisoners Now, Freedom for Vietnamese People Now, Free Father LY, and McCain VC." I eventually left at about 12:30 PM so I could record comments about McCain at the National Alliance of Families meeting. These tapes would be used in commercials against McCain.

Chapter Twelve
Bonding with Vietnamese Community

The day after I confronted President Triet I met in the evening with Ted, Bill Hendon, and I met Col. Earl Hopper for dinner. Earl was a twenty-year veteran of Army Intelligence. Earl's son is a famous POW case. He was known to be alive in captivity during the war but never returned.

I asked Col. Hopper if I could videotape an interview with him, and he agreed. As I taped, he dropped a couple of bombs about McCain. The first was that the Package Routes (aircraft bombing routes from and to two aircraft carriers off the coast of North Vietnam) that McCain had given the enemy in exchange for a promise of better medical treatment shortly after his crash and capture undoubtedly cost the lives of American pilots. Earl backed that up by saying that the rate of shoot-downs in the zone McCain flew increased by almost sixty percent after his capture.

Col. Hopper's wife, Patty, pointed out that POWs receive automatic promotions during their capture consistent with those serving normal duty unless there is reason to believe that a POW is collaborating with the enemy. John McCain didn't receive any grade promotions during or immediately after the five and a half years he was a prisoner. He should have received at least one if not two promotions in that amount of time. Patty said she had a package containing five DOD declassified documents that analyzed McCain's actions while in captivity to support that statement.

One more important issue with McCain was the fact that thirty-plus POWs had crossed the line as far as giving the enemy information and they were all allowed to ask for forgiveness and all would be forgiven before going home. McCain was one of them. There were only eight who defied the pardon and they were called the Peace Committee.

I said to the Colonel, "Some people say that at the very least McCain is a collaborator, and at worst he is a traitor. Do you agree?"

He responded with a very firm "No."

I said to myself, "Shit."

He thought for a second and then said, "I only agree with one part of it, it is the part that he was treasonous," in a very firm voice with tremendous conviction. He then called McCain a traitor.

Earl has been like a father to all of us and at 86 years old, having survived three bouts of cancer, being partially blind, partially deaf, and confined to a wheelchair, I knew this was very likely the last time I would see him in this world. This tape would not only be used against McCain but more importantly be a lasting reminder and legacy of a man who devoted his life to exposing government lies about the disappearance and incarceration of his son and the many other POWs. What tears me apart is thinking that he will die like Jane (Duke) Gaylor not knowing what happened to her son who was also alive in the hands of the enemy, and never returned. I shed a tear every time I think of Jane.

"Of Two Minds on Vietnam"
John E. Carey
Washington Times
June 22, 2007

Today, Vietnam's President Nguyen Minh Triet will visit the United States. This is the first time a head of state from Vietnam has visited the U.S. since before the end of the war in Vietnam in 1975.

Mr. Triet is expected to be greeted by protesters in the U.S. who support Vietnam's dissident community and human rights activists. Despite plenty of good economic and other news from Vietnam, the country has an abysmal human rights record.

The protesters President Triet will probably see in Washington walk a tricky path. Ironically, although Mr. Triet will be free in the U.S. and undoubtedly well protected and cared for, Vietnamese-Americans who engage in human rights advocacy face a strangely coercive dilemma. Many fear for their safety if they return to Vietnam to visit friends and family. Vietnam's Communist government frequently scoops up purported trouble makers and jails them without charges — often for stretches of more than a year.

6/23/07 – Andy Koch called Saturday morning to say that his great uncle, former mayor Ed Koch, was supposed to have met one-on-one with President Bush to discuss the POW issue. He started off the meeting saying that even though Bush owed him for his help in the 2004 election, he wanted the President to do the right thing.

The mayor was supposed to have shown Bush a classified DOD document dated February 2007 giving an analysis of multiple Caucasians that were tall and apparently looked like Americans. Bush said that he was possibly jumping to a conclusion. Koch said he read *Enormous Crime* as he believed the President did.

Koch then said if Vietnam did nothing on the POW issue coming off this meeting, he would go public with information with the help of his friend Rupert Murdoch, the owner of many newspapers. Bush asked Koch if he wanted to go down this path and Koch said absolutely. Then the President suggested that Koch attend the meeting with Triet on Friday, June 22nd, and he accepted as long as he could provide his own interpreter.

Koch supposedly attended this historic meeting and told Triet the same thing he told Bush, with one exception: he told the Communist president he had thirty days to do something or he would go public with this information and boycott all Vietnamese products imported into America.

When Triet said the Caucasians could be there because they wanted to stay, Koch said, "That's crap," something he was known to say on many occasions when he was mayor of NYC.

I immediately called John LeBoutillier to try and make contact with Ed Koch to verify this story, and then called a Vietnam veteran friend to do the same with his contact person. I did say that if this is not a true story, it is one of the most intriguing stories I've ever heard. Of course I had already become skeptical of "Andy Koch," if that was even his real name.

If the story is not true, either this Andy character was just entertaining himself or he was intentionally trying to throw us onto a false track, possibly to get us to do something with the media that would later make us look bad. Since we sat on this with no leaks on our end, placing a thirty-day deadline date in this storyline could be an act of desperation to hook us into releasing this story.

My friend called later that night to tell me he had verified that Ed Koch was definitely not at the meeting with Bush and Triet. He told me that what I did with Triet and my past adventures has made an enormous impact on those who are fighting for democracy in Vietnam. He followed up by saying that his contact in Vietnam knows all about what I did in New York and that I have become a very important player in this struggle for freedom, more important than I could ever imagine. I didn't want to know any more because none of this matters if we do not succeed.

6/24/07 – The Vietnamese-American community has a large party every year the day after the New York Diversity Parade. Peter Nguyen invited me as their Honorary Guest at the 88 Palace Restaurant in Chinatown. Before the event began, I was busy posing for pictures and giving interviews with the Vietnamese media. Someone came over to me and asked if I wanted to meet Le Tong and I enthusiastically said, "Definitely."

Tong was right behind him. I immediately said what an honor it was to meet him and then introduced myself to him. He said he knew who I was.

I gave a speech for a couple of minutes and sat down and enjoyed the night with young Vietnamese men and women. I introduced myself to Mayor Bloomberg's representative and made some complimentary remarks about the Mayor's alleged intention to fund his own campaign to keep himself free of donor pressure.

6/25/07 – The next night I was giving an interview to a Vietnamese radio show about the Triet luncheon incident. The announcer told me that Le

Tong was at the demonstration outside the luncheon, so that was probably why he knew me.

6/27/07 – Andy Koch called and said that his uncle was following a lead with two missionaries in Thailand regarding what they saw in their travels. He said the mayor was considering going over there, and I said that would be a bad idea and that he needed to stay here and use his contacts to expose the issue if he is serious.

Andy then said the mayor was pursuing the possible return of POWs and where they are today. Andy said his father was working on this issue when he died. His father had a friend in the Social Security Department who told him about these returnees getting checks through the SS system. His father checked out the one location in Connecticut that had three men guarding the house. He traced their plate numbers to find out their names and then checked the Federal Registry to determine that they worked for the FBI, DOD, and CIA.

Since we weren't investing any time or money, we had nothing to lose, and by continuing to listen, we might get some clues about who might be behind him, if anyone was.

I called LeBoutillier, who confirmed that the mayor had not responded to John's email from four days earlier. I asked him to follow-up with another email to the mayor stating that someone was using his name relating to the POW issue and if it wasn't true, John wanted to alert him. John said he would.

We were always concerned that someone or some group on the inside would slip us information which verified our claims or otherwise embarrassed the government, hoping that we would run with it… but the trickster(s) would have a way to prove the information was incorrect, so we would be embarrassed and discredited, causing people to doubt even our solid facts.

6/28/07 – I received two articles, *Washington Times* and *Post*, from Tom Burch regarding the demonstration. He also included a very warm letter again thanking me for what I had done. His appreciation and excitement exceeded my expectations of what was accomplished. Considering we are looked upon with disdain from many in the establishment, both government and media, it is always nice to get a pat on the back.

7/4/07 – Ban and I were communicating all day getting Earl and Patty Hopper's interviews on the web site while reorganizing the articles on the home page. We must have contacted each other a couple dozen times through the day and late into the night. As usual, John Nevin made a significant contribution, including the suggestion that we include the link to our web site in the email to all of our friends and media.

Even though Ban worked his ass off all day and night at the end of the process he said how honored he was to work with us on this project. Without him, it would have been very difficult for us to get this ready, and he has been the backbone of our organization. Ban said the work he does with Vietnam Vote is nothing compared to the impact he is having with us. I was surprised how enthusiastic he was after all the work he put in that day.

7/12/07 – I was scheduled to leave the next day for a fundraiser in California to support the family members of the freedom activist leaders of block 8406 who were thrown in jail after a kangaroo court in Vietnam sentenced them with no representation. The Vietnamese-American community in Little Saigon was flying me out to Orange County for three days for the fundraiser on Saturday and a debate at the Westminster city hall on Sunday. I knew this should prove to be an "interesting" weekend, considering that I will be calling McCain and any Vietnamese supporters of McCain traitors. That would indirectly be calling the highest-ranking Vietnamese-American elected official, California State Senator Van Tran, a traitor.

7/13/07 Friday – I arrived at California Long Beach Airport at 8 PM and was picked up by Ky, an activist in this area. He drove me to Phoc Le's nephew's house where we ate, drank straight cognac, and toasted to Vietnam's freedom until about midnight.

7/14/07 Saturday 11 AM – We showed up for the fundraiser at a very nice restaurant with about 300 people. I was one of several honored guests that included a very well-respected pastor and his wife. They have been involved with the community fighting for human rights in Vietnam for years.

After I was introduced, I acknowledged the arrest of Father Ly and encouraged everybody to support the families of the convicted freedom fighters. I immediately asked why America would support one of the most brutal Viet Cong Communist regimes in the world and traced it back to 1995 when we normalized relations with Vietnam opening the door that eventually allowed for WTO status.

I referred to Viet Cong McCain because Clinton could never have normalized relations without the support of McCain. The other talking points were:

1. McCain's embracing of Colonel Bui Tin (tortured and killed for a living during the war) in 1992 and his introduction of his best friend Prime Minister Khai in 2005 were additional examples of Viet Cong McCain's betrayal of the people of Vietnam, the millions of brave Vietnamese and thousands of brave Americans who died so the people in Vietnam could live in freedom.

2. Anyone supporting McCain is either Viet Cong or a sympathizer and also betrayed the principles of freedom and democracy.

3. The VC love McCain and consider him their best friend.

4. What has McCain ever done for freedom and democracy? Nothing! He in fact has supported every piece of legislation the Vietnamese government cared about since he was first elected to Congress in 1982:

- Lifting the Trade Embargo and normalizing relations in the mid-00s.

- Introducing Permanent Normal Trade Relations legislation in 2006 which lead to World Trade Organization status in 2007.

- Supported legislation to facilitate Amerasian immigration to the U.S., something McCain did to help the Communists get rid of a thorny problem while pretending to do it for the Vietnamese-American community.

- Supported legislation that established a cultural exchange between our two countries, laying the groundwork for lifting the trade embargo and normalizing relations mentioned above.

5. Don't count McCain out; he could still win the Republican nomination or be selected as a Vice Presidential running mate; if a Republican won the Presidency, he could be appointed Secretary of State or Defense. Even if he remained a Senator, we would still want to expose him as a phony and fraud.

6. Help me expose McCain and cut off the head of the Communist snake, the political head of McCain. Visit my web site VVAJM.

7. Last but not least, Free Father Ly!

Later, I speculated that perhaps my comments were so strong that Van Tran, California State Assemblyman, might show up on Sunday at the Westminster City Civic Center and I believe it was Ky that said the politicians stay away from this forum for fear of being sued per the instructions of the city lawyers. The thing was, Van Tran is not a city official.

We left there at about 8 PM and visited Quyen Le's friend, Nguyen van Lanh, whose great-grandfather was a Mandarin and special advisor on prophecy in the reign of King Thieu Tri. Quyen Le said that Lanh was an advisor to someone at the top of the Vietnamese government. I did learn later that Lanh traveled to Vietnam on a regular basis; however, I didn't find out who he advised.

Lanh asked me what numbers were in my mind, and I said, "3333," because I've always said three was my lucky number even though it never won me any money, and I have no idea why I selected four in a row. He placed those numbers in a computer and in 10 minutes showed me a print out of my past and future. What he said made sense, but were not extraordinary statements like the fact that I have successfully come through some very rough waters and was now entering very calm waters.

He advised me that I need not take any more risks and to avoid danger. He said to be patient and to allow things to come to me rather than to force the issue. None of it was extraordinary, nonetheless it was very good advice and seemed to help me to relax and not press too hard.

7/15/07 Sunday – Quyen Le, his friend, and I went to brunch at a Vietnamese café. Two of the Vietnamese newspapers had articles on me with my picture on the front page from the fundraiser the day before. The articles were excellent and both mentioned Viet Cong McCain. I was thrilled.

If nothing else happened this would make the trip worthwhile because one paper, *Vien Dong Daily*, had a distribution throughout the United States, Australia, Canada, and even Vietnam. After seeing that, I knew McCain and Tran could not ignore this insult in the heart of the largest Vietnamese-American community outside of Vietnam, Little Saigon. The fire was lit, now it was time to throw on some gasoline.

In our conversation, Quyen Le surprised me when he said he wanted me to join him on a three-month trip throughout Vietnam in 2009. I said okay, but I wasn't planning on coming back. Quyen laughed and said I would be safe. I didn't agree. Quyen left for a couple of minutes, so I asked Lanh when Vietnam will be free. He gave me a very decisive answer, 2012. Since he didn't speak English fluently I asked again. He said emphatically, "It will be free in 2012."

Lanh then made a very strange prediction. He said "There will be a king in 2012, and he will call on you. He will need you and you will go to him." I believe the term "king" means leader, not necessarily an actual king. Quyen returned, and I was too shocked to pursue the issue.

In talking to Ban later in the week, he said his parents talked about people like Lanh having the ability to forecast the future; however, 80% of them were frauds. They did say many were here in America. Ban said that Lanh was most likely legitimate because a con artist would never be so blunt so quickly. They would work the scam. Second and most important, he didn't want anything from me.

Lanh told Quyen that I had a good heart, indicating that I was a good person. He was an older man with a gray beard, very soft spoken and calm as you would expect, but when Quyen told him about my encounters with Khai and Triet he laughed very hard, which seemed very much out of character.

When shaking his hand to say goodbye, his eyes lit up, which I gladly took to mean he liked me. Even though I sensed a possible storm approaching that afternoon at city hall, I absorbed a great sense of calm because of my encounter with Lanh. This meeting would serve me well in dealing with what I was about to experience.

During our breakfast, the Program Host for Saigon Broadcast Television Network (SBTN), Huy Phuong, showed up at Quyen's request and asked me to join him at 1:00 that afternoon for a thirty-minute taped interview that would play that Thursday. I agreed and stated that I needed to get to city hall no later than 2 PM and he agreed. I knew the 1:30 PM meeting would start late because the Vietnamese have a running joke that their events always start one hour late.

We did the interview at the SBTN headquarters in Garden Grove and naturally it was delayed at the start, along with some retakes of some segments, because the host and Quyen Le, who was interpreting, occasionally had some missed communication. I did want to get to the city hall event before the meeting began in order to speak with the other media; however, SBTN is without doubt the largest and most influential Vietnamese network in the world and that time was more important than anything else I could have accomplished.

Huy Phuong drove Quyen and me to the event and we arrived at about 2:30 PM. There were a couple of hundred people standing around outside the Senior Center, so I thought the meeting had not yet started. As we approached the hall, I could see that it was filled to capacity and overflowing outside. I immediately felt a tremendous sense of anxiety as we squeezed through the packed crowd and realized that I had never been exposed to such an explosive or highly charged situation like this before.

As we entered this large center, I looked up to see who was speaking at the podium; it was Van Tran. My heart jumped into my throat, or at least that's how I felt at that time. I remember saying to myself, "Holy shit! We forced the rats out of the basement."

My mind began racing on what I was going to say and how I would deliver the message as we made our way to the front. I thought for a moment about being politically correct and then remembered how I did that in my speech in San Diego. I quickly decided that I will never make that same mistake twice; if I made a mistake it would be that I was too assertive. I knew that when I left California, I didn't want to be forgotten.

I walked directly behind Van Tran as he spoke and positioned myself so that the media was filming both of us at the same time. I believe there were about eight professional cameras filming the event, including SBTN's Little Saigon TV that covered local events. The emcee of the event came over to me to shake my hand and I said in a very assertive tone, "I want to follow Van Tran." He quickly conferred with his committee members at the dais and returned to tell me I would be next and could only speak for five minutes.

Considering we had never discussed my speaking in advance, I graciously accepted. They sat me down directly in front of Tran.

While sitting and waiting for my introduction, I reflected on my conversation with Lanh and I was able to calm myself down to a state that almost felt surreal. As Tran finished his speech, the crowd gave him a very good response. He was admired by most; his only blemish, as far as I knew, was supporting McCain.

The emcee introduced me to the crowd. I was completely blown away by the loud response and had to gather myself again for my speech. Fortunately for me, the emcee told me to sit down again as he introduced other dignitaries in the room. That gave me the time to regroup and compose myself. As I waited to speak, Van Tran sat next to me and handed me his card. He introduced himself.

I said, "I know who you are, I'm Jerry Kiley and we met twice before, once at your Philadelphia fundraiser in 2004 and the other time at Duc Tran's house."

He nervously said, "Oh," and then began explaining who he was again. I looked at him with a frown on my face and said in an almost annoyed tone, "I know who you are." It was an awkward moment.

Perhaps he felt a need to tell me twice because I clearly didn't show him any respect the first time. After the second time, he knew I was blowing him off and had no respect to show.

I was introduced, and I began talking about Father Ly and a brutal Communist regime that beat, jailed, raped, and killed their people and religious leaders on a daily basis. I asked how the American government could support this brutal, repressive Viet Cong regime. The answer was the same as the day before. Viet Cong McCain played the most critical role in opening the door to Vietnam; he and John Kerry were joined at the hip in betraying the people of Vietnam. I continued to hammer McCain, talking about his embrace of Bui Tin and announcing his buddy Khai. I ended by talking about the luncheon for Triet and said, "Free Father Ly."

One thing I did different from everyone else was to take the wireless microphone and walk directly in front of the first row of chairs to be closer to the people and closer to Tran. It was strange that even though he has endorsed McCain, he didn't show any disdain for my aggressive comments condemning McCain. In fact, he looked like he was agreeing with my verbal attack.

After I finished, Tran and I sat together for a while. When he got up and stood near the door getting ready to leave, I followed and told him I was very disappointed in his endorsement of McCain. He said that he was a strong person and that he had expressed his concern at what McCain has done. I answered in an annoyed tone that he still endorsed a man who supports Communists.

Tran told me he was supporting McCain and pushing to support reinstating Vietnam as a "Country of Particular Concern." Tran was pushing the wrong guy. McCain was one of the least likely people to do that. Tran, like so many others, had the false impression that McCain was a friend of the Vietnamese People rather than a friend of Vietnam's communist government. I ended by saying, "While you are at it, tell him to get the living U.S. POWs out of Vietnam." He nodded and said he would.

During my speech, the crowd reacted the same way as the Vietnamese people did the day before. As a group they became quieter as I continued my attack, with a large number urging me on, but they were not the majority. I believe some of that came from the Vietnamese non-assertive or passive approach to American politics. They were used to a strong military state that includes a very invasive security force in Vietnam, not only under Communist rule but even when South Vietnam was free. The free South was infiltrated with VC sympathizers, so the government was constantly trying to find them through the constant monitoring of the state police.

The other reason for the crowd's reaction is that many didn't know that McCain had betrayed them, and they were in shock when I attacked him. They give him too much credit with his involvement in the Communist release of Amerasians to America. I needed to address that problem and make sure they knew who the real John McCain was.

I went with Duc Tran and Ky a few blocks away to visit their version of the Vietnam Memorial honoring everyone who lost their lives in the Vietnam War, including the South Vietnamese military forces and the people of Vietnam. It was very moving, considering how underappreciated the Vietnamese people are in terms of the courage and character they showed risking the lives of their families to escape from Communism to live in freedom. I have a much greater appreciation for what I have and the freedoms I enjoy because of my relationship with a culture that truly knows what a blessing it is to be free.

When we came back to the center, the meeting was over; however, I did get some feedback from one person who said what I was doing to McCain appeared political. I told him about my attack on John Kerry and that both of them are joined at the hip in their betrayal of the people of Vietnam. This is another situation that I also need to address. They know I'm a registered Democrat and will try to use that against me. Good move on their part, no problem for me.

Ky finally made contact with An Nguyen, who has her own SBTN radio talk show and owns her own real estate company. We met her at 6:30 PM for a taped audio interview. She is a very relaxed, quiet, and unassuming person. It was clear that An wanted to get to know me first, so we spoke about my personal life and military service for about fifteen minutes. The taped interview lasted for about half an hour.

We discussed the McCain issue and even my feelings about how America had abandoned our principles of freedom and democracy by supporting two brutal Communist countries, China and Vietnam, with bad trade agreements pushed by big business and special interests who buy far too much corrupt influence in Washington, D.C. When she asked why they would do such a thing, I said, "It's simple; when someone is willing to sell what you want, you will buy if the price is right. Billions are made at the cost of only millions in corrupt influence."

When we concluded the interview, An stopped the tape and talked to me again for about fifteen minutes about the website and the organization against McCain. When we concluded, she suggested that I come back for a fundraiser, and I agreed.

Later in the week, Ban confirmed that An and her husband were very wealthy through their real estate business and that she appeared to be okay as far as not having ties to the Communists. He did caution me that there were many in that line of business that supported the Communists.

7/16/07 Monday - My flight left Long Beach Airport at 9:45 PM and I arrived back in JFK at 6 AM. The next day, Ban said I was so popular I could run for office in Little Saigon and win. Ky and Duc had mentioned the fact that the current Congresswoman in that area will be running and probably winning the Governor's race. They said I could win that Congressional seat.

Ban said if I rented an apartment in that district and applied for a cell phone I would qualify to run. I laughed and said I wasn't interested in running for any political office. I have to admit that the thought of going to D.C. and raising hell was a very pleasant one.

7/18/07 Wednesday – Realizing that there were some issues for me to address concerning the Vietnamese perception of McCain related to the Communist release of the Amerasian children, I began writing an editorial. Since the *Vien Dong Daily* was the national/international newspaper that covered my visit to the Father Ly fundraiser with a front page picture and story, I decided to send them my article to print. The other issues were to hammer McCain for his obsessive support for Communist Vietnam and link him with John Kerry. Last but not least, my goal was to make it clear that I attacked both Kerry and McCain not for partisan politics but for their betrayal of the people of Vietnam.

7/22/07 Sunday PM– I called Ky to ask if he could send me the information about McCain's sponsorship of Senate Resolution 199 that called for a cultural exchange between the U.S. and Vietnam in 1988. He told me that Little Saigon was up in arms with two demonstrations that weekend with 2,000 and 3,000 people in front of the newspaper that seemed to be favoring the Communists. I was thrilled.

7/23/07 Monday – I wrote a letter that ended by saying, "Ask Father Ly" about the hell the Vietnamese people lived in when I found out from Ban that the 100 demonstrators protesting in Saigon were killed by the Communists. They had been arrested earlier in the week for protesting the confiscation of their land by the Communists for no other reason than greed and corruption.

Apparently, the government let some of the older demonstrators go free because they posed no future problem. They enforced one of their doctrines; make sure any problems go away permanently. What Ky didn't tell me was that these demonstrations stateside were caused by the killing of the 100 demonstrators before the weekend.

Ban did a rewrite of the opening paragraphs in the article below. He has been the backbone of this movement to expose McCain. His insight on the Vietnamese community and experience in the political arena has been priceless.

I wrote an extensive article for the Vietnamese community newspaper, Vien Dong Daily, to be sure that readers had an opportunity to see how much evidence there is that John McCain was not their friend.

I told Ban that if they could pay my way to California, I would join them the following weekend in front of John McCain's headquarters.

7/24/07 Tuesday – I found the 6/21/05 DVD of McCain introducing Pham Van Khai at the banquet held in the Mayflower Hotel in Washington, D.C. McCain talks about how he and Kerry played important roles in normalizing relations with Vietnam ten years earlier, and how the U.S. and a prosperous Vietnam are now such great friends. These statements should be enough to convince any Vietnamese who thought McCain was a good guy.

7/26/07 – I told my son Dave about my plans to join Quyen Le for a three-month trip to Vietnam in 2009. Dave asked, "Why would you risk everything? What are you trying to accomplish?" I wasn't quite sure how to answer, but after thinking about it later I realized that the last 24 years I've spent thinking and acting to right one of the most grievous and despicable wrongs our government has ever committed, it now seems almost my destiny to take the next step. Whatever roadblocks stood in my way, I intended to do all in my power to break them down, regardless of consequences. There was no turning back.

7/30/07 – I received congratulatory messages from other leaders in the movement for taking on Triet at the Asia Society luncheon. One, who had contacts in Vietnam, said that what I did had far more impact and significance than I realized. He went on to say that I was by far the most important player in the movement. I didn't know what to say.

A veteran friend said he had verified from an inside source that neither his phone nor mine were being monitored. I had no doubt that he believed it, but I was less than confident of his source. Years ago, this same friend told me that there was a legal tap on my home and work phone. If that was true, my company had to know it, and I would have thought someone would mention it to me, even if in confidence. It didn't really matter to me because I always assumed that might be the case. It's safer that way.

7/31 – 8/2/07 – We experienced telephone problems for three days. When my wife originally called Verizon, they said that the line was clear and okay. I bought a new phone, and that didn't resolve the problem. I called on 8/2/07 and they sent a technician who found the problem at their box in front of the house. Olga said she thought the tech seemed nervous.

8/9/07 – Again we had a temporary problem with our phone service that fixed itself.

8/10/07 – My call home was disconnected.

8/12/07 – Ban said the Prime Minister of Vietnam was arriving in Texas on 9/15/07 and then will go to D.C. Ban will arrange for my expenses to be paid to Texas.

8/23/07 – Duc Tran called and asked that I remove Viet Cong and VC from in front of McCain's name because some Vietnamese feel that should be reserved for the actual VC killers in Vietnam. I wondered if it would fly if I explained that McCain's assistance to them as a POW and since then made him just as guilty as they were.

Duc also said there was a great article written by a Chinese journalist criticizing Chinese people in the U.S. for accepting the Communist regime and its leadership. The article mentioned that Tuan Le and I expressed the outrage of the Vietnamese community and how our actions were an inspiration to the Chinese freedom movement.

He mentioned the bravery of the Chinese woman who protested the Communist President of China Hu Jintao's visit to the White House and expressed his disappointment that there was no sense of outrage from the Chinese American community.

Duc inadvertently mentioned the possible attendance of McCain at a meeting of the Amerasian community in Texas on 9/22/07 in September. He asked me not to interfere in that meeting because it is a very sensitive issue.

I asked Duc in a very angry tone why Vietnamese people who hate Communism would think that McCain is okay after seeing that he is the Vietnamese Communists' best friend. He said when McCain visited Little Saigon three days after my visit in late April, he promised that when elected president he would invite the Communist leaders to the White House and convince them that they need to free the country and become a democracy. Incredible! How can people take at face value promises for future action that are contrary to what a person has done in the past?

9/13/07 - Duc Tran called and said he has been recruited as a reporter for the BBC and Voice of America print media. He said I could also write articles, reach a wider audience, and be even more popular. Duc enjoys notoriety; I do not. He mentioned again about my removal of the VC McCain reference in my open letter to the Vietnamese people so he could reprint it in other media outlets. He commented that I should listen to him and not be so radical.

Duc was a mixed bag. He kept doing things that were very helpful, but would then do something that looked like he was on the other side. I was never able to place full confidence in him.

I asked him if he could get a copy of the video tape of the Asian Society luncheon in June and he said probably not; however, he might be able to get the audio tape that VOA made for that event. He never produced the tape.

What disturbs me most is that Duc's sole purpose at the Triet luncheon was to take pictures when I interrupted Triet's speech and then subsequent arrest. He didn't take one picture, even with the heads-up that I was about to make my move.

He said he could get me into the UN to lobby the countries that will be voting for Vietnam's acceptance as a Non-Permanent Member of the Security Council. My gut instincts tell me to be careful in my dealing with him going forward, something doesn't feel right.

I recalled other situations with Duc where he seemed to be working against my interest, which was exposing McCain. I had serious doubts about who was influencing Duc and his motivation.

9/13/07 - I called my friend Ban and he cautioned me again to be careful because Duc's actions sounded very much like someone trying to control me and neutralize my effectiveness. John Nevin had the same reaction.

9/14/07 - I mentioned to John that I thought we should send a letter to McCain requesting his immediate and vocal support for the placement in Vietnam of international human rights organizations, Human Rights Watch, and Amnesty International to monitor their activity, so we could hold his feet to the fire when he denies our request. John Nevin suggested lobbying all the presidential candidates for both parties to sign a letter simply stating that they supported permanent and unrestricted access to Vietnam for both of these human rights organizations.

All the Vietnamese-American organizations should sign the letter and then send several of their members along with Mike Benge to lobby in Washington, D.C., and around the country at their campaign headquarters. I'm going to suggest that at the meeting on Sunday the 23rd, with all the leaders from around the country present.

9/20/07 - A veteran contact that I placed great trust in contacted me to say he had received an additional seventeen names of purported living POWs from his contact in Vietnam. These seventeen were said to have been originally captured by Vietnamese forces in Laos, but were now in Vietnam. There are 37 names he has not received out of the 54 total mentioned in November, 2005. He said that if this information was true, many people would be surprised because the names are not those most commonly known and suspected of being alive, and they were NCOs rather than officers, as all the pilots would have been. In some cases, these are names of Americans not considered likely survivors. John Nevin later said this might correspond to an incident he had read about in uncorrelated CIA reports involving the alleged capture of a U.S. insertion team inside Laos.

9/23/07 - I joined the leaders of Vietnamese communities around the country at a meeting in Manhattan on Bowery Street. I spoke for about five minutes concerning my support for whatever they wanted to do during the 9/25 demonstration scheduled at the UN to protest the visit of the Vietnamese Prime Minister.

I also spoke at length criticizing McCain and handing out my new cards with the website address, www.AgainstMcCain.com. Most of the people seemed to appreciate my remarks. Some of the leadership didn't seem happy because many of them are obsessed with being politically correct, which makes them politically ineffective. Also, because the Republicans were always considered better supporters of the South Vietnamese during the war, the majority who are active in U.S. politics are aligned with the GOP. So their desire for political correctness was elevated by their desire for party correctness.

9/25/07 - I went to the demonstration and Duc Tran called me over to meet a woman standing next to him. As I approached, he asked if I knew who this was, but I didn't. He introduced me to her, saying that she was the person who was arrested posing as a news reporter on the White House lawn when the president of China visited President Bush. I immediately said how honored I was to meet her, and she returned the compliment.

10/13/07 – Duc Tran called to say that an organization in the Chinese-American community invited both of us to one of their events on Wednesday night, 10/17/07. They want our support for their boycott of the August 2008 Olympics and their Human Rights Torch Run (HRTR) through 60 countries and 100 cities.

10/20/07 – After attending the event on 10/17, I received an email from Sen inviting me to speak at their HRTR rally either on 10/27/07 in D.C. or 10/28/07 in Baltimore. Ban said that the *Epoch Times* is a very aggressive organization and would be an excellent organization to be involved with.

10/22/07 – Sen Nieh, President of the *Epoch Times*, left me two messages over the weekend on my business phone, so I returned his calls this morning to accept his invitation to speak on Sunday, October 28th, in Baltimore.

I expressed an interest in the New York event. Sen told me that I would have five to ten minutes to talk in Baltimore. I asked what he wanted me to speak about after mentioning that I have very strong feelings against my own government's support of the two brutal Communist regimes in China and Vietnam and that the U.S. Congress was politically corrupt. Sen said he wanted me to mention support of the boycott of the China Olympics, the reports issued by Human Rights Watch and Amnesty International, and our own State Department indicating that violations in China have worsened over the past year. He then said how disappointed he was when President Bush accepted China's invitation to attend the Olympics and that he wanted me to address that issue. I assured him I would and would mention similar human rights violations in Vietnam.

10/25/07 - I went out to lunch with an attorney friend who has connections with likely Presidential candidate Rudolph Giuliani. He agreed to encourage Giuliani to take on the issue of human rights in Vietnam and to give him the following write-up by former Vietnam POW Mike Benge.

"Religious Freedom in Vietnam is a Sham"

On September 14, 2007, the State Department issued its International Religious Freedom Report 2007 giving the Vietnamese Communists another free pass on religious persecution and delisting them as a "Country of Particular Concern (CPC)" -- citing "improvements in conditions for religious adherents." This is mainly based on the number of churches that have registered with the Vietnamese government. US policy favors accelerating the registration of churches.

What the State Department didn't say is at what cost to religious freedom this registration entails. In order to register, churches must submit to the Central Bureau of Religious Affairs (CBA) a list of the names and addresses of members, and only those approved by the CBA can attend services. All sermons must be approved by the CBA, and must be given in Vietnamese, including those in ethnic minority churches. Pastors and priests can neither deviate from the approved sermon nor proselytize, and CBA police monitor all services. This is de facto Communist control of churches in Vietnam.

However, the Vietnamese Communist's religious repression is not limited to just the control of churches. While Communist Vietnam's President Nguyen Minh Triet met with President Bush at the White House, Y-Het Vin, a young Hroi ethnic minority man, died from injuries after several days of sustained beatings during official interrogations by Vietnamese police who tried to force him to recant his Christian faith. Y-Het was from Son Hoa district in the coastal province of Phu Yen in south-central Vietnam. This is but one of a litany of arrests, beatings and imprisonments, sometimes deaths of ethnic minorities who refuse to recant their Christian faith. Over 350 Christian Montagnard political prisoners have been incarcerated.

On February 8th, two hundred Khmer Krom Buddhist monks peacefully demonstrated in Soc Treang, Vietnam, asking for religious freedom. The Vietnamese government responded by brutally beating, arresting, and imprisoning nineteen monks. Five were given prison sentences of two to four years.

On Feb 27th, responding to the arrests in Viet Nam, Buddhist monks living in Cambodia peacefully demonstrated in front of the Vietnamese Embassy in Phnom Penh. The Venerable Eang Sok Thoeun, who participated, was found in a temple dead with his throat slit, and Cambodian authorities refused to allow his parents to organize a formal Buddhist funeral service for him. The Chinese call this, "killing the chicken to scare the monkey."

Soon after the demonstrations, the Venerable Tim Sakhorn, a Cambodian citizen who was the Abbot of the Phnom Den North Pagoda temple in Takeo province, was kidnapped by Vietnamese and Cambodian agents and taken to Vietnam in violation of international law. The Vietnamese Communist government had issued an order to Hanoi-installed Cambodian Prime Minister Hun Sen for his arrest (HDTSTW PHAT GIAO KPC So: 502/07-DN). Finally, on August 1, 2007, the Hanoi regime admitted through its official websites (www.vovnews.vn and www.vov.org.vn) that the Venerable Tim Sakhorn has been imprisoned (location unknown). Ironically, the monk was charged with crossing into Vietnam without having any proper legal travel document; the international community has been quiet.

The Vietnamese Communist government does not discriminate between the various religions when it persecutes religious believers. Last March, Hanoi brazenly aired on TV the kangaroo court trial of Father Thaddeus Nguyen Van Ly, a Catholic priest who was muzzled during the proceedings. In Vietnamese, the colloquial phrase for censorship is "bit mieng," to cover the mouth. The picture of Father Ly's muzzling seems a literal enactment of an old cliché. Denied representation during his trial, Father Ly was sentenced to eight years imprisonment.

Despite claims of giving more freedom to Montagnard and Hmong house churches, the fact is the Vietnamese Communist regime has imposed even more restrictions. Christians are now allowed to pray at home, but not in groups, including extended families, in churches (unless government sanctioned), or in public. Routinely, house church Christians are rounded up and beaten, given electric shocks, and jailed when they refuse to join Communist-controlled churches.

Wives of imprisoned Christian Montagnards are being rounded up, and under the threat of torture, are forced to renounce God and recant their faith in public.

On September 24th, the U.S. Commission on International Religious Freedom left for Vietnam, supposedly to investigate religious conditions there. However, unlike Vietnamese officials here, U.S. officials and *delegations cannot freely travel in Vietnam unless escorted by government minders and taken on strictly controlled guided tours. In the central highlands and other contentious areas, delegations are taken to Potempkin villages and model government churches and fed misinformation by government agents posing as religious leaders. U.S. officials often take their word as the gospel. One such agent is Siu Kim, a Montagnard with a church in Plieku, who works for Vietnam's Communist government. According to that government's statistics, the Montagnards are among Vietnam's poorest inhabitants. Yet, Siu Kim has been on four tours to the U.S., paid for by the Communist government to propagandize the Montagnards here.*

In June 2007, Prime Minister Nguyen Tan Dung certified the Vietnamese Communist party's "Religion Campaign Plan," in which 21,811 Communist religious workers will be trained in the political management of religion, with a special focus on ethnic minorities (Vietnam News Agency, 6/13/07).

I am positive that this is not the religious freedom that President Bush envisioned when he took Vietnam's President Nguyen Minh Triet to the woodshed over religious repression and human rights abuses during his White House visit last June. I'm sure that if the President knew what was going on, he would not approve of the Department of State's actions. And I know Pope John Paul II, who championed religious freedom during the repressive era of the Soviet Union, would roll over in his grave if he knew that U.S. policy toward Vietnam favors Communist control of churches.

--Michael Benge is a retired Foreign Service Officer who spent eleven years in Vietnam, is a student of South East Asian Politics, and is very active in advocating for human rights and religious freedom for the peoples of this region. He was captured while helping the Vietnamese people during the Vietnam War and held as a Prisoner of War for many years, much of that time in solitary confinement, until his release in 1973.

11/2/07 –I told Ban we had a plan for after the Presidential election was over to raise money for TV commercials. The ads would show an American family worshiping together in the privacy of their own home when the door is smashed in and the parents and children are dragged out of the house, arrested, and charged with conspiracy against the government, and then brought before a judge and sentenced to jail. The commercial would end by making a plea for the American people to support permanent and unrestricted monitoring of human rights violations in Vietnam by Amnesty International and Human Rights Watch.

I was surprised when Ban asked if that would be believable to the American public. I said we need to take a two by four and hit the American public over the head to get their attention. He agreed and said there was a

Vietnamese group in California who had raised money as a non-profit organization to pay for a billboard with a picture of Father Ly for the last nine months. He said they may be interested in supporting this project. I said we could produce our own commercials and Ban chimed in that we could put them on YouTube for worldwide viewing.

John Nevin said he would check with a professional he knows in Kansas City who might be willing to help us produce some commercials.

Chapter Thirteen
McCain's Presidential Run

11/8/07 Thursday – I traveled to Washington, D.C., at Tom Burch's invitation, for the National Vietnam and Gulf War Veterans Coalition (formally known as NVVC) breakfast the next morning.

I had come early to spend some time with a veteran friend who had important contacts. We talked at great length during a lunch meeting. He revealed that he had received an additional thirteen names of living Vietnam POWs to add to the original four names he had received in 2005.

Four of the seventeen names had been confirmed as being on the Defense Department's "Last Known Alive" list. He emphasized that we needed to keep the faith as we have friends in key positions who are willing to risk their careers and their lives if necessary to complete this task.

Since the November 2005 meeting when we first realized that some of the Communist leaders in Vietnam were considering working with us on the POW issue, we tried to avoid letting ourselves become overconfident of the possibility that this might happen. We were originally thinking that there was perhaps a 10% chance. With the receipt of the second list of thirteen, we started thinking that the likelihood was much greater.

11/9/07 Friday – I sat at Tom Burch's table at the National Vietnam and Gulf War Veterans Coalition, next to his wife, Linda. Bill Hendon gave what he called his last speech and briefing on the POW issue and proceeded to go through all the people who worked on this issue for the last 25 years.

Billy showed a picture of the Fuller remains we'd displayed at a New York City press conference in the Penta Hotel sponsored by the National Coalition in the mid-80s. The press conference involved Ann Hart, Jeff Donahue, a relative of Fuller whose name I don't recall, and Dr. Michael Charney, a world-renowned forensic anthropologist. I'd organized the press conference and Tom Burch was the spokesperson for NVVC.

Charney had said at the conference that the remains were not Fuller's, and in fact were not even human; they were animal remains. I recall that Charney was so incensed he said it looked like someone had picked up some animal remains off the ground, placed them in a plastic bag, and given it to the Fuller family as their son's remains. He said the government officials involved in this sham were a disgrace.

Billy Hendon, Lamont Gaston (former Viet Now and NVVC chairperson), and I went out for lunch. I was amazed that neither Billy nor Lamont knew what was going on in Vietnam. I told them of the Mennonite pastor's beheading, Farther Ly's prosecution, and the general crackdown on civil rights and religious freedom which included registering of religious organizations. Lamont said he had generally followed events in Vietnam but was surprised that the Communists were worse after we gave them the WTO status they so badly wanted.

I said that was just what should have been expected. They were temporarily playing nice, easing up on the human rights abuses, to get what they wanted, and then returned to their old ways after they got it.

11/23/07 Friday – I got a back-channel message that one of our key contacts in Vietnam was saying that there were complications regarding the release of large numbers initially. However, he was still working on the release of the original four POWs whose names had been given to us two years earlier.

We were told—and it's ironic if true—that it was some of the Communist hard-liners who most wanted to work with us on any release since they didn't trust the U.S. government for two reasons: They thought (as we did) that there were too many officials from the old days still in the U.S. government who preferred that no POWs were released because of the black eye it would give them here, both for denying their existence, and for doing nothing to bring them home; and because these same people would not consider it a favor and would do everything they could to make the Vietnamese government and its leaders look bad.

The Vietnamese knew that we, at least, would appreciate a no-precondition act of good faith on their part.

On the other hand, the reformers in Vietnam preferred to deal with the U.S. government to arrange any release since they saw their futures tied to good relations with USG.

12/23/07 – Tom Burch called to tell me that someone he knew was going to release many of the 32 taped confessions McCain made for the Communists when he was a POW. Tom said he hadn't ever seen the tapes; however, he said there's no doubt that the content of those tapes would be very damaging to McCain. Tom wanted to prepare me so I could speak to the New York media about how hypocritical McCain was to paint himself as a war hero. I would push this point to declare that we do not deserve such a President, nor does he deserve to be elected.

Tom was hoping that the tapes would be released before the Iowa caucus vote on 1/3/08, or at least before the New Hampshire primary on 1/8/08, well in advance of the South Carolina primary on 2/5/08. Tom said that McCain was still looking to get back at him for his 2000 defeat in SC when the National Coalition supported Bush and soundly defeated McCain, who had just won New Hampshire. That defeat destroyed any chance McCain had to win the nomination, and Bush went on to easily win every state and embarrass him. Tom said if McCain became President, he wouldn't forget what a thorn we've been in his side over the years.

I told Tom that the outcome in Iowa would play a significant role in the New Hampshire vote for McCain. The independents in NH can vote in either the Republican or Democratic primary. They had a tendency to vote in the hottest race.

If Barack Obama won Iowa, the Democratic primary would be considered the hottest race so the independents would be inclined to vote in that race, depriving McCain of "moderate" votes he needs.

If Hillary defeated Obama in Iowa, then it would be a foregone conclusion that she would easily win the Democrat nomination. In that case, more independents would vote in the Republican primary and help McCain. Considering NH was the only state McCain won in 2000, he could easily overtake Mitt Romney.

Tom thanked me for my analysis and said it was very useful. Having followed all the Presidential races going back to the Nixon and Kennedy debates in 1960, I have a very good idea what is possible and plausible in these primaries.

12/24/07 - I got another update on the interest Vietnam has in releasing the American POWs in their possession. The American government officials who were in recent discussions with the Vietnamese government representatives were headed by the Undersecretary of Defense. The information was that our officials were told point blank by the Communists that they held a number of living POWs, and that this fact was conveyed to President Bush. The response was a communiqué requesting the names of these POWs. My source said that a communiqué demanding information rather than a request for an immediate high-level meeting would have been a strong signal that the U.S. government didn't consider the matter a priority. This would have confirmed the Communists' earlier suspicions, and it was no surprise to us.

It had become clear long ago that too many influential people in the government felt vulnerable to the fallout from the release of prisoners. Obviously, 34 years since all the American POWs were supposed to be released, there was still a mess that needed to be cleaned up.

I mentioned to my source that it seemed likely that the U.S. government reaction would increase the chance that the Communists would do business with us; he strongly agreed.

12/25/07 – I was telling my sons about the possibility of McCain's tapes in a low voice when Dave started to joke about my thinking we were being bugged by the government. I was annoyed at his response because this had come up before. Later that night, I told him that I didn't want Mike's girlfriend in the next room to hear what I was saying.

He didn't realize the significance of her father working for the Federal Emergency' Management Agency (FEMA). I told him that it was a federal agency whose primary mission was to manage events and coordinate the U.S. government response when things got out of hand, whether for natural disasters, industrial accidents, terrorist acts, or domestic insurrection. As a result, the organization would be tuned into any political situation that had potential for high volatility.

I called Ban to discuss Condoleezza Rice's statement in *The New York Times* that the U.S. would oppose Taiwan's entry into the United Nations under that name. Ban said that China had invaded the islands off the coast of Vietnam and was currently occupying them. In 1968, North Vietnam signed over the oil-rich island area to China in appreciation for their support in neutralizing the U.S. threat to invade them. China had threatened that if the U.S. invaded the North they would enter the war in support of their Communist ally. Now the Vietnamese government was claiming that the transfer exceeded the authority of the 1968 regime.

12/27/07 – Benazir Bhutto, former leader of Pakistan, was assassinated today while campaigning before the 1/8/08 election that she most likely would have won, resulting in a democratic government. We were afraid that this tragedy would help McCain, who has been trying to give himself credibility by claiming foreign policy credentials.

1/6/08 – Mike Huckabee won the Republican Iowa caucus by a large margin over Mitt Romney, with McCain coming in fourth. Barack Obama won the Democratic caucus by a similar margin.

McCain won the New Hampshire primary in 2000 against GW Bush, and it looks like he will beat Romney this coming Tuesday, the 8th. If he does, then some are predicting that he will win the Republican nomination. If that happens, and he wins the Presidential election, then all of us who have worked against McCain will be screwed. He is a vindictive man who will spare no expense to cause us trouble.

1/8/08 (Wed) – McCain won the New Hampshire Republican primary with Romney coming in second, and Hillary for the Democrats with Obama coming in second.

I called Ted to relay a suggestion from John Nevin and Tom Ashworth to try to send the veterans' posts in South Carolina a write-up on McCain before the 1/19/08 primary.

1/9/08 (Thurs) – Called Ted and he described a postcard that he was going to send out to the editors of all the SC newspapers with a picture of McCain planning his presidential campaign from his POW cell, implying that he was using that to further his political ambition. The back of the card will contain his record as a POW.

I called Tom Burch, who committed to donating $300 for the cost to produce and mail these cards and perhaps as much as $500 if needed.

1/11/08 (Sat) – Ted mailed out eighty one-page flyers to the editors of SC newspapers.

1/13/08 (Mon) – The media started receiving the information and apparently notified the McCain camp. That same evening, McCain's "Truth Squad," along with his campaign staff, held a press conference declaring war on the Vietnam Veterans Against John McCain (VVAJM) organization. The rest of the week, I answered dozens of phone calls from the print media around the country.

I told Ted that he was a genius in his ability to hit a nerve. On the downside, Ted chose to use a cartoon caricature of McCain on the postcard and a lot of the focus was on the "disrespectful" cartoon rather than on the content.

Having learned from John Kerry's mistake of not responding quickly, they overreacted and created a media feeding frenzy that carried over to the cable stations and all the radio talk shows. Had they ignored us, this certainly would not have had the same impact after the SC Republican primary.

1/17/08 (Thurs) – Ross Perot entered the political arena today by criticizing McCain for being an opportunist, abandoning his ill wife for a rich trophy wife, and abandoning our POWs. This was probably more effective than all of the effort and aggravation we invested in trying to get evidence of other aspects of McCain's character flaws exposed to the public.

1/18/08 (Fri) – I did a half-hour interview with CNN for the "Situation Room with Wolf Blitzer" for that evening's show. The producer, Laura Dolan, tried to conduct this interview the night before; however, my wife didn't want any media in our house because "Inside Edition" was outside our home filming the house and knocked on the door for an interview with me. They left a card and apparently were asked by the police to leave the neighborhood. Our next door neighbors received a call from "Entertainment Tonight" wanting to know what they thought of me.

Laura called the Stony Point Civic Center, five minutes from my house, and received permission to use their lodge for the interview. There were two cameramen, the interviewer (Jim), and Laura. The lighting set-up and many reflection pads were way beyond anything I was ever involved with over the years. It had usually been one cameraman with a tripod, and one interviewer. I knew this was a very serious commitment with a specific game plan in mind. I was skeptical but committed to give them my best shot, hoping that Wolf Blitzer would be fair in his presentation.

I knew that he had three hours, a two hour segment from 4 to 6 PM EST, and then a 6 to 7 PM recap that my wife said went around the world. Considering the media did their normal slanted and biased reporting favoring McCain, our message was never clear. I took the chance because Wolf Blitzer seemed to be giving a balanced view of all the candidates.

Laura said after the interview was over that it would probably run in the first two-hour segment and then again after 6 PM. As it turns out, Laura said the 2.5 minute segment was too long to get it in on Friday and it would air on Monday.

One of Ron Paul's senior campaign staff members who was very friendly to us and our issue invited me to one of Mr. Paul's events in South Carolina. He called again a few days later and very apologetically explained that some of the other campaign staff thought I was too controversial a figure at that time.

Patty Hopper attended the event in my place, and she and Bill Dumas went over the campaign manager's head and spoke directly to Mr. Paul about what happened. Mr. Paul said that he would have been fine with me speaking and that they would welcome my participation in the future. I let them know that this wasn't about egos but about getting the job done. I committed my future services to them if it could help our cause and theirs.

1/20/08 (Sun) – Tom Burch called and wanted to know about my interview with CNN, why I thought it wasn't played on Friday, and why my appearance with Ron Paul was cancelled on Friday. I guess I can call that Black Friday as far as the end result of what could have been a great day.

After explaining what happened, Tom said that from what he and his people could assess, we did a great job with the flyer controversy over McCain's past. He believed McCain may have had a small sympathy vote and that it may have hurt him more than helped. He only won by 3% with a 33% total versus the 49% he received in 2000 when he ran against GW Bush in a two-man race. Even though this race was with multiple candidates, Tom thought that was very significant.

Tom said that the tapes of McCain's confessions were in the hands of a German TV station and that they had considered releasing it last Friday; however, they didn't have enough time to do it correctly. A friend told Tom that he had seen one of the tapes and that it was very damaging. It showed McCain as very serious when making his propaganda statements, then joking with his captors afterward with no apparent stress. It is to our advantage to have someone else release them independently to avoid immediate criticism that political "dirty tricks" were involved. The German delay was to verify that the source of the tapes was legitimate, and that there had not been tampering with the content.

Tom said he understood that they were considering releasing the tape the following day, which he thought was too early to suit our purposes. He thought the shelf-life of the media coverage would only be 72 hours. I disagreed with that assessment because I expected it to be used throughout the primary process in Florida on 1/29/08, and the 24 states on Super Tuesday 2/5/08, and even in the general election if he got the nomination.

Tom thought that McCain would not be the nominee, but we could use the tapes later to derail possible consideration of him as a VP running mate. The good news there is that the other two front runners for the nomination, Giuliani and Romney, both dislike McCain.

Perhaps the most important piece of information was that Ron Paul had visited President Bush to make sure he knew that the Vietnamese Communists were discussing the live Americans they held with our delegation of government officials.

I suspect that Mr. Paul assumed Bush knew, but he wanted Bush to know HE knew.

1/21/08 (Mon) – Wolf Blitzer aired my interview at 5 PM and my worst fears were realized; it was an obvious hatchet job against me. The only thing positive was their mentioning the POW issue as a cover-up, followed that with a statement that we have no proof, but then mentioned that Perot backs us up. They completely misrepresented the fact that there is no proof and probably included Perot thinking it would make him look bad more than it would make us look good.

1/24/08 – Unfortunately, some of the POW/MIA family members thought we were "disrespectful" of McCain, and thought—as I did, to be honest—that too much of the material Ted had used on the flyer and post card amounted to allegations and accusations that could not be proved, particularly about his behavior as a POW. What many of them didn't know was that for some of the things they were calling "unprovable," we already had multiple witnesses or documents. Nevertheless, we even heard from one lady who thought we had created sympathy for McCain that would do him more good than harm.

That is the problem for any complex issue, especially one with strong feelings on the side against you and large numbers of people who don't want to believe. It's necessary to present strong evidence, but there is rarely opportunity, especially on TV, to offer more than sound bites, which just aren't enough to change minds. Presenting a complex case in print is effective, but only with those who have an open mind. Most of the response one sees to such material is ad hominem, out-of-context, or otherwise unjustified attacks on minor points or counterclaims for which there is no evidence.

Telling an uncomfortable truth to a public that has been conditioned to believe a more comfortable lie is a huge challenge. I was able to brush off the criticisms that were coming from McCain supporters, but the complaints and criticisms coming from POW/MIA family members hit me hard. It was the lowest point in my 25 years of dedication to the POW cause, including the twenty hours I spent in a federal jail cell two and a half years earlier.

2/5/08 – Super Tuesday was a windfall for McCain in the twenty-plus Republican primary states. He has all but locked up the nomination.

2/7/08 – Romney suspended his campaign at the Conservative PAC convention; however, Huckabee and Ron Paul are remaining in the race.

2/9/08 – Huckabee took two of the three states today from McCain. Even though it appears impossible to stop McCain, this was a bit of an upset.

Ted called me the night before saying someone wanted to use our 527 Non-Political PAC against McCain to raise money for commercials. I received a call from Tyler Collier, who runs a political consulting firm in Texas.

He laid out a plan of action if we were interested where a coalition of conservative groups around the country would donate money to use in commercials against McCain. The first ones would be about amnesty and McCain's flip-flopping on many key conservative issues. He was thinking about one sixty-second and two thirty-second commercials that would play on TV, primarily in Texas and possibly Ohio.

Tyler said the person who was driving this plan is a director who owns his own company in Manhattan.

When I told him I lived an hour north of New York, he said that was great. He then said his friend would be able to start filming these commercials this coming Wednesday and would take him about a week or more to complete the commercials in time for the Texas and Ohio primaries, less than a month away.

When I asked him how much he expects to raise, he said a minimum of $30,000 and up to $500,000 wouldn't be out of the question. The plan is to air some commercials in Texas with the expectation that it would create a major reaction, resulting in more donations. Tyler is pricing the cost to blitz statewide Texas TV.

2/29/08 – We've raised about $3,000 and have purchased $1,800 in TV ads to run this week through the primary on 3/4/08. We're airing two ads, one made by Ted and the other by Tyler's friends.

3/4/08 – McCain won Texas and Ohio by very large margins and clinched the Republican Party nomination. Hillary won three of four states so her contest against Obama will be settled on the floor of the Democratic Party Convention in August. The 795 super delegates will decide that contest at that time. This helps McCain because Hillary went on the attack against Obama in order to win Texas and Ohio and Obama now has to counter that negative campaigning. McCain will sit back and watch the Democrats waste their money and then use all of the negative comments in the general election starting in early September.

We need to take this six-month opportunity from now until the Republican Convention in September to go after McCain.

3/5/08 – One of my friends, "Greasy" from Kentucky, sent me Carol Hrdlicka's write-up about one of the most famous stories of her husband's shoot down and capture. His picture as a live POW in the hands of the enemy is well known by anyone involved in the issue. I know Carol from many years ago. Probably the last time we met was when I asked Jane Duke Gaylor to chain her wheelchair to the White House fence. Carol wasn't one of the dirty dozen who joined Jane; however, she was there supporting us.

3/6/08 – Ted sent me Carol's email address and I sent her the following email:

Hi Carol, long time since we've seen each other. I would appreciate your sending me your phone number so we can talk or calling me any time after 5 PM EST on the weekdays or any time on the weekend.

We have been making some ads against McCain and in your case it would be an ad against our own government for abandoning our men. If you would be interested in telling the country and perhaps the world about your struggle, I would be thrilled to help you.

There are hundreds of stories that can be told; however, yours is not only compelling, you are the right person to tell it. As a registered 527 PAC we have raised thousands of dollars to date and plan on raising much more over the next six months before the Republican convention.

I would love to make Bush Sr, Bush Jr, and McCain squirm before and after the convention. Let me know if you are interested. This is a rare moment in time and a great opportunity to try and expose these traitors.

Forever loyal,
Jerry Kiley

3/7/08 – I called Carol and we spoke about the possibility of making ads since Ted now had the ability to edit tape to produce our own. I said we could have the family members make their own home tapes and send them to Ted concerning McCain's betrayal during the 1992 Senate hearings and his temper, including the pushing of family members when they confronted him about his destroying the Missing Persons Act bill. This bill would have required 24-hour notification of families when their loved ones were captured by the enemy. It also made the deliberate withholding of information from captives' families a criminal offense.

I also asked Carol if she would be willing to come to D.C. in June, on the government's dime, for the National Alliance of Families meeting so the family members could participate in a press conference exposing McCain. She immediately said she wanted to include Eleanor Apodaca, from Arizona, who she considered a very good speaker. I told Carol I wanted her to be in charge and that it would be her press conference. I explained that we would be there only as a support group to assist them.

I wasn't sure if Carol had lost her fire as many family members have due to years of frustration caused by the lies of their own government. After speaking to her for a couple of seconds I could tell it was the same feisty person who I knew and loved many years ago. That's why I made it very clear that I wanted her walking point for the family members.

3/12/08 – Carol called and directed me to read comments by the family members on YouTube where they posted McCain's berating of Delores.

3/14/08 – I met with a veteran friend close to GOP leadership, who revealed the following:

* The U.S. Under Secretary of Defense (the #2 Defense Department official) led the U.S. delegation in the talks with Vietnamese officials about the POWs they are still holding. There were three separate meetings with President Bush at the end of last year by Ron Paul, Rudy Giuliani, and Hillary Clinton to say that he needs to resolve the POW issue after they learned of the delegation and the substance of the talks.

* Bill Clinton has the Defense Intelligence Agency POW file that McCain had buried during the Clinton presidency. If Hillary is the nominee, she may use it against him after the Republican convention.

* McCain is receiving a psychotropic medication prescribed by the Senate physician; it will not be mentioned in the medical records McCain's people will release next month.

* Another "connected" veteran friend was invited by his boss to attend a fundraiser for Hillary and met her in the receiving line. After finding out that he was a Vietnam veteran, she expressed interest in speaking with him later. Hillary actually found him sitting at a table and sat down with him for a one-on-one conversation. He explained one of the most important issues for veterans was the POW issue and that Bill had hurt the issue when he normalized relations with Vietnam in the mid-90s. She claimed not to know about the POWs at that time.

There were three Congressmen along with several people who surrounded their table listening to the conversation. One of the Congressmen said that it was obvious coming off the Senate hearings by Kerry in 1992 that the POW issue was never resolved, and got several head nods from around the table.

* Former Congressman Bill Hendon was starting a 527 PAC and would receive financial support from Paul Weyrich (former Stanton Group leader, a coalition of conservative groups) and Ross Perot. I had told Bill how he could start a 527 of his own in our long phone conversation when he called me a month ago.

* The *Washington Post* was going to run a story about McCain's temper, and *The New York Times* is working on another story that involves former U.S. Senator Dennis DeConcini, which probably meant it would mention the Keating Five Scandal that McCain was involved in.

* We had friends with good connections to Hillary's campaign, but we need to connect with Obama's.

I called Tom Burch and mentioned the possibility of getting Carol Hrdlicka and several other family members to do a press conference the week of the National Alliance meeting in June. Tom loved the idea and immediately committed $500 to pay for the Press Club room which is the best place to stage that kind of event, since much of the D.C. media are in that building. After telling me how much he liked this event and explaining that it would be a great set-up for their endorsement of a Presidential candidate, Tom increased his commitment to $1,000 and made it clear he could handle more if necessary. I told him I'd like Senator Bob Smith or former Congressman John LeBoutillier to join the family members.

3/15/08 Saturday – I spoke to Carol when I returned from D.C. and told her the good news that Tom Burch had committed $1,000 to their press conference. Carol was happy to hear about that support; however, she was concerned about contacting the niece of Jane Duke Gaylor because the *Washington Post* needed her verification concerning McCain pushing Jane's wheel chair aside in the Congressional hallway. The niece was getting cold feet and was concerned about retribution by McCain. After *The New York Times* got burned for not having solid information when they insinuated that McCain had a romantic involvement with a female lobbyist, the *Post* is not running anything negative about McCain unless they can verify everything.

I spoke to John Nevin that night and he suggested using Jessie Jackson as a possible point of contact to arrange a meeting with Obama, Burch, Molloy, and Muller. John remembered my friendly encounter with Jackson in Getty Square in Yonkers when he ran for President back in the '80s, and the fact that Jackson liked to intervene when he could to get prisoners and hostages released.

Carol Hrdlicka said a former JCRC crash site investigator working for the USG has now come forward to tell her that he was involved in the shredding of David Hrdlicka's documents in Bangkok, Thailand, back in the early '90s. He was told that there were back-up documents in the government files, as revealed during the '92 Senate POW hearings. This is a potential bombshell. He also said that there are still fifty to sixty American POWs alive in Laos.

4/23/08 – I contacted the National Press Club to arrange a room for the family members' press conference against McCain during the National Alliance of Families annual meeting. I selected that time frame because the families are flown in by military transport at the government's expense. Tom Burch committed $1,000 for this event. The smaller room for forty people will cost $450 and the remaining money can be used for hotel and other expenses.

When I told Ted that I was suggesting either "Truth Squad of POW/MIA Families" or "POW/MIA Family Truth Squad" as the press conference organization, he protested by saying that we should put it under our name VVAJM. I said we were damaged goods, and Ted said I was backing off, implying that I had lost my commitment or focus. I said that my goal was to get McCain's "Truth Squad," led by former POW Orson Swindle, who attacked us in North Carolina to attack POW/MIA family members, which would automatically substantiate the earlier examples we had recounted of McCain doing exactly that.

Ted insisted that I was wrong and that by the time we had the press conference in mid-June the VVAJM organization would have more credibility than it has right now, leading me to believe that he wasn't telling me everything he knew. I said even if that were true, I would still want the family members to take the lead at that time. I consulted with Tom Burch and John Nevin and they absolutely agreed with me.

Carol liked using "Truth Squad" in the organization name to play off of the name McCain had given to his group that was trying to counter some of our claims. She said she would let me know the name she and the other family members agreed upon. I found that we could get space at the Press Club on Wednesday afternoon instead of Friday morning, which would be better because it would play in the media on Thursday rather than Friday or Saturday, days which get less attention.

4/26/08 – I sent John LeBoutillier and Bill Bell emails to check out the person Carol wanted to fly in from Australia.

5/20/08 – Today I saw a picture of McCain in *The New York Times* greeting people the day before at the Chicago Board of Trade. What stood out in the picture was the person in front of him staring into the crowd. He is the Secret Service agent who spotted me prior to my entry into the Asian Society building for the luncheon honoring President Triet. Now he's protecting McCain. I have no idea what this all meant.

5/27/08 – John LeBoutillier sent me an email stating that he was pulling out as the emcee of the press conference on June 18th because of the participation of Artie Mueller, the president of Rolling Thunder, who had given President Bush one of their leather vests when they met in the White House.

Later in the week, Carol Hrdlicka asked me if she should ask Al Santoli to join us and I said definitely. Al accepted enthusiastically, stating that he wanted to expose the fact that McCain has not helped veterans. He recently voted against Jim Weber's veterans benefit bill; however, Obama and seventy-plus Senators passed it. Carol also told me that Mike Benge is going to join the press conference. He is going to say that McCain not only sealed his own file, but that he made it impossible for the other POWs to get their own files.

6/2/08 – At the last minute, Tom Burch confirmed with the Maryland District Attorney that I would not have to appear the following morning in court for disturbing the peace at the Winter Soldiers meeting last March where I had created a disturbance in support of our troops abroad. What I disrupted was an anti-war protest with which I largely agreed, but I didn't want opposition to the war to cause the same poor treatment for today's troops that Vietnam vets had experienced when we came home.

6/3/08 - Tom represented me when the DA recommended to the judge that this case be *nolle prossed*, meaning the charges would not be pursued, on the condition that I not enter the college property again for another Winter Soldier meeting in Montgomery County. This implied to me that the prosecutor largely agreed with my actions, since the conditions were almost entirely irrelevant. No one thought the Winter Soldiers intended further meeting in that county, much less at that college.

This would have cost me at least $1,500 to $2,000 if I had to pay a lawyer's fee. I'm five-for-five on arrests with no convictions. I think I'm going to stop while I'm ahead.

Barack Obama clinched the presumptive Democratic Party nomination that became official at their convention in August. Obama and McCain were already going after each other.

McCain gave a horrible speech and appeared stiff and scripted while reading from a teleprompter. It was without a doubt the worst delivery of a speech I have ever seen a presidential nominee give. He took a small group of enthusiastic supporters and silenced them with an unemotional speech. I loved it, even though his sarcasm and odd facial expressions scared me a little, foreboding what I and my friends might be in for if he won.

6/9/08 – I received a call from a "Barbara" who said that she had an affair with McCain in 1976 while he was married to his first wife Carol, who had been crippled in a car accident while he was a POW in Vietnam. She said she first met McCain when she was assigned to him in November 1975, and soon struck up an affair which continued until March of 1976, when he had her assigned to Air Traffic Controller training. She felt as though she had been "sent away," and immediately thought of her competition, Cindy, when she got her orders. She had seen Cindy in McCain's office multiple times and was sure they "had something going."

The significance of this is that McCain claimed—in response to charges that he had a long term affair with Cindy while he was still married to his wife Carol—that he and Cindy had not met until 1979. (He married Cindy one month after his divorce from wheelchair-bound Carol was final.) Barbara said, "So many people knew about Cindy. I don't know how they got away with their revised date of meeting."

If Barbara's story is true, she would have some credibility from having been an official in McCain's campaign and from serving in the Bush campaign after McCain dropped out. At least she wasn't a Democrat trying to hurt a Republican candidate. She said she had spoken to a local NBC affiliate and to Associated Press but both apparently decided not to publish.

She has no eye-witness or correspondence to corroborate her claims, but she says she can describe scars on his body which he claimed were a result of torture. Barbara said he would make general references concerning his alleged torture but never talk about the details.

I asked if she was still willing to talk to the media again and she said yes. I told her she needed to realize that McCain would come after her by calling her every name in the book, and they have opposition research people who can be put on the job of identifying every possible questionable thing in her past. She said she needed to think about it and asked me not to do anything yet. I really hated to discourage her, but I thought I owed it to her to let her know what she would be in for. I told her she would have to be the one to take the next step, but if she did, I would be there to help her all I could.

I asked her if she thought his temper was a problem related to having his finger on nuclear trigger if he were elected, and she said that wasn't the problem. She said he would make a bad President because he had a bad mouth. He had trouble getting and keeping respect from the people who work for him because he had a very nasty, belittling way of dressing people down in front of others.

She said that when she was with him in '75-'76, he talked often about wanting to be President. She said she loved McCain and had a crush on him until she was told by a military visitor at her home that McCain was marrying Cindy. I asked if she thought that was an act of intimidation and she said no at first, hesitated, and then said it was a possibility.

She never got in touch with me again, and I never attempted to contact her or to do anything with her story. Maybe we could have been more successful if we'd been more heartless, willing to make a point at anyone's expense. I thought Barbara was very believable and sincere. I couldn't consider putting her in a vulnerable situation unless she understood what she was up against and was willing to pay the price. It's one example of why I never considered a life in politics: it's too dirty.

6/18/08 – National Press Club Press Conference, Washington, D.C., - After all the problems Carol Hrdlicka and I faced with John LeBoutillier dropping out as spokesperson for the press conference and Eleanor Apodaca almost not showing up due to her daughter's illness, we had a successful event. Al Santoli, disabled veteran and former Congressional aide who wrote part of the Missing Persons Act of 1996, was our spokesperson. He did an excellent job, along with Carol, Eleanor, and former POW Mike Benge.

6/22/08 – I broke down the 56-minute press conference into five segments and posted each to the VVAJM website.

6/26/08 – I put together our first of seven YouTube videos that will be released one at a time over the next few weeks. The first is on McCain's emotional instability, followed by one on his not supporting or even opposing veterans' issues. A third is about his efforts—some successful, some not—to bury the POW files. The last four will be separate videos for each presenter at our press conference.

10/8/08 – I gave a one-hour audio interview with Rider College to be used on their local radio station. Even though I wasn't able to hit every talking point, I did manage to get these across:

* Election is about his temperament, lack of character, dishonesty, and emotional instability

* He is Vietnam's best friend, a regime that tortures and kills its own people for their religious beliefs; monitors the internet for the words like freedom and democracy;

* He was a key figure in normalizing relations with Vietnam in 1995, opening the door for loans and trade, culminating in World Trading Organization status in 2007;

* He reluctantly followed in his father's and grandfather's footsteps, both of whom were Navy Admirals;

* He was given a very questionable appointment to Annapolis Naval Academy where he set the record for demerits and placed fifth from the bottom of his graduating class of 800;

* He got a very questionable flight school placement, crashed four planes in his career, and was involved in a fifth accident on the deck of the USS Forrestal;

* The last of his four crashes was in October 1967 over Hanoi, where he admits to ignoring his radar so he could "drop his load";

* On his fourth day of captivity, he gave the enemy military information for the promise of better medical treatment (a treasonous act according to our Constitution);

* He admits in his book that he got better medical treatment than the other POWs and claims he feels guilty about it;

* He received 28 medals for twenty hours of flight time, almost one and a half per hour;

* He recorded several "confessions" that were played over Hanoi radio and in the POW camps; ·

* We know that almost anyone can be broken under the right conditions, but McCain was one of only a handful to make recorded "confessions" and propaganda statements. I said that Jane Fonda's betrayal of the American POWs when she turned over their notes to her to the Communist captors during her visit to Hanoi, was one of the worst imaginable acts, then corrected myself by saying that the betrayal of one POW of another was far worse than what Fonda did; it is the more despicable by far.

* In June of 1969, the *New York Daily News* reported that a "Song Bird" was giving the enemy propaganda tapes, and it became common knowledge in the Pentagon that the offender was John McCain. That is said to be why McCain didn't receive his normal promotion while in captivity as the other POWs did, and wasn't promoted until after President Carter took office in 1977;

* While it is true that McCain turned down an early release, so did many others, as they were ordered to do. McCain's Senior Ranking Officer (SRO) Ted Guy, whom I met with on two occasions, said the POWs were to be released in the chronological order in which they had been captured, and accepting early release out of order would result in court martial when they came home;

* Phil Butler went to the Naval Academy with McCain and he also knew him as a POW; he said no one from their camp was tortured after Ho Chi Minh died in September 1969, prior to the last three and a half years of McCain's five and a half years as a POW; Butler also said he could never see him as a Senator much less President of the US because he was crazy;

* Both of McCain's SROs (Col. Ted Guy & Swede Larson) substantiate Butler's claim that no one from their camp was tortured; Ted Guy told me personally that McCain was also missing from camp for long periods of time with no explanation;

* When McCain was released in March 1973, the US mainstream media created the myth that McCain was a great hero; they now apparently feel obligated to perpetuate that myth or risk exposing their own lies. The best example is the late Tim Russert (world renowned for his penetrating interviews) who said on his "Meet The Press" show that McCain spent five and a half years in a black box with his hands tied behind his back; McCain then dishonestly used that in one of his TV commercials during the South Carolina primary this past summer, knowing that it was an absolute lie;

The dislike and disdain the POW/MIA families and activists developed for McCain wasn't because of the myth he helped to create concerning his time in Vietnam, but there's no denying that the phony "war hero" image gave him authority in the minds of many people. He earned his poor reputation among the families and vets most tuned in to the Vietnam POW/MIA issue by supporting every piece of legislation that benefited Vietnam and opposing every government move that could have aided POWs still alive in Southeast Asia.

McCain became an obstructionist and our worst nightmare; the former POW war hero called us every name in the book while claiming we were motivated by financial gain, which would be funny if it weren't so infuriating, given the thousands of dollars many of us spent out of our own pockets trying to get the U.S. government to do its job.

McCain's unstable and seemingly irrational behavior includes warmly greeting, hugging, and laughing with Bui Tin, one of the camp guards where he was held, who had a special reputation for brutality.

In the same time, in a Senate hearing, he cruelly berated Delores Alfond, whose brother was shot down and never returned. In 1996, he pushed the wheelchair of Jane Duke Gaylor, and shoved Jane's niece against the wall in the Senate hallway, all because they were gathered with several other family members to encourage McCain not to oppose the Missing Service Personnel Act. (He subsequently managed to attach an amendment to the Act which gutted the provision that would have made any cover-up of POW/MIA information a crime.)

Why would McCain shun the family members and align himself with the people he claims tortured him? Bill Bell (an official in the Defense Department's Hanoi missing personnel office) said he has personally seen film of POWs surreptitiously taken in their normal camp environment, suggesting that any questionable behavior behind the scenes would have likely been recorded. The Vietnamese were intelligent, shrewd, and well-trained by the KGB and by Cuban advisors, and may well have a clear record of any embarrassing indiscretions that could later be used to apply pressure to subject. People who know the real McCain certainly have reason to wonder why his behavior has been so out of character for the person he pretends to be.

10/14/08 – McCain/Palin conducted a fund raiser at the Grand Hyatt Hotel (Grand Central Station). I spoke to John Nevin and decided not to go. This was the same hotel where I disrupted the Chamber of Commerce meeting to promote business investments in Vietnam. At this point in the presidential race, only three weeks until the election, even if I were successful, the media would either ignore me as they did in 1988 (see below) or McCain's people would turn it around and use it to demonstrate the insult to one of the greatest war heroes of our time. Also, the Hyatt is a difficult place to maneuver through because of the way it is set up.

10/16/08 – The Alfred E. Smith fundraising dinner at the Waldorf Astoria hotel was hosted by Cardinal Egan and highlighted by the appearance of the presidential candidates, Obama and McCain. This was the scene of my first Stealth Activist episode in 1988. I decided not to go for the same reason mentioned above; however, this one was tempting because the Waldorf has many nooks and crannies where my chances to succeed were much better than the Hyatt. My overall chances would have been greatly diminished because the Secret Service has my dossier and picture and would be looking for me.

11/4/08 – Obama won the Presidential election in a landslide electorally (365 to 173) and by a substantial 6% difference in the popular vote (53% to 47%).

11/5/08 – I received a call from a "connected" veteran friend who said he had been told by a source he considered reliable (at least he thought the source believed what he was saying) that a number of Vietnam POWs had been secretly returned to the U.S. over the years and were anonymously put in the federal witness protection program. The rationale and explanation was that an agreement had been made with the Vietnamese not to publicize the fact that POWs were held after the war, and if that promise were broken it would undermine further planned releases.

This would conflict with much of what we were being told by contacts in Vietnam about the level and content of discussion about the subject of U.S. POWs there. What made it most suspicious is that this is exactly the kind of story people in our government might make up to convince us that they were doing the best that they could and that it was paying dividends.

If these alleged returnees existed, they hadn't been allowed to make contact with their families or friends, or let it be known publicly that others remained behind. It's pretty hard to believe that a very high percentage of these people would agree to such an arrangement. What would they do with anyone who didn't… execute them? Our best guess was that it was an elaborate hoax by U.S. government officials to get us to back off.

11/15/08 – My Vietnamese friend Ban called to tell me that there had been a coup in Vietnam involving two Vietnamese generals four days earlier. There was flooding around Saigon and Hanoi and these generals used that as an excuse to mobilize their vehicles to assist the victims. Using that as their cover, they tried to rescue four POWs in the Hanoi area, one of which was confirmed to be an American intelligence officer. They wanted to present them to the world community in order to embarrass the hardline Communist faction that prefers pursuing improved relations with China rather than with the U.S. Ban said he understood that the two generals had been killed, but he wasn't sure.

This sounded as though one of our important contacts in Vietnam could have been directly involved since a big part of his rationale for working with us was allegedly to see Vietnam pursue future good relations with the U.S. rather than with China.

11/23/08 – I spoke to a friend who might be able to confirm or refute the report from Ban. This friend said, very causally, that the POW issue had been discussed within Obama's transition team, but they had no idea how to handle it. It wasn't known whether anyone had been tasked to gather information and/or figure out their best course.

11/24/08 – John Nevin and I spoke about how the issue of POWs in the witness protection program could be used very effectively by USG officials to convince President-elect Obama and others that by changing this program we would jeopardize those remaining in Vietnam. We didn't believe the story was true, but it was easy to see how it could be used as a tool to encourage Obama's people to keep "hands off." However, even if it were true, our efforts to get the rest of the living POWs out of Vietnam through semi-private channels would eliminate the rationale for continuing secrecy and free any witness program POWs to return to their families.

11/26/08 – Spoke to John LeBoutillier about my plans for next June. I explained the strategy involving Carol Hrdlicka's son, who we could correlate with the President. Obama's father had abandoned him, and our government had abandoned Hrdlicka. In essence, both young men had to grow up without a father, and now Obama was continuing the abandonment. John liked the theme, but he did ask were we trying to influence Obama or piss him off. I said if he has not addressed the issue or at least met with the family members, then I was going to make sure we got his attention by making it personal. John said okay.

12/15/08 – We initiated an e-mail and phone call campaign to Obama's transition team in support of a good friend of our issue to encourage his appointment to one of two possible Administration positions. I contacted Ban to ask him to get the word out in the Vietnamese-American community that a good friend needed support, asking them to call or e-mail. He said he had direct contact with 5,200 families and would reach out to all of them.

12/28/08 – Sunday – We heard that there had been over 20,000 calls and e-mails made on our friend's behalf, which was considered an unusually large number for such a subject. I called Ban to tell him the news and asked him to send out another request for calls and e-mails.

Chapter Fourteen
Miscellaneous

1/30/09 - Friday – I received a call from Ken Robinson, the attorney who won my federal trial back in 2005, requesting my presence today in Washington, D.C., to give a statement concerning his $20,000 fee to handle my case. Apparently, he placed the money in the wrong account and the DA is looking to take his license to practice law. I have no relevant information to offer except to say that the $20k was a flat-fee we agreed upon, no matter whether we settled or went to trial.

He offered to pay my expenses and salary for a day-trip to Washington, but I told him to pay only my expenses because I could take a vacation day and not lose any money. I told him that even though he was paid for his service as my lawyer, he did me a big favor to take the case for only $20k.

I distinctly remember him telling me that he owed it to his best friend, who died in Vietnam, to defend me. On several occasions, he told me that he made many visits to the Vietnam Veteran Memorial ("The Wall") to talk to his friend. He told me of the guilt he felt that his friend had died while he remained safely at home with a deferment. It's strange to hear someone who was never in the war talk about his survivor's guilt. Similar guilt haunts many combat veterans whose friends died in front of them.

Every time Ken mentioned his visits to The Wall, his eyes would well-up. When I mentioned honoring his friend, he got a lump in his throat and could hardly talk.

I met with Ken's attorney, Jacob Stein, to review the facts concerning the signed agreement and payments made by my legal defense fund. It turns out that Ken had his assistant sign and send a letter to Quyen Le, with a copy to me, without his review. The letter incorrectly said that Ken was charging his usual hourly fee of $500, which would have made the $20,000 we paid him a retainer that must be placed in an escrow account. When I received the letter, I immediately called Quyen Le to confirm that we were being charged a flat fee of $20k and not being billed by the hour. Quyen Le confirmed that and said he would contact Ken and straighten it out.

Since our agreement was for a flat fee of $20,000, no escrow account was necessary, so Ken deposited the money directly into his personal account. The person leading the witch hunt is someone he worked with in the seventies who resents Ken because of his success in the private sector.

Ken also told me that he had made an actual error by drawing $5,000 out of his escrow account, thinking that our $20,000 had been put there. This raised a red flag at the bank—withdrawals from escrow have to be documented—and could give the appearance that my money should have gone into the escrow account. Ken admitted to making this mistake, and said he could accept being censured for it with a slap on the wrist and a warning, but that he would not accept anything more serious without a fight because the error was an honest mistake with no harm done to anybody.

Mr. Stein (he told me to call him Jacob) asked me all about the wine tossing incident with Prime Minister Khai and got a kick out of hearing about my planning it days in advance. As usual, everybody laughed when I recounted my complaining to the irate security guard that my $1,000 plate of chicken was overcooked.

In the middle of our conversation about Ken's situation, Jacob stopped, looked at me, and asked, "Where do you get the courage to do that stuff?" He succeeded in surprising me.

I paused to gather my thoughts and said, "I don't know, I've been at this for 25 years, but growing up in the Bronx probably didn't hurt."

We engaged in a conversation after Jacob asked why Vietnam would keep our men all these years. I told him that President Nixon had sent Henry Kissinger to Paris in January 1973 with a letter which promised the Vietnamese $4 billion in "postwar reconstruction aid." This was to meet the North Vietnamese demand for signing the Paris Peace Accords, which formally ended our involvement in combat in Vietnam. Of course, the Vietnamese didn't take it on faith that the U.S. would pay the promised money, so they held hostages to ensure payment.

They had witnessed incidents during the war in which several of our personnel were placed at great risk, sometimes resulting in multiple casualties, in attempts to rescue one downed American pilot, so they knew the high value our military placed on their comrades. They thought, incorrectly as it turned out, that holding back half of the prisoners would force the U.S. to pay as the French had paid to get their prisoners out after Dien Bien Phu.

They were still trying to get the money at least as late as 1981, when they offered to return an unspecified number of POWs for cash.

I told him that our best information indicated that a substantial number of POWs were still alive, despite their advancing ages, and were being treated reasonably well. There was a "reform" group in Vietnam of people who'd been too young to have been affected by the war and therefore held little resentment related to it who favored improved relations with the U.S. This group was arguing for their release. Opposing them was a faction of hardliners who thought that releasing them held great potential risk and offered little hope of gain.

Jacob, who is 84, talked about his friend "the Colonel" who he jogs with every day. The colonel had told him that during the Bush Presidency he had been close to Oliver North. North had asked him to visit Nicaragua without telling him what the mission was about, and as it turned out, the mission put him at great risk. He felt betrayed by North.

Before I left, Jacob gave me a book he put together and a DVD of a speech he had made at American College the previous year.

The meeting ended with Jacob telling me to take my prepared statement back home, make any changes, sign it, and then mail it back to him. He shook my hand and graciously said that he enjoyed meeting me, and I returned his comment in kind. I was impressed by his politeness and humility, even though I didn't know much about him at that time.

We went to lunch and Ken told me about Jacob Stein. It turns out that he was the defense counsel for one of the Watergate lawyers, Kenneth Parkinson, accused of conspiracy along with Erlichman, Halderman, and Mitchell. The lawyer he represented was the only one exonerated; the other three were convicted of conspiracy. Ken said that Jacob was one of the most respected lawyers in D.C. and a long-time friend who mentored Ken back in the '70s.

1/31/09 - I began writing a yearly review for a lady who was on my staff at work. She was a very good employee, and as I recounted her accomplishments during the year, I commented that this was a breakthrough year for her in personal growth primarily because she overcame her fear of speaking to a large group of people.

That started me thinking about where I had come over the last 25 years. My involvement in pressing veterans' issues had forced me to develop new skills, but more importantly, had put me in many positions that forced me to summon the courage to press on even when the skills that would seem to be required were lacking.

One example sticks in my mind because I very comfortably did something that in the early days of my adulthood would have terrified me. The event was a retirement dinner for the vice president of my company. Since I had known him for over thirty years, I immediately volunteered to say a few words at the dinner to "roast" the retiree, a long-held tradition. Even though I suspected that the president of the company would be there, I definitely didn't expect that the CEO and a senior VP of our parent company would attend.

The routine I did in front of these notables and about 100 other people was risky. I did a comparison of the retiree to Father Guido Sarducci of *Saturday Night Live* fame. If I didn't pull it off it could be embarrassing to a lot of people besides me. The upside is that the bigger risk, the bigger the potential reward. I was relaxed and confident; I didn't blow a single line. The persistent laughter made me think immediately of what the veteran's movement had done for ME.

As fate would have it, the chairman of our parent corporation followed my act and indirectly gave me a compliment by beginning his speech saying, "That's a tough act to follow."

The President of our company said a few words, and as soon as he finished he came directly to my table to say he had enjoyed my presentation and he was followed by one of the Senior VPs. I was on cloud nine. Looking back, the thing that amazed me most was how calm and in control I was in my delivery. What an amazing journey for the kid from the Bronx who started as a Clerk B union employee, the lowest title in my company.

2/24/09 - Tuesday – I called John Nevin to update him about the prospects for one of our veteran leaders to receive recommendation for a high-level appointment in the Veterans Administration from President Obama's transition team.

John and I knew he could become a critical cog in turning around VA's decades of inefficiency and neglect. We talked about the slow deterioration over the previous thirty years that had resulted from VA funding increases falling behind cost of living increases, followed by the need for more VA services that resulted from the large number of combat casualties. The delays in processing disability claims were starting to be mentioned occasionally in mainstream media, and we took that as a good sign.

I mentioned the surprise and disappointment I had felt seeing Presidents Reagan, Bush, and Bush—who'd talked a good game in favor of service personnel and veterans—failing to demand the VA get what it needed, and the irony that the Clinton Administration had made a breakthrough in formally recognizing the long-term damage of Agent Orange. Now maybe our friend could get in a position to help veterans with real action rather than politically-correct rhetoric.

The one thing we worried most about, if he even got the appointment, was that John McCain would be on hand during the confirmation hearings. There was no doubt about the animus McCain had for him.

3/23/09 - I was getting almost daily updates about reactions to our friend's file as it made its way through the various bureaucratic levels, and about the many thousands of phone calls and e-mails we had generated in support from around the country to the VA and White House. Everything continued to look positive, but I was trying to avoid becoming too confident, knowing that disappointment was a real possibility. In the end, it wasn't to be. Of course, we suspected that McCain may have played a role, but we never got any detail about why it got short-circuited after earlier looking like a near certainty.

5/10/09 Sunday – One of my best sources received a message from Vietnam. A VIP will be visiting the U.S. later in the year and wants to meet with us. A positive response was sent on our behalf, in which our urgent request for the names of the POWs being considered for release was repeated. Our last information indicated 50+ men under their jurisdiction, and the possibility that additional individuals held under "other authority" might be included.

Chapter Fifteen
Passing of a True Hero

5/12/09 – Sad news, Ted Sampley passed away after receiving a quadruple bypass at the Richmond, VA, hospital last week. I'll go to North Carolina for Ted's funeral. He was the most influential leader among the POW/MIA activists, and I think it's fair to say that without him, our movement would have been several steps back even from the tenuous position we were then in.

5/16/09 – I picked up Mike Benge, former POW, in Virginia, and we arrived in North Carolina early afternoon. We stayed at the home of Timmy Trip, a longtime friend and activist buddy of Ted's. That evening we all attended a dinner in Ted's honor giving us a chance to tell our Ted Sampley war stories.

Ted's mother, daughter, and son were there, along with all his friends, who were mostly veterans. I relived the story when Ted was arrested outside the hotel where Bush Senior was telling the POW/MIA family members to shut up and sit down when they interrupted his speech. Bush was running for reelection and had the gall to say he was doing everything possible on the POW issue.

Ted was arrested for protesting in the street rather than the sidewalk. The police placed him in a paddy wagon and left it unguarded. I told the 100 protesters to surround the paddy wagon and we began to shake it, yelling, "Free Ted!" He later yelled at me when we bailed him out of jail because he could not hear us and thought there was an earthquake with people panicking.

I told them how one of the detectives got in my face when I said, "You've made a big mistake."

In a very aggressive tone, he said, "What are you going to do about it?"

I said, "Leave him in jail." They all froze and just looked at me in disbelief until I said, "He's your problem now; we never wanted him."

I said I had a million stories to tell about Ted and Jerry's adventures, but we didn't have enough time to tell them all. I did recall our conversation every time we would get together to raise some hell. I would start off by saying, "I was arrested last time; it's your turn today."

Ted would look at me with that evil stare he had and say, "I distinctly remember I was arrested last time." If one of us was arrested, the other one would take care of any media interviews and bail out the perpetrator. I began to lose it emotionally when I said Ted was the one person I could always count on to cover my back.

What I didn't say was that Ted would be my first choice if I were in a foxhole surrounded by the enemy because I knew there would be a lot of dead bodies lying around before anyone laid a hand on me. We would always go out drinking after all of our events over the years and he would occasionally tell about his hit and run operations in Laos on VC camps. He did two tours in Vietnam as Army Special Forces and his weapon of choice was a knife. Nothing more needs to be said.

5/17/09 – As Mike Benge and I arrived at the Baptist Church for Ted's funeral service, there was heavy rain with thunder and lightning. It rained all day and into the night, a truly miserable day.

There were ten people who were scheduled to make remarks. Among them were former Congressman Bill Hendon, Tracy Usry (former Senate committee investigator), and two from the Vietnamese community who I had encouraged to speak. I volunteered to go second because I had planned on beginning with some humor to break the tension.

This newly-built church had digital TVs that we were told were often used during worship services. Behind the main stage was a huge screen that flashed about a hundred pictures of Ted. I was surprised to see myself in so many of them. I had even forgotten the context of some. Ted and I were behind what looked like bars in one, and Sharon reminded me that when we threw Frisbees onto the White House lawn they took us inside the gate and made us wait until the Secret Service agents could take down our names and ask us some questions. They released us as soon as they were through.

There were about 1,000 people in attendance. I began my talk by saying how honored and delighted Ted would be to see so many people who traveled from around the country to come here for him. I said we came not to mourn his loss but rather to celebrate his life. I then said having known Ted for 25 years I knew exactly what he would say at this moment, "I don't want no damn Yankee giving my eulogy."

I would answer him as I always did in the past, with a very heavy Brooklyn accent saying, "You talkin to me?" while I looked over the podium at his open casket and pointed to him, and then to me.

I said, "I guess you are all wondering why I would drive all the way from New York considering Ted would always call me a damn Yankee; it's because for the first time in 25 years I finally get the chance to say what I want, without being interrupted."

My final remarks were that Ted had found religion late in life and a peace I had never seen before. Even though many people didn't know that he was very artistic, his greatest works of art were sitting in front of us, his son and daughter. As I started to talk about his son Lane, who literally grew up in front of us over the years, I began to lose it emotionally.

I ended by saying that every time you see a POW/MIA flag, think of Ted. He played a major role in making the public aware that our live POWs were left behind.

A couple with young children approached me, asking if I was Jerry Kiley. When I responded the woman said, "My father is Tom Ashworth, and he speaks about you all the time. After seeing you today, I understand why he has so much respect for you."

I said, "Your father is the salt of the earth, and one of the finest people I have ever met."

Tom Ashworth grew up in a small country town in Arkansas where honesty, loyalty, perseverance, and strong family ties were premium values. He earned Bachelor's and Master's degrees in economics and political science, joined the Marine Corps, and was admitted to Officer Candidate School. Following OCS, he received pilot training and became a helicopter pilot in Vietnam.

Tom has done some of the most important original research in the National Archives on the history of the POW issue, primarily through formerly classified documents and sometimes documents that should have been classified but were overlooked in the process. His work revealed that the United States has a long and consistent history of leaving POWs in enemy hands after armed conflict, going back at least as far as Operation Archangel in northern Russia in 1919.

These include at least several thousand taken from German POW camps by Soviet troops as they moved west near the end of WWII. They were taken to the Soviet Union and used for purposes about which we have little solid information, but speculation runs the gamut from teaching technical aspects of U.S. military hardware and tactics to simply becoming a part of the Soviet slave-labor economy.

At least 944 were left in North Korea following that conflict, and apparently about 500 following the Vietnam War, including those held in Laos and a small number in China.

Tom has testified several times before Congressional committees, done hundreds of radio and television shows, and been an honored guest speaker at dozens of veterans' events. Tom's most important quality as a historian is his near-obsession with never being wrong in any statement of fact. All writers and speakers let their own opinions slip into their presentations, but few are as careful as Tom to avoid letting opinions appear to be claimed as fact.

Tom Ashworth has uncovered much of the unfortunate history of the U.S. handling of the problem of leaving prisoners in enemy hands.

5/18/09 Burial at 3 PM in Wilmington, NC – This was the most difficult situation, especially for the family. Ted's mother said she would rather be dead than to see her son die.

One of the stories I didn't talk about was Ted's complete turn-around in the last few years of his life. He went from drinking, staying up all hours of the night, and cursing a blue streak to become a person who didn't hang out, didn't curse, and went to sleep early. I challenged him one day when he called me a damn Yankee, saying that some people consider damn to be a curse word.

He agreed and said it was a curse word but he wasn't cursing. I knew Ted was setting me up; however, I took the bait and asked why it wasn't a curse word when he used it. Ted asked, "Didn't you ever hear up in Yankee land about the play on Broadway called 'Damn Yankees'?" I said yes. He looked me with a twinkle in the eyes and said, "I'm very fond of that play, and I'm just quoting its title, you 'Damn Yankee'."

On my ride to North Carolina and back, Mike Benge talked extensively about his service in Vietnam during the war. He was captured when he returned to the local village to warn them to evacuate the villagers because the VC was coming. Mike was in captivity for over five years until he was released in 1973 with 590 other POWs. He spent time in the black box, one of the most devastating forms of torture. Because he was a civilian, the Vietnamese considered him a spy and treated him more harshly than many others.

Unlike most of the returning POWs, Mike stayed true to his cause of exposing the brutality of the Vietnamese government and the U.S. government's failure to bring all the POWs home, but it was more than that. If it couldn't be done, he could have forgiven mere failure. But refusing to make a serious effort and telling the myriad of lies over the years to cover-up the fact of their existence earned Mike's deepest resentment. However, unlike many of us, Mike has never let his emotional reaction to this tragedy affect his judgment about the best way to go forward.

5/23/09 & 5/24/09 Sat & Sun – I arrived in D.C. for Rolling Thunder weekend just before noontime and helped sell t-shirts at the booth where Ted would have been. This is their biggest fund raiser to pay for Ted's activities in the veteran movement, and several veterans' organizations he supported. Saturday was so busy that we sold out the next day by noon before the Rolling Thunder run.

Early Sunday morning, I went with Eric Cantu down to the Wall for his first visit to see the names of his seven friends who died in Vietnam. Ted had been encouraging Eric to visit the wall for the last ten years and made him promise to do it this year.

Several days before, Eric had tried to go to the Wall but could not do it. As we approached the entrance, his hand began to shake so much that I had to grab his cup of coffee that had spilled all over himself. We slowly walked through the path while he wept. I told him that the apex was a very special place where people felt a strong attachment to those they had lost.

When we arrived at the other end, he said he didn't want to go back through until later that day.

When I hugged him, he broke down in my arms and cried. I told him that would never go away no matter how many times he visits the Wall. I've been there at least a hundred times, and I shed a tear every time I visit. I told him early in the morning before the sun comes up is the best time to visit so you can be alone when you talk to your friends.

As the motorcycle run began in front of our booth in Thunder Alley, Ted's son Lane and daughter Wendy took Ted's wreath with his picture and stood in the middle of Constitution Avenue while the motor cycles thundered by in tribute to Ted's work as an advocate for all veterans. The ride was dedicated in his honor and was a fitting end for someone who created so much thunder and lightning in fighting for our men in Washington, D.C. He can never be replaced and will never be forgotten. There wasn't a dry eye looking on as Lane and Wendy saluted the riders.

5/25/09 – Tom Burch called and I updated him on the funeral and all the issues surrounding Ted and the financial mess he left behind because he didn't make out a will.

5/28/09 – I had lunch with an attorney friend and told him about my method of breaking the tension at the funeral. He said even he would not attempt that for fear of the consequences. Considering how confident he is about public speaking, I was surprised that he ruled out that kind of humor.

I know the funeral service of one of your best friends is not a situation to take lightly; however, there was never a doubt in my mind that I would figure out a way to lighten the atmosphere. I know Ted would have laughed his ass off while telling me how bad I am. I knew he would have wanted me there to help everyone through a difficult time, so I knew my mission and knew that I had to be on point.

Mike Benge gave a beautiful and appropriate eulogy for Ted at the annual meeting of National Alliance of Families, one of many organizations Ted was instrumental in getting off the ground, and for which he provided financial support over the years:

Ted Sampley
Someone wrote a song that could have been about Ted. Without success, I've tried finding the rest of the lyrics that included "he's a poet, a painter, a pirate…" Ted was that and a whole lot more. He was known to write a little prose once in a while and paint a few pictures. He was also a master potter, a farmer, a historian, and a traditional story teller, even though he may have wandered from the truth once in a while. You say Ted couldn't have been a pirate. Well, Jan Scruggs of the Vietnam Memorial thought so and sued Ted for pirating the image of the statue of the three

soldiers to put on T-shirts; an image in Ted's mind that belonged to everyone – especially the Vets and the families of the POW/MIAs.

Ted was a soldier, a Green Beret, a seasoned combat veteran, highly decorated after two tours in Vietnam, 10 years in the Army, and he was proud of it. He was an organizer who helped establish Rolling Thunder and the National Alliance of Families. He was a journalist and newspaper publisher dedicated to the plight of the POW-MIAs. And best of all, Ted was a thorn in the side of the Vietnamese, Lao and Cambodian Communists, Washington bureaucrats, DOD, DPMO and especially Senators McCain and Kerry who did what they could to bury the POW/MIA issue. In 2004, McCain called Ted "one of the most despicable people I have ever had the misfortune to encounter." Ted thought this was a badge of honor.

Ted was an activist with integrity and was a true believer in causes, not only that of the POW/MIAs, but the struggle for freedom, democracy, human rights and religious freedom in Vietnam, Laos and Cambodia, and against these brutal Communist dictatorships.

But most of all, Ted was a hero to the families of the POW/MIAs, veterans and others who believed POWs were left behind and that the bureaucrats weren't doing anything to bring them home nor were they honest in accounting for our missing servicemen.

I don't know how many times he got arrested, locked up, or just missed getting there, for he believed that unless the POW/MIA issue was kept in the news, the Washington bureaucrats would bury the issue. Often the police were sympathetic to the cause and would go through the motion of detaining him only to turn him loose a short time later. Ted wasn't out for personal recognition and realized the need to get the faces of others in the news on the issue, or soon the media would sour on him, so he often stood back and encouraged others to "talk the talk and walk the walk." Stealth man Jerry Kiley knows this well and shared a cell with Ted on one occasion, but most often, after planning with Ted, he set out on his own and got arrested anyway.

When Vietnam's vice-prime Minister Tran Duc Luong came to D.C., the first high-ranking Vietnamese Communist official to be allowed an official visit, Ted was demonstrating with a group of Vietnamese-Americans in Front of the Washington Hotel where the Communist officials were staying. Ted wanted to show the demonstrators an example of civil disobedience. The police kept them on the other side of the street when suddenly Ted jumped the police cordon and rushed toward the Hotel while waving the big yellow flag of the Free Viet Nam. He was tackled by the Secret Service, but several Vietnamese-Americans, inspired by Ted, also broke through the cordon and rushed to his rescue, including a couple of petite ladies who stood between the secret service and Ted on the ground screaming, *"He's our friend, you arrest him, then arrest us!"*... *He was held in a police van for about half an hour and then released.*

He occasionally went back to Vietnam, Cambodia and Laos and was sometimes arrested for illegally crossing borders.

His mother, Dorothy Pate Smith, said to me, "Ted could be mischievous at times;" now that was an understatement. Here's some of his mischievousness:

Ted blocked National Security Council director Frank Carlucci's driveway with 1,800 boxes of "care packages" for MIAs and POWs who Sampley believed were still alive.

Ted chained himself to the White House fence and once delivered several bamboo cages filled with hunger strikers to the front lawn of White House chief of staff Donald Regan's house.

Ted was true to his beliefs and he had integrity. He was taught to fight to win and he won more than he lost.

Ted was set on righting wrongs and he successfully challenged the Pentagon on the identity of the "unknown soldier" in the Tomb of the Unknowns at Arlington National Cemetery. Using service records, maps and other documents, Sampley pieced together evidence that the unidentified serviceman was Air Force pilot Michael Blassie, who was shot in 1972. Reluctantly, the Pentagon confirmed Sampley's research through DNA analysis in 1998. The Tomb of the Unknown Soldier for the Vietnam War is now empty.

Ted was often blamed for things he didn't do, such as interrupting Senior President Bush's talk at the National League of Families by shouting "No more lies!" It couldn't have been Ted, for at that time the police had him bent over the hood of their car out front; it was a group of Alliance POW/MIA family members. Bush lost his cool and shouted, "Shut up and sit down!" And he also lost his reelection.

Ted was wrongly accused of making millions off the POW/MIA issue and selling T-shirts and Vietnam era memorabilia at the Last Firebase at the foot of the Lincoln Memorial, at Thunder Alley, and on his website. This couldn't be further from the truth, for Ted put all his money back into the movement for Veterans, POW/MIAs and the ordinary citizen. Ted died basically penniless because he put his money where his mouth was.

Ted's energy seemed boundless. Ted was also an entrepreneur and started and owned several small successful businesses in a rundown section of Kinston, NC, including a restaurant and a printing shop, but once they got going, he turned them over to someone else to run. Ted discovered the rotting hull of a Confederate warship, the CSS Neuse II, and organized an effort to build a replica of that ship. It now sits on a nearby lot that has become a tourist attraction. He was also instrumental in efforts to establish a museum of Confederate history. He helped champion the rebirth of downtown Kinston. In an article in his hometown newspaper, a city council member said, "Ted had one of the biggest hearts of anyone I have ever met;" "He would put up a very gruff exterior, but if anyone ever broke through it, he had a heart of gold."

Ted was loyal a man with passion, and the last few years of Ted's life were focused on being a father to his son Lane and revamping his religious faith.

The Rolling Thunder ride this year was in dedication to Ted and all he has meant to the POW issue and all veteran's issues.

Jerry Kiley, the one-time cellmate of Ted, said that Ted was admired, and thought of as the leader of the POW/MIA activists by those that were most aggressive. As others have said, we lost a great man, a fighter. He was described as today's "Brave Heart" and a true representative of the Spirit of America. He gave no quarter, made a few enemies, but had a hell of a lot more friends and admirers. He fought for his country, he fought for his missing comrades in arms and he fought for his life until the very end. We are all deeply saddened to lose such a great friend – it was the passing of a great American patriot. And when we see a POW/MIA flag flying, we'll think of Ted.

Ted was the prime mover, organizer and manager of "The Last Firebase." It was a "vigil" that was located between the Lincoln Memorial and the Vietnam Veterans' Memorial "Wall," manned 24/7/365 for almost a decade. The only time the booth wasn't open was during hurricanes or blizzards. The selling of POW related items helped raise the public awareness of our men left behind and provided essential financial support to POW/MIA activists and their activities around the country. Larry Bice, Margaret Nevin, Donna Long and many others help run that booth. Their efforts helped educate an apathetic public.

Ted had incredible energy and drive. The fact that he was self-employed gave him the time to work on special veterans' projects, most of which centered on the POW issue. He was an incredible person. His death left a definite void in a movement that now risks the same fate. I have a hollow feeling in the pit of my stomach knowing that I have to go it alone from now on, with no Sampley safety net to catch me if I fall.

Chapter Sixteen
White House Initiative

5/27/09 – I spoke to Carol Hrdlicka about going to D.C. the week of July 23rd for the National Alliance of Families meeting so we could either attend a meeting in the White House, or she could support me when I chained myself to the fence if the meeting didn't happen. I told her it was critical that both Carol and her son attend and she assured me that if I gave them enough notice, they would. Carol wanted me to do it sooner so I said that if I could I would.

I called Valerie Jarrett and followed up with an email requesting this meeting. Carol said that if we were to have a meeting we should suggest that Ross Perot be given the authority by the President to negotiate for the release of our men in Vietnam. Carol, who was close with Perot, said she would call Ross and ask him if he was willing.

6/14/09 – I sent Carol Hrdlicka the email requesting a meeting with the President. After speaking with John Nevin, I agreed that their chances are much greater than if I were to send it for them or even plan to attend with them. My name had the potential to set off alarm bells. Even though maximizing their chances was the right thing to do, I found it difficult because I felt that my experience at applying pressure in these situations would be a real advantage.

Carol sent the following email to someone named Matt, a White House communications officer, who'd responded to my initial attempt to make contact with Ms. Jarrett:

Matt, I would appreciate your sending this to Valerie Jarrett for her review and response.
Thanks,
Carol

Ms. Jarrett:
The President and Mrs. Obama have made a very strong commitment to those serving in the military and their families. In addition, they have made it clear that transparency and openness will be a hallmark of the Obama Administration.
One issue which has for three decades been anything but transparent is the fate of Vietnam War POWs who were known or thought to have been in captivity, but never came home. The families of these men have been depicted as hysterical, emotionally fragile, and unable to accept that their loved ones are dead. The fact is that we are rational, logical, and naturally

unwilling to accept that our government has failed to forcefully press the SRV for detailed information about our loved ones' fates.

We can discuss dozens of such cases in great detail, however; one of the most compelling cases involves my husband, David Hrdlicka, who was shot down on May 18, 1965. The photograph below has been confirmed to be David, taken after he was captured. Since Vietnam kept meticulous records of all their captured POWs, the question is, what happened to my husband and why has he not been returned to his family?

President Obama and my son David Hrdlicka, Jr. have something in common: they both grew up without their fathers. In the President's case, his father abandoned him; David's father was abandoned by the United States government. The President has an opportunity to bring this issue into the light of day.

My son and I would like to meet with the President the week of July 23ʳᵈ, 2009, during the National Alliance of Families yearly meeting to discuss this issue. We are not looking for a photo opportunity; we want to sit down and discuss the POW issue in a substantive way.

I would appreciate your letting me know what day the President might be available for such a meeting. Please respond either by email or you can call me at my home (Optional). Thank you for your consideration.

Sincerely,

Carol Hrdlicka

6/15/09 Monday - Carol sent this email on Monday and went outside to mow the lawn. When she came in, she found that Matt had already called her almost immediately after receiving her email.

I called John Nevin and then I conveyed to Carol our recommended strategy of keeping her comments to Matt positive and brief. She will simply say that she wants to talk about the possibilities with the President on how they can press the SRV on the live POW issue.

6/30/09 – Carol's son David sent the following email to try to arrange a meeting. Even though Matt, our White House contact, called Carol immediately after she sent her email, he failed to respond to numerous later emails and phone calls to his office. This is the last email we sent; I planned to try calling Valerie Jarrett the next week if there was no response to this:

Date: Tue, 30 Jun 2009 08:46:39 -0700

Matt: I understand my mother has contacted you for a meeting with the President and asked that you forward her letter to Valerie Jarrett. I am asking that you include my letter to Valerie Jarrett.

To: Valerie Jarrett

White House

I am the son of David L. Hrdlicka, captured in Laos on May 18, 1965. My father wasn't released from captivity. I served thirteen years in the United States Navy as a carrier pilot and I am presently a captain flying for American Airlines.

President Obama and I have some similarities in history. I also grew up in Kansas without a father and understand the hardship of making a path in life from disadvantaged childhood. The circumstances of my father's absence are the direct result of poor leadership of the United States government. He was shot down and captured in Laos while enforcing flawed policies of our leaders of the time. At the end of hostilities in the region, the captives in Laos were never negotiated for. Our unwillingness to admit or compensate the people of Laos for the pain and damage we inflicted on their country then resulted in the abandonment of some of the finest Americans this country had to offer.

I truly believe that as a direct result of the Obama presidency this country has regained the international credibility needed to address and resolve this issue. The OLD SCHOOL approach simply has not worked. This is a veteran's issue of the highest magnitude. The Laotian people deserve the recognition and apology long overdue to open the door to real progress on both sides of the ocean.

My mother and I request the opportunity to visit with President Obama regarding this issue without the intervention of organizations that claim to speak for us. I think now is the time to table fresh ideas and build a relationship with the people of Laos. My father was a good man and deserved more from the country he served so faithfully.

Sincerely,

David M. Hrdlicka

7/8/09 – Matt called David and left a message for him to call back. The irony was that the message addressed him as Captain David Hrdlicka, because that is his title as a commercial pilot; however, that was also the rank of his father when he was shot down in Vietnam. David was out of town but planned to call Matt when he returned from a three-day flight schedule.

8/5/09 – I spoke to Carol Hrdlicka and told her we have another opportunity to try to pressure the White House to meet with her in September on POW/MIA Recognition Day.

8/30/09 – We received word to expect a visit before the end of the year from a "friendly" in Vietnam who has the ear of some important members of the Vietnamese Politburo. We were asked what we thought of

President Obama and our planned response was that Obama didn't have any history or personal vulnerability on the POW issue.

We considered mentioning the recent release of two American journalists from North Korea after President Obama sent former President Clinton as his emissary. The most important fact to convey was that there was no retribution or recrimination against North Korea after their release. A public relations problem turned into a public relations success.

9/25/09 Friday – I participated in a rally in front of the UN, joining the Vietnamese community in protest of President Triet's speech. I spoke about human rights violations and the need for us to put pressure on the brutal Communist government.

I began my speech honoring Ted's dedication to the Vietnamese-American community with a moment of silence. Ted was always there in case we saw an opportunity to make our point. I still have many friends, but none who could cover my back like he would in a tense activist activity. I felt very lonely without him.

At the end of my speech, I challenged President Obama to use his good relationship with Vietnam to influence them to improve human rights and to release the imprisoned dissidents and American POWs. I said that I was willing to chain myself to the White House fence if necessary to make our point as I have with two other administrations. There was a seven minute SBTN YouTube video that showed most of my speech.

11/5/09 – The Yankees won their 27th World Series. I made one last futile effort to contact Valerie Jarrett through email; however, I do not expect any response of substance. I'm sure I will receive the customary response directing me to a web site to express my thoughts. After all this effort, it is extremely discouraging to see political considerations once again trump common sense, efficiency, and the best interest of veterans.

The change we hoped for with Obama cannot happen because, as I've known for the last decade, we can elect new representatives with good intentions but they are quickly undercut or corrupted by a system that cannot be changed.

In the last several months, I had been thinking more broadly about the current political situation. I was thinking that what was needed was a national movement among the many people who must have been thinking, as I was, that the most important thing that could clean up the mess was to break the strangle-hold special interests have over our elected officials.

12/31/09 Thursday – I called John Nevin to see what he thought about a third party as a vehicle to promote such a movement.

John said he didn't know whether a third party was the right approach, but liked the idea of reducing the power of money in politics as the rallying cry. If money is speech, as the courts have held, and if corporations are people, as the courts have also held, the First Amendment prevents any substantial reduction in the influence money can buy in our system. Success could only come after either or both of those court decisions were reversed. Spending money to voice an opinion at least makes more sense than "corporations are people," so the latter should be the centerpiece of the effort. There were VERY few individuals with the amount of money that the big corporations could spend to get their way, or just push things in their direction. Reversing "corporate personhood" would clear the way for placing statutory restrictions on corporations' participation in the electoral process.

He also said that a second change would be helpful, and VERY easy to sell if people only knew the current reality. Legal restrictions on candidates' use of campaign contributions are much too lenient. Candidates have broad discretion in how they can be used, and there are many loopholes (and even broader interpretations) that allow these funds to be used in ways that personally benefit the candidates and their families. One example that has gotten some public notice is the practice of hiring family members to "work" in campaigns in what is referred to in the organized crime world as "no-show jobs."

I asked him what he thought of the name "Revolutionary Party" and he said he thought it was too radical sounding, but there was one thing he said was appealing about it. The U.S. intelligence "Echelon" system used key words in electronic transmissions to red-flag conversations that should be assessed for potential domestic or foreign threat to the U.S. or the government. "Revolutionary" would certainly be one of those words and would drive Echelon monitors crazy if it became the name of a substantial political party, being used thousands of times every day.

If a third party wasn't feasible, and John didn't really think it was, we needed to explore other ways to approach these problems. We would work within the political system, as I had for the last 25 years, occasionally using peaceful civil disobedience if necessary to push a point.

5/5/10 – Since my feeble attempt to get Carol Hrdlicka into the White House, I began considering who would be best to represent our point of view.

I had no doubt that the President's thinking had already been corrupted by the same government individuals and agencies whose job it is to keep pushing the big lie.

I thought about the Secret Service agent, John Syphrit. If I could somehow arrange a meeting between him and the President, we might be able to generate some movement to an issue that has been nearly dead for years.

After speaking to John Nevin, he mentioned using Ross Perot as an intermediary to set the meeting up. I knew that Carol Hrdlicka spoke with

Perot on occasion; however, I needed to get the agent's approval to proceed with this idea.

After some back and forth communication, John Syphrit, despite being less than optimistic about its effect, said he would do as requested out of respect for us.

I called Carol Hrdlicka immediately and she said she would try to reach Perot. Sometimes Perot will call her back immediately, usually the same day.

5/16/10 – Bill Hendon called me to request my participation at a book signing of *Beyond the Killing Fields* by Sydney Schanberg, Pulitzer Prize-winning author of *The Killing Fields*, on the following day.

I attended with Bill, and as soon as they began the Q & A I stood up first and made a statement about the secret underground prison in Hanoi that DOD and the USG denied was there, claiming that the water level was too high. There were reports of multiple American POWs held there after the war. I asked Schanberg if he would join Bill Hendon and me in visiting that underground prison with McCain—who agreed with DIA that it didn't exist—and he said yes.

Schanberg spoke about the POW issue for about ten minutes.

Sydney inscribed his thanks for my support of the POWs in the new book Bill bought for me. When he was signing the book, I asked if he could help arrange a meeting between John Syphrit and President Obama. He gave me his card and I sent him the following email on 5/20/10:

Mr. Schanberg,

I was honored to finally meet you at your book signing last Monday and grateful for your inscription. As we discussed, I'm trying to arrange a meeting between President Obama and John Syphrit.

I met John Syphrit several years ago and was very impressed with his intelligence, professional appearance, and dedication to the issue as witnessed by his willingness to sacrifice the career he loved. John is ready, willing, and able to discuss the 1981 meeting and his subsequent treatment for his willingness to tell the truth in 1992. You probably know John was eventually moved to the Chicago office and then forced out of the Secret Service.

We know any POW information given to the President by DPMO or any other USG agency is corrupted and slanted. John is one person who can give the President first-hand information that is not corrupted. I believe, as you do, that the President is a good man if given a chance.

If there is anything you can do to help arrange a meeting between John and the President, I believe it might do more than anything else within our ability to move things in the right direction.

Please give me a call after 5 PM weekdays or anytime on the weekend if you need further information or have suggestions.
--Jerry Kiley

5/21/10 - Sydney called the next morning and spoke to my wife to ask for my work number. I spoke to him for about thirty minutes during my lunch time and he said the following:

· He interviewed John Syphrit in 1992 and was told about a new White House system that unintentionally taped the conversation in the Roosevelt room in the White House in early 1981. John decided not to use the tape held by a friendly at that time. That's when Sydney said he knows how to protect his sources and would not go out on a limb without corroboration. He said after Richard Allen recanted his testimony in 1992, he could not make a credible case on John's information.

· A couple of months ago, a Silicon Valley engineer contacted him after reading one of his POW articles and said he was interested in using that information to do an entire issue in *The American Conservative*, a conservative on-line magazine. That was scheduled to be released soon and should cause a stir considering McCain is in a heated Senate race for the Republican Party nomination in Arizona.

· He wanted to make a point that at age 76 he was still totally committed to the POW issue and would take off his pants in Macy's window if he had the right information. We both laughed and I said I'm happy that you still have that fire and commitment after all these years. He then said some very nice things about me for sticking to it in the face of so much adversity for so long.

5/21/10 – Carol called to say that Perot declined using his personal intervention to arrange a meeting with the President and suggested former POW and current congressman from Texas, Sam Johnson. She said for John to call Sam's people the next morning to arrange a call with him.

Over the next few days, there were calls going back and forth between Carol and me and Tom and John. Through it all, we established that John wasn't going to solicit a meeting with the President. He would attend if invited; however, John wasn't going through the normal protocol of trying to convince the Congressman and then three to four White House staffers. Promoting it himself would set entirely the wrong tone. I agreed.

I told Carol that Tom had confirmed through John that the Schanberg write-up on the 1981 meeting was accurate, so repeating that same information was unnecessary. I told her that I believed John had additional relevant information that was classified and he would not share it with anyone but the President.

Tom said that the Treasury Department could press charges against

John for revealing Top Secret information, even to a Congressman who had a top security clearance. That's why he was supposed to be subpoenaed in 1992 to testify before the Senate Select Committee on POW/MIA Affairs. John's only protection, other than speaking directly to the President, was that subpoena. The committee refused to subpoena him, apparently not wanting to put on the record what he had to say.

5/25/10 – Carol said that Sam Johnson is a Republican Congressman who does not have the pull to just get a meeting, he has to go through the normal White House protocol. I said that we should put this on hold for now because John clearly is not going down that path.

Two days later, Carol called me late at night to say Perot had reconsidered. He was going to see what he could do to set up the meeting. The first step was for Perot and Syphrit to meet.

I spoke to John Nevin and we speculated about what might have changed for Perot to become interested after passing the first time around.

5/28/10 - Tom returned my call from the 27th and said he would check with John Syphrit on how he would want to arrange this meeting with Perot. We all thought that Perot probably had the connections to get the meeting with the President.

John wanted Tom to attend if there was a meeting with the President in order to state what we wanted. Tom and John were strategizing that we could say we wanted the President's support for the current legislation, supported by a majority of Congressman, to open a new investigation into the POW issue.

I need to tell Tom that the chairman of the investigation needs to be someone we have absolute faith and confidence in (i.e., Ross Perot or Col. Peck), otherwise it will be a waste of time as we found out in 1992's Senate Select Committee. This would mean it would have to be a "Blue Ribbon" Presidential Commission reporting its findings only to the President.

5/29/10 – Bill Hendon called from Washington, D.C., on Memorial weekend and asked if I was coming down to D.C. because he and John LeBoutillier had hired a professional crew to make a Memorial Day film for YouTube. I told Billy that the only reason I would have gone to D.C. was to chain myself to the White House fence and that got a big laugh from him. He said he still wanted to include me at a later date to say a few words and I agreed.

Billy marched into C-SPAN's office to see the person in charge of booking. He believed someone was preventing the airing of a "Book TV" event the network had already taped of Schanberg's discussion of his new book, the one that Billy and I attended. He was refused access, which means they will not air the show.

6/3/10 – Tom called to tell me that Perot and Syphrit made contact and both were very satisfied with the outcome. Perot also spoke to Tom and asked why he would need to be at the meeting with the President and Tom said he is John's lawyer. Perot accepted that answer and gave Tom his cell number.

Perot said he was confident that he could get a meeting with the President, but suggested that Tom give a heads-up to the Chairman of the Joint Chiefs. I wasn't crazy about that idea, only because I've had so many reasons over the years to distrust almost anyone in an official position in D.C. However, Tom said there are good guys and bad guys in government positions and some of the good guys have been helpful to us. I observed that besides McCain and Kerry, DOD had been our biggest problem and I couldn't help being skeptical of the Joint Chiefs on this issue.

6/3/10 – I spoke to John Nevin about what we could ask for from the President and told him what I'd told Tom, that if any Congressional hearings were held on the POW issue, the Chairperson would be critical. John said it had to be a Presidential Commission because a Congressional Commission would only be Chaired and made up of members of Congress. For an independent commission, the President could appoint Perot. Colonel Peck would be excellent, but there was no way that political protocols would allow the President to appoint an Air Force colonel to head a Presidential Commission. He would be told that it HAD to be someone with a big name.

I mentioned appointing Perot as Special Emissary, a position he had been willing to accept under President Bush in 1989, but that position had eventually been given to General Vesey, who we thought had sold us out. John agreed that would be the best case scenario; Perot had some contacts in Vietnam that no one else had.

We agreed that I needed to be sure all of "our guys" knew what a strong potential asset Sydney Schanberg could be for us, and how committed he was to getting and publicizing any new information that could be corroborated.

6/4/10 - Carol returned my call and told me that Perot thought his conversation was more productive with Tom than John Syphrit. I told her that was probably because John will not discuss the issue over the telephone, but Tom can be more open.

Carol said she was going to suggest to Perot that Sydney attend the meeting with the President but I reminded her that Sydney passed because he needed corroboration. Carol believed he could add to the meeting by giving his independent view as a Pulitzer Prize-winning journalist. It would be hard to disagree with that logic. I made a note to myself to make sure Sydney understood that he would be there to discuss the issue in general, not as support for anything John had to say about the '81 meeting.

I told Carol that there was going to be an intentional delay in arranging this meeting but didn't tell her why. She asked whether it had anything to do with an overseas operation, and I said no. Carol followed up by saying that there were a number of other factors that will hopefully all come together.

6/9/10 – Tom called to discuss the following:

· The gatekeeper or Secretary to the Joints Chief of Staff who would make the arrangement for a White House meeting with Perot is Col. Sutherland.

· Based on feedback from our inside friends, Perot is generally considered over the hill by the White House and does not have the influence to get a meeting with the President on his own.

· The most likely scenario would be a meeting with Obama's Chief of Staff, Rahm Emanuel. I said my impression was that he is cold and ruthless, the last person we would want to deal with. Later that night, John Nevin agreed and said Tom should do everything possible to go through either Valerie Jarrett or David Axelrod.

· Vietnam still admires and respects Perot; they see him as an important person primarily because of his success in business, and they hope he might play an important role in future economic development. His involvement could generate a VIP invitation from the Prime Minister.

· Even though John Syphrit never heard the tape from the 1981 Reagan cabinet meeting, he was 99% sure it existed.

· Another strategy we could use is the committee formed by GW Bush near the end of his administration, when the committee deliberately insulted the Vietnam government after they had made serious overtures to discuss live POWs. The offer was then withdrawn and never put back on the table.

· If DOD gets wind of this plan, they will likely contact the White House or the Chiefs of Staff to prevent a meeting.

· Almost five years ago, we received information that 54 American POWs were still alive and received some of their names; even if we wanted to release those names to the media they would not be interested and without absolute corroboration they would most likely treat it as though we had made it up.

· I mentioned Carol Hrdlicka's desire to get Perot to include Sydney Schanberg in any meeting and Tom said that Sydney represented the old strategy and would be much more valuable as an independent outsider reporting any breaking news. (John Nevin disagreed.)

· One of our reliable friends had a meeting set up in Toronto with a visiting Vietnamese official. He would determine as soon as possible after arrival whether any serious discussion was likely, and if so contact me to join him. I could take the next flight up.

· Perot called Tom to tell him that he is ready to help in any way possible, including the use of his name to use as leverage, his private plane, funding a government sponsored invitation to Vietnam, or anything else that develops from the Toronto meeting. Tom said involving Perot was a stroke of genius, even if it didn't work out exactly as we originally planned.

John Nevin suggested that we needed to find out for sure whether Perot was giving us permission to use his name. He said it was completely out of character for Perot to trust anyone except his closest long-time friends and business associates to speak on his behalf.

Chapter Seventeen
2nd Meeting with 2nd Vietnamese General

6/9/10 - The intermediary in Canada has called repeatedly to verify that our representative is definitely coming. We hope that there must be something special planned. As we made clear to Perot, there would be no quid pro quo for anything the Vietnamese offered. We will help facilitate the end of this long nightmare and nothing more. We are hoping that Vietnamese officials see it the way we do: that it will be in their best long term interest to make this move.

6/15/10 – Tom returned my call and I asked him if he was absolutely sure Perot had given our representative permission to use his name. He confirmed that Perot had agreed and our representative was aware. I said that this is out of character for him; and he must have a lot of confidence in us. We agreed that it was fine with both of us if it worked out that Perot ultimately got the credit.

I called John Nevin that night and he was astonished that Perot gave us that authority. He said it was Perot's style to let only his most trusted associates speak in his name.

6/18/10 Friday – I received the scheduled call from Toronto: no significant movement; I would not be needed.

6/19/10 Saturday– Our representative in Toronto called to say that he and the contact were joined by another high-ranking military operations person who allegedly had responsibilities regarding the POWs' current status in Vietnam. He was said to be of equal rank or higher than the person we met in the 2005 meeting. This person spoke fluent English so no interpreter was needed. This meant that there would be far less potential for misunderstanding on either side. We speculated that he had been educated in the U.S. and set in motion an effort to verify his past activities and present credentials.

The numbers that he gave us in this meeting: 36 in Vietnam, 14 in Laos, with 12 of the 50 choosing not to come home. They are 70 to 78 years old with a number of them in bad shape physically. Later that night, John Nevin commented that including those 12 made the entire situation more credible because it's less likely they would include that if this were some kind of scam on their part.

On the other hand, Sydney Schanberg, one of our staunchest supporters, is saying that his sources indicate that none of them are still alive. He made this remark in his new book, *Beyond the Killing Fields*, saying that he'd been told they had been executed some time previously, and implying that he found the source credible.

With all due respect to Sydney, we had learned the hard way over the years that some people quite credible on other subjects could not be trusted on this one. I understood Sydney's trusted contact to be CIA, and CIA was very dirty on this issue.

The military operations person claimed that he was there with the full authority of the Vietnamese Politburo. They understood that there would be no money or other consideration involved, and simply stated that they needed to return these men as a gesture of goodwill to the American people. They didn't believe that President Bush's failure to positively respond to a Vietnamese overture near the end of his second term could have been an innocent mistake.

He was well aware that there were still people in U.S. positions of influence who preferred that POWs not be returned. That was why they were choosing to deal with us instead of government to government.

Because of an arcane, seldom-enforced U.S. law, the Logan Act, we must be clear that we are offering no quid pro quo, nor even advice or suggestions. If the Vietnamese government believes, as we do, that it is in their interest to take this step, we will facilitate the logistics any way we can. We were hoping that the Vietnamese would see Perot's involvement as possibly leading to some future economic initiatives in Vietnam, a worthwhile fringe benefit.

The official said that their intention was to return all the men; however, they would first return a smaller number who were healthy both mentally and physically. We reasserted our three terms: no money would pass through our hands, they would give us the identification of the men in advance, and we would receive an official invitation only when it was time to release them. We also suggested that it would be helpful here if the first group was made up of pilots who would be difficult to paint as defectors. The official understood, and that when the time came we could choose the delegation of our choice as long as we led it.

6/21/10 Monday – Our representative in Toronto called me to say that there had been a second meeting on Sunday and it had been extraordinary. The meeting took place over 24 hours after their initial discussion on Saturday, so the official had time to consult with someone in Vietnam; there was an implication that it was the Minister of Defense.

He said that we would get the entire list of 50 POWs in 30 days; however, we felt that was overly optimistic considering the snail's pace at which Vietnam's bureaucracy usually moves.

The official indicated that if this plan were approved, their SRV ambassador would notify the Department of Defense and State Department that the initial group of POWs would be released to us unconditionally. Our representative wisely suggested that the timing we would prefer for that notice would be when our delegation arrived in Vietnam.

The time frame mentioned was January 2011. We preferred a date that carries significance, such as Christmas or January 27, the anniversary of the signing of the "Paris Peace Accords."

We were getting positive indications from friendlies in-the-know regarding our contact's credentials and his role of substance regarding POWs in Vietnam and possibly Laos.

After updating Perot, we were told he was totally on board.

That night, John Nevin said I should be one of the people in that delegation to Vietnam. Tom has always said since the original meeting in 2005 that I would be most effective at contacting the family members because of my good relationship with them, contacting the media, and organizing multiple press conferences at home. Even though I had to agree that was probably best, I'd give my right arm to join that delegation if that miracle were to happen.

6/24/10 – John Nevin's suggestion that I should go to Vietnam was purely based on the fact that he thought I deserved to go. At first, he didn't see the need for me to stay home. I said that Tom wanted me to arrange a press conference back home after his expected conference in Vietnam and to field questions from the media as well as direct them to other sources for information.

Since this wasn't going to happen until the beginning of 2011 at the earliest, we agreed to think about how this might manifest itself. John said that the media would be coming to us for a change, wanting information, and someone definitely needed to be available to talk to them during the long period that the homebound group was in the air.

I tried like hell to stop thinking about the possibility of POWs' release, but I couldn't get it out of my mind. Besides my devotion to my immediate family, my life for over 26 years has been devoted to those men.

6/27/10 Sunday – I got what looked like very good news today:

· Our network of people supporting our effort confirmed 85% of the information discussed last weekend in Toronto.

· The next step was for final approval, a written document from the SRV, and the complete list of the 50 men in the same format as the original 17 names we received: Name, Rank, Unit, Date of Birth, Hometown, Date of Loss, Country of Loss, Loss Coordinates, Status, Category, Other Personnel in Incident, and a one-page chronology of the capture.

· There was even a contingency plan, if the USG tries to undermine the effort, to release the men in a foreign country already determined by them but not named. Almost all of our contacts and sources thought this was the best opportunity we had ever had to finally bring these men home. Even though we were disappointed by the relatively small number reportedly surviving, we didn't think it likely that the Vietnamese had good reason to hold any back at this point.

As I looked at the list of the original 17 names I could not help but wonder how many of them had died since we received those names. Even worse, how many have died since the partial return of our men in March 1973. It makes me sick to my stomach to think how many could have been saved had President Nixon, Henry Kissinger, and numerous government officials, politicians, and the media not written these men off as an acceptable cost of war.

6/28/10 – The thought that there was any chance these men might come home was overwhelming and I was trying to avoid too much confidence that it would really happen. I often thought back over the 27 years since I first learned we had left men behind, and all the people and events who influenced me in that time. The kid from the Bronx had traveled a lot of roads he'd never have imagined going down.

I always think back to the high school student who told me about my future. He may not have had a clue what my actual destiny would be. It doesn't matter; I listened and continued to open doors as he encouraged me to do throughout my life. He indicated that most people never achieved their potential because of their fear of the unknown. His advice that opening one door would lead to other doors or opportunities was my driving force all these years. The more doors opened, the more opportunities. I don't know if I would have wound up here without his planting that thought in my mind.

7/5/10 – We heard from Perot that he was willing to provide aircraft and, if it became necessary, any mid-flight stops and security. (Vietnam was considering Singapore as a possible third-country release point.) One of our sources reported that things were moving fast in Vietnam, some good, some bad. Even though it appeared they were making an effort to compile the list for all the POWs, there was some push-back from the conservative wing of the Communist party.

The primary problem seemed to be that these characters preferred upgrading Vietnam's relationship with China, rather than the U.S. They preferred the authoritarian form of government of China to the more liberal and democratic U.S.

There was said to be a plan in the works to send another official, perhaps one less friendly to us, for an additional meeting and to have the Vietnamese Prime Minister request the approval for this from our State Department. Even though another meeting might mean delays, it certainly wasn't being considered to tell us they weren't going to go through with the plan. On the other hand, the idea of putting our State Department on notice made us nervous.

I called John Nevin and we discussed the potential downside of having the Vietnamese notify the State Department of this. It would give DOD and the politicians in D.C. an opportunity to find a way to undermine the entire project. John thought it naive to be concerned about this... he had always assumed that "they" already knew everything that we were doing.

John felt very strongly that releasing only a few at first was detrimental to what the Vietnamese were trying to accomplish if they stated that every single piece of information they had on all U.S. MIAs would be provided. Even if additional time was needed to compile it, there was no reason to delay the release until it had all been gathered. He believed that this would stop any immediate criticism and eliminate many of the questions that were sure to follow.

Last but not least, John said releasing our men held in Laos could be a problem. The Vietnamese always claimed they had no authority in Laos. In meetings with Vietnamese officials at the UN they always told us, "You will need to speak to the government of Laos about this."

We discussed our concern that the real purpose of an additional meeting with us and prior notice to the State Department might be intended to use us as leverage to get something else from the U.S. government. There could be no doubt that the Vietnamese had finally figured out that influential people here didn't want POWs released, and it was possible that they saw the threat to do so as a way to gain that leverage.

John and I agreed that a release in Hanoi would give them maximum ability to control what happens; showing our delegation being treated respectfully would be good cosmetics for them. Releasing them in a third country would create an impression of something less than complete openness. For their purposes, it needed to be clear that they were acting for humanitarian reasons and a sign of good faith to the American people, with no conditions attached.

I told John that our Vietnamese contacts wanted our help in formulating the public statement announcing the release. He felt better about the potential problem of releasing our men from Laos, and the general strategy to initially release a few with no broad statement on all the information. He again expressed our need for caution regarding the Logan Act. There would be influential people here who would not be happy with us.

7/8/10 – I've been thinking about my role at the time of the release. As much as I would like to go, I would be more useful here. It was also possible that my various public confrontations with Vietnamese officials here might make my presence there problematic.

If Vietnam is going to take any action in January, that was only six months away. I need to start preparing a strategy and talking points for the media, family members, and head off any possible attacks to derail this initiative. I definitely want to put together all the information on what McCain did to derail this issue for the last 20 years, and his comments about those who have fought to get these men released.

I told John Nevin that the wine tossing incident would rule me out as an option to go on any trip to Vietnam because it would jeopardize the mission. John reluctantly agreed. He said that as much as he thought I deserved to go, it might cause problems, and, more importantly, I had to be available for media contact until the delegation returned.

John also mentioned something I hadn't realized: he considered it a certainty that Perot was going to notify the U.S. government what was happening and his role in it. There was a chance that he would wait until the last minute to minimize possible damage, but he would NOT do something like this without giving notice. Despite the many shenanigans he had seen over the years, he was still at heart a True Believer.

7/13/10 – I got word that hard- liners in Vietnam were arguing against putting together the list of POWs, saying that it would be an embarrassment. There was no discussion of wanting any money for the POWs; it was all about saving face.

The debate has been going on for over a week and was reportedly intensifying as time goes on.

Our Toronto contact was supposed to give a report to two committees but postponed both meetings because of the ongoing debate. He was considered a moderate as are all those who favor the release.

7/15/10 – I received word that there was an interesting, positive twist. Vietnam is said to have ordered a private investigation of NVVC in the USA and Canada to determine whether we can really deliver on our claim that our voice would be significant in shaping the reaction to the release of our men, especially within the U.S. veteran community, to be positive and appreciative rather than hostile and accusatory.

This was a good sign because it means the possibility is still alive and that's all we can hope for at this time. We knew, and hoped the Vietnamese understood, that the Vietnam veteran reaction would be critical in influencing the overall public response if men were released.

I obtained a copy of President Nixon's 1973 letter delivered to Vietnamese "peace talks" negotiators by Henry Kissinger, promising to give Vietnam almost $5 billion in postwar reconstruction and other humanitarian aid. I was prepared to say that even though we feel it was very wrong for the Vietnamese government to hold our men so long after the war, it's easy to understand their wanting to retain some leverage to force fulfillment of the promise made to them. They had tried, most directly in 1981 when Reagan took office, to resolve the issue by returning the men and receiving the promised aid. They were rebuffed.

If things didn't work out in this series of discussions, we thought it might be either good or bad that a change in political leadership in Vietnam was scheduled to occur the following year. It would be bad in that we might have to start over with a new set of characters, or it might be good that we at least would have had a second chance.

I called John Nevin to discuss using my activist status to our advantage. With the passing of Ted Sampley, I had unofficially inherited the moniker of "leader of the POW/MIA activist movement." He believed that Vietnam would ultimately determine that the NVVC is the strongest voice of the Vietnam veteran community. John believed promoting me to the Vietnamese decision-makers as a leader who has the respect of the family members and activists is more advantageous than my influence with Vietnam veterans because the media will give most of their attention to the families. Also, the activists would initially be the most vocal and possibly set the tone for the rest to follow.

I felt confident that the National Alliance of Families would at least listen to our counsel and felt it likely that most families would follow. It couldn't hurt that Tom, on behalf of the Vietnam Veterans' Foundation, had provided financial support to their organization.

7/18/10 Sunday – I learned that Hillary Clinton, then Secretary of State, had scheduled a trip to Vietnam. Our concern was that someone in Vietnam would bring up the POW situation in some manner. Not only could they get a less than encouraging response from her, it could also be a problem if it resulted in DOD being alerted to anything they didn't already know.

Unfortunately, there were people in DOD, especially in the DIA, who were excellent at screwing things up and discrediting people. We couldn't imagine that anything good would come from Hillary's visit.

7/23/10 Friday - I arrived at the National Alliance of Families meeting in Arlington at about 11 AM while DPMO (Defense POW/Missing Office) was concluding a presentation that, as usual, spoke only about recovery of remains and not a word about the possibility of living POWs. Over the fifteen years, I had attended almost every yearly conference and they said the same things. They pretend that everything possible is being done to inform the families, but when they are caught red-handed in a falsehood, they claim innocent mistake or conflicting information or blame it on new people that had been assigned to the issue.

Bill Hendon confronted DPMO as I arrived with overhead photos of an underground complex as it was being constructed, and further pictures of the finished product. He attacked one of the panelists as having supported the USG statement under oath that the water table in that area would not support a complex that could hold POWs.

This was the USG's argument used to disprove and discredit solid POW reports in that area. Billy challenged the panelist to fly with him to Hanoi to see for himself; naturally, he declined. I challenged him again, saying that a former Congressman just called you a liar, and he declined again.

Later that afternoon, after DPMO left, Ann Holland told her story of how she had been lied to about her husband, and that officials had withheld from her critical information indicating that he survived at Site 85, a now-famous US intelligence outpost. Her story included how a lie about her husband's fate, which included the loss of one of his arms in the skirmish as his post was over-run, even affected her grandchildren, to the point where one of them continues to have nightmares. Her story brought me to tears, both then and as I write this.

Unfortunately, the National Alliance's biggest project, the passage of House Resolution 111 asking for a Congressional Committee to investigate the POW/MIA issue, had enough signatures (280) in support of the resolution; however, they had no chance to pass it because Speaker of the House Nancy Pelosi refused to fund the committee.

When one of the people in the audience said that he knew where Pelosi lived in Georgetown, I said if any family members wanted to go that night I'd join them. Lynn O'Shea immediately said their group didn't believe in that kind of activity.

I explained how we'd already visited Jim Baker at his house and spoke to his wife, and also demonstrated at Reagan's Chief of Staff's house, just to get their attention and let them know we take this personally. In the end, the families decided against a visit to Pelosi's home.

This reminded me that if we were fortunate enough to pull off this POW release project, I was going to have to control my emotions. I had, and still have, some anger of my own to deal with. Since I hoped to take the lead regarding the families and media, I would need to keep my emotions in check. It would certainly help that a good part of my anger is directed at people in the U.S. who caused this to fester unresolved for so long.

During our lunch break I approached Lynn, who is clearly the leader of the Alliance even though she is not a family member, and told her Tom Burch wanted to meet with her at 5 PM.

When they met, Tom opened with a very cordial statement saying how important it was to keep the Alliance meetings and organization together and that he wanted to help in supporting that effort. He gave Lynn a check for $1,000 and said that if they needed more help to please ask and he would gladly do what he could. Lynn was very gracious in accepting.

Tom told Lynn that if there was ever any movement by Vietnam to release some of our men, our group would very much like to work closely with their family organization. I commented that we all agree that there is little chance our government will be voluntarily involved in their release, so our best hope was for the Vietnamese to realize it was in their best interest to do so.

Lynn said they agreed with that position and would gladly join us if there was any movement by Vietnam.

At dinner, Tom filled me in on some details he had preferred not to discuss on the telephone. Apparently Vietnam had already decided to allow a second political party as a counterpart to the Communist party; however, Tom said the other party is doomed to second-class status. It would attract many of the moderates who were inclined to support the release of our men, and would be made up primarily of supporters of a more open government to foster more external interest in business and investment in Vietnam. Many Western businessmen were reluctant to make a commitment to a Communist government that might nationalize their assets at any time.

One of our key contacts in Vietnam had no political authority but was very close to many Politburo and Central Committee members. He had an unusual private sector job which called for personal relationships with many of them. We thought we were getting a pretty good read on the various factions in Vietnam regarding a possible prisoner release. Those most friendly to us were not the top dogs, but there was a very influential group that, although not openly supporting a release, seemed to have no objection if that decision were made.

Chapter Eighteen
Roller Coaster

7/24/10 Sat – On the drive back from D.C., I thought about the reluctance of many Western businesses to invest in Vietnam, and thought back to the four events I had disrupted whose purpose was the promotion of investment opportunities in Vietnam. As a matter of personal pride, I hoped I had contributed to that reluctance. More importantly, if the Vietnamese thought my actions had played some role, it might make them more eager to have me involved in shaping the post-release reaction in the U.S., assuming of course, that they understood that my intent was toward appreciation, not accusation.

7/25/10 Sunday – Tom called to tell me an interesting story. During Hillary Clinton's visit to Vietnam for a regional security conference and to celebrate the 15th anniversary of the reestablishment of diplomatic relations between the U.S. and Vietnam, she met privately with Vietnam's Foreign Minister. When he mentioned in vague terms that Vietnam might know the location of some U.S. soldiers from the war that they could give passage home, Hillary supposedly asked for another interpretation of what was said because she didn't understand.

After it was repeated, her response was to say she wasn't sure how the U.S. would handle it, didn't know anything about it, would have to check further. Staff members of the two officials met afterward to discuss a range of issues, but there was no further development regarding POWs, or whatever the Vietnamese side preferred to call them.

A *New York Times* article on Saturday said Hillary suggested that the USG intervene to facilitate mutual talks on the Paracel and Spratly Islands dispute between China and Vietnam. China is upset with Hillary because they claim the islands belong to them, there's nothing to discuss, and furthermore, their territorial issues are of no legitimate concern to the U.S.

I knew Hillary would report to DOD regarding the POW reference made by the Foreign Minister. This could result in some kind of precipitous action by DOD that we'd need to be ready to respond to. We might need to discuss it immediately with our friend overseas to gauge any reaction there and to discuss our next move. We agreed that we should keep our eyes and ears open but do nothing until/unless DOD made a move that would require our response.

John Nevin believed that Hillary absolutely understood and gave what would be the best response to deflect the need for an answer. I thought that even if she didn't understand what the Foreign Minister was saying, her staffers should have been able to clarify what the Foreign Minister meant. In either case, I told John I thought there was a very good chance DOD/DIA would do something after Hillary reported.

He agreed and said the most troubling fact is that Vietnam mentioned it to her knowing that the USG has no interest in bringing home POWs. We came to the conclusion we feared most: they are using us for leverage to get what they want. In other words, the Foreign Minister's comment wasn't an offer, but a threat. This was the same red flag that was raised when we found out Vietnam was considering sending one of their generals to meet with the State Department in October, while they were privately telling us that they wanted to work only with us.

John felt that the best move in a cover-up sense was for DOD to actually accept these men. That would prevent Vietnam from taking advantage of the "threat" of releasing them. Then, if they are truly as heartless and committed to the cover-up as we think they are, they could segregate the most credible ones—mostly pilots and other officers—sending them somewhere else for "debriefing" without releasing their names or numbers to the public. The most hardcore POWs are probably dead, so some of the remaining ones could be called "voluntary stay-behinds," making their return easier for DOD to explain. This would also be the safest move for Vietnam: return them directly to the USG because they have made it clear in a number of ways that they want good economic relations with the U.S., even if the political relationship remains tense.

They know that some influential people would be angry if they released the men to us rather than to the government. DOD would wind up doing exactly what we were going to do. Praise Vietnam for the humanitarian gesture and say that complete records of every POW/MIA they had information about would follow shortly.

Even though John was upset with that prospect, it would still accomplish part of what we wanted. Even if DOD twisted the story around and hid those POWs with the most compelling and credible stories, the POW movement is burned out and is running on fumes.

Bottom line: we needed to get some of them home and then worry about what to do next. It ain't over until it's over.

John wanted me to check with Sydney Schanberg to see what he thinks Hillary's role is in this situation. I want to get additional information before making that call.

On another front, a U.S. team of researchers who had been granted limited access to Soviet archives had run across information that appeared to relate to U.S. POWs being moved from Vietnam to the Soviet Union, and another reference was to U.S. POWs of Germany during World War II who had been "liberated" from the German POW camps by Soviet troops as they moved West and had been taken to the Soviet Union, possibly for later release.

Russian officials repeatedly denied holding live American POWs from the Vietnam War; however, one of the generals who'd attended arranged a private meeting; he said to continue to push because they were going in the right direction. He said these Americans are married and have children. They might not be interested in returning to the U.S. unless their entire families, including grandchildren, could come with them.

8/1/10 Sunday – Tom called me this morning: he'd just heard that our deal was dead for now.

He speculated that Hillary's visit might have had something to do with it, but had no confirming info. He tried to put a positive spin on this by saying a new regime was scheduled to take over the next year and the serious consideration to release our men can be revisited at any time.

He'd been told Hillary really didn't know what the Vietnamese Foreign Minister was talking about at their private meeting.

I called John Nevin, and he wasn't buying any of it. He believed there was very little chance that Hillary didn't know. Even if Vietnam was using us as leverage, it had to be for more than one comment about the Spratly Islands and another about their progress moving toward a "functional Democracy."

After 27 years, I've come to expect this frustrating outcome. It will always be a roller coaster ride.

8/3/10 – Tom learned the Vietnamese investigation of NVVC wasn't only ongoing, they were digging deeper than before. If this was true, Vietnam had not yet ruled out the possibility of the release, unless, of course, they had a plan to use us in some other capacity which we couldn't even imagine.

8/6/10 – 8/11/10 Sydney Schanberg was scheduled to be the guest speaker at the November 10th coalition luncheon and I was slotted for his table. We planned to solicit Sydney's help in making direct contact with *The New York Times* before the story breaks, and I would be the contact. Perot had said he could help in getting Turner Broadcast Systems on board.

Tom said the investigation was focusing on some questionable deals our Toronto contact had been working overseas and whether the NVVC was involved. He assured me it wasn't.

8/20/10 Friday – We heard that the Politburo's fourteen members voted on whether to return the men. They'd come up two votes short, even though they had voted to send the official to meet with us in June. The Politburo operates by consensus on matters considered of greatest importance, and unanimous vote is much preferred because the Central Committee of the Communist Party, of which the Politburo is an organ, can over-ride Politburo decisions.

9/13/10 – I left for Washington, D.C., with my son Mike to assist my former lawyer Ken Robinson in the case brought by the Bar Association for improperly withdrawing funds from his escrow account. I was there to testify that the money represented a flat-fee for my defense, rather than a retainer against charges that would be incurred.

Mike and I had time to visit the Smithsonian on the morning of the 14th before my 2:00 PM testimony in the federal court. I gave my account, stating that Ken had every right to the money because it was a flat fee with no contingencies rather than his usual hourly fee of $500.

I explained that we initially agreed that in July 2005 I would pay him $7,500 if the Assistant DA dropped the case before we appeared before the judge, $15,000 if he dropped the case before my October trial, and $20,000 if we went to trial.

The prosecutor asked if I had hired any other attorneys, and I said Tom Burch from the National Vietnam Veterans Coalition represented me in another case and the charges were dropped.

He then said, "I mean a criminal attorney."

I said "No," but then thought for a few seconds and said I had hired a local criminal attorney to handle some mischief my sons had gotten into. I explained that we did set up an escrow account in that case, so I was familiar with the process.

When the prosecutor pressed me as to why I paid Ken before the trial, I said that the money had been raised for my defense. I was going to have to pay Ken eventually anyway, and I didn't have any place to conveniently put it temporarily. The prosecutor was trying to paint the picture that Ken insisted on getting all his money or he would not represent me. I said that from the beginning Ken said that if we were unable to raise the money he and I would work something out. He always indicated to me that he was representing me, no matter what.

The prosecutor continued to pressure me why I would pay him in advance and I finally said with conviction, "I'm a man of character and I wanted to make sure Ken received the money we had promised." The prosecutor's body literally snapped back, shocked by my answer. I could see Ken in the corner of my eye with a clenched fist mouthing the word, "Yes." The prosecutor was so stunned he began shuffling his papers trying to regain his composure.

One of the three judges finally prompted him by asking if he had any more questions and I believe he asked another question that seemed irrelevant and then said, "No further questions, your Honor."

Following my testimony, Karen, Jacob's assistant, said I did great. I simply stuck to the truth.

Ken took Mike and me out for a steak dinner that night and told me I did great. Sadly, he told me that some of his big-time clients would not even say hello if they passed in the street, even ones he had successfully defended. There seems to be a different breed of people among the "movers and shakers" in D.C.

9/17/10 – I called Ken to ask what happened, and he said the three-judge panel didn't render a verdict, which he thought was good news. They wanted both sides to submit briefs within thirty days detailing their positions. I said I was guessing that they would either exonerate him or give him only a brief suspension. He said that was Jacob's opinion, too.

9/19/10 Sunday – The Vietnamese Legislature was scheduled to assemble in October to ratify a change in their constitution to allow the formation of a second political party. One of the officials named as friendliest to our project is supposedly to be the leader of that new party. If that happens, he would have to be given an official position in the government, but how much influence or authority he would have in that position was anybody's guess.

We learned that the Politburo vote that temporarily turned down going forward on our project wasn't a formal vote but merely a head count. This was good news because it meant that the "no" positions hadn't been hardened by a recorded vote.

John Nevin said the formation of a second political party was entirely cosmetic; the Central Committee of the Communist Party of Vietnam (CCCPV) would remain firmly in control of all important decisions. If its formation had the desired effect of improving Vietnam's image in the West, it could have a detrimental effect on our issues (POWs and improved human rights for the citizenry). Getting what they wanted without those two difficult steps would make it less likely they would take them.

9/30/10 Thursday – A write-up ("5 Things You Should Know") in *The New York Times* entitled, "Kissinger: Vietnam Failures Are on US," said that in a speech at a State Department conference the day before Kissinger had said that America's central objective to preserve an independent South Vietnam had been unachievable. He said the U.S. wanted compromise, and Hanoi wanted victory.

Kissinger's most interesting comment was, "Most of what went wrong in Vietnam, we did to ourselves," such as underestimating the tenacity of the North Vietnamese leaders.

10/12/10 – *The New York Times* had a front page picture of Secretary of Defense Robert Gates shaking hands with a three- or four-star General, Liang Guanglie, in Hanoi.

10/13/10 – *The New York Times* published an article on page A9 talking about the improvement in U.S./Vietnam relations. Paraphrasing the article, it quoted a Vietnamese government statement that we are enjoying an excellent period of bilateral relations, and quoted Hillary Clinton as saying that Vietnam's progress was "breathtaking." The warming of relations has been slowed by Vietnam's suspicion that we are trying to use the human rights issue as leverage to accomplish other things. They saw that tactic used to bring down Communist governments in the Soviet Union, Yugoslavia, and former Soviet satellites.

Also, the chief remaining postwar issue for the U.S. continued to be a full accounting for our military service members still missing from the war, even though that concern no longer carried the power that it once did. The remaining postwar issue for Vietnam was the demand for more assistance in addressing the effects of Agent Orange that was causing widespread birth defects as well as other after-effects of the war. Gates visited Vietnam for the gathering of defense chiefs from ten Southeast Asian nations and Russia.

I naturally had to wonder whether the release of our men was discussed in private talks.

Bill Hendon called me and asked if I could attend a press conference in D.C. with him the following day. I told Billy that I was ill and had taken a rare sick day from work.

I spoke with Tom about Billy's press conference and he thought there were too many themes, including the underground prison facility in Hanoi and discussions about possible U.S. assistance to Vietnam acquiring the capability for nuclear enrichment.

11/4/10 Thursday – I received a communication from a veteran friend allegedly "in the know." He said he'd gotten word that a meeting among a group of high-ranking Vietnamese officials was scheduled for the following day and that the POW issue was on their agenda. He said that the issue appeared to have taken on a life of its own without the intercession of our best friend there. The pro-Western trade faction in the Vietnamese government wanted to release POWs as a step toward getting "Most Favored Nation" (MFN) trade status with the U.S.

There were articles over the previous week indicating that South Korean families had recently visited their loved ones in Communist North Korea who had been captured in the early 1950s. This is significant because the media released the names and information about some of these men. Apparently four of them were considered dead, and the South Korean government was being forced to consider changing the status of many of its Korean War troops from KIA to POW/MIA.

This was a turn of events that might possibly cause a domino effect of releases by Communist governments around the world. I wasn't confident that we could connect the dots, but Cuba had unexpectedly released fifty political dissidents in July, Kim Jung IL had made a second visit to China in August, and a few months later information was released regarding family visits to South Korean POWs who'd been held for over 57 years by North Korea.

I'm about to become a grandfather very soon. I ordered my son Dave to make sure his wife didn't deliver on the 10th because I would be in D.C.

for the coalition luncheon. Sydney Schanberg was to receive an award. Dave said, "No problem." He would just load her up with pain-killers and muscle-relaxers the night of the 9th. We had a good laugh.

11/10/10 – I spoke to Sydney at the National Vietnam Veterans Coalition luncheon, and I told him Vietnam veterans need heroes like him to break through some of the rampant deception and corruption in politics and media. He graciously denied the "hero" label but acknowledged the problems I mentioned. I told him I might need to call on him for help in the future, and he said to let him know when we had anything significant.

I saw Sydney, whose eyesight is failing, waiting to meet with John Syphrit, the former Secret Service agent who had been present in the 1981 White House meeting. I took him over to John and excused myself to let them talk. Tom soon joined them and intervened when Sydney asked for John's telephone number. Tom was John's legal counsel and didn't want John to speak publicly about that event without him present. Sydney wasn't happy.

11/20/10 -- My son and daughter-in-law delivered my first beautiful, healthy granddaughter, Madison Brook Kiley.

11/22/10 Monday – We got more "good news, bad news." A meeting had taken place among Vietnamese officials and they reportedly agreed to implement the release plan; however, the time frame established was distant. This group would make their recommendation directly to the Prime Minister who wasn't only expecting it, he supposedly wanted it.

11/23/10 Tuesday – My "insider" veteran friend called because he allegedly had an important update. The Prime Minister asked for a complete listing of all the Americans, their status, and their physical conditions. My friend said it would take weeks to gather all that information from both Laos and Vietnam, which might explain the delay I'd been told to expect.

If this turned out to be a very tight time frame, we would need the names and other relevant information about the first small group. We would need to visit their families in person to explain what was about to take place and make sure they were on the same page with us. They needed to realize the importance of not sounding hostile toward Vietnam. If the cosmetics don't go well from the Vietnamese perspective, the release of the larger group could be jeopardized. We will need to do some investigative work to identify and locate the closest family members, which won't be easy.

12/5/10 – I received word that the Vietnamese Prime Minister had allegedly met with a group of military officers who were in the minority among their peers in opposing the release. The word was that the PM dismissed their objections and said he wanted the information about these men ASAP.

The CCCPV wants detailed information on these men. Many of the younger Party officials never knew they existed and think it was a foolish risk to hold them alive since the end of the war. The PM appears to favor the plan to turn the men over to a U.S. non-government organization.

Despite the advancing age and difficult living conditions for men left behind, we thought the number of survivors was low. A combination of all the intelligence and live sighting reports over the years and the seeming logic of "release half, hold half" makes us believe that about 600 in total were kept. (591 were released in "Operation Homecoming" in 1973.) This number of 600 may or may not include additional prisoners held in Laos. We thought, and were hopeful, that in gathering the names, locations, and status of all the detainees they would find that they actually had more than our sources had told us.

12/26/10 Sunday – I received a message that the Prime Minister was recently given a list of 120 MIAs still alive. This seemed to me like surprisingly fast work. Supposedly only about half of them wanted to come home, due to the fact that many had eventually been allowed to have families, which they were not now willing to leave.

1/12/11 – The 1981 offer to President Reagan when he first took office came through the Canadian embassy. We recently received word that besides the 1981 offer, there had been several others we didn't know about.

2/6/11 - We heard that Prime Minister Nguyen Tan Dung and President Nguyen Minh Triet are both in support of the release. The General Secretary of the Communist Party and the Chairman of the National Assembly had not made a commitment either way. The good news for us is that the PM was elected to another five-year term.

Tom was invited to the Reagan Building in D.C. for a special 100 year party for what would have been President Ronald Reagan's 100th birthday, had he lived. The reason Tom received the invitation was that he had been a delegate to the Republican National Convention that nominated Reagan for President. There were six of Reagan's former cabinet members in attendance, three of whom Tom knew. He made it a point to meet with them as well as the former Convention Chairman because he suspects that his every action is being monitored and reported. It's funny because our friends are watching them watch us.

Three of the cabinet members at the celebration were there in 1981 when Hanoi's offer was discussed in John Syphrit's presence. I hope John will someday talk off the record to me about his life experience. It has to be an incredible story. When I think about the character of people like John Syphrit, my eyes tear up. When he made the decision about revealing the occurrence of the meeting, he didn't know what price he might have to pay. As it turned out, he was only given a lateral transfer to a position with less prestige, but the same pay. We think he wasn't pursued criminally because doing so risked moving what had been treated as a back-page story to the front pages of U.S. newspapers.

3/5/11 – We were trying to contain our excitement. If everything we were hearing was true, it looked as though it was really going to happen. All four of Vietnam's top people, including the PM and General Secretary of the Communist Party, were said to be in favor of releasing these men. Even the new President-to-be in June, Truong Tan Sang, favored this move.

The bad news was that our best sources are telling us it won't happen until at least the end of the year. Perhaps some changes in the personalities near the top of the Vietnamese political structure—scheduled for June—are causing the delay.

The original discussions included statements which implied that they would release a small first group—perhaps as few as three men—to gauge the reaction. We were recently hearing that they were considering six, eight, or even ten men, or possibly even the entire group. Also, Vietnam supposedly made contact with the political leadership in Laos and got the arrangement they were looking for to insure that none would be left behind in the region to cause future problems. Along this same line, some officials were suggesting that even the half who didn't want to return should be forced to do so.

A strange piece of information I had not thought about: Tom said all of these POWs will be millionaires because they are considered active military and would receive 40-plus years of pay with the normal increases in rank. Non-commissioned Officers would be sergeant majors and officers would be full colonels.

Tom said we would need to be prepared to deal with the possibility of 120 POWs released at one time. First, that would raise transportation problems that we hadn't considered, and when we got closer we would need to let Perot know that his assistance would be needed. Secondly, there was no way we'd be able to reach even the majority of next-of-kin. Thirdly, many of the family members we were able to reach would be suspicious, especially if they were not among those who had been most active in the fight to get POWs home and therefore probably wouldn't know Tom and me from Adam.

For those who didn't know us or weren't aware of all the deceit and machinations on the issue over the years, I suggested that we be prepared to provide copies of the twenty-page chapter six from Sydney Schanberg's book, *Beyond the Killing Fields*, which gives a solid but concise recap of the government cover-up. Tom agreed that might be very helpful.

We'd been told we would receive advance notice with a visit by someone from Vietnam when the plans were finalized. Before that, but when it began to look closer, I would have to take Lynn O'Shea of the National Alliance of Families into our confidence because her help would be critical to finding as many family members as possible. This will give us the opportunity to share with the National Alliance any credit we receive for making it happen.

However, we need to make the point that credit also goes to the government of Vietnam for reversing long-standing policy and forgoing the opportunity to receive the billions in aid they had been promised. The Vietnamese government decided to deal with a non-profit veterans' organization rather than with the U.S. government so that there could be no legitimate suspicions about the possibility of their having sought any quid pro quo.

One of our semi-official Vietnamese contacts discussed wanting to involve Perot after the release in some issue that they knew the USG would not be interested in. Extreme caution was called for here because of that very issue of quid pro quo, and, if necessary, the Vietnamese would need to be warned to be careful about involving Perot in anything that wouldn't look right.

On our side, when the question arose, we would have to let it be known that we were not looking for any book or movie deals. Without having direct knowledge, it's easy for the public to believe anything government naysayers might claim to make us look bad, such as that we were only in it for the money. The public is a little less trusting of government and political figures than before, and people hearing that we'd been dedicated to this cause for 28 years would at least give us the benefit of the doubt.

Veterans' issues have been central to much of the more recent skepticism. Besides the government lies that a substantial minority knew about the POW issue, there had been Agent Orange, Gulf War Syndrome, numerous veteran health care issues, and the unbelievably long delays in reviewing veteran disability claims. Add to this Iran/Contra, revelations about using unknowing military personnel in radiation and mind-altering drug experiments, the syphilis "study" at Tuskegee Institute, and the well-known lies that got us involved in the most recent Iraq conflict, and it's easy to see why they have used up all of their "trust me" chances with a lot of people.

3/26/11 – Everything seemed to be moving along at the normally slow pace, typical of the Vietnamese government. It had been four months since the PM first approved the release following his demand for more information.

Our Toronto contact received a call from Vietnam, questioning him about NVVC. As I mentioned earlier, the contact had been involved in some questionable financial dealings overseas. He confirmed that he had no financial ties of any kind with us and gave a positive general report.

A little interesting cloak and dagger: Tom made a reservation for two at a Vietnamese restaurant in D.C. whose owner was believed to be friendly with the Vietnamese Communists. Many suspected that the capability existed to audio tape conversations of restaurant customers, and Tom was proceeding on the assumption it was true. Either way, it couldn't cost anything to be careful. He made the reservation in advance to give time for people at the restaurant to check out who he was and to assign him to a table at which his conversation could be monitored. He took a trusted advisor and when they arrived at the restaurant, they were led to a table that had a card with his name on it. So far, so good.

In the course of the conversation, Tom and his friend said all the things we thought the Vietnamese would want to hear. The substance was that we would treat the release as unconditional on humanitarian grounds. He said the release of a small group of highly credible prisoners, men who had actually been in detention all this time, would play best here. To release anyone in the first group who could be characterized as a voluntary "stay behind" would reduce the favorable "liberalization" impression created by freeing actual prisoners. If the Vietnamese chose to release everyone who wanted to come home in one group, we would not object and could arrange transportation. He stated his preference for an official release in Bangkok because we have people there who can assist with logistics and who can insure positive reports in the Thai press.

Tom left feeling like it was the first time he could remember ever hoping that he'd been recorded.

Tom's law firm had accumulated $50K in flight credits over the years that he would be able to use to help defray transportation costs for any leg of the trip that could go commercial rather than charter. I suggested that we arrange for two aircraft for each leg of the flights, if we could manage the cost. Things do seem to get FUBARed at the worst times, and having back-up arranged could be critical. Perot had already agreed to assist in this, but we were pretty sure he didn't expect the large potential numbers.

I called and told John Nevin about my suggestion to call this second release Homecoming II, which was the name of an organization started by his wife, Margaret. (The first prisoner releases in three stages in 1973 had been called "Operation Homecoming.") John has since remarried to the daughter of a pilot missing in Laos. I was surprised when he didn't immediately like naming this second release; however, he then realized the media would want to label the event, and changed his mind. He thought Homecoming II would be appropriate.

After I told him about Tom's orchestrated visit to the Vietnamese restaurant he said what I was thinking: if we're not being lied to this is an amazing story. We knew Tom was being 100% truthful regarding what he believed to be the facts, and we couldn't imagine how anyone could manage to misdirect us through so many sources. However, we did have to keep in mind that there were those in both Vietnam and the U.S. who would benefit from our activism being silenced while we awaited supposedly revolutionary events.

It's a shame we wouldn't be able to tell the story of what actually happened, but John said that in four or five years things would change enough that it would be okay. Telling the whole story would put some of our sources in jeopardy, and we wouldn't need to reveal names or even positions to tell the story. Anyone who wanted credit for his/her role could make it public and we would back them up.

3/27/11 – A veteran friend with inside connections reported bizarre, possibly devastating news. The new incoming Vietnamese President was objecting to NVVC's involvement because he blames our Chairman, Tom Burch, for his son's death!

Tom was an officer in Vietnam during the Tet Offensive in January/February 1968. There was a U.S.-controlled POW camp holding 2,000 prisoners in Le Trang. Tom was familiar with the area even though he and his commanding officer, a colonel, were in a different command location.

After Tom's command received intelligence indicating that a VC operation was ready to launch in the Le Trang area, the entire staff became embroiled in a loud verbal debate over the most likely intended target. Tom insisted that it would be the Le Trang prison camp and the majority of the other officers thought it was something else. The colonel ultimately decided to send fifty men to reinforce the twelve guards then serving at the camp.

Tom was right and the reinforcements successfully defended the camp. Tom actually received a Bronze Star for saving the twelve men, the camp, and what would have resulted in 2,000 enemy soldiers escaping to fight against us. The incoming president's son was one of the VC killed in that fight.

Unfortunately, it was the Bronze Star citation, a public document that detailed the event and credited Tom with the decision that made this detail known to the Vietnamese during their investigation of NVVC. There was a new analysis underway toward working the release with one of the other major veterans' organizations, or even with the U.S. government.

When I spoke to John Nevin, his assessment was that it is possible that part of what we thought was a loyal network here in the U.S. could be trying to delay things for their own reasons. I said one possibility was that someone we trusted was actually working with people who wanted to prevent a release.

4/1/11 – Good news! The information I had gotten about the president-to-be in Vietnam had been garbled, and it was actually the current President whose son had been killed. The new President, who would take over in June, had no problem with us.

Reportedly, the CCCPV just found out about the list of names we were given in 2005, and they thought that was a mistake; however, it would probably work to our advantage because we didn't violate their trust and go public with that information. Maybe this new reason to trust us would override the current President's objections, which were personal rather than politically calculated.

This was the first day of my retirement after 44 years with the same company. In talking to Tom, he said he might have a retirement vacation for me... to Southeast Asia. We both laughed, but I later wondered whether he intended more than humor by the remark. I hope there's no reason Tom thinks he might be unable to lead the delegation. I hoped that things would stay as we had planned. Tom should lead that delegation.

Earlier in the week, I was thinking about the low-intensity investigation of me that Vietnam supposedly performed. I felt sure that they thought of me as an activist rabble-rouser without direct political influence. I thought about everything I did over the years that would have appeared on their radar and made a difference to them.

4/7/11 – There was a retirement party and luncheon for me, which the President of the company attended. I was surprised because he and I had been on far different tracks in our careers and we hardly knew each other. The kid from the Bronx did good.

I was grateful that my company had never raised objections to my activism, even though they had to be politically sensitive to anything controversial. I was very fortunate to have been able to keep their name out of the media all these years. On several occasions, members of the media tracked down my place of employment, but after asking that it not be published, surprisingly, it wasn't. Considering that I had envisioned the possibility of losing my job under a worst-case scenario, I was lucky to have made it 44 years without embarrassing the company.

John Nevin is one of the most grounded people I've ever known and he has been the one person I've constantly kept contact with over the 27 plus years I've been involved in the issue. He has earned my trust by being brutally honest with me so I not only value his input I also value his judgment. His response, when I'm way off base, is usually, "Hell no." With that as a backdrop, I told John if we were successful in what I called Phase I release of all POWs, then I would move on to Phase II, which would be to work for peace, prosperity, and freedom for the people in Vietnam. To my surprise, John said that was a worthy pursuit and offered the possibility of making a real impact. I said that would be a heck of a finale to my secret career as an activist, and he agreed. But, he said, that will never be a full time pursuit.

"There are veterans' healthcare and employment issues that you'll be in up to your neck." We both laughed and I had to agree.

The 2007 prophesy that I would be invited to visit Vietnam by its supreme leader in 2012 was still in play. Quyen Le told me that his friend who'd made this prediction regularly visits someone highly placed in the Vietnamese government. Maybe he knows something we don't.

Thinking about going to Vietnam under Communist rule, no matter what the circumstances, and saying goodbye to my sons and wife at the airport, would bring tears to my eyes; the risk was undeniable, and even though it was small, I couldn't avoid thinking about it. I mentioned this to John Nevin in the context of me being harmed and his response was, "Hell no. They're not going to let a public relations coup become a public relations nightmare." As much as I respect his opinion, it did little to relieve my fear.

4/10/11 – John sent me the email below. This is not good for us. DOD visited Deputy Foreign Minister Nguyen Quoc Cuong in Vietnam on the POW issue. Any publicized contact with DOD at this time is not a good sign. They may have fallen back to the use of the POW issue as leverage against the USG to get something they want. "Give us what we want or we will embarrass you by releasing the men," without actually saying it.

I called John and he said he never believed our contacts' claims that DOD didn't know what we were up to. I said that it was also possible that Vietnam had called for this visit in order to play their leverage game.

Date: Sun, 10 Apr 2011 07:24:15 -0500

Subject: Uh oh

http://english.vovnews.vn/Home/US-Department-of-Defence-senior-official-visits-Vietnam/20114/125583.vov

US Department of Defense senior official visits Vietnam

Robert Newberry, Deputy Assistant Secretary of Defense for the POW/MIA, is on a working visit to Vietnam from April 4-8.

While in Hanoi, Robert Newberry met with Deputy Foreign Minister Nguyen Quoc Cuong, held talks with Deputy Defense Minister Lieutenant-General Nguyen Chi Vinh, and worked with the Vietnam Office for Seeking Missing Personnel (VNOSMP).

During the meetings, the US official on behalf of the US government thanked Vietnam for its efficient cooperation in searching for Americans missing in action (MIA) in Vietnam.

He pledged to do his utmost to contribute to increasing mutual understanding and friendship between the two governments and peoples.

Deputy Minister Cuong affirmed the Vietnamese government's consistent policy regarding the MIA issue, adding that with its humanitarian traditions, the Vietnamese side will continue to cooperate in the MIA issue with the US. He reminded the US to pay appropriate attention to meeting

Vietnam's request relating to humanitarian issues, war consequences, and Agent Orange victims.

On this occasion, the US handed over to the Vietnamese side memorabilia collected by US families which may belong to Vietnamese soldiers during the war.

During his visit to Vietnam, Newberry attended the 10th commemoration of the MIA helicopter crash in central province of Quang Binh.

The source of this, vovnews, is an organ of Vietnam's state, so we could be confident that there was nothing unauthorized in it.

I forwarded the email to Tom.

4/12/11 Tuesday - Ted's son, Lane Sampley, called me to request that I attend his Eagle Scout ceremony on April 23rd. This was one of those strange occurrences, because although I had not thought of him in quite some time, I had been thinking of him and his dad just the day before. Ted had died almost two years earlier.

I had deliberately stayed away from Lane because I knew he wanted me to get arrested so he could join me. He really wanted to prove himself, but putting an arrest on his record wasn't the way. Despite the long drive from New York to North Carolina, there was no way I was going to miss that Eagle Scout ceremony.

4/25/11 – At Lane's Eagle ceremony, I was asked to say a few words about Lane's character.

Naturally, I mentioned how proud Ted would be and how proud all of us in the POW issue were to see Lane grow into manhood. I mentioned that Lane was now carrying on for his dad and displaying the same character he did.

Unfortunately, I got choked up when mentioning Ted, just as I did at his funeral two years earlier. I saw Lane wipe away a tear just after my voice cracked. He maintained his composure, which was very hard under the circumstances. If controlling your emotions is a sign of manliness, then Lane is more a man than I am.

Years before, Ted had discovered the rotting hull of a Confederate warship, the CSS Neuse II, and organized efforts to build a replica of it that now sits on a nearby lot. It's become a tourist attraction in downtown Kinston, NC. The project Lane completed to get his Eagle badge was to raise the money and support to help build a memorial plaque in his father's honor in front of the ship that had been his pride and joy. With a gleam in his eye—whenever he wanted to goad me—Ted would refer to the CSS Neuse II as the Yankee Killer.

I stayed with Lane Friday and Saturday nights. He, his mother Robin, and I went to their farm after the ceremony and hung out with their hens, roosters, goats, and donkeys that evening. Lane claimed, to his mother's surprise, that he could drink a can of beer in three seconds. After betting her he could do it, he punctured a hole in the middle of the can with his car keys and drank it in four seconds. Lane, like his dad, can hold his liquor, but I'm not sure that's a good thing.

I said, "You came up short. You claimed three seconds and it took you four."

Naturally, being Ted Sampley's son, he came at me and challenged me to do better. I never liked chugging beers, and I knew there was no way I could beat him, so I said, "I don't want to embarrass you in front of your mother." Robin took the heat off me by telling him to go play with the roosters or donkeys. We had a good laugh, something Ted would have enjoyed.

Chapter Nineteen
Slipping Away

5/1/11 – Osama Bin Laden was reportedly killed by our Navy SEALs in a night raid on his compound in Pakistan. Celebrations broke out throughout the country in patriotic response.

The following day, President Obama posthumously awarded two Medals of Honor for heroic action during the Korean War. I found it curious that in one of the presentations he mentioned several issues relating to persistence and determination, followed by a statement that we should never forget our missing soldiers.

This may have no meaning; however, I still think about the most recent visits to Vietnam by Secretary Gates and Hillary Clinton and would find it hard to believe that nothing was said to them about our POWs. Since they were able to keep a secret on hunting down Osama, they can easily do the same if an offer were made to them about the release of our men. I'm trying not to read too much into the President's comment, but a certain amount of paranoia is unavoidable.

5/5/11 Thursday – Tom called to say that he'd heard from a friend in Vietnam that the leadership had been given a positive assessment of NVVC's possible role in the release initiative.

Tom made a second visit to the Vietnamese restaurant and, as hoped, was seated at the "special" table.

5/29/11 – I got word that there had been a meeting about a week ago of Vietnam's political leadership in which a decision had been made to do nothing for now regarding the POWs. The supposed reasoning was that the possible reward didn't justify the risk of the public reaction going the wrong way. It was also claimed that they didn't have confidence that—as the proposed leader of our delegation—Tom's ambitions wouldn't tempt him to play the event to their detriment. Tom is very meticulous in what he says and his commitment to honor his word. I was disappointed, but not surprised, that they didn't realize that.

The messenger also said something that, if true, we hadn't previously known. All the actual prisoners were and had been for some time held in Laos. This conflicted with repeated public claims Vietnamese officials had made over the years that they had no authority and little influence in Laos.

After this new information, I began to experience a loss of my optimism, weary of all the ups and downs over the last six years. It seemed to me that our greatest opportunity to get our men home had come and gone this past year. Disappointment and frustration started setting in, and I became more doubtful about the veracity of "insider" reports from this point forward.

5/31/11 – I spoke to John Nevin about the most recent developments and we began to look at this entire process, cynically speculating that we might have been set up by somebody in the complex web of sources we had been counting on. Maybe those with political or economic interests overestimated our potential to monkey-wrench the development of more favorable relations between the two countries and had gone to extremes to use our hope to keep us quiet.

We experienced several more ups, downs, and misdirections during the remainder of 2011, but my loss of confidence and declining hope prevented me from getting too wrapped up in any of it.

1/31/12 – I attended a retirement dinner for an old friend. Over the years, I've participated in the traditional "roasts" of retiring colleagues. However, this time I was stumped and could not come up with anything in the humorous style I preferred. I was planning to just say what a great person he was and leave it at that.

Just before I was about to speak, one of the younger workers thanked the retiree, Paul, for being like a father to him. So I led off with that line—that Paul had been like a father to *me*—knowing that I looked older than Paul and he's one year older than me. This got the reaction I hoped for, so I worked it by staring in stone-faced disbelief.

5/1/12 - In what I was thinking of as "one last shot," I sent Tom an email with a proposal to try to put pressure on the Vietnamese. The idea was to present a letter to the Vietnamese Ambassador at the UN for forwarding to Hanoi. The letter that John Nevin and I put together was more direct and demanding in tone than we'd ever used with them:

We've been very patient and trusting of your government's good intentions over the last seven years. Our trust and patience has been based upon our conviction that the course of action we hope your government will take is also the course of action which will best serve your country's interest.

We've been largely silent, and when we spoke of the issue of greatest concern to us we have done so with caution and moderation. We are troubled by thoughts of the deteriorating health of aging Americans in your country. Further delay risks failure through attrition so we know you will understand our growing concern. Time is of the essence.

We need clarification regarding your government's intentions, and we need assurance that real steps are being taken toward the solution that we have previously been assured would be forthcoming. In addition, we would welcome any suggestions you might have for us to be helpful in expediting this process, providing that we can do so without any risk of damage to our own country's interests or the interests of those who rely on us.

5/4/12 Friday – I missed two phone calls from Tom on May 3rd and finally spoke to him on the 4th. His view was that things were not nearly as hopeless on the current track as I felt, and a harshly-worded letter might do more harm than good.

This sent me firmly back into the pessimistic doldrums that I had been in for some time. I had several brief conversations with sources, but nothing definitive, and being off the roller coaster gave me a badly needed respite.

Memorial Day weekend 2012 – Over dinner with Tom, John Syphrit, and Dave Kauffman, Tom had me retell the story of the 1988 Alfred E. Smith dinner. Tom loved hearing how I kept asking questions even though the Cardinal was scolding me each time and his angry reaction when I called him out on his promise to help the POWs.

Tom and Dave told stories about their experience in Russia doing research and making contacts concerning the U.S. POWs taken by the Red Army from German POW camps at the end of WWII, who were then shipped to the Soviet Union and never released.

On Memorial Day, I attended the Vietnam Veteran Commemoration ceremony at the Vietnam Veterans Memorial in D.C. This initiative by President Obama, commemorating the 50th anniversary of the first engagement of U.S. troops, would be implemented over the next thirteen years to reflect the span of the war from 1962 to 1975. Its purpose was to educate our citizens on the high price paid by Vietnam veterans during and after the war.

The Commemoration Committee was encouraging Vietnam veterans to talk about their experiences when they came home.

John Syphrit spoke to me about the importance of our legacy as Vietnam veterans and the need for us to educate young people about the war, how we were treated when we came home, and the tragic issue of our men left behind. John said he would like to see a book written about this; however, he said he wasn't a good writer, implying that I should consider that task. I told John that I wouldn't take on the job of an entire book, but I'd work on putting something together.

I sent John Syphrit and Tom Burch a write-up about my experience on return from Vietnam. They both liked it, and I told them they were welcome to give it to the committee or anyone interested.

June 3, 2012 – Secretary of Defense Leon Panetta visited the former U.S. naval base at Vietnam's Cam Ranh Bay to encourage greater cooperation in recovering U.S. remains. He was also there to discuss resolution of the territorial conflicts with China, which was reported by the media as historic. Even though Panetta's previous job in the Obama administration was CIA Director, he never mentioned the POW issue. He has to know that some POWs are still alive. Any visit to Vietnam by a senior U.S. official seems likely to harm our already dwindling prospects.

Thinking about this gave me a charge I hadn't experienced in a while, and I felt myself wanting to do something drastic to try to embarrass the current administration into doing something. I voted for Obama in 2008 and called anyone voting for McCain a traitor to our cause. That should eliminate any perception that I'm a Republican surrogate.

I had several conversations with John Nevin about the possibilities for doing something effective. In the end, we were forced to conclude that the only real hope at that point lay in a favorable decision by the Vietnamese. Nothing I could do here would have any real impact. John's input helped me to analyze the situation rationally rather than emotionally.

John has not only been a good friend, he's been a mentor. My success professionally, and whatever success I might be able to claim as a POW activist, is due to John's help. Our friendship is solid because it was forged in the heat of battle, where we got to see each other at our best and worst. John has been brutally honest when critiquing my opinions. His unbridled honesty helped me avoid looming pitfalls.

I will forever be grateful for his help in sorting fact from fiction.

July 11, 2012 – I called Tom about an article John had sent me as a heads-up. The article detailed some of the issues surrounding the China/Vietnam dispute over territorial sovereignty in the South China Sea. China has physical control of the sea and the surrounding islands, so they encouraged oil companies from around the world to bid on off-shore drilling rights. Meanwhile, Vietnam's legislature voted to claim sovereignty over all waters within 200 miles of their coastline.

An escalated conflict with China would give Vietnam additional incentive to get U.S. military support. Leon Panetta's June visit to Vietnam could have something to do with that incentive. My gut tells me this escalation and Panetta's visit will probably complicate the process to release our men, but Tom's opinion was that these developments would have no effect on what we were trying to do.

We had heard that high-ranking Vietnamese military officers had asked for a briefing regarding plans to release the men. Apparently, they had been left out of the high level meetings when these decisions were made. This seemed odd given the level of influence the military leadership typically had, and even more so given that they had control of the camps where the majority of the POWs were held. Good news/bad news one more time. It was good news that they had asked for the briefing since our understanding was that they were generally in favor of our project, but bad news that they had left out of the earlier discussions.

Another bad sign: one of the younger Politburo members thought to be leaning our way had apparently tried to meet with Panetta during his June trip but had been prevented from doing so.

July 12, 2012 – If I wasn't already paranoid with Panetta's visit to Vietnam in June and China's escalating conflict with Vietnam in the South China Sea, Hillary Clinton visited Laos a month later, allegedly to encourage resolution of over 300 U.S. servicemen missing in that country. This was part of a week-long visit to Asia related to U.S. economic interest in the area. Laos is one of the poorest countries in Asia with little political power, being very much under Vietnam's thumb. Hillary's visit wasn't a good sign.

August 3, 2012 – I heard that senior generals in Vietnam who favored the project had asked to delay the release until March 1, 2013. We couldn't get info regarding the significance of that date.

8/7/12 Tues – John Syphrit called me at my son's house while I was working on removing nails and screws from the rafters. I had sent word to him through Tom that I had a number of questions. John had called to say that he visited New York three or four times a year and we should get together on his next trip. I agreed and then asked him if he would be coming any time soon. He wasn't sure but would let me know well in advance, and I could ask him anything when we met, emphasizing the word, "anything," and he would answer anything he could.

8/31/12 – I sent John Syphrit an email asking whether he would be comfortable with our communicating by telephone, and he responded a couple of days later by saying to call him anytime.

9/5/12 – I phoned Syphrit and he was surprisingly forthcoming, addressing a number of things I thought might be too sensitive for the telephone. He said he and Tom Burch first met back in 1979 while assisting a veteran making a movie. Apparently, Tom was on a Reagan transition team in case he won the election, which he subsequently did. They both attended a big meeting at Page Airways (reputed to be a CIA front) at National Airport with about a hundred people on hand to discuss the possibility of POWs left behind. John said Tom basically ran the meeting and their relationship was bonded at that time.

John said that he and a number of Secret Service colleagues had officially and unofficially followed the careers of several of the POW activists going back to the beginning of our involvement. He wasn't able to say how, or who, but he strongly implied that they had quietly supported, and sometimes helped facilitate, our lawful activities.

For example, he briefed Tom before his trip to Russia years ago to warn him of potential problems. Tom has always felt that the trip to Russia and meeting with their military people to discuss American POWs sent to

Moscow during the Vietnam War was a success. One of their generals unofficially told Tom he was on the right track.

Al Gore asked an intelligence person who would know whether there were any POWs alive and he was told no. Even when retired head of the Defense Intelligence Agency, General Eugene Tighe, who had access to those reports, came clean to say there were live POWs, he was dismissed as a demented old man.

John referred back to a conversation he had with General Westmoreland, saying the military was supposed to be used for the good of the citizenry and the country, not for the good of the military. Westmoreland said there should be a special course given at West Point to educate the cadets on that principle.

John was a naturally pessimistic person. He believed the release would not happen because of the conflict between the young reformers and the old hardliners, and the fact that Vietnam and the U.S. would be in bed together by next year. The older group in power wants a secretive way to release them while the younger group wants a big splash to short-circuit possible repercussions at a later date.

On the bright side, he said he had several friends "in-the-know" who supported us and believed this would happen either by the end of this year or beginning of next.

John and I had previously discussed our desire to document our unfortunate experiences on our return from Vietnam, and he asked whether I was still in contact with Sydney Schanberg, saying that he would be a good person to help with that project. I said I would see whether Sydney would be interested.

John thought he had told me about his experience on his return, but he hadn't, so I asked.

His job during the war was Military Intelligence. His group would fly in by choppers immediately after a battle to assess worst-case enemy movement. He indicated it was a very risky business because the area wasn't always secured.

After six months in country, sometimes sleeping in trees, he was blown out of his chopper at about 100 feet from their landing zone. Subsequently, he was flown to Walter Reed Hospital in D.C. for a few weeks and then transferred not far away to Forest Glen Research Center for five to six weeks.

During his stay there, the wounded vets were crammed into a room where even some of the most basic assistance wasn't provided. There was excrement in a corner of the room with men urinating on themselves due to the lack of proper care. The person in charge of their well-being would say with conviction that stress was good for all of them in transitioning back to society. John was so upset with this person he eventually punched him to get out of that facility.

I observed that as extreme as that was, it was almost typical of the callous disregard our government seems to have for veterans. The handling of the POW issue, Agent Orange, Gulf War Syndrome, PTSD, high levels of veteran suicide, and the appalling conditions in some VA medical centers and Walter Reed Hospital, were signals hard to misunderstand.

His last few comments were very interesting and sensitive. He had information he couldn't discuss regarding McCain's time in Vietnam, the 1981 White House meeting, and the circumstances in which additional names of living POWs in Vietnam had been acquired since 2005.

9/22/12 Saturday – POW/MIA Recognition Day this year was the day before but the local American Legion Post in my area celebrates this day on Saturday to draw the most people. There were about sixty or so in attendance. I had a few beers at the bar before the event when a strange thing occurred. The bartender spilled a glass of red wine right next to me. I laughed and said to the Nam Knight motorcycle club member to my left that it reminded me of the incident involving Khai. I told him about it and my arrest and trial.

Shortly after that he turned his back to me, clearly indicating he had a problem with what I said. I'm not sure if it was because he didn't believe me, or because he was a policeman who found any arrest offensive, or both.

I laughed to myself, thinking if he didn't believe me imagine if he read my journal. I could definitely see where a person reading this would think I'm delusional, a fabricator, or at the very least an exaggerator. I'm beginning to reread the diary and actually find some of it a little hard to believe myself.

I came to this event with low expectations. After all these years, the American Legion would be focused entirely on remains. The post commander began by placing an empty chair to his right and then had one of his people place a specially designed black cloth with the POW logo over the top of the chair. He said this was a tradition that all posts reenacted at every American Legion meeting. He then read the Legion's official statement that they will never rest until we resolve what happened to our POWs, those missing in action, and a full accounting of everyone who served. The speakers included all wars going back to WWII. I was very impressed that they didn't buy into the USG position to focus only on the remains.

In 1991, I had spoken with American Legion executives Dave Christensen and John Summers about taking a stand on the POW issue to draw in the Vietnam vets and save their dying organization. This meeting with Dave and John influenced the membership side to take a much more aggressive stance in holding the government's feet to the fire.

There are those who will say that our publicizing our government's deceitfulness on this issue ultimately does more harm than good by undermining people's faith in their government. My friend John Nevin is very definitely in the other camp. He says there are few things in life more dangerous than misplaced faith, and that is most true regarding faith in those who have great power.

10/31/12 – We had the most devastating storm ever to hit the northeast. I purchased a generator for our refrigerators, heating, and lights. I had to travel past the overpass where the released Iranian hostages traveled on their way to West Point in 1981. On my way back, I stopped and walked to the overpass as I had done with my sister and two sons over thirty years ago. Considering this was the moment in my life that stirred emotions in me that would never go away, I was a little emotional when revisiting this site.

11/6/12 – On Election Day, I voted for the Libertarian candidate as a protest, even though I do not believe in all their positions. The two-party system has betrayed our democracy. The Democratic and Republican parties differ on many of the less important issues, but on many of the most important issues they are often in lockstep. They are both heavily influenced by the same special interest groups who bankroll their campaigns or deliver big projects and jobs to their districts. The big issues that would create positive change for the middle class are dealt with and tabled for another time. Both presidential campaigns along with outside non-profit fundraising groups spent three billion dollars. I don't know what I can do to help stop this hijacking. If there is an opportunity down the road to make an impact, I will consider my options.

11/9/12 – Bad news: another delay or maybe worse. A number of senior military officials have changed their position and no longer support the planned release.

For the first time my skepticism reached the tipping point. I finally concluded that there was a better than 50% chance that someone—here, there, or both—had been intentionally stringing us along for their own purposes but never intended for a release to occur. John Nevin had reached that conclusion some time ago but didn't want to inject pessimism in case he was wrong.

I told Tom that I thought the time had come to devise a plan to put added pressure on the Vietnamese. He neither agreed nor disagreed, but said he might consider going to Vietnam to see whether that would stir things up. I said that if he couldn't or didn't, I would consider going there myself.

Any trip to Vietnam would be potentially dangerous for me, considering my history of harassing their top leaders and ambassadors. I hoped this last option does not come about because as I became older I'd become less bold than when I was younger.

I believe releasing the names of the POWs given to us in 2005 would be a starting point to get their attention. We had long agonized over what to do about the list of names we had been given. We thought the list was probably valid, and if so we felt we owed it to the families of those on the list to let them know that we had them. However, there was no name on the list of anyone related to any of the families with whom we'd become acquainted over the years, so we thought we could safely assume, even fear, that many of those families wouldn't believe us and simply think we had some disreputable agenda.

It was a real dilemma, and each time we discussed it, we concluded that the most responsible thing to do was to wait until we received a "final" list prior to a confirmed release date. One thing was certain: we couldn't use the names as leverage against the Vietnamese or U.S. governments without first contacting every family member we could find, and that would be a huge undertaking.

11/11/12 – The first time I realized we left our men behind was exactly 29 years ago. It's been a long journey, one that's been emotionally draining.

Last night, I spoke to John Nevin about possible options if the release does not happen. He recommended delivering a letter to the Vietnamese Ambassador on January 27, 2013, the 40th anniversary of the signing of the Paris Peace Accords.

The letter should state that, absent decisive action on their part, we planned to start within ten days contacting the families of the men whose names had been given to us. This would create a firestorm, and it was anybody's guess whether the heat would fall mostly on the Vietnamese government, the U.S. government, or us. The other members of our team would need to sign off on this idea, but both John and I felt that if we had no contact by our New Year, then it would be time for us to go on the offensive.

11/12/12 – President Obama won reelection. I'm relieved because the military establishment was behind Romney and I feared he would have gone along with the chicken hawks and declared a war with Iran. We have had enough wars. Maybe Obama would be at least less influenced by the hawks, the Pentagon and the military contractors.

It was rumored that Senator John Kerry might be given either the Secretary of Defense or State. Either way, this will not be good for me, given the high profile opposition to him I orchestrated earlier. At least he'd be a little less dangerous to me and my friends than his pal McCain would have been. McCain hates us and has a very vengeful nature.

11/14/12 – John Syphrit called. I mentioned discussing plan B with our friends if plan A does not work and he strongly agreed in principle. I said a visit over there could be risky and perhaps a letter with a target date would be the way to go. I told John that I had not thought of the letter when initially discussing this; however, I suggested he think of the content or any other feasible options and we would meet the beginning of January if nothing favorable had happened by then.

11/21/12 Wednesday – Sydney Schanberg returned my call. I took John Nevin's advice and relayed the idea of a book to Sydney in terms of the past and how it relates to the current situation with returning vets being called heroes, but receiving so much less than heroic treatment.

I told him about John Syphrit's and my experiences when returning home and our desire to leave a legacy of helping other vets, and Sydney emphatically said it was a great idea. In an apologetic tone he said because of his deteriorating eyesight he could not commit to such an undertaking. Sydney explained it would take a major commitment that would require flying around the country to conduct research. He promised to send me the names of some quality people who might be interested in such a project.

11/27/12 – On Thanksgiving Day, one of my neighbors and I started talking. In the years past we had many political conversations so he knew I had been a hard core Goldwater supporter; he knew I was no "bleeding heart."

To put this conversation in perspective, Obama had just won his second Presidential term in office earlier in the month.

My neighbor started by saying it always bothered him that I voted for Obama in 2008, knowing that I had never voted for a Democratic candidate for President previously.

Even though I was surprised at having to defend my position, I realize now that I had been guilty in my earlier conversations with this neighbor of being too cautious when describing my feelings toward John McCain.

I told him the high bar I set years ago trying to decide who to vote for has been lowered to the point of deciding who is the least corrupt candidate. In my opinion, a social worker from Chicago who had only been in the Senate for a couple of years was likely to be less corrupt than a Senator like McCain with all those years in Washington, D.C., and I knew a lot about McCain that made him worse than any other Senator. I said McCain was part of the problem, not part of the solution.

My earlier faint hope that Obama would at least try to begin to clean up the corruption in D.C. had been dashed, so I voted for a third party candidate in the recent election as a protest vote. The Democrats and Republicans each raised over one billion dollars for the 2012 Presidential campaign. There's only one way to raise that kind of money: selling favors.

My neighbor expressed his dissatisfaction with Obama and repeated his confusion over my voting for him. I said assertively, "John McCain is the biggest scumbag on the face of this earth."

I explained that McCain not only stabbed his fellow POWs who had been left behind in the back, he also stabbed the POW/MIA family members, veterans, and others fighting for the freedom of those men. I described some of the issues.

At that point, I broke off our conversation. I include it here to leave no doubt about my opinion of John McCain. I consider him one of the most despicable people I know. If I ever allowed myself to hate a fellow American, as we were hated when we returned from Vietnam, John McCain would be at the very top of my list. No one even comes close, not even John Kerry, who would coast into second place.

12/7/12 – Spoke to John Syphrit and said I was drafting a letter to the Ambassador of Vietnam as an option to consider if plan A does not develop. I asked him if he would be available at the beginning of the year and he indicated he would be completely moved into his new house by the middle of February. John did indicate he could break away for a day if necessary and accepted my offer to come to him if I could convince Tom to join us.

12/26/12 – I called John Syphrit to discuss plan B. I hoped I could convince our team to take action in the beginning of the year to force some response from the Vietnamese government. John seemed reluctant to take any action, telling me a story about dripping water in the desert and when someone tried to make it better the water stopped dripping. He clearly didn't want to take an action that could ruin our chances of success.

However, I raised the issue of the USG's greater involvement in Vietnam, including military maneuvers in the South China Sea, an indirect threat to China. Hillary Clinton had visited Vietnam several times over the past year, and President Obama had recently attended an economic conference of Eastern Asian countries, excluding China. I thought the handwriting was on the wall; the USG was going to give Vietnam everything they ever wanted some time soon, probably in 2013, and he agreed.

John was the one who first alerted me to that fact earlier this year. If the USG gives Vietnam what they want, there will be no reason to return our men. John agreed and said maybe we could take a trip to Vietnam the middle of next year. I mentioned my apprehension about visiting Vietnam, with all the potential problems it presents.

I gave John a brief outline of a letter I drafted and he said that some of our guys could lose their security clearances if they were seen as being involved with negotiations with a foreign country. I reminded him that there were never negotiations, just informal discussions regarding what they had in mind. No classified information is involved, and there has never been implication of a quid pro quo of any kind. John felt it wouldn't be necessary to be technically guilty of anything for it to cause problems for us.

John said we should wait until after March before considering a plan B. John repeatedly said I would need to talk to our friends about these matters and I agreed, but with the understanding that we have a limited window to act. We don't know when the USG is likely to give Vietnam what they're asking for.

2/13/13 – President Obama gave his State of the Union speech last night and mentioned opening free trade markets in Asia and Europe. With John Kerry as the new Secretary of State, that means Vietnam will be at the top of his priority.

2/15/13 – I contacted John Nevin to work on the letter that I planned to deliver if there was no movement in the following month. I was writing it as coming only from me so that none of our friends could be put under pressure because of it. I was prepared to take all the heat if I have to go public with this information.

Ambassador Nguyen Quoc Cuong;

As you may know, I am the Director of Communication and Media Relations for the Foundation of the National Vietnam, Iraq, and Afghanistan Veterans Coalition. Our organization has been in contact with representatives of your government regarding U.S. veterans' issues.

In November 2005, we met with Major General Tran Dai Quang and his delegation in Washington, D.C., to discuss the unconditional repatriation of living American POWs from the recent war in Southeast Asia. At that time, General Quang said there were fifty-plus Americans held in Laos and indicated that your government had the ability to accomplish their release. In a private meeting later that night, as a sign of good faith, he revealed many of their names and locations.

In June 2010, we also met with a Brigadier General in Toronto. The general reiterated that more than fifty American POWs were still being held in Laos and confirmed that your government could achieve their release. At both meetings, we made it clear that we would facilitate logistics for their unconditional return to include ground and/or air transportation. We will provide these services without condition. We told both generals that our coalition would consider this courageous, humanitarian act a powerful sign of good will to U.S. veterans and the American people. This will be an important step in putting the unfortunate past behind our peoples.

We received strong assurances that these steps would be taken, but many years have passed. Time is of the essence due to the advancing age of these men and our patience has been stretched to its limit. We realize that there is some disagreement among your country's leaders regarding how to proceed. This ongoing internal conflict undermines our confidence that the proper steps will ever be taken.

While we have no desire to make things more difficult for your country or its leaders, we cannot continue to quietly accept further delays to the repatriation of our comrades in arms. Therefore, in the absence of visible and positive steps from your government, with reluctance we will proceed with the full release of this information in thirty days from the date of this letter to business, media, and U.S. government leaders, as well as the families of the men whose names we were given.

Bold action is required to change long held perceptions. You have a remarkable opportunity to demonstrate in unmistakable terms the true face of Vietnam's humanity and international good will.

We look forward to hearing from you no later than (due date).

Sincerely,
Jerry Kiley

2/17/13 Sunday – Bad news again, Vietnam's decision-makers were in the middle of a blame game involving the usual suspects: the old guard, the new guard, and the military.

There was a group of American investors who wanted to meet with the Vietnamese government leadership to discuss the POW issue, but so far there had been no luck arranging it. I inquired whether Perot was involved and word came back that he wasn't.

I had unfortunately failed to record the name of the General we met in Toronto so I asked some friends whom I knew would have it. I was told that this was very sensitive and we should have consensus among our team before releasing that name. I countered that there was extremely high likelihood that the governments of both the U.S. and Vietnam knew about it, so from whom would we be concealing the name? I was told we needed to talk about it. I thought that's what we were doing.

One big problem: if I sent the letter threatening to release the names of the still-living POWs given to us by the Vietnamese General and there was no favorable response from Vietnam within the thirty-day time limit, it would be essential to contact as many of the families of those men as possible before going public with their names. That will be difficult and time-consuming. Also, given that we couldn't actually prove the names were given to us by the General, and didn't know for sure whether the list was even valid in the first place, it was predictable that some families would be more angry with us than with the Vietnamese—whether or not they believed us—and some would over-react in the other direction. It was a real dilemma, and I knew I'd take heat from almost every direction. My life as I know it could be completely turned upside down, but it looked like "now or never." I was determined to follow my own advice not to leave this world with regrets.

3/9/13 Saturday – I met with friends in D.C. for breakfast and showed them the letter I was proposing. I knew it would not be met with glowing approval; however, I needed to shake things up. I heard previous arguments repeated, namely the possibility of endangering security clearances. I was also fully briefed on a parallel initiative which I had misunderstood because of the way we sometimes had to limit information when speaking on the telephone. It wasn't a bad idea, and had I previously grasped the details, I may not have forced this meeting.

In the end, I accepted the team judgment to hold off on the letter for the time being. We discussed some ideas for some actions we could take domestically and settled on Memorial Day demonstrations at the White House and Vietnamese embassy.

4/8/13 – I spoke to Artie Mueller, president of Rolling Thunder, and he liked the idea of the demonstrations at the White House and Vietnamese embassy, but he indicated that he had no time for planning or organizing on his end. I assured him I would handle it. He said he would pass the word in his organization, and he agreed to post information I sent him on the organization website.

4/11/13 – I spoke to insider friends to see what they knew and thought about Obama's State of the Union comment regarding the establishment of a free trade agreement with several Asian countries, including Vietnam. I was told that the agreement with Vietnam was a done deal and that we could be embarrassed by trying to stop something that was unstoppable. I was taken aback by this comment. I was thinking later that day how much I missed Ted Sampley. Had he been alive, he would have been the first person I'd call for advice.

It took me a couple of days before I said, "Bullshit!" It would be a disgrace for us to do nothing. One thing I have learned over the years, when things look the bleakest, it's time to turn up the heat and fight for what we believe.

I did a draft of the write-up for Artie and as usual John Nevin fine-tuned it. I got the fire in my belly after thinking, "What would Ted do?" I joked with John, saying I was channeling Ted. Later on, I was thinking that even though Ted and I were fairly equal in terms of hard core activism, no one could touch Ted on dedication and almost obsession to the POW issue. This cause was his second child.

I also called John LeBoutillier to see if he knew anything about the pending deal with Vietnam, and he said I definitely should proceed with my plan to raise a stink even if it was a done deal.

4/24/13 – I sent the following to Artie Muller for posting on the Rolling Thunder website.

"Last Best Chance"

President Obama and Sec of State Kerry are now on the verge of including Vietnam as a member of the proposed Trans-Pacific Partnership that will not only substantially improve Vietnam's trade, it will give them everything they have ever wanted.

Next year at this time, the new deal will be complete. This Memorial weekend is our last best chance to make our voices heard at the White House, Congress, Pentagon, State Department, Vietnamese embassy, and Politburo in Hanoi on behalf of living American POWs.

Our message will be clear: we strongly oppose any new deal with Vietnam until our living POWs are returned, and the POW issue will die only when all of us are dead.

We are requesting that all riders drive by the Vietnamese embassy (1233 20th St, NW) at least once during the weekend and make your presence felt by revving your engines and honking your horns.

We are also asking all of you, whether you're a rider or spectator, to join us in front of the White House Saturday afternoon (May 25th) at 2 PM in Lafayette Park to show the President what we think of this final act of betrayal against our brothers abandoned after the war ended in 1975.

Jerry Kiley
National Vietnam Veterans Coalition

4/25/13 – In the end, Artie Muller told me his webmaster had a personal problem and wasn't available; Artie's lack of support was something I had prior reasons to expect. When Tom was informed, he was very disappointed, considering how many times he had helped Artie and the Rolling Thunder group. People who hang around Washington, D.C., too long sometimes come to see themselves as a king protecting a kingdom. This was the final straw in a long series of disappointments with Artie.

8/13/13 - I decided to try to compile my ten years of journal-writing into book form for my grandchildren and their children. As usual, John Nevin said he would help me edit the material.

8/18/13 – I met with Mark Sauter, a long-time friend, author, and journalist, to inquire about how he self-published his book on the American POWs the U.S. abandoned after the Korean War. Mark is one of the foremost experts on that subject.

The main reason I met him in person was to discuss the struggle I was having in deciding whether, how, and when to release the seventeen POW names the Vietnamese General had given us. After he heard all my pros and cons, he definitely believed I should do it, and agreed that contacting as many of the families of those men as possible beforehand was essential.

March 2014 - I went snowmobiling with my son near the Adirondack Mountain range. When I reached the top of a mountain, I looked out to see a breathtaking view of the mountains heading north as far as the eye could see.

When I joined my son and his friends at the bottom of the mountain I said, "We're very lucky." The boys asked why and I explained that we were lucky to be born in this country. I could not help qualifying that with a criticism of how our politicians are doing everything they can to screw it up.

3/18/14 – I happened to turn on the TV and saw President Obama at a ceremony awarding 24 Medal of Honor recipients, 21 of them posthumously. The following is part of his speech that I transcribed:

Of the 24 American soldiers we honor today, ten never came home. One of them, Corporal Baldonado from the Korean War, is still missing, reminding us that we have a sacred obligation to keep working to give the families of our missing service members from all wars a full accounting of their loved ones.

With all due respect, this was just more words to pretend that the big issue is recovering the bones of the dead. When it comes down to what I think I'm entitled to expect from my government, I will keep it simple: TELL US WHAT HAPPENED TO DAVID HRDLICKA! His family has stated repeatedly over many years since his capture that they are absolutely sure, 100%, that this is David Hrdlicka in captivity.

Chapter Twenty
Betrayal of Our Returned War Veterans

April 23, 2014 – A Veterans Administration doctor, Sam Foote, who recently retired from the Phoenix, Arizona VA Health Care facility, said at least forty U.S. veterans died there while on a secret waiting list devised to cover-up delays in the system. His claim that this facility destroyed documents has created anger among veterans groups throughout the country.

Dr. Foote said that Dr. Petzel, who is Under-Secretary for Health, reporting directly to VA Secretary Shinseki in D.C., "should have been forced out right away," because "he was the chief cover-up artist."

5/15/14 – I sent the following letter to my local newspaper, *The Journal News.*

Senator John McCain Missing In Action
5/15/14
To: letters@lowhud.com
Please print in your Letters section. Thanks
Jerry Kiley

On May 9th, I saw John McCain on TV comforting the widow of a veteran who died waiting for help from his local Veterans Affairs (VA) hospital amid the scandal that there were two waiting lists kept to cover-up a very lengthy wait for medical treatment.

Much of this inadequate VA health care can be laid at the feet of Senator John McCain. As of 2008, he had the worst voting record of the 535 members of Congress for voting against increased health care funding for veterans.

The alleged "war hero" status that John McCain enjoys has given members of both major parties and the mainstream media a ready excuse to follow his lead when opposing veteran issues.

Widely perceived as a natural friend and supporter of veterans, John McCain has been anything but. It may be no coincidence that the worst of the VA "secret list" scandals uncovered so far occurred in Arizona, his home state.

John McCain is not only Missing In Action on veteran health care issues, he has been MIA regarding the abandonment of living American POWs after the Vietnam War, PTSD, Gulf War Syndrome, veteran homelessness and unemployment, and the current high rate of veteran suicides (22 per day).

*In 2007, he uncharacteristically admitted failure of his own
responsibility when the Walter Reed health care scandal broke.*

*A real "war hero" would have been out front fighting for his fellow
veterans on all these issues instead of playing to the media only after
scandals surface.*

5/15/14 – This scandal has grown even larger and spread to at least
four other states. Secretary General Shinseki testified before the Senate
Veterans' Affairs Committee and embarrassed himself by passing all
questions of substance to his subordinate, Dr. Petzel, and generally looked
like a deer caught in headlights.

When questioned by the senators on this committee, he acknowledged
doing nothing since he found out about a month ago despite the fact that one
of the senators said there were fifty Inspector General (IG) reports since
2013 addressing this problem.

His only answer was to wait for the Inspector General's (IG) report in
two months. The problem is that the IG is part of the system and based upon
the many reports coming out of the previous investigations over several
years, nothing was ever done to address this issue.

Perhaps the most damning information came from an internal memo
sent by William Schoenhard, Deputy Under-Secretary for Health, to the
chiefs of VA facilities in 2010. The following are excerpts from an NBC
NEWS online article first published on May 13, 2014, entitled, "Memos
Show VA Staffers Have Been 'Gaming System' for Six Years."

Internal memos show the VA had been playing whack-a-mole for at
least six years with employees using dozens of different scheduling tricks to
hide substantial delays in health care for America's veterans. And whenever
the VA tries to stop its staffers from "gaming the system," the staffers come
up with new techniques.

Whistleblowers around the country are now accusing the VA of
hiding a backlog in patient care with bookkeeping tricks, and a former
doctor at a VA facility in Arizona says the delays may have contributed to
the deaths of forty patients.

In an April 26, 2010, memo, William Schoenhard said, "It has come
to my attention that in order to improve scores on assorted access measures,
certain facilities have adopted use of inappropriate scheduling practices
sometimes referred to as 'gaming strategies.' ... This is not patient-centered
care."

Schoenhard then listed two dozen different tactics identified in a 2008
study that facilities around the country were using to cut down on the
officially recorded time that patients had to wait for care.

"Please be cautioned that since 2008, additional new or modified
gaming strategies may have emerged, so do not consider this list a full

description of all current possibilities of inappropriate scheduling practices that need to be addressed. These practices will not be tolerated."

Under oath, Shinseki claimed not to know about the memo even though he acknowledged knowing Schoenhard.

Dr. Petzel, Undersecretary for Health, sitting next to Shinseki, acknowledged seeing the 2010 memo; however, under further questioning Petzel and Shinseki said none of the 3,000 people they'd disciplined included scheduling problems that they were aware of. In other words, they never addressed this problem.

The next day, Petzel resigned. There is no punishment involved because he was planning on retiring before the end of the year anyway. What we need to look at is who knew, when did they know it, and how much money did they make in bonuses while they covered this up. That raises the stakes to criminal behavior. Someone needs to be held accountable in a court of law.

Several days later, I spoke to John Nevin about wanting to do something to highlight this problem, suggesting perhaps going to Phoenix to help organize the families who'd lost their loved ones.

John said I would have a greater impact on the national stage by first creating an alliance with one of the Iraq /Afghanistan veterans groups. We decided I should set up a meeting with leaders of that group and ask John Syphrit and Mike Benge to join me.

5/22/14 - John Syphrit and LeBoutillier both returned my calls. John Syphrit said he wasn't going to jump on the bandwagon demanding Shinseki's resignation until he sees the IG report due in several months. I asked if he was interested in joining me at a meeting with IAVA and he declined, stating he would rather work behind the scenes to set up a high-level veterans committee that would be given full access to any and all VA facilities around the country.

When John LeBoutillier called me, I asked if there was anything I could do to help him. John had stated on Fox TV that the veterans should be granted access to the same exact health care system Congress has for themselves. Even though it's very unlikely Congress would pass such legislation, John challenged anyone in Congress to say they deserved better healthcare than our military.

John did say he had something brewing on the POW issue and if anything broke his secretary was instructed to call me immediately.

5/23/14 – I emailed the Iraq and Afghanistan Veterans of America to request a contact to set up a meeting with Tom Tarantino, the IAVA Chief Policy Officer.

5/29/14 – *USA Today* reported that delaying medical care to veterans and manipulating records to hide those delays is "systemic throughout" the VA health system in the preliminary Inspector General's report.

The IG report also found that there were 1,700 veterans at the Phoenix facility who are patients there but not on any official waiting list even though they need to see a doctor. The IG is now working with the Justice Department to determine if this falsifying of records is criminal. Of course it is criminal, but whether prosecutions result will depend on who is influential among those most in need of CYA.

The drum beat calling for Shinseki's resignation is much louder now. McCain, never one to miss a chance to talk big on behalf of veterans, has now jumped on the bandwagon. As mentioned earlier, his voting record clearly indicates it's only talk.

5/30/14 – A *USA Today* article by Gregg Zoroya reported that the number of medical facilities now being looked at for possible violations has risen to 72 from only ten violations two weeks ago.

Later in the day, Shinseki resigned and is being temporarily replaced by his Deputy Secretary Sloan Gibson, who has been with the VA for only three months.

5/31/14 – As reported in an article today, the House of Representatives voted to freeze bonuses to senior VA executives for five years. It turns out that the director of the Phoenix VA facility received $8,500 in bonus while under an open IG investigation.

An unrelated event this morning will take away from the media blitz of the VA scandal. Sgt. Bowe Bergdahl, the only American POW from the Afghanistan war, was traded and released for five Taliban members we previously held as prisoners in Guantanamo, Cuba.

As far as I know, this is the first time we publicaly traded for one of our POWs.

In a statement, President Barack Obama said Bergdahl's recovery "is a reminder of America's unwavering commitment to leave no man or woman in uniform behind on the battlefield."

If the timing wasn't intentional, it was a very fortunate coincidence for the Administration that this occurred when it did, breaking the cycle of non-stop reporting on the VA scandal. A big brouhaha developed over whether Bergdahl was a legitimate POW, a deserter, or a hero. I think he was more victim than any of those. He was fascinated with Pashtun culture and left the camp unarmed. I suspect he fully intended to return after a "visit" with locals.

6/8/14 – Since I never saw my earlier letter to the editor published, I sent a second letter, believing that McCain's involvement would compromise efforts to make a substantial positive change in the VA system:

"Senator John McCain's Hypocrisy"
John McCain is again the shining knight coming to the rescue with compromise legislation on Veterans Administration health care. Earlier this

year, John McCain and forty of his Republican colleagues blocked a vote on a bill calling for over two dozen new medical facilities to help a healthcare system burdened by veterans of the Iraq and Afghanistan wars.

John McCain led Washington Senate Republicans in blocking a bill to expand healthcare and education programs for veterans, claiming that the $24 billion bill was too expensive.

Much of this inadequate VA health care can be laid at the feet of Senator John McCain. As of 2008, McCain had the worst voting record of the 535 members of Congress for voting against increased health care funding for veterans.

I hope McCain does not gut Bernie Sanders' legislation as he did with the POW/MIA Missing Service Personnel Act (2005) when his amendment completely reversed a provision that held government officials criminally responsible for withholding information from family members.

John McCain is widely perceived as a natural friend of veterans; however, he is MIA on veteran health care issues, abandonment of living American POWs after the Vietnam War, PTSD, Gulf War Syndrome, veteran homelessness, unemployment, and current high rate of veteran suicides of one per hour.

A real "war hero" would have been out front fighting for his fellow veterans on all these issues instead of playing to the media only after scandals surface.

6/9/14 – I received an email from the Assistant Editor of my newspaper, stating that she could not print my second letter because my first one was published on 6/2/14.

6/10/14 – I called the customer service number for *The Journal News*. The woman who answered was very polite, but she could not give me a name and number to call in case I needed to take my concerns to the paper's owner, Gannett News Service.

6/11/14 – A bill pushed by Bernie Sanders and McCain passed the Senate and is going to the house. This bill is similar to the one McCain voted against in February, with one significant improvement to get immediate relief for those vets waiting over thirty days for help. I still have to see how it plays out because of my skepticism of McCain and the Republicans. On the other hand, it's not unlike McCain to do an immediate about-face if he thinks it's in his interest.

6/24/14 – I called John Nevin to tell him I had decided to do a press conference to release the list of POW names. He said it is probably a go big or go bust situation, and that he didn't necessarily believe it was a good move.

After I suggested that we could benefit from all the talk from President Obama and others about leaving no man behind, he seemed to be a little less doubtful. If we didn't act before the Bergdahl story was forgotten, we may never have as good a chance. I have always felt that President Obama and Michelle were good people caught up in the political frenzy in D.C., but there was no disputing that there had been many disappointments.

Even though John didn't share my point of view—and he held firm to the necessity of contacting the families of the men on the list before we went public—he immediately came up with the idea of using quotes from current Secretary of State John Kerry, who was directly involved in the cover-up. John said we need to get experts on the POW issue for Vietnam, Korea, and WWII. We agreed that Mark Sauter was a good choice for both Korea and WWII, perhaps Al Santoli for Vietnam, and Tom Ashworth for Laos. I had already considered participants, including Carol Hrdlicka, Lynn O'Shea, and Mike Benge. John said we should try to get John Syphrit and former Senator Bob Smith.

I called Sydney Schanberg to discuss the situation mentioned above and without knowing what the meeting was about he asked if I could come that afternoon. I met with him for about an hour and a half. Even though I told him I had to get clearance from some friends before I gave specifics, he seemed intrigued with the general overview.

We agreed to meet again before I took any action, which I thought would be in a two to three week time frame. That next meeting would involve giving him all the details.

6/25/14 – A *USA Today* article dated the day before said an independent investigator found that the VA ignored whistleblowers reporting improperly cleaned medical instruments and year-long delays in evaluating psych patients. A VA spokesman claimed that the problems caused no potential harm to the public health or safety. "Public health or safety" are weasel words that didn't address the issue in question.

Carolyn Lerner, who leads the U.S. Office of Special Counsel, wrote a letter to President Obama on Monday saying that the VA's Office of the Medical Inspector used this "harmless error" defense acknowledging that problems existed while claiming that patient care is unaffected.

She also said, "This approach has prevented the VA from acknowledging the severity of systemic problems and from taking the necessary steps to provide quality care to veterans."

As reported by *USA TODAY*, the scheduling clerk for the Phoenix VA acknowledged she maintained the secret list of veterans who waited months for appointments. She turned over evidence to the IG, including a statement that her entry of "deceased" was later changed by someone to "entered in error" and "no longer needed" to cover-up the number of deaths.

6/26/14 – The general counsel for the VA resigned yesterday. He resigned the day after Carolyn Lerner's letter to the President became public. Apparently the general counsel approved the "harmless error" defense.

6/27/14 – I asked if Carol Hrdlicka could join me in a press conference around the theme "No One Left Behind" and she said perhaps in three or four weeks because one of her mares just had a new foal. I told her there was more to the press conference that would be revealed at a later date. Fortunately, Carol trusts that whatever I'm involved in is worth her trip across the country.

6/28/14 – I called Al Santoli to see if he would available for a press conference in about a month. Al is well respected and very knowledgeable concerning our POWs.

6/29/14 – President Obama is nominating Bob McDonald, former Proctor and Gamble CEO, for VA Secretary to replace Shinseki.

On a more humorous note, Bob McDonald was Vice Chairman of P&G when I attended the infamous "red wine incident" banquet in 2005. The table at which I had taken a seat was for Proctor and Gamble employees. Perhaps I should send Bob a letter thanking him for the dried chicken I ate at $1,000 per plate and for the red wine I never got to drink.

7/1/14 – I spoke to John Nevin about Paul Rieckhoff (CEO, IAVA) appearing on Bill Maher's show "Real Time." I liked his feistiness in arguing his point of view. I told John that the standard I use to judge a veteran as a potential leader is how he or she will stand up to John McCain. Unfortunately, McCain is a rabid dog when he needs to be and the person opposing him cannot wilt under that intense pressure.

John and I agreed that Paul was tough enough to take on McCain, if necessary.

7/3/14 – My local newspaper printed a story by *USA Today*'s Kevin Johnson indicating that U.S. Magistrate Judge Deborah Robinson ordered that a Benghazi terrorist, suspected in the attack on our U.S. embassy, should be detained indefinitely.

I only mention this because Deborah Robinson was the judge who decided I wasn't guilty in my federal trial. It's unusual that within a four day period both Judge Robinson and Proctor and Gamble, who had ties to my three-day trial, were prominent in the national news.

Sydney Schanberg called this afternoon to follow-up on our meeting last week. He asked me some questions about what I was going to do and the source of the information we had received. When I told him our source was Vietnamese and that it had nothing to do with an extraction, he said he was comfortable with that information. I indicated that he would be informed about the details when I had clearance from my group to take him into our confidence.

Sydney said he was working on an article regarding Bergdahl.

7/23/14 – *USA Today* reported that the nominee for VA Secretary, Robert McDonald, was warned by Senators about the problems that await him if he is confirmed sometime in August. When asked why he wanted this job, he said, "I desperately want this job because I think I can make a difference." "I think there's no higher calling. If not me, who?"

I found this last statement interesting because over the years when I've been asked by my close friends and wife why I do what I do, my answer has been the same, "If not me, who else is going to do it?"

My wife will always follow that by saying, "There has to be someone else who can do this besides you." In the past, there were others like Ted Sampley, but now it has fallen to me to push the envelope.

I returned from vacation, having spent almost two weeks away from my granddaughters I often babysit for. After going to the park and playing with them I realized again how lucky I was and how much I didn't want to change what I had come to love so much.

I also realized that I need to notify the seventeen families whose names we were given. I was caught between a rock and a hard place with no easy solution in sight.

8/4/14 – John Nevin told me Pat Buchanan was on one of the cable stations, saying that one of President Nixon's great accomplishments was bringing home all the POWs from the Vietnam War. I reminded John about my meeting with Buchanan in the White House when he was President Reagan's Press Secretary. Paul Weyrich, who was the head of the Stanton Group, a very powerful conservative organization, complimented me after the meeting was over, saying I wasn't intimidated by that environment as he had feared and that I did a very good job in pressing Buchanan on the POW issue.

Buchanan had every opportunity to do something about the issue in the 1980s; however, he followed President Reagan's lead and did nothing. Even though I generally like his outspoken views, he is part of the problem in D.C. because he definitely is not part of the solution.

August 2014 – During the month, John Nevin and I discussed the possibility of a press conference. We agreed that with the media fixated on U.S. bombing of ISIS and the turmoil in the Ukraine, it was going to be hard to determine the right time to begin the process of contacting the POW families.

Initially John talked about including our experts on the POW issue from WWII and the Korean War; however, I wasn't comfortable with the possibility of diluting our message about the names of the men given to us in 2005 and 2007.

Even though John makes very compelling arguments to support his suggestions, I subsequently told him there are times I will do something based on my gut feeling rather than sound logic.

In our last conversation, he said staying focused on those names for the purpose of the press conference made sense, but the rest of the story still needed to be told.

Carol Hrdlicka called to say even if she wasn't able to attend that we could SKYPE so she could see the press conference and participate. To my surprise, John said I should do it without Carol so the message about the men is not diminished. He said many in the media were aware of Carol's story and they would treat it as "old news, previously debunked." (John and I were clear between us about what the word "debunked" usually meant: some Pentagon spokesperson simply said something wasn't true without offering evidence to support the claim, and media types unfriendly to our position would use "debunked.")

9/23/14 – President Obama spoke at the Clinton Global Initiative in New York to discuss the need for the basic freedom to worship and speak your mind without retribution. I happened to see this speech live as he listed those who had died and those who are currently detained or imprisoned. I cringed until he mentioned Father Ly at the very end.

It's ironic that it was President Clinton who normalized relations with Vietnam, legitimizing their brutal, godless regime. There was still a chance that President Obama would hold Vietnam accountable. That would mean no Trans-Pacific Partnership (TPP) for them until they substantially cleaned up their human rights (rights abuse) behavior. Even though Father Ly is perhaps the best known, there are many more who are imprisoned for simply practicing their religions or merely mentioning freedom or democracy.

Even though there is little hope that someone will step up to secure the release of our men, the TPP could be used as leverage if that scenario were to present itself.

10/2/14 –My birthday. I turned 68 years old, or as I like to say, more than two-thirds of a century.

I saw talk show host Montel Williams give an impassioned plea for President Obama to get directly involved in securing the release of an American veteran who is being held in Mexico for possession of a weapon. Montel said the veteran was already diagnosed by the USG as having PTSD and being incarcerated in a Mexican jail will only exacerbate that problem.

I could not help thinking that if veterans do start a nationwide movement to aggressively pursue all of our issues, Montel would be an excellent spokesperson.

10/9/14 – My wife mishandled a boiling pot of water that fell on her chest and one arm. This was a potential game-changer not only for her but for everyone she knows, especially me. A full recovery will take at least a year. I later learned that in this same time John Nevin's wife Karen broke her leg, and would be non-weight-bearing for twelve weeks. We were both promoted to cooking, cleaning, and nursing.

10/30/14 – Sydney Schanberg called me today to find out how I was doing with my book. I told him I thought I was in the final stages. When I told him I had expanded the meaning of the title *Betrayal* to include all veterans' issues from all the wars going back to World War I, he responded enthusiastically. He basically said it's about time.

I told him chapter six of his newest book would be the beginning of my book, word for word, exactly as he wrote it. At this point he said, "I can't wait to read it." Before I released the book I would send him a digital copy to read.

Sydney's eyesight is failing but his wife reads to him much of what he receives, and there are software programs available that could convert text to audio. Strange as this may sound, I was very interested in hearing not only his opinion, but his wife's. She has been his anchor and seemed generally to know just about all he did on sensitive subjects.

Sydney then said he was pursuing the Nixon tapes from March 1973 that would reveal his conversations about the POW issue. Those tapes have not been released to date. Given the large number of sensitive tapes that have been released, I naturally suspected that failure to release these was no coincidence. Sydney said his investigations always follow a path that no one else has taken. He was trying to contact people high up in the Pentagon to find out why they had not been released and to ask what gives them the authority to hold them. This sounded like a great idea; however, it seems they always find a way, no matter what the law. After all, torture isn't torture.

I was planning to ask Sydney for an endorsement for the cover of my book; since he called me, it seemed like the right moment to ask. I said, "I would be honored if you could say a few words that I could include in the book." He responded by saying, "Back at you."

I said that the one thing that had always resonated with me in our conversations over the years is the respect he had shown for Vietnam veterans who were knocked down, got up, and never gave up fighting. I'm sure Sydney understood that I hoped he would include this in his comments and ultimately that future generations would look back and see this as our legacy.

Even though my wife was just admitted to a rehab center after skin grafting and lying in bed for the last three weeks in excruciating pain, I have to finish this book because, as John Nevin told me, "This has become much bigger than a journal for your grandchildren."

12/16/14 – I called John to tell him that the final 100 pages will be the most difficult. He answered the phone, "Yo."

I said, "Yo, yo."

John said he was busy and to call him back at 9 PM. I said okay and then said, "If you had answered, 'Yo, yo,' then I would have to say, 'Yo, yo, yo'."

He laughed and I said, "Don't take it personally; it's a New York thing."

This is probably the best example of how important John has been to me over the years. We have a mutual respect for each other; John has been my mentor over the years, helping me and supporting me even when he wasn't 100% behind the way I wanted to go. Our friendship has bonded over the last thirty years. My judgment has sometimes been clouded by my emotions and John has always kept me grounded.

I can guarantee you that without John Nevin, I would not be writing the final pages of this book. I don't think he knows how profound his influence has been in my life. [John's Note: You can't make a silk purse out of a pig's ear and you can't polish a Hershey bar... Excellent raw material provides excellent potential.]

12/16/14 – My local newspaper said that—according to the Inspector General's report from the day before—the VA made false or misleading statements when they said 23 veterans had died because of delays in their health care dating back to 1999. In fact, they only went back to 2007, so the actual number of deaths back to 1999 would be much greater. Speculation was that we might never know the real number. At that point, we had to assume that every statement made by the VA was unreliable and hope things could be changed in the future.

3/7/15 – The previous five months were a game changer. I was consumed with caring for my wife through her healing process as well as babysitting for two of my granddaughters.

I was able to find time to work on my journal and discussed with John Nevin whether there might be an advantageous date to establish as a goal for the book's release.

We also agreed that it was time to go forward with contacting the families of the seventeen names we were given years ago. I have to be honest that the thought of releasing this information scares me because the reaction could be catastrophic. The USG and its minions will normally ignore any challenge to authority, but if simply ignoring doesn't work, "kill the messenger" is a common tactic.

My critics would have the additional advantage of having two high-profile characters with unlimited media access who already have an axe to grind with me: John Kerry and John McCain.

One of their common lines of attack has been that we are preying on the family members in order to make money. Without a doubt my involvement in veterans' issues, particularly POW/MIA, has cost me a considerable amount of money. I'm very fortunate that my house is paid in full and that I receive a substantial pension after working for 44 years for the same company. This, along with Social Security has put me in a very sound position financially, so I've been able to pay many of my own expenses, even when operating for one of the organizations I've worked with.

But that's not a real issue. It's just a false charge that will sound as though it might be true, and that's all the critics care about.

I'll probably lose some of the money I invest to turn this journal to book form, but, as Mark Sauter told me, I have a responsibility not only to the family members but also as a matter of history to put much of this on record. If I actually profit from the book, I'll divide the proceeds between the Wounded Warrior Project and an education fund for my three granddaughters.

Perhaps worse than an attack from the USG could be a very negative reaction from the families of the men whose names we were given years ago. Some would criticize me for not informing them years ago, and some would claim I was making it up for some reason of my own. Those would hurt more than anything the USG could say about me, but some of it is inevitable.

I could also expect both positive and negative reaction from veterans. At this point in my life, four years into my retirement, I absolutely do not want this attention; however, I need to do what is right regardless of the ramifications. That thought is what pushed me forward for the last 32 years of my life, and I wasn't going to change.

With all of this weighing on me, I contacted Lynn O'Shea of the National Alliance of Families to solicit her help in locating as many families as possible. I wanted to set up a meeting but was sorry to hear that she had some rather serious health problems and her scheduled therapy would last at least another three weeks. Lynn said she would contact me when she returned home.

Lynn is one of those people with whom our movement has been blessed who have neither family connection to any of the missing nor military or veteran background. She has simply been moved to right a wrong. (John Nevin's first wife Margaret is another one.) They are simply American patriots who have unselfishly devoted themselves to a cause. I've been surrounded by these patriots, many of whom, like Lynn, have shown incredible character and endurance in the face of adversity.

No doubt seeing their commitment and dedication helped me summon the will to continue even during our darkest periods.

Lynn recently released a book that was the product of many years of her research: *Abandoned in Place*. As of this writing, I have not read it but John Nevin tells me it is outstanding. He says it is available on Amazon and would be an excellent read whether a person knows little or nothing about this issue or wants to expand already extensive knowledge.

3/9/15 – *USA TODAY* has been relentless in reporting problems with veteran health care issues. An article written by Donovan Slack reported that the Veterans Administration has not and apparently does not want to release the results of 140 VA healthcare investigations. It is impossible to know how many serious problems exist without seeing the reports, and this leaves potentially dangerous problems to fester.

Catherine Gromek, a VA Inspector General spokesperson, said, "We have not analyzed these reports and therefore cannot offer a specific description of the kinds of reasons." Another spokesperson said they would not release any reports that they determined are unsubstantiated. No one would be able to question their judgment if the reports are not released.

My experience over these many years with various elected and appointed officials and agents of our government has made me quite skeptical of taking what they say at face value. If it weren't for the whistleblowers, we'd know far less than we do now, but the Obama administration—despite campaign promises of openness—has been one of the worst in punishing them. Transparency is hard to achieve when government officials are allowed to get away with lies that have nothing to do with national security, but are only to avoid the embarrassment of the citizenry knowing the truth. No more lies!

3/12/15 – Another article in *USA TODAY* by Gregg Zoroya, this one titled, "Soldiers Face Crisis in Substance-Abuse Care," states that the 20,000 soldiers applying for help each year at Army substance-abuse clinics experience a program in disarray.

Their investigation stated that thousands of veterans requiring treatment were turned away. Worse, they found that over two dozen had received poor care that resulted in suicide.

4/20/15 – I called Lynn O'Shea to see how she was doing and I was told that she had an adverse reaction to the medication she was taking. She'd wound up in the hospital on two occasions since our last conversation.

If the USG and public officials decide to verbally attack us as they have in the past, remember Lynn O'Shea and the family members, veterans, and concerned citizens who devoted their lives to this cause and are no longer with us. I shed a number of tears in writing these three paragraphs.

4/21/15 – John Nevin was sad to hear of Lynn's setback. He mentioned that trying to contact the families, whose names were given to us by the Vietnamese General, would be awkward at best. We agreed to wait for the release of the book to contact whatever families we could find, and would send them advance copies of this journal.

4/26/15 – My local newspaper ran a front page story on suicides in America. It turns out that veterans are over three times more likely to kill themselves than non-veterans.

This probably comes as no surprise to the people who know that, on average, one U.S. veteran commits suicide every hour of every day, 365 days a year.

5/29/15 – I met for dinner with some of the colleagues I'd worked with before my retirement. Before the evening began, I met with Ray Depew, who reported to me for many years. We sat at the bar talking about our books. I told Ray about my deep concern regarding the well-being of my family and the problems that my book could bring. Ray leaned forward, looked me in the eye, pointed his finger in my direction, and said with conviction, almost with disdain, "The Jerry Kiley I know is not afraid of anything or anybody, and you have to complete that book!"

My response was a nervous laugh, a smile, and I simply said, "Okay."

My best friends over the years would never be that brash. It took Ray giving me a swift kick in my ass to get me going again. Ray is over thirty years my junior but his enthusiasm motivated me to complete my journey, wherever that leads me. Two days later, I sent John Nevin the next group of pages to be edited.

Even though I never directly told Ray, I was proud of who he had become. He was beginning to harness all the energy which seemed unlimited at a younger age. In our relatively short professional relationship, I referred to him as "Grasshopper." It was an unspoken compliment to him that what I saw of his growth prevented me from thinking "Grasshopper" even once that night.

6/2/15 – *USA Today* ran another article concerning a VA study on the brain damage improvised explosive devices (IEDs) had on the Iraq and Afghanistan veterans. The study conducted by VA scientists and published in *Brain: A Journal of Neurology,* indicated early aging in the brains of Iraq and Afghanistan war veterans. Even some who didn't show any symptoms of concussion were affected with memory loss at an early age.

Benjamin Trotter, who is a VA bio-medical engineer and lead author of the study, indicated that those veterans with blast exposure are experiencing brain deterioration at a faster rate.

William Milberg, a Harvard Medical School professor, said if Alzheimer's or other dementia-like illnesses appear five to ten years earlier, "This would have tremendous consequences for society." He also said, "We would have to develop on a much larger scale ways of taking care of people."

To me this is very disconcerting because the VA system is already underperforming due to management failures and funding levels.

The article continued, "An estimated 2.7 million Americans served in Iraq and Afghanistan. Nearly 1.9 million are now veterans, about 60% of whom have or are receiving VA treatment, according to the agency."

Also many veterans say that over the course of several deployments the number of explosions they survived rose into double digits.

6/30/15 – Last week President Obama issued a presidential directive and executive order stating that the U.S. government will no longer threaten criminal prosecution when families of American hostages held abroad try to negotiate and pay ransom for their release.

The government's official position is unchanged—no negotiations for hostages—even though they have violated that policy before.

7/1/15 – *USA Today* reported that the embattled chief watchdog for the VA, General Inspector General Richard Griffin, resigned after 43 years as a federal government employee.

His resignation comes one day after a group of whistleblowers, from more than a dozen VA medical facilities, urged President Obama to fire Griffin because he went after whistleblowers rather than the problems they reported. Griffin also failed to cooperate with oversight and instead conducted investigations in a "horrifying pattern of whitewashing and deceit."

As I mentioned earlier, President Obama has gone back on his campaign promise of transparency and open government and instead has gone along with, and perhaps has promoted, the corrupt culture of Washington, D.C. This is no clearer than in the current climate of punishing the messenger in order to hide the truth from the American people and U.S. veterans.

I'm not suggesting that Obama is the only one at fault. All the previous Congresses and Administrations, whether they be Democratic or Republican, are also responsible; however, Obama had over six years to address this situation and he didn't.

We should make sure that as veterans we fully support these brave whistleblowers who have put their careers and families in the cross-hairs of people who can crush anyone who gets in their way.

I have always reserved the hero status to those who served in the heat of combat and those who put their lives at risk domestically to keep us safe; this group of whistleblowers comes very close to being heroes.

When I did a search on the internet for Obama/whistleblowers, I was shocked to see dozens of articles criticizing Obama for being the worst president in prosecuting whistleblowers, and sometimes even the journalists who received the scandalous evidence. **One of these articles said there were over 1,500 complaints made in 2014 about the VA, more than any other department in the U.S. government.**

7/8/15 – *USA Today* reports that Obama said, after a meeting with the leaders of Vietnam's ruling party at the White House, that Vietnam has become "a very constructive partner." Obama also said they had candid discussions about human rights issues, including freedom of religion and incarceration of political prisoners.

They also discussed the proposed Trans-Pacific Partnership of a dozen countries, including the U.S. and Vietnam, that is supposed to include a threshold for human rights; however, since the TPP is a confidential document that has been viewed by only a few, it is impossible to say whether Vietnam clears that low bar.

If Vietnam does get in, then perhaps the criteria for human rights is that they didn't kill enough of their own people to disqualify this brutal, godless, Communist regime.

The founding fathers, who rebelled against the English king, would be horrified to see how we are propping up these barbarians in the name of financial reward. Many have said that the majority of this reward will go to the greedy bastards that are ruining this country.

Ironically, the king of England we fought against in the Revolutionary War was a boy scout compared to those committing the egregious government-sanctioned human rights violations in Vietnam.

7/14/15 – A Washington Associated Press article said that the Department of Veterans Affairs may have to close some hospitals next month if Congress does not appropriate $2.5 billion to close a shortfall for the current budget year.

The VA told Congress that an increased demand by veterans for health care, including costly treatments for hepatitis C, created this shortfall. The VA is also considering furloughs and hiring freezes to close a funding gap.

The VA is also considering using up to $3 billion from the new Veterans Choice program, which was a $10 million Congressional appropriation in response to the veteran health care scandal last year where VA hospitals falsified records to cover up the delays.

The VA needs flexibility from Congress to close the budget gap, Gibson said, adding that the VA said Congress needs to act "in the next three weeks to avoid drastic consequences" and lawmakers from both parties faulted the VA for failing to anticipate or fix budget problems.

Rep. Jeff Miller (R-Florida), chairman of the House Veterans Affairs Committee, said he was troubled at the "VA's continued lack of transparency and refusal to be forthright with Congress," but said, "Veterans must not be penalized for VA's ongoing mismanagement."

"This is far from the first time VA has disclosed problems far too late and turned its blatant mismanagement into a fiscal emergency," Miller said. He called on President Barack Obama to "step up and become engaged" in order to "ensure VA's incompetence does not shut down hospitals and deny veterans the care they have earned."

Our government in general and the VA specifically are so bogged down in their own bureaucratic incompetence that committing fraud to cover up failures has become a way of life.

Lack of transparency comes up again in a department that Obama promised would deliver efficient health care to its veterans.

Where is the fake hero John McCain, Chairman of the Armed Services Committee? He's where he usually is: leading from behind, reversing previous positions that fostered the deceptions surrounding veterans' issues in the first place.

Maybe our first step should be to express our disappointment and anger at the dismal failures of our government officials in a veterans march on Washington, D.C. If the egregious deficiencies in veteran health care aren't enough to mobilize U.S. veterans to demand of our elected leaders much improved performance, accountability and honesty in fulfilling their promises, I have little hope for the future of our country.

NO MORE LIES!

Chapter Twenty-One
Final Comments

My wife, who was a registered nurse for ten years in a very busy New York emergency room, said, "You can always tell the character of a person by the way they treat their parents."

I would say, "You can always tell the character of a government by the way it lives up to its promises." The United States government lied about the POW issue, lied about the effects of Agent Orange, lied about Gulf War Syndrome, and lied when they said our war veterans would receive the health care commensurate to their honorable service to our country.

It's taking six to twelve months to process health care and compensation claims for our Iraq and Afghanistan War Veterans, while the number of suicides climbs. A government that truly cared about its veterans or felt obligated to honor its promises would never allow that to happen.

The Phoenix VA scandal only confirms how corrupt our government is.

The Vietnam veteran mantra is, "Never Forget," and it applies equally to the service of our fallen comrades, the way we were treated when we came home, the lies about our abandoned POWs, and the shoddy medical treatment so many veterans have received—or NOT received. "Never leave a man behind" is not some convenient, feel-good phrase for politicians to use; it's what we believe in our hearts and souls.

The United States government began losing its soul when the decision was made not to recover some living American POWs after WWI, and then when tens of thousands of American and British POWs were held by Stalin and denied return to the US after WWII. That's when officials in the Departments of Defense and State decided that the political cost of recovering them made it advisable to consider them casualties of war and abandon them to their fate. This same mindset prevailed after the Korean and Vietnam Wars.

It would appear that the hunger for power and riches in the minds of far too many has been the breeding ground for unstoppable ethical decay in our government. I have no surefire solution; however, I believe the group with the greatest ability to turn things around is the veteran community.

I've always had a positive impression of Barry Goldwater because of his brutal honesty. The dirty negative campaign launched against him in 1964, the famous "daisy" commercial that ended with a mushroom cloud, was the turning point in negative advertising.

Unfortunately, to see why it's used and why it works we need only look in the mirror. That's not likely to change any time soon, but at least we can work toward reducing the destructive influence of the biggest single source of funding for that negativity, the big corporations.

To successfully do that it will be essential to first reverse the ridiculous 20th century court ruling which has since equated a corporation and a person in the eyes of the law. "Corporate personhood" grants the rights of real individuals to non-human entities, and as such they have First Amendment rights that prevent restricting their political activities.

Many millions of dollars are spent by these entities to elect or defeat targeted candidates. Too many of the successful candidates will take special note of those who helped them. One can argue either way about which is worse: the corrupters or the corrupted, but either way it must be stopped.

I read an article in *USA Today* that said one of these super PACs was directly involved in trying to toss out members of the Elizabeth, New Jersey, school board. The length and breadth of this legalized manipulation of our government is more pervasive than I thought. Money equals power and power equals control. Some of the wealthiest corporations are subverting the electoral process by funding political advertising and corrupting many of the beneficiaries of their largesse.

The most powerful industries that have corrupted our democratic system are banking, oil, and the military complex, with pharmaceutical and insurance not far behind.

In his farewell address to the nation, President Dwight D. Eisenhower warned that the U.S armaments industry, which he called the "military-industrial complex" whose growth he believed was necessary following WWII and the birth of the Cold War, could become too influential and powerful, weakening or destroying what it was intended to protect. He worried that both foreign and domestic policy could become "the captive of a scientific-technological elite."

Indeed, the armaments industry and related military contractors have become a substantial driving force behind building the political push to engage in U.S. military conflicts abroad, which inevitably increase the demand for the goods and services they sell. I would be hard pressed to explain how any of these conflicts have made us more secure or served our collective well-being.

A strong case can be made that the military complex has little regard for the blood spilled by the soldiers who fought and died.

If we don't do something to turn this around, the long slope of our decline will only get steeper. We must make truth, ethics, and honor our highest priorities in the candidates and issues we support. A logical first step is to expose and stop the lies about the ultimate betrayal, the abandonment of the living POWs and the war veterans who came home to an inferior health care system.

If we as veterans do not fight for our brothers in arms who desperately need our help, then we cannot expect the American people to stand up and fight with us to save our country.

In the end, my involvement in the politics of veterans' issues wasn't about money, power, or partisanship, but what I saw as my obligation to take care of my brothers less fortunate than myself. When I thanked God for saving me from the horrors of war upon returning in one piece, I promised to help my fellow veterans.

Unfortunately, it took me fifteen years to recover from a very disturbing homecoming before I was compelled to begin my journey.

Acknowledgements

To my family, especially my sister Mary Lou, who has been there supporting me from the time I came home from the war and throughout the tumultuous years since.

To my close friends Terry Foxe, Alex Rivera, and Don Neubauer, who gave me encouragement during my darkest hours.

To the family members of our missing men, who kept the POW issue alive until the Vietnam veterans could pick themselves up off the ground and join in the fight.

To the millions of veterans, concerned citizens, and the Vietnamese-American community, for their tireless efforts to free both our living American POWs and the oppressed people of Vietnam.

To John Nevin, who has helped me in many ways for thirty years.

To Tom Burch, who has been a dedicated and resourceful veteran leader for three decades.

To Ted Sampley, whose dedication, courage, and energy often pushed me to my own limits.

Finally, to my friend Ray Depew, for his encouragement.

And to the many dozens who joined the fight:

Bruce W. Adams, DDS, Delores Apodaca Alfond, PhD, Patricia O'Grady, Eleanor Apodaca, Tom Ashworth, Scott Barnes, Margaret (Nevin) Bates, Michael Bates, Bill Bell, Mike Benge, Bill Bennett, Larry Bice, John M. G. Brown, Tom Burch, Dino Carluccio, Michael Caron, Gino Casanova, Doctor Michael Charney, Michael Clark, Jim Copp, Lee Covino, Evelyn and Bob Cressman, Congressman Bob Dornan, Dr. Sam Dunlap, Jeff Donahue, Bill Dumas, Bob Dumas, Fuller family, Katherine Fanning, Robin Owen Goodman, Elzene Gourley, Kenny Green, Col. Bo Gritz, Col. Laird Guttersen, Col. Ted Guy, Col. David Hackworth, Leigh and Lynn Hampton, Ann Hart, Congressman Bill Hendon, Dave Hendrix, Ann Holland, Col. Earl and Patty Hopper, Col. Robert L. Howard, Carol and David Hrdlicka, Congressman Duncan Hunter, Quyen Le, Congressman John LeBoutillier, Chuck Lewis, Sheila and Caronzo Lewis, Donna Long, Ron Martz, Mary Matejov, Captain Eugene McDaniel, 1st Sgt. Melvin McIntyre, John Molloy, Jerry Mooney, John Musgrave, Lynn O'Shea, John Parsels, Bill Paul, Ron Paul, Col. Millard "Mike" Peck, Ross Perot, Mary Ann Reitano, Col. Rob Risner, Col. Nick Rowe, Ted Sampley, Wendy and Lane Sampley, Jim Sanders, Al Santoli, Mark Sauter, Chuck and Mary Schantag, Suzi Sharp, Marian Shelton, Sen. Bob Smith, Major Mark Smith, Beth Stewart, Karen, Lynn and Sherrill Standerwick, Larry Stark, Bill Sullivan, John Syphrit, General Eugene Tighe, Tuan Tran, Lance Trimmer, Tim Tripp, Tracy Usry, Mike Van Atta, Paul Weyrich

Supporting Statements

"As a result of my service in the United States Marine Corps during the Vietnam War, I came to know three Marine recipients of the Medal of Honor: PFC Raymond M. 'Iron Mike' Clausen, Major Stephen Pless, and Staff Sergeant Karl Taylor. Though my admiration of these men is boundless, I have known no man or woman more resolute, dedicated, or courageous than Jerry Kiley. There are no better Americans."
-- Tom Ashworth, former helicopter pilot

"I met Jerry in 1990 during the POW/MIA meetings in Washington, D.C.; Jerry has been a staunch supporter of the men left alive in captivity and has continued to work over the years to do whatever it took to get the truth out concerning the abandonment of these men."
-- Carol Hrdlicka, wife of Col. David L. Hrdlicka, POW Laos

"Earning the name 'the Stealth Activist' from his fellow POW/MIA activists, and called a 'scumbag' by Senator 'Song Bird' McCain, Jerry Kiley earned this distinction by infiltrating through the perimeter of numerous official and semi-official events, secured by Secret Service agents, to raise the issue of our abandoned brothers with high-ranking American officials and foreign diplomats."
-- Mike Benge, former POW

"Jerry Kiley is the single most courageous and heroic Vietnam vet I have ever met. I am proud to call him a great personal friend, and a friend of ALL vets and their issues."
-- John LeBoutillier, former Congressman

"Jerry Kiley's efforts on behalf of the Indochina POWs put us all to shame."
– Bill Hendon, former Congressman